HISTORY AN

# History and Belief

*The Foundations of Historical*
*Understanding*

Robert Eric Frykenberg

WILLIAM B. EERDMANS PUBLISHING COMPANY
GRAND RAPIDS, MICHIGAN / CAMBRIDGE, U.K.
WITH
THE INSTITUTE FOR ADVANCED CHRISTIAN STUDIES

© 1996 Wm. B. Eerdmans Publishing Co.
255 Jefferson Ave. S.E., Grand Rapids, Michigan 49503 /
P.O. Box 163, Cambridge CB3 9PU U.K.

Published in cooperation with
The Institute for Advanced Christian Studies

Printed in the United States of America

01 00 99 98 97 96     7 6 5 4 3 2 1


Library of Congress Cataloging-in-Publication Data

Frykenberg, Robert Eric.
History and belief: the foundations of historical understanding/
Robert Eric Frykenberg.
p.     cm.
Includes bibliographical references (p.   ) and index.
ISBN 0-8028-0739-3 (pbk.)
1. History — Philosophy.   2. Historiography.   3. Belief and doubt.
I. Title.
D16.9.F79  1996                           96-2594
901 — dc20                                CIP

# Contents

*To*
## *Carol*
*in the Faith, Hope, and Love we share*

*Introduction*

# Historical Understandings and World Views

*Only when detailed researches are connected with a hypothesis that does purport to make the world make sense can the historical profession be said to earn its keep . . . [O]ur predecessors rendered that service by creating national histories for their respective constituencies and locating them firmly within a universal frame* **that in every case derived from a simple secularization of the Christian epos.** *It is high time for historians to reflect anew about how the world's history can be adequately conceived. Unless we seek . . . to construct a believable portrait of the human past on a global scale, we will have failed to perform our function adequately.*

W. H. McNeill
(Royal Historical Society Lecture, 1981)

## I. Background and Focus

Over the past several years, work upon relationships between various conflicting doctrinal, ethical, and ideological systems and processes of historical development and structural integration within societies of India and within other societies have raised some basic questions about the conflicting ways in which human beings have thought about the past. As manifested in various forms of religious and social conflict

1

(Hindu-Buddhist, Hindu-Christian, Hindu-Muslim, caste-noncaste, tribal-nontribal, and other kinds of conflict) in several specific localities of India, much of my own research over the last forty years has been informed by looking at struggles over questions of ideological and social distinction, with special reference to social distance or (sacred) space. I have studied historical situations in which "wrongful" use of buildings, conveyances, dress, inns, roads, schools, temples, or any of a host of facilities (e.g., blood sacrifice, prostitution, slave labor, and so on) became focal points for civil aggravation and conflagration. Recently I have studied structures of belief and loyalty to see how conflicts broke out and how such conflicts can be better understood, especially within the context of various current fundamentalist movements in South Asia.

## Current Interest

All of this has led, quite naturally, to an interest in different perceptions of history as these arise out of different systems of value and out of different world views. Research seminars conducted over the past thirty years have almost invariably led to broader questions about the ways in which different peoples have recorded events or have thought about their own perceptions of the past. Logically, discussions have led to questions about the underlying role of religion in the framing of epistemic and metaphysical understandings of "what has happened." By religion, I mean those bedrock commitments and doctrines, both ideological and institutional (whether theistic or nontheistic), held by individuals and by communities, which actually hold societies together or which, when weak, fail to do so. Religion, in this sense, has provided the conceptual and definitional framework for the historiography generated within each civilization.

## Central Question

Exactly *how* ideology, or religion in a broad sense, has served to inform the historiography of each major civilization is the central question of this study. Each culture has produced its own unique kind of historical understandings, and consequent historiographies. From earliest antiquity down to our own day, a number of legacies of what was understood to be "historical" can be perceived. Each has made its own distinctive contribution or left its own peculiar form of historiography. Historical understandings surviving from antiquity were succeeded, or superseded, by historiographies no less distinctive. Some of these attained what may be seen as "classical" standards for assessing events. Flowing out of an intermingling of Hebrew and Hellenistic elements came several streams of historiography. Out of a common Greco-Roman or Judeo-Christian trunk came separate branches: Western-Christian, Eastern-Christian, and Islamic historiographies. Each of these combined its own unique kinds of blending of perceptions about past events. The designation "classical" is often broadened, sometimes confused, and even obscured, in our day, by its application to important non-Western legacies in historical understandings — those of "Classical" China and "Classical" India, if not those of "Classical" Arab or Persian Islam. Other particular historical traditions, such as those of sub-Saharan Africa and pre-Columbian America(s), can only be mentioned, since it is impossible within the modest compass of this study to bring all structures of historical understanding under scrutiny.

## Conceptual Focus

The purpose of this work is to trace, compare, and describe different conceptions and to examine different ways of understanding historical events. Closely connected to different ways of understanding, almost unavoidably, are differing concepts of "society," if not also of "humanity" itself. This work also attempts to make comparative assessments of tensions between different, sometimes contradictory conceptions *within* major historiographic traditions. At the same time, on another level of analysis, different conceptions of obligation, as seen in various forms of contractual, consensual, and other instruments of governance, cannot be ignored. None of these levels of analysis, nor the several methodological problems which they entail, are simple. They cannot be viewed merely from within a single, unidimensional or culture-bound (Eurocentric) epistemology. But neither can tensions in outlook which have developed *between* various major cultures be fully comprehended or properly appreciated without reference to tensions that developed *within* the historiographies of each of the cultures concerned.

In India, for example, arguments over the nature and destiny of mankind are found both within indigenous or so-called "Hindu," Indo-Islamic, and Indo-Christian conceptualizations and in encounters between these major cultures. The very existence of any common concept or "doctrine" of humanity can be seen as an issue of severe contention. Briefly and simply put, whether or not there is any room for a concept of a common "humanity" within the polarity of conceptions which lie between ideas of divinity and ideas of animality, as manifested within stratified notions of mankind *(manisha)* and as portrayed in the doctrine of *varnāshramadharma*, is open to question. By implication, different species of mankind are ranked hierarchically between the categories of "animality" and "divinity." So postulated, *varnāshramadharma* was a concept developed by Brahmans. A system of "color coding" categories (and ranks) for all forms of "birth" *(jāt)* was devised for the purpose of classifying, according to inherent properties of purity or pollution, all "birth groups" or "castes" *(jātīs)*. By such thinking, birth groups could no more be crossed biologically than different species of animals: Manu compared such miscegenation with attempting to interbreed birds with snakes.

Yet, on the other hand, while this doctrine undoubtedly played a dominant role in forming cultural understandings of India's past, there was another doctrine which, even if less dominant or more recessive, cannot be ignored. *Sadhāranadharma* spelled out those duties which could be considered common to all mankind — good conduct, honesty, loyalty, kindness, truthfulness, or avoidance of anger. By such logic, it could be argued that Brahmanical systems of metaphysics in India no more mandated the necessity of a caste system for all mankind than Christian principles obliged the enslavement of blacks in Africa or America. Yet, the "Hindu" sense of time and destiny, as found in the *puranic* historiography, is undoubtedly very different from that found in other major historiographic traditions. Moreover, in encounters with the normative demands of *dar-ul-Islam*, as reflected in Indo-Islamicate understandings of the past or in later encounters with the normative values of the West, guardians of custom, religion, and tradition *(sanāthana dharm)* faced unprecedented challenges to their long dominance.

## II. Conceptual Problems

In distinguishing between "events" or "what has happened" and "what is known about what has happened" (especially within human affairs) — between the two senses in which the term *history* is commonly used — our focus of attention is upon what is "known," rather than on "events" or "what has happened," as such. The accumulated forms and structures of understanding events are what concern us. What history is, of what it consists, or of what it does not consist, what basic elements have constituted historical knowledge (and historical scholarship) and what the limitations upon such knowledge are: such questions are problems of definition and, as such, are both metaphysical and epistemic.

Questions about what historians can or, more to the point, what historians *cannot* do are questions that seem never to be fully or properly addressed (at least to our full satisfaction). Approaches and arguments about historical understanding have also been pursued very differently. Several kinds of activity are involved, each continually open to critical review, if not revision: *(1) Discovery, Selection, and Validation of Information:* What we call data, evidence, or sources involves us in different methods of gaining understandings of the past, of validating previous findings, and of testing or not testing earlier findings. These elements of enterprise are themselves subjects which have been open to continual argument. *(2) Analysis and Logic:* Applications of critical "tools" for the identifying and selecting of data/evidence — concerning artifacts of past human actions, records of past human and "inhuman" behavior, and samples of past human thought — have varied in each and every age and in each and every area of the world. *(3) Bias and Detachment:* The role of inclination, interest, or ideology, and how they are reflected in institutions, can hardly be overemphasized. In attempts to accumulate historical knowledge, the use of memory, records, or other devices and resources is manifold. In order to reconstruct a sense of past human events, to provide a "collective memory" of those events, or, as much as possible, to avoid suffering from "collective amnesia," humans generate some sense of "meaning." Events that have meaning provide a sense of "validation" for the present, if not also for the future. Human existence, by drawing upon understandings about the past, depends upon and draws inspiration from belief. In the broadest sense of the term, "religion" can be seen as the oldest kind of vehicle for the conveying of belief and ideology. *(4) Creative Interpretation and "Plausibility"*: Of central concern in understandings of the past are visions of the future, together with attempts either to control destiny or, at the very least, to be on the right side of destiny. *Historicism* is our name for systematic attempts to see patterns in events and to make predictable understandings about the direction of events, looking to their development and culmination. It is but one consequence of such endeavors. Historical understandings that are "historicist" are found within the great prophetic movements: from Moses to Marx, these movements have embodied such features. Understandings of God and history, faith and history (Niebuhr), or the historian and the believer (Van Harvey), are but a few of the recurrent examples of this kind of concern.

## Historiography

What people have themselves done to understand the past and what people have *not* done to gain understandings of events serve as the empirical base for this study. This kind of study is sometimes seen as "history of history," "knowledge about knowledge," or "understanding the understanding" of past events. Our research traces the growth of different kinds of historical understandings, understandings held by different peoples, in different parts of the world, and in different times. In addition to what is today accepted within the conventional boundaries of the historical discipline, what is done by so-called "practicing" and "professional" historians, this kind of search for historical understandings reaches out in many directions and recognizes the usefulness of understandings which have sometimes been ignored or shunned. Recognition of the importance of memory, folklore, and oral tradition, for example, can be seen as alternative ways to approach understandings of the past which have, at least until very recently, not been acceptable to modern historians. These approaches are now again being opened up.

On another level, this work falls between fields. It is neither as historical as many historians may wish nor as philosophical as many philosophers may wish. That is to say, it is neither sufficiently filled with the detailed or systematic or theory-driven descriptions of what historians have written to please professional historians; nor is it a philosophy of history which deals, analytically and sufficiently, with closely reasoned arguments among and between philosophers about the epistemology, ontology (or metaphysics), and logic of human thinking about the nature of events as these occur or have occurred in space and time. Yet, at the same time, it is both: an attempt *is* made to describe how peoples in different cultures, and in different eras, have approached their understandings of the past.

## Comparative Analysis

What contemporary historians now know and understand about the human past can be compared with such understandings as they once existed. Comparative evaluations require attempts to discover and see past historical understandings as they were perceived by their beholders and creators. Here again, the role of "religion" broadly defined, as a vehicle of historiography, can scarcely be ignored. The place of theocentric, ethnocentric, anthropocentric, and other kinds of understandings can be approached, appreciated, and assessed, each in its own terms. Such assessments can serve to better inform the grounds of historical understandings as these exist in our own day.

Exactly what concepts are to be tracked and examined comparatively has never been altogether clear-cut or comprehensive. Some kinds of concepts are but cloaks for doctrine. Among these, for example, are those of "humanity" and "society," "community" or "polity," "change" or "destiny." *(1) Conceptions of humanity* (anthropological and/or moral theory): These trace progressive "humanization" or "dehumanization" of mankind: a constant and recurring preoccupation in almost all history, with variations depending upon conflicts, distortions, and questions raised in any given time and place. *(2) Conceptions of community and society* (social theory): These are distinctions made between those who "belong" and those who "do not belong," between "insiders" and "outsiders." Between "chosen people" or "choice people" and non-chosen peoples; between Israel, especially Judah, and Gentiles (or *Goyim*); between believers and nonbelievers (pagans, heathens, kafirs); between the righteous and the unrighteous — the "blessed" and the "cursed"; between those who are patriots/citizens and those who are aliens/foreigners; between "proletariat" and "bourgeoisie": distinctions such as these have always been germane within structures of historical understanding. *(3) Conceptions of commonwealth, kingdom, realm, or state* (political theory): Here one finds such concepts as the "City of God"; the "City of Peace" *(Jerusalem);* the "abode of peace" *(Dar-ul-Islam)* as distinct from the "abode of war" *(Dar-ul-Harb);* or the "mandate of heaven." Many other different, or similar, conceptions have been developed within structures of historical understanding. *(4) Conceptions of change and/or destiny:* Forms of change, whether seen as redemption, rescue, restoration, resurrection, or revolution, even progress and development, or something else, are deeply ingrained into human understandings about both the past and the future. A "trajectory" of events in the past can be seen as pointing the way to further events. Events projected into the future, described by such concepts as eschatology and millenarianism, have come into vogue within some structures of historical thought. Almost inextricable from other concepts — concepts such as those concerning an ideal "mandate of heaven" or an ideal "realm of peace" — these pertain to utopian notions. They can be found stretching from the Abrahamic conceptions of the "promised land" to recently held beliefs such as those conceptions describing the deterministic inevitability of a "classless society."

## III. Presuppositions and Problems

### Limitations

Historical understandings are never absolute and never complete. They are always tentative — sometimes highly so and sometimes hardly at all. Historical knowledge, in technical terms, is never entirely certain. It is never entirely free from question. This always being so, in some measure, the task of the historian is to maximize plausibility. Within such a frame of reference several kinds of problems arise:

### 1. Definition, or conceptuality

Epistemic and metaphysical dimensions in human events and human relations are features without which historical understandings and the accumulating of historical knowledge would not be possible. Concepts generalize, summarize, or categorize "facts," putting them into various kinds of combinations, structures, systems, processes, and the like. As generalizations, or as generalizing symbols, concepts, as such, are never implicit within or necessary to those conceptual elements which we call "data," "evidence," or "facts." Here there is a certain circularity, or circumlocution. Concepts, in short, describe elements which they purport to represent, elements which are also conceptually marked. As parts of those rational enterprises which are carried on by intelligent observers, structures of language are a problem. Critical reviews or revisions of past historical understandings left by a given culture (sometimes called "historiography" or "history of history") do not escape the traps and trammels of language.

## 2. Evidence, or factuality

Language is not the only methodological obstacle when attempts to compare structures of historical understanding are made. No "data" nor "facts" — descriptions of events which are described by means of propositions or statements based on observation — are incontrovertibly or indubitably true, at least in any ultimate sense. Historical understandings contain no such items. Such being the case, questions of relative authenticity, proximity, complexity, and totality become germane. More germane to structures of historical understanding are space gaps and time lapses. The "actual" processes or "reaction times" of elements within an event or within a chain of events; numbers and kinds of variables and their controllability, also degrees of uniqueness of elements within an event or combinations bearing upon a chain of events; and relative degrees of "comprehensiveness" (or totality) of available evidence (or information): these are but a few issues affecting relationships between observer and event when historical understanding is acquired. *A complete, accurate, authentic grasp of all data described in evidence (both in its complexity and in its totality) can never be altogether certain.* Thus, data recorded in a test-tube experiment can be such that it is "repeatable." Due to its relative simplicity and totality, such an event is also more completely and easily understood. No such controllability of complex data is even remotely possible, much less probable, for a rerunning of the Partition of India in 1947, the Battle of D-Day in 1944, or the Battle of Waterloo on June 8, 1815. Yet, data can be accumulated and compared; assessments of historical understanding can be made; and measures of plausibility can be weighed or found wanting.

## 3. Subjectivity vs. objectivity

"Outlook" in the observer as historian is crucial. From selecting data, classifying its relative significance, and giving shape to understandings of an event itself, what is *seen* as worthy of scrutiny and what is *not* seen or "overlooked" has profound implications. This can be viewed both positively and negatively. At the very least, a self-awareness and self-consciousness of outlook poses a challenge, but not necessarily a counsel of despair and futility. Any challenge to surmount the mundane or the sordid, and to recognize if not rise above limitations, calls for decisions. Even "scrupulous" attempts to be fair, critical and self-critical, and open-minded are never perfect. Willingness to subject prior assumptions and previous understandings, including convictions, doctrines, ideologies, and prejudices, to ruthless examination is never quite sufficient. Historical claims remain inherently tentative, and partial understandings remain humble. To suspend final or ultimate judgment, especially that which is moral and condemnatory, and to strive for technically exact and precise answers, acutely rational insights and critical self-awareness are required. An attitude that is profoundly, if not inherently, skeptical of human achievements, however wonderful these may seem, is essential for reliable historical understandings. All the best institutional constructions of mankind, with all their highest possibilities, including the finest accomplishments of historians themselves, are open to question. What is generated in strivings for historical understandings is an attitude, an outlook, and a self-awareness that affects the kinds of questions that are asked, the qualities of data that are selected, and the shapes of conclusions that are drawn. This attitude influences any careful observer of events. Contextualities of time and place and perspective — even what is embedded within the observer's unconscious inclinations — can escape scrutiny. The very recognition of the need for detachment, even if merely an abstraction or ideal never fully attained, constitutes a historic intellectual (and metaphysical) achievement.

Put differently, if all historians considered exactly the same data, if they all counted, numbered, and weighed exactly the same evidence, made exactly the same observations, and came to exactly the same conclusions in exactly the same way — inasmuch as all historical understandings were entirely certain, complete, correct, and beyond doubt — we would not have a story of past experiences or achievements, disappointments and failures. Neither would we have historical argument, historical explanation, or historical insight. Rather, what we would have is merely another look at the same old records, a rerunning of recording machines. The information might be altogether accurate and precise. It would also be altogether boring and dull. Without the questioning of assumptions, the salt of human life itself would have lost its savor.

## 4. Meaning and purpose

The statement by Professor William H. McNeill with which this study begins encapsulates the essence of a challenge. His words to historians serve to show how much any work of this nature is bound inextricably with structures of historical understanding that are linked to the world views and the "great traditions" within which those understandings have developed. Or, in other words, assumptions about the origin, development, and destiny of mankind, assumptions that comprehend or include ideologies and institutions in holistic terms, are but another definition for religion. Religion, in this sense, has always provided the underlying foundation, or ground, for the drama of history.

### Historical Interpretation

One of the most important tasks of a historian, in any age, is the interpretation and/or reinterpretation of events. What is understood about events — past, present, and/or future — can be assessed in the light of the central concepts and doctrines of some all-embracing system of thought. Such systems of thought are usually in the form of some ideology, or religion. Exactly *how* this task can be accomplished — by a historian, as a historian — is the question which is of concern here.

Since the task itself is, essentially, philosophical or theological or, in Marxist idiom, "theoretical," some thinkers may doubt whether it is possible for work of this nature ever to be done by a historian. If such doubts are entertained or hold any validity, perhaps there are also grounds to justify a study of this nature *as a historical* investigation.

## 1. Historical belief and historical religion

In some sense every religion, and every ideology, is historical. In an even stronger and more central sense, all the basic claims and doctrines and institutions are not only, in and of themselves, events, but also, even if only in the slightest sense, contain references to historical events and to historical persons. These kinds of historical events (and persons involved in them) bear upon the ultimate significance and claims to validity made on behalf of any given religious (or ideological) system in itself. Questions concerning the historicity of historical claims can give rise to several conditions.

One condition that a historical belief possesses, in order to hold validity, is the claim that certain events have occurred and that certain persons have existed. For example, historical claims concerning actual occurrence of the Incarnation as an event rest upon a prior acceptance of claims concerning the actuality of the birth of Jesus. Likewise, claims about the efficacy of the Crucifixion as the Atonement presuppose the death of Jesus as a prior event. Again, any claims about the historicity of the Resurrection will rest upon a prior understanding concerning the death and burial of Jesus. In negative terms, there is always a sense in which any historical inquiry can, both in principle or theory, as well as in fact, refute claims as to the historical "truth" or "validity" of Christianity by showing that these claims rest upon invalid, false, or insufficient evidence — by showing that the evidence (or data) for the actual occurrence of events or of persons does not exist. In short, showing that these events or these persons did not or could not have "existed" or "happened" is a way of showing that the historical claims central to Christian faith are false.

There is a sense in which the vulnerability of historical claims to historical refutation is inherent to the nature of all historical understandings. Such vulnerability in history is comparable to the vulnerability in epistemology or in doctrine to claims that are, in a similar sense, essential to a religion. Claims that are not vulnerable, in principle, to refutation of some sort (whether historical or otherwise), however much there may actually be such claims, are not historical claims. Claims that are seen as *necessary* claims (or "truths") — that is, claims or statements that are valid "in all possible worlds" — are not claims that contingencies of existing evidence allow historians to make. Claims concerning events which can be denied or refuted are claims which can be seen as contradictory. Claims made within an ideological or religious system concerning events are not the kinds of claims which, like those of philosophy or theology, must be able to stand as valid (correct or true) in all possible worlds. Rather, historical claims are claims that, in spite of whatever else might have happened, are seen as having occurred within this world and within a given framework of particularities in space and time. Such claims, claims of historical validity, cannot be generated solely out of those kinds of truth-claims which are seen as *necessary* claims.

This kind of perspective, with all its semantic convolutions, can be seen as separating some kinds of ideology and/or religion from others. In Classical Greek thought, for example, *important* claims to truth were seen as being of those kinds which are *necessary.* This kind of thinking was and is, on the whole, in sharp contrast to Judeo-Christian thought. Yet, even in this, the thought of Tillich, and of other theologians of an outlook comparable to his, can be seen as lying closer to the thought of Plato and Aristotle than to the heritage that he professed to represent. Historical kinds of perspective, as noted above, place ultimate significance upon *temporal* and *historical* phenomena, rather than upon that which is *eternal.* Moreover, historical understandings of this sort assign ultimate significance to events which are specifically temporal, as distinct from concerns which were merely everlasting. This kind of perspective, again, can be seen as having been in sharp contrast to the "historical" thinking of Hegel.

The vulnerability of a historical perspective has sometimes been expressed in terms that make religious doctrines seem to be *only probable.* Doctrines may even be declared to be vulnerable. That is to say, since only necessary kinds of claims to truth are known or fixed with absolute certainty and since certain religious doctrines are not seen as being claims to truth of that sort, some doctrinal claims can never be known or, more to the point, can never be held with utter certainty. But the same kind of vulnerability, probability, plausibility, or lack of final certainty also applies in our understandings of all physical objects — of all events and persons, and even of ourselves. Vulnerability to empirical confirmation, or disconfirmation, can be correlated, in principle, with any and all kinds of solid information about historical events. Indeed, the higher the degree of certainty one gets with the one, the higher the degree of certainty with the other.

Yet, for all that, historical understandings are always contingent, always vulnerable. "Certainty" in this context, therefore, means the same as "without possibility of error," "with appropriate confidence," or "with plausibility." The *latter* is relevant, even though the former kind of certainty is the kind more often used for beliefs, conceptual systems, doctrines, and systems of ideology, religion, or "theory." Attempts, therefore, to *deny* the vulnerability, in principle, of claims concerning historical events by denying that ideological or religious doctrines (claims, etc.) possess such invulnerability or by trying to bridge some alleged gap between evidence and faith by sheer "enthusiasm" or sentiment (cf. Kierkegaard) have tended to become both confused and unnecessary (cf. Lessing's ditch).

## 2. Historical meaning and historical analogy

In making a distinction between "events" — "what has happened" — and "what is known/understood about events" or "what is known about what has happened," questions arise about how these two meanings are related. About "events" or "what has happened," the first meaning of history, it would be preposterous even to suppose that everything can ever be known, much less discussed or encompassed within the second meaning of the term. In relative terms, only an infinitesimally minuscule proportion of "what has happened," even of "human events," can ever be even known about, much less "understood." Among "known-about events," "known events," or "known history," two kinds of understanding are in conflict. If an event can be "known" and/or "understood" as "known history," there is a sense in which it is an event of a kind which has other, or multiple, instances. That is, it is an event of a kind which either happened "before" or happened "somewhere else." Moreover, it is an event of a kind which, by its very nature, was such that it had happened *more than once before* and, more probably, several times. If this, or something like it, had not happened before, it would be almost impossible to describe. Hence, an event about which we have very little information, can best be understood and perhaps can only be understood in terms of another event of the same kind. Perhaps, but not necessarily, such an event is one which was described or experienced previously, as a contemporary occurrence. Perhaps it is something about which *more* information may be available.

Only in this way, some would argue, have people been able to construct and fabricate even the most simple of descriptive "concepts." Concepts of greater complexity or of higher levels of abstraction are, quite obviously, more difficult to construct. Hence, each event with which we deal in "known history," or each collection of "known events," no matter how particular or unique each event may ostensibly be, can be seen as having belonged to some "kind," some "category" or "class" of events, the membership of which it has possessed or shared something in common with other similar events (of its own kind, or in its same category). This principle concerning the nature of "known events" or "known history" is sometimes called the *principle of analogy,* or *comparability.* If the principle is accepted, entirely and without reservation, then known history cannot include certain kinds of events which might be described as "religious," "spiritual," or "supernatural" as describable or discussable events. Any event that is so unique that it has had no analogy and nothing with which it can be compared, by such reasoning, could not become part of known history. In conflict with this principle, if not contradicting it, would be any claim that a "known event" was and is altogether and completely and entirely unique (however much this may yet, in fact, actually be so).

Carrying this line of philosophical thinking further, one could assert that an event has belonged to history — to "what has happened" or to "past events" — only if it falls within the provenance of and only if it has been, in principle, accessible to and part of a history which can be understood. If this line of reasoning is valid, then one would have to hold and, indeed, one would be obliged to hold that certain kinds of events about which claims of occurrence have been made (e.g., the Resurrection) are events which never did occur. An insistence, or assertion, of this requirement has been (and is) sometimes called the *principle*

*of verification,* or simply *historical verification.* According to this principle, an event can properly be said to have occurred only if it is possible
to discover, and to show others, that it occurred; and one can show
others that such an event occurred only by use of a methodology which
includes the principle of analogy/comparison. Some claims of ideology
and some claims of theistic religion, by and large, cannot accept both
principles. Thus, in such cases, it has been possible for certain kinds of
religious claims and certain kinds of historical claims to have points of
contact (and concurrence) and points of potential conflict. Other points
of potential, but not necessary, contact between claims of ideology
and/or religion and claims to historical understanding, achieved by
means of the methodology just described, pertain to *purpose in history*
and *moral judgments.*

Whether purpose is somehow manifested in events, or in what we
know about events, and whether understandings can be acquired in
such a manner that they are accessible to methods of the historical
inquiry just described, is an issue which can either be open or closed
within any given ideological or religious tradition. It is an issue which
is related to the question about whether there are "laws" or general
principles about the nature of "events" or about "what has happened"
in the past. Also, whether known events and/or known history, however
it is gained and conveyed, either in oral or written form, can properly
include moral judgments upon, or assessments of, persons and events
are also matters which may be either open or closed within any given
ideological or religious tradition. On all such questions as these, what
can be understood about "what has happened" in the past (historical
knowledge) and how what we understand is, or can be, linked to ideological or religious belief itself prompts us to exercise extreme caution.
Due humility, restraint, and measured skepticism are attitudes essential
for any higher understanding of historical events. In such matters, "we
see through a glass darkly."

## 3. Comparability and continuity

How can the "absolute correctness" of one ideological or religious system (e.g., cf. Troeltsch) in relation to other ideologies and religions be
claimed? And how can similarities and differences between such systems

of ideology and religion, in their claims to the authoritativeness or to uniqueness of one system of ideology or religion over all other systems of ideology or religion be treated? How can any comparative and critical assessments of claims to religious forms of historical understanding be made? These are questions which defy neat or simple answers.

### (a) Phenomenology

One challenge to such a claim or perspective emerges from a comparative-religion/history-of-religion approach. This approach is one in which each religion "instantiates" certain *forms* or *patterns;* and such forms and patterns comprise the "essence" of (*all*) ideology or religion, no matter how much emphasis is placed upon the particularities or uniquenesses of any single ideological or religious tradition (cf. Eliade, or at least some uses made of his view). If the religious significance of any given ideology or religion lies in certain *forms,* and if these forms are shared by all ideologies or religions as such, then an assumption (or presumption) is being held that no single ideology or religion can be unique or authoritative in the sense in which other ideologies or religions are not. Here, methodologies of various social sciences, such as those of anthropology or phenomenology (and, in some views, part also of historical methodology), can be brought into play, even if (and when) such methodology runs counter to more exclusivistic and fundamentalistic systems of analysis, belief, or logic.

### (b) Continuity and discontinuity

Another challenge pertains to the adequacy of a view which has claimed that whatever occurs in history, in the meaning and sense of "all that is past," can be explained in terms of, or seen as connected and related to, an unbroken *sequence* of events. Each event, by such thinking, is seen as being linked to all the events that preceded it. This line of thinking concerning linkages of continuity would include, as events, those kinds of phenomena which are described as doctrines that are basic in any given ideology or religion. Historical events, being woven together in a seamless cloth (so to speak), occur within a *context* which leaves no room for discontinuities. This would mean that historical events, such as divine acts, supernatural events, or spiritual insights, would, could,

or might necessarily create religious understandings. Attempts to deal
with this issue have, so far, not been adequate. Some have attempted to
do this by positing a "complementarity" in which historical and ideological or religious claims *cannot* be allowed to be in conflict (cf. McKay).
Others have tried to do so by putting "events," "known events" and
ideological, religious, or theological understandings on somewhat different levels of analysis (cf. Butterfield). Yet another approach has been
to reject any notion that there is, or ever could be any absolute or
unexceptionable historical continuity in the flow of events, in the sense
of our being able to understand "all that has ever happened" within "all
of the past that ever was," moving from remote antiquity into a no less
remote future.

As the following chapters will attempt to show, there have been many
structures of historical understanding. One can also trace the rise of an
emphasis upon one kind of structure over another; most of these structures that have been constructed, described, or imagined, have coexisted
throughout the long epochs during which mankind has had to rely upon
historical understandings. Both for the sake of survival and for the sake
of a sense of well-being, forms of historical understanding have always,
to a lesser or to a greater degree, been contested. There is no lasting
peace, nor even any perpetual truce in struggles over historical understandings. These, we believe, have been going on through the ages and
are still continuing in our own day. Never before, indeed, have struggles
over conflicting structures of historical understanding been more acute.
In what follows, a thread of narrative lies behind attempts to describe
and evaluate each of these different kinds of structures.

*Chapter 1*

# History as History:
# A Double Definition

*To the historian every event, every action, is to be studied
not as an external thing, not as a mere part in some system
of mechanics, but as a thing incomprehensible save as it goes
into or comes out of human minds. . . .*

Herbert Butterfield, 1949

*H*istory as a term causes much confusion. Many thinkers who should
know better use it in sloppy ways. Careless habits of ordinary conversation and popular usage allow one term to convey different meanings.
This is done without realizing (or showing) when one meaning has been
exchanged for another. Since *history* can have such very different meanings,
and since it can be used without any one particular meaning always being
clearly spelled out at the time it is being used, one should hardly be
surprised at the many misunderstandings that result. The all-too-common
propensity for misapplying, mistaking, and misunderstanding this term is
especially remarkable when it occurs so frequently among those who, as
scholars, might perhaps be expected to know better but who, for one reason
or another, fail to clarify and distinguish the different meanings they are
using and when they are doing so.[1]

---

1. Questions about the avoidability of such errors is a problematic issue in itself,
one over which scholars (philosophers and theologians, psychologists and other partic-

Nevertheless, at the very outset, it is important to delineate the amazing variety of conceptual and definitional and connotational features that are to be found within this one single term. The word *history* is often used to mean (or is confused with) *existence* itself; and/or also, more commonly, with *events* (or even series of events) which comprise existence.[2] Events are actions, clusters of actions, or occurrences (in space and time, or in the mind). They are things that have already happened, things that are now happening, or even things that may yet happen in the future. An event can also be, and indeed often is, used (or confused) with time (or space) itself or with a total cluster or process of events — that continuum-through-time-and-space-of-all-events — which comprises all existence. On the other hand, a much more profound confusion arises out of a failure to distinguish between history as event — including whatever has or does (or will) exist or "happen" — and human *experiences* and *understandings* of events. Before experiences of events can turn into understandings of events, several processes of action (which are themselves events) need to occur within the mind. Experiences of an event, which come into the conscious mind, are events *observed* or *perceived* — *or even imagined*. Observings and perceivings and imaginings are turned into what some may consider to be "more solid" forms of "knowing" — into *knowledge*. But even this cannot become common or public (as distinct from personal and private) until it has itself been made conveyable and then communicated. What are conveyed, in one form or another (whether verbal, pictorial, or whatever), are *descriptions* of events — or *facts*. Descriptions, or facts, may or may not be validly supported by *evidences* of events. The evidences for the occurrences of events may or may not be explicit or implicit in what is conveyed. Whatever the case, what are now sometimes

---

ipants, in both "hard" and "soft" sciences) have continually struggled, without reaching a consensus. Important as this issue may be, however, I shall not pursue this matter further, except to suggest that, from linguistic or literary perspectives, semantic confusions surrounding any single term are common features within all language use, especially if and when and where terms are seen not as single units of expression but as semantic triggers for "word clusters" which are better understood within particular verbal contexts.

2. See meaning 4, *a* and *b* in vol. 1 of *The Compact Edition of the Oxford English Dictionary: Complete Text Reproduced Micrographically* (hereafter abbreviated *OED*): a. "a series of events (of which the story is or may be told)"; and b. "The whole train of events connected with . . . a course of existence."

fashionably known as *representations* (and what are essentially *factualizations*) of actual events are intrinsic to our *understandings* of those same events.

*Inquiries* about events, their quality depending upon varying measures of curiosity, imagination, and rationality, can be accompanied by *explanations* of events. And explanations of events, especially if and when they are plausible, can require all sorts of further mental exercises. These exercises, if and when ordered and well organized, call for various kinds of intellectual discipline (within the arts and sciences). But, whether or not some or all of the above steps occur, understandings of events arise from some kind of human interaction with or experiences of those events. This is so even whether or not experiences of events are direct and immediate, or remote and indirect. Moreover, some explanations of understandings of events can themselves lead to questions and concerns over the criteria for judging the actualities or qualities of some particular events — or even of all events. *Beliefs* about the very actualities or qualities of events and criteria for determining what qualities make for *significance* in those events then become crucial. Beliefs can then embody concerns about the nature of events and questions about *all* events that have ever happened or about just some small slices or selections of events; they can eventually even evoke concerns, if not beliefs, about the very nature of existence itself. Moreover, beliefs about events, about orderings of priority among events and about what events are or are not of great importance, or what is of ultimate significance, can then go so far as to reflect upon what are considered to be events of ultimate meaning. Questions about relationships between ideas about existence, events, and experience, arising out of what are seen as "larger" — philosophical, psychological (emotional), or personal — concerns, can then hold "world-viewish" features of momentous consequence.

All of this etymological backing and filling, this repetitious "heavy breathing" about concepts, can be tedious. Yet such exercises serve to emphasize how, all too easily and all too often, history as object can be confused with history as subject. The hard substance of "what is past" and "what is passing" — "what once happened," "what is happening," or even "what is yet to happen" — is too often confounded with the soft substance of "what is known or understood about what has passed or is passing" or "what is known about what has happened (or may yet happen)." Existence itself is an event; and events that are its component elements can be misconstrued for experiences, for evidences, or even for explanations of events. To repeat, miscommunication of this kind is so common that, in much everyday conversation, individuals too often are not even aware of having moved: from talking about "history as event" to talking about "history as experience," "history as evidence," or "history as explanation"; from talking about "what is past" to talking about "what is known about what has passed." To think more carefully about these distinctions, it is useful to look at various roots of the English word itself and to search for ways by which this word has come to have so many possible meanings.[3]

Technically, the English noun *history* comes from some form, whether verb or noun, of a single Greek root and its branches: *istor* (ιστορ), *istorie* or *istoria* (ιστορια), and such.[4] Exactly what the original meanings may have been is still a matter open to debate.[5] The word seems to have been used by Homer, as a verb meaning "to witness" ("know" or "learn"). The origin of the word is mainly linked to that famous work on the Persian Wars which opens with the words, "These are the *istoria* of Herodotus." Herodotus used the word as a noun: he meant "inquiries," "investigations," or "researches."[6] The word, as such,

---

3. Yet, even as we begin such an exercise, we face a problem of approach. Whichever approach may be selected, bias of perspective seems unavoidable. Any study being written in America, in English, and addressed to an English-reading world, must necessarily proceed from the parochial "known" and culture-bound worlds of its readers. Any such study unavoidably communicates within contexts and perspectives of readers in the "West" (wherever this may be), as distinct from perspectives held in various parts of the non-Western or Afro-Eurasian worlds. Circumstances dictate what is, in effect, a self-consciously practical and tactical decision — namely, to focus upon the English word *history* and to seek to discover how it has come to be what it now is.

4. *OED*, s.v. "history."

5. Whenever and however the term(s) was first used, a matter still far from settled, I am indebted to several colleagues, especially Kenneth S. Sacks (Brown) and Stephen Humphreys (now at California-Santa Barbara), for enlarging my view of such issues. Louis Gottschalk, in *Understanding History: A Primer of Historical Method* (New York: Alfred A. Knopf, 1950), 41ff., briefly explores the origin of *istoria (historie)*.

6. *Herodotus: The Persian Wars*, trans. George Rawlinson, with an introduction by Francis R. B. Godolphin (New York: Modern Library, 1942), ix. Herodotus, the fabled "Father of History" (often also reviled as "Father of Liars"), opened his classic with the words, "These are the *istoria* [inquiries, investigations, researches, etc.] of Herodotus. . . ." Whether or not he was the first to use the term, which seems doubtful, it is from this usage that the title of his work came and with which his fame is

may have originally been used to designate anything in the world that was "witnessed"; and it may then have been applied to any more systematic (or scientific) account of things that actually existed in the "natural," "real," or "seen" world.[7] Whether or not the order, system, or world being considered happened to consist of chronological events and whether or not events could have been better described by means of narrative episodes is not at all clear (and may have been incidental). Whatever the case, by the time of Thucydides, understandings conveyed by this noun consisted of nothing more nor less than facts, carefully arranged combinations of facts, and arguments based thereon. (This old meaning of *history*, though perhaps now somewhat rare, may still be found in the modified usage, "natural history.") By Roman times, with the transfer of this term into Latin, *historia* had come more strictly to mean "story" or "narrative" of past events in the form of an account, story, or tale in which incidents (either real or imaginary) would be sequentially related.

Interestingly, the English word *science*, coming from the equivalent but later Latin noun *scientia*, seems, at least originally, to have meant much the same thing. The term *science*, however, seems to have retained more of its original meaning. Thus, it continues to be used more regularly to designate systematic accounts (or explanations) of phenomena. Moreover, it now seems, more often than not, and yet not always nor even necessarily, to be applied to synchronic or nonchronological kinds of observation. This bias seems to pertain even though, ironically, much "scientific" description is actually narrative in character. One may also note, in this connection, that what we now call "natural science" and "natural history" was also once known as "natural philosophy." At the same time, of course, many older meanings of the word *history* have been blended together, changed, or disappeared. So seen, *history*, as we now use it, is the word often used both for the "recalling" or "recounting" of things past and as that more formal and systematic setting down of understandings about events. Both descriptions and explanations are

---

connected. For recent work, see Francois Hartog, *The Mirror of Herodotus: The Representation of the Other in the Writings of History*, trans. Janet Lloyd (Berkeley: University of California Press, 1988), xv-xxii.

7. Sometimes, however, the term seems to have been extended so as to apply to the "unseen" and/or also "supernatural" worlds, or at least to such forces. Both Homer and Herodotus seem to have done this.

contained within meanings of this single term. Usually of a lower-level, more particularistic, or non-universal character and usually set down within some sort of chronological or narrative framework, history is a disciplined and formal "branch of knowledge which deals with past events, as recorded in writings or as otherwise ascertained."[8]

Another source for understanding our English word *history*, one that is just as common, seems to have come down to us from the German word *geschichte*. This noun, stemming from the verb *geschehen*, means "to happen." It seems just as likely to be what many may really have had in mind when they have wanted to refer to "what has happened" or to "the past." By putting these two very different roots together, it seems clear that what is meant by history as "the past" — as "what has happened" (history as *geschichte*) — also depends upon forms of "systematic learning" and "narrative learning" which history as "witness," as "inquiry," as "facts," as "understanding," and as "narrative" (history as *istoria*) has acquired. History as the understandings of events, whether discovered, uncovered, or recovered, is thus put into more formal, systematic, and/or narrative structures which have been drawn from memory or written records.[9] This Nordic form, both in its content and its meaning, can be found within the traditions of many other cultures. It is perhaps nowhere more clearly, closely, and explicitly paralleled than in the Sanskritic term *itihāsa*, meaning "as it happened."[10] (Classical Greek and Indian roots and usages are more closely examined in chapter 7.)

8. *OED*, s.v. "history." But even these now conventional features are sometimes being scorned and, alas, are too often missing in the work of some academic and professional historians today, especially those who seem to be writing only for their academic peers rather than for a society that wishes to know about its past.

9. For further elucidation, read F. H. Bradley's famous pamphlet, "The Presuppositions of Critical History" (Oxford: James Parker & Co., 1874); also found in *Collected Essays* (Oxford: Clarendon Press, 1935; and Don Mills, Ont.: J. M. Dent, 1968), 7-8. Michael Stanford, *The Nature of Historical Knowledge* (Oxford and New York: Basil Blackwell, 1986), uses "history-as-events," or *res gestae*, and "history-as-story," or *historia rerum gestarum*, to make the same distinction. He, in turn, cites G. W. F. Hegel, *The Philosophy of History* (Dover Publications, 1956), 60.

10. Sir Monier-Williams et al., *Sanskrit-English Dictionary* (Oxford: Clarendon Press, 1899), s.v. "itihāsa." I am indebted to my Wisconsin colleague, Professor V. Narayana Rao, for insights on this subject. As explained and indicated in the preface, the circumstance of my being a historian of India means that, quite understandably, I shall be inclined to draw many of my comparisons and examples from that field of specialization.

Apparent but deceptively simple distinctions discerned from such root sources as these may be helpful. But they are only a beginning, hardly scratching the surface of problematic issues surrounding the definition of history. Implications much more profound and sweeping than may seem evident at first glance can perhaps be better appreciated by closely exploring some of the finer gradations into which this double concept can be broken and by then pursuing various ramifications.

## I. History as Event: Past and Present, If Not Future

History, in this "objective" sense, is as compelling and deep, as complex and rich, as all existence itself. Indeed, there is a sense in which History embraces, and is identical with, all existence. All things that now exist — and all things (substances concrete or abstract) that have ever existed[11] — come within the purview of what "has happened" (*geschehen*). In this sense, all existence, both past and present, can be understood to be History. In this sense, all things that have ever possessed "being" (or have "come to be") are historical. History is all that has ever existed, all that has ever actually happened, and all that has "passed," all that has "come to pass," or all that can be "*located* in the past" (or in the present). History encompasses all of the ceaseless flow and changing forms and qualities which any and all events (or things) might have possessed. As such, History includes any and every past event anywhere in this universe (or in any other universe). It includes the tiniest squeak or spark that might have occurred in the remotest corner of space at the remotest moment of time. If all of existence began with a "big bang" or if any

11. What can be either included in or excluded from this compendium of "all things," of course, is "God." The question of how a single Supreme Being, as Creator or Maker and Sustainer of "all things" that "now exist," "have existed," "have happened," or even "will happen," fits *into* or remains *outside* of history is, more strictly, a theological question. How, for example, an "eternal" or "everlasting" Being, "who was, who is and ever shall," or who existed "before all things" or who "created all things," can be any more than "historical," limited to phenomena manifest in space and time, is not a question that a historian can answer. Yet, even so, the question of whether God, as ever-existing and pre-existing, is also an event is also a question that perhaps cannot be answered. Again, the question of whether what "exists" is *something* that is an event — some object, substance, or abstraction that "has happened" — is, it would seem, complex and tricky. More issues surround this question than can be fruitfully explored here.

other single event — or any combination of events — brought the universe into being, then it is at that precise moment and place that History, in this sense, is seen as having begun. This is so no matter however many countless trillions of ages or light-years ago this may have been. But, if something — anything or anyone — *caused* that "bang," then "the past" goes back even further and one can then try to see if, and when and where, some beginning or original cause can be found.[12]

Some have even speculated that there was *no* beginning. Such thinking, when pursued further, has led to the argument that, since there never was a beginning to the universe, there can never have been such a thing as an initial start of History. And since no beginning can ever be found, moreover, even events themselves are no more than illusions (unworthy of serious notice). Of course other thinkers have also implied that, therefore, there can be no such thing as History (as in "the past"); and that the past is merely another figment of imagination, something dreamed up and existing only in the human mind. History, and all existence, from this perspective, is nothing more than a purely metaphysical abstraction. It is what *advaita vedanta* thinkers call *maya*.[13]

Nevertheless, whatever one believes concerning this matter, the concept of History, in the sense of all of existence and of all events in all of the past (and present), can then also by the same logic be seen as including each and every smallest particle or micro-"zillionth" of any event. It can be seen as implying that tiniest flicker of light. That something which instruments have not yet discovered but which may have

12. So considered, or investigated, a thinker looking at such phenomena can just as easily be labeled "cosmologist," "mathematician," "philosopher," "physicist," "scientist," or even "theologian." Meanings applied to what is done in such seemingly disparate disciplines as history and physics and science and theology can thus be seen as virtually becoming, more or less, the same.

13. "Hindu" philosophical and religious literature abounds with references to this central concept. Summaries of these may be found in such standard texts as those of A. L. Basham, *The Wonder That Was India* (London: Sidgwick and Jackson, 1954), 328; Pratima Bowes, *The Hindu Religious Tradition* (London and Boston: Routledge and Kegan Paul, 1977), 164-78; T. J. Hopkins, *The Hindu Religious Tradition* (Encino, Calif.: Dickenson, 1971), 99-101, 119; K. M. Sen, *Hinduism* (Harmondsworth: Penguin, 1961), 37, 83; S. Radhakrishnan and C. A. Moore, *A Sourcebook of Indian Philosophy* (Princeton: Princeton University Press, 1957), 589-97; and H. Zimmer, *Philosophies of India* (Princeton: Princeton University Press, 1951), 19; Heinrich Robert Zimmer, *Myths and Symbols in Indian Art and Civilization* (New York: Pantheon Books, 1946), index under *maya*.

originated trillions of light-years ago is also historical in an objective sense.[14] It can also be conceived as including any elemental idea or spark of imagination, even any mental quirk, whether large or small and whether or however expressed (or not expressed). So conceived, History is existential to the very point of including the exact moment — if there is such a thing as a "point" or "moment in time" or even "process of time of transition" between the future and the past, from what is about to be to what has already just been or has just gone by — when something comes into being or ceases to be what it was. All existence, in short, consists only of events that have already occurred or are in the process of having occurred. This can be seen as so, whether or not these events have ever as yet been perceived, whether they have as yet been experienced or whether evidence of their having happened is ever discovered. This is so whether or not these events have yet been described or explained and thus made to come within the scope of human knowledge and understanding.[15]

Included in this meaning of the concept is another feature, something that has already been alluded to. This is a feature which is, nevertheless, "present," "here" or "there." Whether or not it can readily be identified or isolated so as to be perceived, it is something found, something pertaining to all the past or all past events about which there has been much speculation and theorization, especially among philosophers, scientists, and theologians. This is that feature that can be perceived as a series or a sequence of *connected events* which, for want of other labels, can be labeled *multiple events*. Historians, philosophers, scientists, and theologians alike call this feature "process." It is something that all thinkers ponder, especially when they have grappled with problems of change and continuity, with questions about causation,[16] with speculations about direction (or

14. This point is a variety of the same old argument about whether or not the falling of a tree in the forest can be considered a historical event, even if that event was never heard or observed.

15. R. Stephen Humphreys, "The Historian, His Documents, and the Elementary Modes of Historical Thought," *History and Theory* 19, no. 1 (January 1980): 2. Bradley in "The Presuppositions of Critical History" goes so far as to question whether this distinction is even possible. Whether, indeed, these words imply belief in a primordial element of history — the event — is something which, in itself, perhaps requires a measure of critical analysis and philosophical validation not pursued here.

16. Maurice Mandelbaum, "Causation," in *The Anatomy of Historical Knowledge*

teleology), if not about destiny and purpose to events (and to all of existence).[17]

Of course, a definition of History that includes all things that have ever existed and all events that have ever happened — whatever their direction of "development" or "evolution" — must embrace elements both inanimate and animate. Events are both cosmological and geological, physical or metaphysical (i.e., mental events, abstractions, and ideas conceived by the mind).[18] Quite obviously, any exclusive confining of the use of the term *History* to this meaning alone, even while it often occurs both in popular usage and also in philosophical and scientific discussions, is not adequate.[19] The definition is simply too broad and too imprecise to be very useful. That to which it refers is too vast and vague to be comprehended. Even for ordinary everyday discourse, use of the term *History* in this broadest sense of "everything that has existed," without narrowing or qualifying or refining adjective(s), leads to much confusion.[20]

And yet, use of the word *History* in this broadest sense *is* valid. It does occur and, indeed, is quite common. One cannot simply wish it

---

(Baltimore and London: Johns Hopkins University Press, 1977), 49-142, 169-94, 199-204, gives a full discussion of this subject. Also, W. H. Dray, "Causal Judgment in History," in *Philosophy of History* (Englewood Cliffs, N.J.: Prentice-Hall, 1964), 41-58.

17. Those thinkers who have been preoccupied with such large questions about the nature of the past (existence and events) are sometimes designated as being preoccupied with "speculative history" as distinct from "critical history," and with metaphysical approaches to History as distinct from empirical inquiries into History.

18. Pure physicalists or materialists consider mental events and intellectual abstractions to be little more than complex biochemical or electrochemical (and electromagnetic) alterations of balances and changes within the cells of the brain (which is sometimes metaphorically likened to a computer possessing both "hardware" and "software" components).

19. "Speculative history" of this kind, as distinct from "critical history," can be traced back to the earliest philosophers. Associated with such names as Hegel, Toynbee, Vico, and hosts of other modern thinkers — including many thinkers within Judeo-Christian traditions — such thinking has never been fashionable among practicing historians. Dray, "Causal Judgment in History," 1-2.

20. As already indicated, the concept of *natural* history already includes everything that exists and, as such, is almost synonymous with *natural* philosophy and/or *natural* science. But other adjectives, such as *biological* or *geological* history and such, serve to narrow the focus to that part of the past that is of special interest. In the fields of *speculative* history, where teleological issues are wont to be raised, philosophical and theological issues of a very different order are raised.

away, ban it by fiat, or legislate it out of existence. While there may be good reason to find an altogether separate term — "the past"[21] (or some other word) — to designate this broadest sense of the concept, any attempt to implement a common, altogether exclusive acceptance (and use) of any other more precise word so as to convey only this meaning seems impracticable. Such being the case, we must work with what we have. Until some alternative gains acceptance, we must try to make do with the conventional word, with all its conceptual baggage. Difficult as this may be, use of the word *History* to designate all that has happened in the past *(geschehen)* must continue.

For our purposes, therefore, the term *History*, with an upper-case or capital *H*, and the terms *event* and *past*, as referring to "all that has happened" *(geschichte* or *itihāsa)*, can be used interchangeably. Also for purposes of convenience, one can try to make sure that labels for this broadest of all meanings for the concept are clearly marked, and that specific modifying adjectives are placed in front of the terms *History* and *past* or *event*, as also *history* as some form of understanding about History. Thus the particular kind of focus upon History in this "objective" sense needs to be identified; and then, more narrowly defined and subdefined, with subcategories specified as precisely as possible.

Once this task is undertaken, the broadest aspect or category of this first definition of History can then be broken down. By carefully breaking all existence into bits, by dividing and subdividing all that has ever existed and all that has ever happened into segments and into categories and subcategories, one can separate geological History from cosmological History — separating existence on this planet from whatever has existed or may have existed anywhere else in the universe. Then, within geological History,[22] one can separate what has happened to things that live or have lived (animate things) from what has hap-

---

21. Words like "destiny" or "teleology," for example, link past, present, and future. J. H. Plumb, in *The Death of the Past* (New York: Houghton Mifflin, 1969), has argued about how "domination of the past" and the "critical historical process" which is "destructive of the past," has caused a "weakness of the past" and "death of the past." Such expressions add confusion to our understandings and usages. What he is really referring to is the hold or influence that perceptions or understandings of the past have exercised upon minds.

22. Normally this term is applied only to things of the earth, either on or below its surface crust, which do not live (especially to minerals and rocks and such).

pened to things that could not and never could have lived (inanimate things). Again, all that has happened to beings that live or have lived can be further separated into subcategories and sub-subcategories. Eventually, one arrives at only those things which have happened to that one category of life which we call "humankind" (or humanity).

But when we finally come to what has happened to make humankind more than merely a minor appendage to animate existence and more than merely an animal segment of biological events, we come to the central focus of almost all historical concern and interest. Whether in folklore or literature, music or poetry, art or science — in any and all kinds of ways of looking at the past — this is where most of the "objects" which are the "subjects" of thinking and writing about History can be found. What is there in man's past that is distinctive? What is it that makes mankind "human"? What might have happened in the past to make mankind into something that might even be *more* than human? And finally, what is it that has tended to make mankind much *less* than human? Concern or interest in persons as individuals and in families as communities of human beings has ever prompted certain people to take special pains to *remember* and to discover, rediscover, or uncover the nature of past experiences and understandings. Efforts to recall, to record or register, and to understand certain details concerning past existence and events, especially those events to which special meaning has been attached, seem always to have interested human beings. As far as we know, interest in History, especially in their own particular pasts, has always been a preoccupation, if not an obsession, among communities of human beings.[23]

Even so, by far the most of all that has happened even within the human past of mankind is far beyond any hope of recall. And if this is so for the "human" past, how much greater is the loss beyond discovery or recall of all the rest of The Past (for all that is included within the focus of Cosmic and Natural History)? Few even among those human beings who possess enormous memories and brilliant minds can remember, much less "re-create," more than the tiniest parts within the total sum of experiences or perceptions of events even from within their own separate pasts. Most of each person's perceptions are so short-lived

23. Reasons for interest and obsession are discussed in the section on belief and significance. Cf. pp. 12-14, 261ff., and 304ff.

as to leave almost no durable impression; and what impressions can be retained are often very badly distorted and flawed. If this is so even at the time, or shortly after the time, when most events are experienced — since most events leave hardly any impression — how much more profound is the vanishing of events and experiences from memory or record with each passing day and week, to say nothing of the passing of months and years beyond counting? Experiences of generations long dead and gone, most of which have passed unremembered and unrecorded, vanish with hardly a trace. Most of them will remain undisturbed, beyond any historian's touch. Most of the human past, in other words, is simply lost. It is beyond any hope of recovery. Its reconstruction is, therefore, virtually unattainable.[24]

Yet it is this very kind of existence, this human past of events relating to special forms of self-awareness and self-consciousness, that is of such paramount interest to mankind. What might have happened to make behavior *nonhuman* (less than "acceptable," whether "subhuman" or "inhuman") or what may have awakened efforts perceived as having been *superhuman* ("heroic" if not "godly") never ceases to arouse curiosity. This Human Past is ever an object of further exploration. Expeditions are made to search it out and such attempts are forever being expanded. Elements of its substance are ever being isolated and broken down into rarified and special subcategories. The process of conceptualizing, of defining and subdefining, to refining and sifting things from the past, things that have existed and events that have happened, is a never-ending human quest. It is something that goes on continually, sometimes at enormous cost. Larger chunks of finite existence are being cut into ever smaller bits and pieces. And these smaller components of those events that comprise past existence are then being subjected to ever closer scrutiny. The smallness of objects or forms of past human activity that can be subjected to rational analysis or upon which attention might be more closely focused sometimes seems to have no limit other than the limits of human imagination. Each of these ever smaller sub-subcategories or sub-subdefinitions of events — each tini-

---

24. Of course, even though it is *lost*, what is lost still contains *meaning*. Questions that can be raised, however, pertain to how significant what is lost may be in human History, how this is enhanced by the simple recognition of its being lost, and how much meaning the question itself serves to bring by the fact of our linking what is lost to natural history.

est particle of History — can be given its own label.[25] The process of doing this can be intellectual and rational or it can be emotional and sentimental. It can be (and often is) itself perceptual and conceptual. It can be creative, interpretive, and inventive. It is, of course, an intrinsically *human* kind of activity. And, as such, even past historical understandings of the past have themselves become objects of creative investigation, of imaginative interpretation, and of laborious deconstructions and reconstructions. Our past understandings of the past are those parts of our own past that often interest us most.

But, as often as not, each of these little particles of the human past can itself be lumped together and either some or all portions of the whole can be vaguely referred to as History.[26] This is done even when, in reality, each distinct kind of focus *within* what is actually "Human History" ought to be more clearly specified. Thus, for example, what has happened to human behavior due to certain kinds of genetic mutations in hybrid grain (which we call the "Green Revolution"), what kinds of social institutions should exist (families, tribes, nations, etc.), or how behavior may be influenced by ways in which biochemical mutations within certain kinds of blood cells (T-Helper cells: a kind of leucocyte) are infected by other cells (causing a worldwide epidemic) may be parts of the past that are of special interest. Wars, famines, epidemics, brutalities, crises, sufferings, and indignities, paralleled by feats of heroic courage, opportunities squandered through sloth and stupidity, escape from misery and oppression, fundamentalist movements, and innumerable hosts of other interrelated events — either in *my* country or in someone else's — can provide a wide scope for the scrutinizing of human events. It is by focusing upon such events — any or all of which have made mankind as human or inhuman (if not inhumane) as it is or of what mankind is struggling to be — that we attempt to find our identities. Thereby, we provide ourselves with our most common definitions of "the Past" and give ourselves our most common coinings of meaning for the word *History.* It is about this kind

25. But as we shall see below, it is this process of "labeling" — this experiencing, perceiving, remembering, recording, explaining, portraying, and telling — that is the gist, the sum and substance of history in the second great sense.

26. Most common of all connotations and denotations of History, in this sense, have pertained to the political narratives of countries, nations, peoples, and states in their relations to each other.

of past, this History *(geschichte)* of human affairs, that efforts are made to acquire greater insight and learning and understanding *(istoria)*.

Concerning History in this common sense of the term, Boyd C. Shafer wrote: "History is all that has happened to men: all of man's experience, all of man's actions, political strivings, economic organizations, social groupings; all of man's ideas, good and bad, logical and illogical. In short it is everything in man's past."[27] His meaning of the term comes closest to the central focus of this study. But it is also this meaning and this central focus which, in and of itself, brings us to our other major definition for the concept of history.[28]

## II. History as Perceptions of Events

The second major meaning of the word *history* is clearly and exclusively cognitive. There is a huge difference between "all that has existed" and "all that is *known* about *part* of what has existed" or "all that is *understood* about *some* of what has happened." The term *history* (lower-case *h*) might just as properly be called "historical description," "historical explanation," "historical interpretation," "historical knowledge," "historical narrative," "historical understanding," or something similar. History, in this sense, is a specific kind of *human* activity. As such, it rests upon *perceptions* of events and upon the ways in which perceptions of events are turned into *conceptions* of events.[29]

There are at least two levels of historical perception: First, there are those *experiences* of events, out of all experiences of events, which have somehow been either directly *remembered* or *recorded*. Such experiences can be either personal or communal, the latter being experiences-in-common shared by two or more persons or by larger groups

27. Boyd C. Shafer, "History, Not Art, Not Science, But History: Meanings and Uses of History," *Pacific Historical Review* 29 (May 1960): 159.

28. But it is just at this interface between the two major meanings of the term — history as existence *(cum* event) and history as explanation *(cum* experience and evidence leading to knowledge) — that the great confusions of miscommunication and of people "talking past one another" usually occur.

29. If I can be charged with giving a privileged status to "events" (each and all) and, in so doing, with holding an *a priori* assumption, I can only reply that "the past" consists of nothing other than "events" and that historical understandings rest upon perceptions of nothing else.

of people. Second, there are those *evidences* of events — evidences of remembered experiences of events — which have either been left by humans (as artifacts, records, etc.) or which have been left not by humans but by "nature" (animate or inanimate events not due to human agency) and which, on one occasion or another, have been valued as holding significance. It is mainly from experience and from evidence of experience, in short, that perceptions are gained about what has happened in past (or is happening in current) human affairs.[30] Yet, also arising from remembered experience and recorded evidence is a third element which is essential for the acquisition of historical knowledge. This activity is sometimes called "historical explanation" (or "historical interpretation").[31]

Explanations of events, as already indicated, must draw upon either experience or evidence, if not upon both. But whether or not explanations are anything more than "mere" descriptions is a matter open to debate.[32] Some consider that descriptions alone, in and of themselves, serve not only as keys to how one arrives at historical explanations but also can be seen as comprising the very essence of historical understanding itself (see chapter 9).[33]

Others, for whom description alone is not sufficient and for whom more than description is required to give us proper historical understanding, insist that some further intellectual activity, whether in various forms of *analogy* (comparisons, correlations, differences vs. likenesses, parallels, resemblances etc.) or of *analysis,* is necessary (if not unavoidable). Such activity, they would argue, requires one to look at *kinds* of events and then to develop abstract formulations that reflect general laws or principles; and these laws, constructed out of concepts, categories, and even catego-

30. A fuller treatment of this fascinating subject is contained in R. W. Southern, "The Historical Experience" (the text of the Rede Lecture, Cambridge), *Times Literary Supplement,* 24 June 1987, 771-73.

31. And/or "interpretation," something we will explore more fully in other sections below.

32. Alan Donagan, "Explanation in History," in *Theories of History,* ed. with introduction and commentary by Patrick Gardiner (New York: Free Press, 1959), 428-43, (reprinted from *Mind,* 1957), gives perhaps the most sophisticated treatment of this subject and, in so doing, deals with the Hempelian (or extreme positivist) position.

33. Michael Oakeshott, *Experience and Its Modes* (Cambridge: Cambridge University Press, 1933), 154, takes the opposite, anticritical and antipositivist position: "The moment historical facts are regarded as instances of general laws, history is dismissed."

ries of concepts, can then be made to encapsulate or give meaning to events and can be made to symbolize the complexities and interrelations of events.[34] Those who stress the sufficiency of description alone counter with claims that of course analysis is inescapable but that analysis is invariably implicit within any properly made description. Concepts and categories, modes of expression, symbols and metaphors, they contend, are merely embedded within accurate descriptions of events and hence, in and of themselves, invariably provide explanations of those events.[35] It would perhaps be an oversimplification to say that the difference, then, really lies between those who think that there are historical laws (or Historical Laws) and those who do not think so. Yet, positions taken by most historians have usually fallen somewhere between these polar extremes.

Whatever the case, *if* historical explanation rests upon perceptions of remembered experience, perceptions of recorded evidence (of remembered events, experiences, and "natural occurrences"), or both, then it is perceptions of existence and of those events that comprise existence that must be "discovered," "established," or "fixed" in human minds. It is perceptions themselves that must be remembered and recorded. It is perceptions of events that must be "described" or "explained." Whether taken directly in the form of experiences that can be described firsthand or whether taken indirectly in the form of evidences that are the remains (or artifacts) and records of experiences, historical understandings can still be seen as resting upon perception.[36] However acquired and established, perceptions serve to concentrate our conscious impressions or realizations (sensations, etc.) of experiences and thus, as such, provide the bedrock for what we believe to be "factual." Thus, even if perceptions are *not* in themselves facts, they provide us with what we decide to be and what are (sometimes) described as "facts"

34. Carl G. Hempel, "The Function of General Laws in History," in *Theories of History*, ed. Patrick Gardiner (New York: Free Press, 1959), 344-56 (reprinted from *Journal of Philosophy*, 1942), presents this position in its most extreme, positivistic form.

35. R. Stephen Humphreys, "Elementary Modes of Historical Thought," 2. This is one of his main arguments.

36. As already indicated, simple evidence can be animate or inanimate as well as mediate and immediate in character. But evidence that a boulder fell and caused a deep crater, for example, can combine immediate evidence and previous observation and/or experience of how such craters are made.

(or "data" to those whose perceptions are viewed as being more "scientific" in character).[37]

"Facts," especially those that are essentially and invariably "historical," can, as we have already indicated, also be considered to be of "scientific" value. But facts are not necessarily scientific simply because they are accurate or reliable. Whether or not facts are indeed scientific must depend upon the degree to which they conform to general laws, principles, or theories — or, in other words, how classifiable and "predictable" or replicable the events being described may be. Historical knowledge, moreover, also consists of the skillful (artful, logical, or plausible) arrangement and management of "facts" derived from experience and evidence.[38] Skillful management is required in order to draw inferences or make interpretations and, also, in order to pursue arguments and come to conclusions based upon statements about "*the* facts." Moreover, collections of "facts" drawn from experience and evidence can so be arranged or organized that they are then seen to possess some inner or cohesive or self-evident logic. Thus, for example, particular attention can be given to sequence ("process") and to other kinds of internal or logical connections and relationships that can be found to exist between facts. (Indeed, perceived interconnections and relationships between facts themselves sometimes suggest causality.) This is what is often meant to result from effective historical description or historical explanation. This is that kind of activity that can produce historical understanding.

*       *       *

So far, we have only begun to explore the simple distinction between (1) <u>Hi</u>story as events in the past and (2) <u>hi</u>story as explanations of

---

37. Even in our ordinary, everyday language, we do assume that our perceptions, whether right or wrong, are factual and, hence, the source of our "facts."

38. Arbitrarily, if only for purposes of analysis, a distinction can be made between "event" and "fact" — between what has actually happened (in "the past") and what has been perceived to have happened. Some make no distinction here, between event and fact, since both are seen, ontologically, as "actual" or as "real." But this can involve a fallacy of confusing the object perceived with the perception. Both may be real and both may be events; but they may not necessarily be the same event. Yet how one goes about sustaining the distinction can be another matter (and may not be all that easily done).

**perceptions of events** — between *the past* and *understanding the past*. These two definitions are basic to its most common everyday meanings. But they are only a beginning. While each can be further refined, it is the second definition that pleads for much more careful elucidation. Historical understanding consists of at least three distinct parts. However we may wish to see them — whether as aspects or branches or categories or definitions (or, more properly, subdefinitions of the second definition) — each of them falls within the perimeters of history; and, therefore, each needs to be explored. "History as Description," "History as Narrative (or Story)," and "History as Belief (or World View)" are epistemic characteristics which, in and of themselves, are essential elements within any valid attempt to achieve better understandings of the past. Together they enable us to better appreciate the fuller perimeters in the nature and limitations of historical thinking as a profoundly human enterprise. They are the foundations upon which understandings of the past can be made to rest.

*Chapter 2*

# History as Memory:
# A Primal Necessity

*Exile is caused by forgetfulness, and the secret of redemption is memory.*

Baal Shem-Tob

U p to this point, the central focus has been to explore what history is, and to do so with special reference to definitions essential for a proper use of the concept. Distinctions not made, at least not often in everyday usage, between history as "what has happened" or "what is past" and history as "what is known or understood about what has passed" cause much confusion (chapter 1). But these initial perspectives, as far as they go, are hardly more than the start of our quest. Of what use are definitions and distinctions if we cannot discover how they apply to ways in which understandings of events in the past have been acquired? How were such understandings first sought? How have primal understandings changed? What skills and tools were first used for the acquiring and utilizing of understandings of past events?

In looking at how and where historical understandings actually originate, our quest begins by turning to how and where history, through countless ages, has actually been "produced" and "practiced," in its most primordial and simple forms. Despite the many "ages" before our own that have passed, it is clear that the most basic elements with which historical understandings began are still as much in use as ever.

From earliest times down to our own, each people has had its own peculiar reasons for wanting to remember, recall, and recount "what has happened." Certain events, just a choice few out of the flood of events occurring within the past of each people, have been selected to serve this need. Each age has had its own peculiar way of understanding what it considered to be *the* important features, both of its own pasts and of other pasts, that it thought were worth knowing.

Each particular people, as also each particular person (as one of the component elements of a people), has selectively or unconsciously forgotten and lost, or at least buried and repressed, far more than it has retained out of the many details of its own past. It has lost even greater proportions of those pasts that were not its own, that at various times and for various reasons it may have uncovered. This loss, this "forgetting" of traces of things that have passed, especially of those portions of things that were once treasured, is a story in itself.[1] Some legacies not originally treasured have later been rediscovered and, for various reasons, have then become highly valued. But when things lost are later missed, partially rediscovered, and valued, or when they are then known to be irrecoverable, such losses produce regretfulness and wistfulness, even soulful lamentations. Things once lost and now missed, or sought, are features of emotion peculiar to all human beings. Both in individuals and in communities, this feature of haunting and of mourning what is gone is common to every people in every age. What a person or a people now is (or might be) — both in personal or communal identity and in continuity — is felt to be intimately bound up with things that once were.[2]

This being so, what any particular people have wanted to know about what has happened in the past and why their understandings of the past have been constructed in one particular way instead of another is itself a kind of historical inquiry. This kind of inquiry is, in fact, historical inquiry about historical inquiry. For whatever was the form of the content, or the content of the form, given to perceptions of the

1. David Lowenthal, "Forgetting," in *The Past Is a Foreign Country* (Cambridge: Cambridge University Press, 1985), 204-6. See note 3 below for more details regarding this book.

2. Mary Warnock, "Memory into Art: Paradise Regained," chap. 5 of *Memory* (London: Faber and Faber, 1987), 76-77, probes this feature in considerable depth. See also Liz Gill, "What Is Memory?" *Times* (London), 17 March 1988, 20.

past by any given people of a bygone age, those perceptions were themselves an evidence of (or reflection upon) what they themselves thought was most important. What people felt were their own most fundamental beliefs and their own views of the world provided the very foundations for that history which that people most wanted to possess and to know. A deep and primal compulsion, a necessity to probe for something felt and valued deep within all of us, something nourished by the powers of human memory, has served as the driving force that moves the wheels of historical understanding.[3]

## I. Probing for Events That Happened in the Past

Primal and primordial forms of historical understanding — as ways of retaining, regaining, or simply gaining some knowledge about the past — have always been with us. And they remain with us still. Primal history is still practiced by everyone. Not only is this so, but it is being practiced virtually all of the time. It is the only kind of historical understanding that most people possess.[4] Every individual, as a person, practices it. Every family holds on to it, preserves it, and circulates it, in one form or another. That it may not be done very well, that it may also be done badly or clumsily by most people does not alter this fundamental fact. Moreover, most of the history that has ever been (or is still being) practiced and most of the understandings of the past that have ever been held, in any given generation, have been of this sort and have been confined to "related" kindreds and lineages ("families"). Virtually all such history soon disappears and is gone. It falls into oblivion and is lost forever.[5] This fact, however, does not change the basic reality of

3. David Lowenthal, *The Past Is a Foreign Country* (Cambridge: Cambridge University Press, 1985), is the best treatment of this subject I have seen so far. See part 2, "Knowing the Past," pp. 185-262, especially chap. 5, pp. 193-209: "How We Know the Past — The Past as Experienced and Believed — Memory" [Personal and collective; Memory and identity; Confirmability; Types of Memory; Forgetting; Revising]; and pp. 210-37: "History and Memory" [as less than the past, as more than the past, etc.].

4. Carl L. Becker, "Everyman His Own Historian," *American Historical Review* 37 (1932): 221-36; reprinted in *The Historian as Detective: Essays on Evidence* (New York: Harper & Row, 1969), 3-23.

5. Lowenthal, *The Past Is a Foreign Country*, 206: "Oblivion is the fate of many events of utmost consequence when they happened."

its common if superficial practice as a primal form of historical understanding by virtually all human beings.[6] The essential question, therefore, has to do with how and why it is that *some* kinds of historical
knowledge are acquired, preserved, and transmitted, both more accurately and over longer periods of time. This question is of crucial importance.

The beginnings of all historical understandings, therefore, can be
seen to fall into two categories: First, there are processes of *remembering
and recalling and recollecting and recounting* what has passed some time
ago. What happened five minutes ago is, quite obviously, much easier
to recall than what happened five hours ago; and what happened five
weeks ago is much easier to recall than what happened five months ago;
and, unless one is getting old, what happened five years ago is much
easier to recall than what happened fifty years ago. What happened five
hundred years or five thousand years ago, however, is another matter.
Since no single life, and no person's brain, lasts that long, what actually
happened within brains that have turned to dust lies altogether beyond
the pale of direct memory. What happened within minds of those who
have died is a matter even more complicated and has been open to much
philosophical argument.[7] Even artifacts and records, except perhaps for
those of clay, stone, or precious metal, crumble and vanish, never to be
recovered.

Second, there are processes of probing and *searching for origins,
for personal or corporate identity and continuity, if not causality and
sequentiality* — for the sequential traces of how certain specific things
actually began.[8] Curiosity about how all things began — a subject sometimes called *cosmogony* — or about how some things came into being
is all pervasive. But, even more narrowly, there is an overpowering
curiosity about one single thing: how *I*, myself, as one, single, individual

6. Jan Vansina, "Memory and Oral Tradition," in *The African Past Speaks: Essays
on Oral Tradition and History,* ed. Joseph C. Miller (Hamden, Conn.: Archon, 1980),
262-79.

7. The body-mind issue, not to mention literatures pertaining thereto, is too vast
a subject to be explored here. However, a rather succinct summary is found in Warnock,
*Memory,* 1-14, 15-36, 127-28.

8. Asking about how things begin — especially how categories or sets of things
begin — is an altogether different kind of question. Such a question asks for observable
regularity and generality, for general theories, rules, principles, and laws. That is not the
same as asking how this particular thing began.

person — as a living being, self, or soul[9] — came into being. How *we*, as a corporately related entity — as a community, family, kinship, group, people — got to be where we now are is a yearning almost as amazing in its vitality and strength. This yearning is strong in each and all of us. Here also, concern arises and concentrates upon happenings or upon series of happenings that first commenced long before any one person's own memory began to function. Those happenings that lie before, behind, or beneath the initial awakening of one person's own memory of the past[10] perforce rely upon the rememberings, upon the recallings and recollections, made by others. The capacity of others to recall and recollect and recount — and, indeed, to *re*-create — and communicate some sort of image or picture, albeit in words, about happenings that another person as one individual could not possibly have experienced firsthand is a matter of remarkable importance. That being so, the words and/or pictures used to convey matters remembered need to be both clear and convincing. If they are to be effective, they must be accurately revealing and reliable. They must be exciting and interesting. But, most of all, they must inspire confidence and trust.

In simplest terms, these two sets of processes — the preserving of information (in memory or in records) and the searching for roots and origins — are epitomized in two most elemental and primitive kinds of questions asked by any parent and by any child. The typical questions, "What is that?" "What have you done today?" or "What happened to you?" elicit responses that, if accurate and true, convey historical understanding about most recent events. And a child's questions, "How did I get here?" or "Where did I come from?" will, when answered with reasonable accuracy and clarity, lead to further questions, such as "Where did you come from?" and "How did you get here?" A string of further questions will then follow, each probing more deeply into one's past until, ultimately, questions about the origins of all events, all life, and all things are broached.

Questions of this sort seem, and indeed really are, at first blush, common and elemental. They are so primal (if not primitive), so seem-

9. William Earle, "Memory," *Review of Metaphysics* 10 (1956): 3-27 [190, 94]. B. S. Benjamin, "Remembering," *Mind* 65 (1956): 312-31; reprinted in *Essays in Philosophical Psychology* (London: Macmillan, 1967), 171-94.

10. Endel Tulving, *Elements of Episodic Memory* (Oxford: Oxford University Press, 1983).

ingly simplistic, that it is easy to quickly and impatiently dismiss them out of hand. Yet, the closer one looks into what they really involve and how they are best answered, the more this initial attitude is apt to fade. Both kinds of questions pertain to processes of inquiry that are intrinsically profound. Both kinds of processes of inquiry involve techniques of investigation which, while they have become more and more sophisticated in recent times, are themselves still very old and very basic. They are so elemental and, indeed, so primordial in character. Yet they involve procedures which are altogether essential to the beginnings of historical understanding.

## II. Remembering and Recollecting What Has Passed

Answers to questions about how historical understanding begins or how it first originated, even if they themselves cannot be documented or supported from evidence, are not difficult to imagine.[11] However skimpy the evidence about how *our own* "world" of persons may have really first begun, our own immediate experience tells us much that is primal, if not primordial, both in basic simplicity and in complexity.[12] The roots of this kind of understanding lie in our own mental processes and in our own ways of recalling and recounting to ourselves and to others those events about which *we know* (or, at the very least, which we think or believe we know) to have actually happened. It is in the remembering and in the searching for what others remember about how things began; it is in the

11. What follows, it must be emphasized, is largely speculative. It is a reading back into the past of assumptions based upon human experience, ideas assumed to have verity in previous times. Perhaps the biggest assumption is that there is a common anthropology. There is no way to verify that the earliest of all human beings, at all times in the past, thought as we think, or that they wished to remember exactly as we wish to remember and understand. Indeed, it could well be that peoples in climes and times different from our own have thought in remarkably different ways. At the same time, various disciplines and technologies developed in our day, especially those which tell us how highly sophisticated supposedly "primitive" and preliterate societies really were, even ways of looking at the past, are exceedingly useful. This is skillfully argued in Claude Lévi-Strauss, *The Savage Mind* (London: Weidenfeld & Nicolson; Chicago: University of Chicago, 1966).

12. C. B. Martin and Max Deutscher, "Remembering," *Philosophical Review* 75 (1966): 161-96.

recalling, the "telling" and "retelling" that historical understanding is born within each of us.[13] How accurate and "true" (or how mistaken and "false") this remembering and recalling may be is another matter.

Again, while it is not difficult to tell, at least in some measure, what happened just a few moments ago or even, often, to produce evidence showing exactly what has just happened, difficulties multiply rapidly the further back in time and the further removed in space a given memory is placed from the actual details of the events being described. Recent research into the nature of human memory seems to indicate that there are great differences between short-term and long-term memory.[14] Moreover, recent scholarship has been able to probe ever more deeply into the open boundaries that lie between perceptions and recollections with special reference to those ontological ambiguities or those qualitative similarities and continuities which, as "ideas" or as "images," they seem to possess in common.[15]

If, on one hand, a person or a people does not take special care to remember something or take the time to drill long-term memory with exact details, only a few moments need elapse after an event has made an impression upon the mind before it can be seemingly forgotten forever and thought to be virtually irretrievable. On the other hand, there is a sense in which "nothing is ever blotted out," so that everything ever experienced is somehow "stored," even if it is not, except in exceptional circumstances, capable of retrieval.[16] Moreover, if a person or a people does develop a science of memorization, then it becomes possible to

13. Herbert Butterfield, *The Origins of History* (London: Methuen, 1981), 17-22.

14. Geoffrey R. Loftus and Elizabeth F. Loftus, *Human Memory: The Processing of Information* (Hillsdale, N.J.: Lawrence Erlbaum Associates; distributed by the Halstead Division of John Wiley & Sons, 1976). Distinctions between "Sensory Store," 11-33; "Short-Term Store," 34-55; "Long-Term Memory for New Material," 56-84; "Recognition Memory," 85-106; and "Long-Term Memory for Meaningful Material," 107-18, are based upon the results of careful scientific research done over a twenty-year period.

15. Lowenthal, *The Past Is a Foreign Country,* 193-94. Ulric Neisser, ed., "Memorists," in *Memory Observed: Remembering in Natural Contexts* (San Francisco: Freeman, 1982), 377-81; Michael M. Gruneberg, Peter E. Morris, and R. N. Sykes, *Practical Aspects of Memory* (London: Methuen, 1978); Jean Piaget and Bärbel Inhelder, *Memory and Intelligence* (London: Routledge & Kegan Paul, 1973).

16. Mary Warnock, *Memory,* 77-78, cites an instance of this kind of potential given by W. H. Hudson, *Far Away and Long Ago: A History of My Early Life* (London: Everyman, 1939).

retrieve and transmit enormous amounts of information from the human brain. This seems to have been done many thousands of years ago, both in parts of Africa and in India. Brahman ritualists, for example, seem to have memorized phenomenal amounts of information, both retaining and transmitting such "memory-held" materials by means of sound systems. These, later reduced to writing, are to be found in the *Sama Veda*.[17] We now have reason to believe, therefore, that by use of special technologies, vast collections of exact details could be passed down from generation to generation, with considerable assurance of accuracy, and that this could be done for centuries (if not for millennia). Thus, it is possible to understand how nonliterate and/or preliterate societies were able to recount and retell what they remembered, thereby conveying enormous amounts of detailed information about events of the past. They could then transmit this, we have reason to believe, from generation to generation through long periods of time.[18] Much of what we now know about the premodern African past, for example, has come down to us in this way. Moreover, we now have good reason to believe that, for thousands of years, historical understandings in Africa were so well conveyed in this way that there may not have been much incentive to reduce language to writing.[19]

17. This contains a "science of sound" which enables replication of pronunciation in tone, tempo, and tune so exactly that, its practitioners believed, the very power of the universe could be harnessed. Years ago (in 1961), the late J. A. B. Van Buitenen, professor of Sanskrit at the University of Chicago, used to illustrate his lectures by indicating that if the memnonic devices and technology of the *Sama Veda* were applied to the Chicago telephone directory, the whole of its text could be committed to memory and that the process of memorizing it would take about five years; moreover, he indicated that, once so memorized, it would be possible to recite the text either forward or backward from any given point.

18. Jan Vansina, *Oral Tradition as History* (Madison: University of Wisconsin Press, 1985) is a revised rendition of Vansina's now classic *Oral Tradition: A Study in Historical Methodology* (Chicago: Aldine Publishing Company, 1965; London: Routledge & Kegan Paul, 1965; and Harmondsworth, Middlesex: Penguin Books, 1973), a translation, by H. M. Wright, of his *De la Tradition Orale: Essai de Methode Historique* (in *Annales due Musee Royal de l'Afrique Centrale*, 1961).

19. For a brilliantly supported argument surrounding this issue, read Jan Vansina's more recent work, *Paths in the Rainforests: Toward a History of Political Tradition in Equatorial Africa* (Madison: University of Wisconsin Press, 1990). Also see the review of this work by Roland Oliver, entitled "Survival in the Rain Forest: The Birth of an African Political Tradition," in *Times Literary Supplement*, 22 February 1991, 6.

   Nevertheless, long-term remembering and recalling has always had
to be, of necessity, a collective or corporate — even a social and political
— enterprise. After all, when one, single, individual person has died,
the brain cells of that person — with their capacity for memory — have
also died. All that the memory and mind of that person had previously
recorded, including all its special gifts, insights, skills, technologies, and
understandings, have also been lost.[20] At the same time, just as it has
always been difficult for one person to keep all details exact and all
sequences straight, it has also been difficult for a group — any collec-
tivity of persons, whether one's own family or some other kind of group
— to do so. This has been so, even when one assumes the harmonious
and honest working together of many minds. In any common endeavor,
even with careful teamwork, when all strive to help each other in checking and cross-checking details about past events, events that all members
of the group have experienced and have, in some measure, retained in
their own individual memories, difficulties can still arise.[21]

   It is reasonable to assume that difficulties impede the maintaining
of accuracy in recollecting from memory. Difficulties in remembering
descriptive details about events can be assumed to increase in direct
proportion to several factors: (1) the size of the group that has been
trying to maintain its collective memory; (2) the quantity of detailed
information being preserved by means of memory; (3) the amount of
time that has elapsed between the events dredged up from the past by
memories; and (4) the substantive quality or relative abstruseness of
the information being recovered from memory. Any remembrance of
details that might have been lost, especially when they could have been
lost for some time, obviously becomes increasingly and progressively
more difficult to recall. Recovery becomes harder and harder until the
recalling itself becomes all but impossible. Therefore, continuous exercises, often in ceremonial or ritual form, become more and more
essential in direct proportion to factors of complexity and difficulty.
Otherwise, the recalling and recollection of things that have happened

   20. To use other words, quite obviously, when one body ceases to breath and
begins to disintegrate and return to dust and when the brain also ceases to function, so
that all the wonders it contains are lost, something happens that can perhaps be described, but never fully explained. No words seem adequate to entirely and fully interpret
what has then happened to the person who was once living.
   21. George Halbwachs, *The Collective Memory* (New York: Harper, 1980).

in the past become so faint that, for the most part, they are lost beyond hope of recovery. Memories fade and historical understandings are lost. As what is sought becomes ever more obscure and remote, times to which one might once have returned vanish altogether. What we hold in our heads as information about the past is like water from a river cupped into our hands, from which drops keep falling back into the river, drops that keep moving into the ocean, where drops of water lose their separate identities, and never again can be recaptured in our hands.

In other words, we can assume with some confidence that most of the peoples who have lived before us, and who might have wanted to know more about things of the past, have had enough difficulty just trying to remember the *most exciting events* or *most important things* that occurred during their own lives. Trying also to discover some of the important things that might have happened before they were born has usually been less crucial. We can assume, therefore, that peoples in all ages and all times have been able to remember and recount to each other only details about the most exciting things that have happened in their own lives. These are the things that only they themselves have experienced and witnessed firsthand. Moreover, except for the senile, they have been able to remember much more *before* they have related those things that have happened to themselves or those things that have been seen and told to them by others. They have done this, even if what they have been told has not been quite so well remembered, even if it has been exaggerated or embellished. They do this, even if what they have been told is assumed to represent only the *most noteworthy* things of the past. Noteworthy things — things that have provoked extreme excitement, extreme delight or dread, exquisite pangs of pain or pleasure, feast or famine, flood or flight, defeat or victory — are things that are more difficult to forget. But still, it is in order to hear about such things that, from generation to generation, the young sit at the feet (or upon the knees) of their elders. It is thus that they hear of amazing and wonderful things that happened long, long ago.[22]

Observations of this sort seem too simple and too speculative. Despite what is known about the human memory, there is still much

22. Mary Warnock, in her book *Memory,* gives us a much fuller and more penetrating account than can be done here, within these few paragraphs.

that we do not know. Our best findings and opinions can seem like so
much guessing. Yet it may not be too farfetched to assume, with some
certainty, that the earliest peoples of our world and those who were
preliterate (and who, even now, are deemed by some to have been very
"primal" if not "primitive") could look with wonder and insight at those
experiences that most inspired or terrified them. That they then remembered to pass on insights about what they had seen — about the lands,
the waters, the stars, the animals and birds and bugs and fishes and
much more — should not seem surprising. Can we assume that peoples
in earliest times of human and social consciousness were any less able
to make logical and rational generalizations or any less able to come to
sophisticated conclusions than people today? Can we assume that their
conclusions about how recurrences and regularities in events happened,
and about why some events happened over and over again, were necessarily less valid than our own? If there are valid reasons to presume
that conclusions drawn in earliest ages of consciousness did not enable
people to interpret the past or to draw wisdom from it which would be
less valid than conclusions that we ourselves are able to draw, these have
yet to be made clear and their cogency demonstrated by the scholarship
that we now possess.[23]

So, this, we presume, is how historical understandings first begin;
and how they first began. It is how most historical knowledge is still
generated and passed on. What was remembered was told and retold
— and this remembering and recollecting and retelling still continues:
in every person and family and people. What was handed down from
age to age within each blood-related or ethnically rooted family, household, kinship, or lineage[24] became part of the collective lore and the
collective wisdom of that primally related group and was its own
peculiar heritage. This is no less true today. Members of such families
or "extended families," as small groups, drew upon a common identity.

23. Roger Shattuck, *Proust's Binoculars: A Study of Memory, Time, and Recognition
in "A la recherche du temps perdu"* (London: Chatto & Windus, 1964). Marcel Proust,
*Remembrance of Things Past*, 3 vols., trans. from French 1913-27 edition by K. C. Scott-
Moncrieff and Terence Kilmartin (Harmondsworth, Middlesex: Penguin, 1983).
24. Our term "family" is used only with caution and hesitation. The term, with
its Latin root, possessed a very different set of meanings than that which we now attach
to it. Family and estate and household, with servants and slaves and minions great and
small, were substantially linked in one, often huge, agrarian institution.

They generated emotions of comfort and pride from the fact that they were all, at least usually, related to each other by ties of common "blood," common experience, and common legacy. If one family became very powerful and rich, so that they ruled over many other peoples and over vast territorial domains, their stories became the stories of kingdoms and empires and of peoples living under their authority. And what they told and retold, what we today may say was their own particular "folklore," was also what they perceived as being their *history*. Later, when such lore was embellished and exaggerated and when some of the oldest traditions that they kept repeating became bigger than life itself, some elements of these things also now began to be seen as becoming part of what some now call "myth" or "religion." Whether or not these elements were sometimes mingled with beliefs and convictions based upon rational analysis or were sometimes mingled with half-baked opinions and fanciful "rubbish," distinctions between one kind of element and the other are as prone to be confused in our own day as in any other. Imaginings of the past, even today, are not immune from delusion and self-deception.

The oldest of these kinds of lore, in other words, occasionally acquired dimensions of epic and mythic proportions.[25] Some tales of the past have grown so tall and have become so fantastic that only superior (or subordinate) beings, only gods and demons, could have done the things that are purported to have happened. Indeed, tales of such dimensions have tended to pertain to things and to happenings beyond ordinary human comprehension. Even if the purposes of their telling were sometimes to mystify or obscure, rather than clarify, we need hardly be surprised. Forces too huge and too mysterious, too vast to understand much less control, so that only unseen powers might possibly explain them, have often provoked speculation. In such circumstances, people turn to those who specialize in plausible explanations and interpretations, to those who can convey a sense of confidence by their ability to control, if not to "demystify," the unknown. Thus, in one way or another, understanding of what has passed also has had a tendency to be linked to the building and maintaining of world views,

25. Burr C. Brundage, "The Birth of Clio: A Resume and Interpretation of Ancient Near Eastern Historiography," in *Teachers of History: Essays in Honour of L. B. Packard*, ed. H. Stuart Hughes (Ithaca, N.Y.: Cornell University Press, 1954), 226 n. 5.

ultimate values, and religious beliefs. (And, obviously and understandably, all of this kind of activity still continues to capture attention and
fascinate people in our own day.)

It is when the past has been remembered, recovered, recalled,
recollected, and *re*-created in this fashion that distinctions between
what is human, more than human, or less than human, between people
and gods (or demons), or even between abstractions of a more universalistic nature, have become obscured. Stories of experiences that
happened long, long ago, about hoary events of bygone years, could
then also be transformed into actions. They could be conveyed by
means of ceremony and by performances of ritual, so that historical
understanding could then become bound up in actions and deeds of
a much later time. Opinion and belief, myth and history, could become
so bound together, so confused and so intermingled, that they might
seem to have become the very same thing. Thus, if dire and terrible
events had once occurred, actions taken at a later time could become
a means of trying to make sure that such terrible things would never
happen again. Collective memory about the past could thus become a
way of trying to gain control over events in the future. For this reason,
episodes in major narratives and epics have often, and indeed have
usually, tended to include all kinds of seemingly extraneous materials.
Not only do they contain substories or sub-substories, each deftly
woven into the much larger tapestry of a grander master epic or of
the higher oral tradition, but they also contain all sorts of tiny bits of
mingled insight and ritual.

Among the most ancient narratives of this sort, each containing
hundreds of tiny bits of extraneous and historical material mingled
together, are the great epics and sagas of the past. Within the fabric of
each such tradition are many sorts of memorable lore, each cunningly
woven and blended together. Here one finds anecdotes, aphorisms,
ballads, battle cries, chants, dances of victory, droll jibes, exultings and
wailings, fabulous fables, sublime hymns, incantations, laments, parables, parodies, poems, prayers, and lyric verses of song. All of these, in
one way or another, can be related to remembrances of heroic deeds,
or to dire tragedies, of a bygone, earlier age.

Usually, at the center of each such collection, one can find the
memories of one person, someone whose life was so grand and heroic
and bigger-than-life, and yet so tragic, that the fascination of later

generations for this personage never seems to end.[26] Is this not why, in every culture, there are legends like those of Arthur or Beowulf, Rama or Krishna, Achilles or Ulysses (and many more) which are repeated again and again? Are not such legacies forever recapturing the imaginations of each new generation? Fact and fiction — categories perhaps clearer and more distinct in our own day, at least in ideal terms, than they once were — have in times past been deftly and wonderfully woven into apparently seamless and continuous pieces of fabric, so that, sometimes, only those scholars who specialize in such things can separate them.[27]

To recapitulate, therefore, we can acknowledge, if only by a massive assumption that cannot be disproved, that every person — and every kindred ("family," "folk," "community," "nation") and people — possesses, and has always possessed, a unique history by which a particular past is understood. No one is now, nor ever has been, without some sense of a personal past, some sense of having shared in a common set of things that have happened and things that have made that person or that person's people what he or she now sees or thinks that they have become. This remembered past is a "shared tradition," of something recalled and recounted over and over again. Call it anecdote, epic, legend, lore, myth, saga, or story, it is a narrative legacy that has been treasured. Later, after developing tools of memory, rhetoric, and literacy, some of what has been carefully remembered has been preserved in more highly stylized oral forms; and, still later, these have been written down. Either way, this legacy has been put "on record" by being reduced

26. Warnock, "The Story of a Life," in *Memory,* 127-46.
27. Chapter 3, "History as Story: A Narrative Art," explores this boundary more fully. Undoubtedly, the *Iliad* and the *Odyssey,* attributed to Homer (whoever he was?), are the primal examples of this in the West. J. R. R. Tolkien, "Beowulf: The Monsters and the Critics," Sir Israel Gallancz Lecture, presented 25 November 1936, published in *Proceedings of the British Academy* 3-53, discusses the significance of recapturing, renovating, and restructuring a culture's pagan past. In my own field, colleagues are demonstrating how hoary memories in Telugu and Tamil culture are being both recaptured and reinterpreted for our own day: e.g., Gene H. Roghair, *The Epic of Palnādu: A Study and Translation of "Palnāti Vīrula Katha, A Telugu Oral Tradition from Andhra Pradesh, India"* (Oxford: Clarendon Press, 1982); *Śiva's Warriors: The "Basava Purāna of Pālkuriki Somanātha"* (Princeton: Princeton University Press, 1990), translated from the Telugu by Velcheru Narayana Rao, assisted by Gene H. Roghair; and David Dean Shulman, *The "King" and the "Clown" in South Indian Myth and Poetry* (Princeton: Princeton University Press, 1985) are only a tiny set of samples.

to formalized symbols. Then later, whether in oral or written form, this record has remained as part of that very essential "stuff," the material out of which later historical understandings have subsequently been constructed.

Many of the oldest cultures in the world, such as those of equatorial Africa, seem to have remained satisfied with their primal forms of historical understanding, passing them down for millennia. The "literature" which they held in elaborated systems of memory until very recently seem to have served well. Something durable of what was remembered is still accessible to them, and to some of us. Some amazingly detailed and exact and full accounts of the past which particular peoples have possessed, containing vast amounts of historical understanding about themselves, can still be found. Jan Vansina and other scholars have shown how oral traditions have been capable of other various kinds of validation. These, when later checked and subjected to critical testing by many of our most sophisticated and "modern" technologies, have proven themselves to be truly amazing structures of historical understanding.[28]

## III. Recalling, Recounting, and Recording What Happened

Memories of regularity and repetitions of similar experiences have always been intimately connected to notions concerning the past. Day and night, sunrise and sunset, full moon and crescent moon, life and death, growth and decay, dry season and wet season, hot times and cold times: the regular comings and goings, ebbs and flows, risings and fallings in the turning cycles of events in nature and in human affairs have been marked and noted and remembered. All of this has gone on for so long that no one can tell us exactly when such things first began. The counting of regularities, such as cycles, the finding of correlations, and the reflecting upon what such things might mean are activities so old that, for long periods of time, it is difficult even to imagine exactly how they could first have originated. Yet such imaginings (now formalized into "theories") seem always to have occurred. Even the primal origins of "counting" — of measuring and numbering things (and then,

28. Jan Vansina, *The Oral Tradition.*

of developing ideas of numeration into systems: binary, quinary, decimal, duodecimal, etc.) — are so remote, so buried, beyond memory, in the past that even with our very best tools for recalling and rediscovering the past, we merely speculate and wonder about the details of how such things could have started in the first place.[29]

The measuring and numbering and weighing of "time" and "times" is a case in point. After the counting of possessions, how did the counting (and sequential numbering) of such natural events as days and months and years, or the dividing or multiplying of these events into parts — that is, hours (as parts of days) and weeks or fortnights (as numbers of days, or as parts of months); and cycles of months (making years) or cycles of aggregated years (such metaphysical entities as decades and centuries and millennia); and all other extended or fixed segments and spans of time — first begin and then develop? Yet the very counting and numbering and naming of years, it is reasonable to assume, were developments that, in and of themselves, were of great significance.[30] To be sure, if people were to remember certain events more accurately, someone had to start the counting and numbering and naming of events — how many days, weeks, months, or years had passed *since* or *after* or *before* some other memorable event had occurred would serve as a system of markers. Usually, "important" and hence memorable events which had marked minds most were those perceived by all in a community, by common agreement, to have been so — some major crisis or some "natural" happening. Some birth or some cataclysmic or catastrophic consequence, such as a "never-to-be-forgotten" famine or fire or flood; some dreadful battle or awful earthquake or pestilence: any such event would stand out in every mind. So also would the founding of a dynastic household or city. Such an event provided each and every person belonging to a local community with a common focal point for measuring and counting other, lesser events. Questions of how

29. For a clear and relatively simple history of numeration systems, see also *World Book Encyclopedia*. Certainly the Hindu-Arabic development of the place-value principle (or decimal point) and the "zero" (or symbol for "nothing" or "not any") must rank among the greatest of all inventions.

30. For elaboration, see *Macropaedia*, vol. 15 of *The New Encyclopedia Britannica*, 15th ed., s.v. "Calendar"; and *Micropaedia*, vol. 2 of *The New Encyclopedia Britannica*, s.v. Babylonian, Assyrian, Hittite, Egyptian, Greek, Roman, Jewish/Christian, Muslim, Hindu, Chinese, Mayan, Mexican systems, etc.

long things lasted, questions of duration and sequence, then begin to take on some new kinds of meaning. In relation to cycles of regularity that "everyone" could understand, special and unpredictable turnings away from regularity could then be marked by reference to those things that could be measured, counted, and numbered; and among important points of reference, all countings could then be duly marked down, named, and recorded in memory.

The question of just how and when people began to mark things down and to record memories by means of written marks — whether days and months and years, or anything else — cannot be answered. After all, even marks (or tallies) recorded upon the bark of a tree trunk are a form of "writing"; moreover, if marks were placed in one place or upon one object for scores or hundreds of years, they were eventually prone to disappear. This could well have been what happened with respect to almost all of the earliest marks and to all earliest forms of "writing," especially when made on perishable materials. Such records, of course, were eventually, and in all probability, prone to be lost; and such records and artifacts would remain lost to later generations. Yet, eventually, the question of durability arises and the use of materials that would not decay seems to have become an issue in itself. If monuments could be made to last, and if dwellings and tools could be made to endure the ravages of time and use, then surely markings could be made to last from generation to generation, so as not to be lost. This kind of marking or recording would have become a matter of importance at a very early date, even before the technology of writing itself was developed. Durability of materials, whether made of stone or of noncorruptible metals, can be seen as one kind of "tool" which, along with writing, could be made to serve the collective memory of a society.[31]

Markers for counting were probably among the first long-term records. But there is also a sense in which artifacts, buildings, coins,

---

31. Lest one take a condescending attitude toward those who first tried to make, keep, and preserve records, a closer look at the quality of records kept in our own day can be instructive. It is interesting that paper made two and three centuries ago — out of parchment or on 100 percent rag paper — has lasted much longer and is in better condition than paper produced in the twentieth century. Our paper and newsprint, with its high acid content, even our microfilm and digital records, will not last as long as older manuscript records. The long-term durability of records in electronic or computerized form is also questionable.

dwellings, and monuments (as also works of art and decoration), while not perhaps intended as aids for remembering the past, have served as records nonetheless.[32] Moreover, depending on how one wishes to define writing, such records can also be seen as an early form of writing. Thus, despite much speculation, we cannot be sure exactly how and when written kinds of records first came into being. We can perhaps only go so far as to presume that by the time words could be written down (whether in pictorial or phonetic form), markings for purposes of remembering things had already been in use for some time. However such developments originally came into use — a matter still subject to debate — none can deny the quantum leap in historical understanding that became possible when things "immediately" remembered could also be "written down." Of course writing became, in and of itself (not to mention its by-products), a technological revolution of tremendous significance.[33]

It is important to remind ourselves at this point that neither the procedures for remembering and recalling nor the procedures for recounting and recording, as such, can be confused with the content or with the nature of historical understanding. Nor can we assume that such things as remembering or recording, by themselves, can have anything to do with procedures for critical and self-critical evaluation. All kinds of things can be remembered or recorded without any deepening of our understandings about the past or any increasing of our insights or wisdom relating thereto. One can remember to do hosts of ordinary, mundane, routine, or even trivial things — avoiding a chilling draft, watching one's step, listening to instructions, closing doors and windows, or counting one's change — which, in most contexts, are simply matters of common or practical self-interest. Likewise, one can keep all sorts of old records — ticket stubs, canceled checks, shopping lists, former addresses, appointment books, travel maps, or household directions — which are no longer valid; and these would thereby normally serve to provide better knowledge about the past. While it might be true

32. For later historians, especially for modern historians, of course, there can be no doubt about the value of such materials as historical sources for better historical understanding.

33. Albertine Gaur, "Origin and Development of Writing," and "The Main Groups: Their Characteristics, History, and Development," in *A History of Writing* (London: The British Library, 1984, 1987), 13-134.

that past experiences could have taught us something about the consequences of *not* remembering such things or of *not* keeping such records (and one may even concede that these items too, in their essence, were historical data or sources), we can still justly question, for historical purposes, the need or value of preserving useless antiques and old curiosities. As artifacts, such items can convey some sense of the way things once were or the way people once lived, some sense of days gone by. But, at the very least, artifacts as records convey only very limited amounts of understanding.

Nevertheless, it should perhaps also be noted that one person's useless old curiosity is often another's priceless treasure. Much depends upon where values lie. Thus, things remembered and recorded in one age can often seem, at least to those of another age, like very odd items and strange blendings. Items needed for ceremonials or festivals, careful measurements and quantities — so many baskets of grain or so many cattle for sacrifice or so many flasks of wine to be poured out in libation, so many days after a particular new moon — seem peculiar indeed. Why, we may well ask, were such items of information preserved? Items of information from five or six thousand years ago, blendings of such apparently important and mundane matters, were recorded in detail, we assume, for some purpose. But what this purpose may have been may not be easy for us to comprehend. Details deemed crucial to another age, perhaps so crucial that they were never to be forgotten, can seem bizarre today. Only as one begins to see why, in far and bygone days, seemingly trivial items were of such significance can historians begin to climb into another age and see the world as it was once seen by another people.

But, to return to the key question, have there not always been, one might well ask, certain kinds of events or certain experiences which all peoples in all ages have shared, things deemed so significant that they simply could not afford to forget them? Are there no universal criteria by which, down through the ages, we might be able to discover things that virtually all people have deemed to be of crucial importance to their own sense of well-being? Here, it would seem, one can perhaps suggest the possibility of some criteria that are already time-tested. We can posit tools that, when applied to various human situations in any age or in any clime, have proven to be valuable for identifying items of "historic" significance. At the heart of this issue (as is indicated in chapter 4) is recognition of a basic set of clearly universal human needs:

first, the need for an elemental minimum of *security* in body and mind; and second, the need for an elemental minimum of physical and emotional (or spiritual) *satisfaction*. Without minimal amounts of safety and satisfaction (comfort and/or contentment), individuals and groups see themselves as threatened. Without such things, people consider that they are encountering some major crisis or some major, if not mortal, danger. As Samuel Johnson so aptly noted two centuries ago, it is the prospect of immediate death or mortal danger that so "wonderfully concentrates" the mind.[34] Quite obviously, such events — matters of life and death — are difficult to forget.

\*          \*          \*

Historical understanding, it is worth noting again in conclusion, has its primal origin and starting point in memory. All history begins — and has always begun — in the mind and memory of each individual person and in the collective memory of particular groups of persons. Or, as Jan Vansina puts it, "The study of memory teaches us that all historical sources are suffused by subjectivity right from the start."[35] Memories, as collective actions, thus also become "institutionalized." Gathered together in one place or another, they have then been shared and transmitted over periods of time, sometimes precisely but often also imprecisely. While there may be, ironically, no direct way to fully verify such a generalization purely by means of empirical data or historical evidence, there is also no way of disproving it. "The prime function of memory," David Lowenthal argues, "is not to preserve the past but to adapt it so as to enrich and manipulate the present."[36]

34. Samuel Johnson: "Depend upon it, Sir, when a man knows he is to be hanged in a fortnight, it concentrates his mind wonderfully," in *Letter to Boswell* (19 September 1777), in James Boswell, *Life of Samuel Johnson*, ed. G. B. Hill, rev. L. F. Powell (Oxford: Clarendon, 1934-50), 3:167. Also quoted in *Oxford Dictionary of Quotations*, 2nd ed. (London and New York: Oxford University Press, 1970), 273.

35. Vansina, "Memory and Oral Tradition," 276.

36. Lowenthal, *The Past Is a Foreign Country*, 210. Citing Ian M. L. Hunter, *Memory*, rev. ed. (Harmonsworth, Middlesex: Penguin, 1964), 202-3, Lowenthal continues: "For from simply holding on to previous experiences, memory helps us to understand them. Memories are not ready-made reflections of the past, but eclectic, selective reconstructions based on subsequent actions and perceptions and on ever-changing codes by which we delineate, symbolize, and classify the world around us."

Recognition that history is memory and that it starts in memory emphasizes, once again, a proposition central to this study: namely, that virtually all historical understandings that have ever come to us from any place or time — whether from the earliest dawnings of human society or from the latest "advances" of our own day — have been gathered and held and preserved by individual persons and by quite small groups of kindred or related persons (whether these be designated as "families," "lineages," "dynasties," "elites," and/or similarly restricted circles of persons). That historical understandings have also been (and still are) produced, preserved, and passed on by persons in control of corporate entities (e.g., churches, companies, societies, and institutions of that nature) in no way nullifies this proposition. All institutions, after all, are formed, organized, and led by individuals or relatively small groups. We have no way of knowing whether or not the "best" or most accurate insights of any age were represented by the words that have come to us from ruling families or, sometimes, from relatively small corporate groups not related by blood ties. Whatever the case, whether those "families" that left us their records happen to have been royal or imperial dynasties, ruling over vast domains through the agency of enormous bureaucratic structures, or merely tiny and relatively weak but still articulate (and literate) families of humbler means or lowlier circumstances, the basic fact remains: historical constructions, down through the ages until modern times, have been made by and for families and relatively small groups of people.[37]

Moreover, most of all the historical understandings preserved within families or small groups about themselves remain as primal, if not primitive, in form as they ever were in past ages. Such history has remained and has been held, mainly if not entirely, within the personal memories of those whose actions, experiences, or observations of events were most directly involved — or, later, in the records of those individuals who could write such things down. Moreover, it is from relatively small circles of individuals, specialists in every age, that later ages have been able to gain some idea of how they themselves under-

---

37. Even institutions, such as states and empires, churches or monasteries, business organizations or political parties, have possessed and carried this "family" or "local" kind of character.

stood their collective or separate pasts. It is to records and writings of the earliest of these kinds of small groups that we will turn in the next chapter.

Before doing so, however, a brief glance at the main categories of things remembered from the past may be useful. As kinds of historical memory, later reduced to writing, these kinds of understanding are as much alive and as actively produced today as ever. All are primal forms of historical understanding. All can be fitted into the larger contextual frameworks of history as it is produced in our own day. In a very primordial sense, virtually all understandings of the past combine or consist of just a few, rather simple forms:

(1) *Annal:* An annal, for the most part, is merely a relatively simple listing of deeds. Set down in chronological order and in literary form, annals describe deeds done by one person (or deeds about or on behalf of one person), with one deed following another deed. They also describe deeds of person after person, usually in sequential order. The person whose deeds are listed is almost invariably a very important person. In today's jargon, such a person is a "VIP," at least in his or her own eyes. Indeed, this is usually a ruler (or a priest or steward, etc.), someone with power over some domain or over some person who could order servants, acting on his or her behalf or surrounding him or her, to write or inscribe his or her deeds so that none would forget them. (It is often amazing indeed to see on what good terms such a person could be with himself or herself.)

(2) *Autobiography and Biography:* Consisting of recollections about the past of one person by that person, this kind of history usually dwells upon, or pertains to, that one person's perspectives (including personal virtues or, occasionally, some faults). Yet such history as memory is rarely very "successful" or useful, either to the person doing the recollecting or to others, if it does not at the very least provide some sort of contextualization and detachment in the form of a tapestry of observations about other selected events, even if only from the past immediately surrounding that person. For this reason, even the "worst," least reliable kinds of autobiographical memories have usually served to convey at least some solid information about past events that are beyond dispute. While the focus of biography is again upon the life of a single individual, as a person, what is recounted is done by another person, or even by several other persons. Implicitly or explicitly, this kind of understanding about the past

has tended, perhaps more deliberately, to integrate the life of the one person which is its subject into a framework of larger historical actions and events, contexts and processes.

(3) *Epic and Myth:* While again often a tale about one single individual, the focus shifts to events and persons larger than life — namely, to one or more heroic characters and deeds. As often as not, if not always, this is a "hero-tale" or a larger-than-life saga. It is about many persons (occasionally including gods and demons) and about many events which may have occurred within a single generation, providing a background for the deeds of its central character, or for events which may have transpired across many generations. Recalled from a very remote and misty past, this kind of historical understanding, first transmitted orally and handed down for centuries beyond counting, has sometimes, in one of its poetic recensions, later been reduced to writing, usually in a form of rhythmic meter if not also in rhyme. Yet, as already indicated above, many (if not most) epics and sagas have not been written down. They remain in the lore of local peoples almost everywhere. Without going into various symbiotic and theoretical discussions with which the concept of myth has increasingly been surrounded in recent decades, we can arbitrarily define myth, quite simply, as a tale about the doings of divine or semi-divine beings in relations with human beings. (More will be said about this kind of memory in a later chapter.)

(4) *Chronicle:* Here, at last, we move to the limits of memory and to the threshold of the earliest kinds of third-person accounts about events connected to ruling persons and groups (dynasties, elites, families, etc.). Chronicles, moving beyond mere memory, have often attempted to explain how or why things turned out as they did. Again, usually transmitting actions and events in simple chronological form and without any necessarily definite or strong or obvious criteria for the selection of data, chronicles argue from evidence and from "facts." As such, while usually attempting to make careful observations about recent or contemporary events, chronicles often combine personal memories with "hearsay" memories of others or, in other words, focus upon events that have taken place during the life of the writer. Yet chronicles have sometimes also given accounts of times previous to the time of the chronicler. As such, therefore, chronicles can now be seen as one kind, probably the earliest kind of historical understanding, that which today is seen as "genuine" and/or "written" history — history that

combines narrative art and descriptive science with teleologically pre-dictive and rhetorical features.[38]

Clearly, historical understandings, in any and every age, have arisen out of memory. Such understandings have been generated in the various ways by which people remember, recall, recollect, record, recount, re-construct, and *re*-create, in words, those events deemed to be notewor-thy. Several primal categories in which historical understandings have been found, at least when coming down out of memory, from oral to written forms, can now be examined more closely. These give us clues about how earliest historical understandings of antiquity were first con-structed.

38. Brundage, "The Birth of Clio," 226 n. 5.

# Chapter 3

# History as Story:
# A Narrative Art

A basic conceptual element in history — indeed, *the* most basic and essential element — is narrative, or *story*. This usage of the word, now somewhat more obsolete and obscure, seems to be a direct descendent of the original Greek ιστορια (*istoria*) and subsequent Latin *historia*. Exactly how, when, or why the word became separated from its ancestral root is a fascinating "story" in itself.[1] Yet the fact remains that it has never ceased to convey some of the original meaning found in its parental root; and "history" has never ceased to mean "story." We can learn from almost any standard dictionary that the noun *story*, meaning "history" as well as "researches," is its more original if more obscure and obsolete meaning. In simplest terms, a story is "a narrative, true or presumed to be true, of important events and celebrated persons";[2] "a narrative of events in their sequence." Moreover, the word *story* pertains to the action of "relating" or "telling" or "writing" or "describing things historically" — adorning the present with "scenes from the past."[3]

However, in the expanded and fuller sense of the concept as it is defined today, story as history is a description of a sequence of actions, events, experiences, incidents, or episodes which have happened in the

---

1. While it is not necessary for us to fully trace the fascinating etymology of this term, it covers over six columns (more than three pages) in *The Compact Edition of the Oxford English Dictionary [OED]*, vol. 2, 1971.

2. *OED*.

3. *Chambers Twentieth Century Dictionary*, ed. E. M. Kirkpatrick (Edinburgh: Chambers, 1983), 176.

life or lives of one or more persons, either real or imaginary, which have occurred in typically *human* situation(s) (or predicaments), and in which *contingencies* (unexpected changes or reactions to change) have affected those situations in such a way as to eventually lead to some sort of conclusion. By its very nature, a story commonly brings to light hidden aspects of an original situation and its personalities; shows up consequences to change, bringing to light further cumulative consequences; and leads to sudden, unexpected contingencies, predicaments, and turns, so that a chain of further actions, thoughts, and predicaments is provoked. Just as predicaments (and even institutions), like people, acquire a kind of life of their own, so it is that responses to predicaments — however good or bad, successful or unsuccessful — gradually bring a story to its ultimate conclusion.[4]

The various elements and facets within a story that serve to make it a special form of understanding are the subject with which we are concerned here. The sense in which history is a "historical" or "true" story is very strong. Indeed, as a form of art, a story is an attempt to imitate life as it happens or as it once happened. As such, it draws upon the creative powers of experience, imagination, insight, and memory, along with any or all resource materials that are available, in order to reconstruct life as it was lived in the past; moreover it follows, recounts, or traces a line of actions, taking them from some beginning point (place and time) through various unexpected and surprising contingencies and turns to some ending point. Narrative, if appreciated and comprehended in all of its manifold implications, can thus be seen as *the* quintessential vehicle for acquiring and transmitting understandings of the past.

In its classic mold, any story — be it anecdote, saga, or tale — attempts to capture and hold the imaginations of those recipients who are its listeners or readers by relating life in the present to things that have already happened at some time (and place) in the past, whether recent or distant. However true a story may be, it makes its appeal to the past in terms understandable to contemporary human experience. Harking back to ageless conventions and formulas, an archetypical story commences its primary function of conveying understanding by simul-

---

4. W. B. Gallie, "What Is Story?" in *Philosophy and the Historical Understanding* (New York: Schocken Books, 1968; 2nd ed., 1969), 22ff.

taneously capturing and holding attention, by entertaining and exciting emotions, and by informing and instructing its recipient listeners or readers. It can do this with some stereotypical invocation comparable to those words recited to children: "Once upon a time, . . ."[5] By employing a familiar cliché, set phrase, or ritual invocation, history as story moves from the familiar to unfamiliar and awakens, brings back, or calls out of the past echoes of something which now no longer exists and restores awareness of things which once were and are no more. Implicit within this sense of history, indeed, are appeals to elemental emotions, feelings which seem to lie deep within each and every human being. Mingled among such deep and innate feelings, one can suggest, are especially profound and primordial sensations: anxiety, curiosity, and mortality. Curiosity about the unknown, as also about darkness and death, seems to be universal within all of us: perhaps some need to come to terms with what lies both within and beyond mortality, a refusal to accept the finality of death and a hope that there is a part of us that is "deathless," something that lives on and that needs to be appropriated and better understood. What moves us to exquisite delight, to experiences of ecstacy, or to fear of impending tragedy can wonderfully "concentrate our minds." It is this striving to know, this wish to resurrect what is dead and gone, that compels our attention and awakens imagination. History as story appeals to something beyond death that is deathless.

Often forgotten in our day is the fact that the way in which we understand history — the way all purposive action and thought is understood — is basically and profoundly different from the way in which we understand natural phenomena. To understand what happened is to understand, at least in some measure, how it happened and even why it happened. To understand in this way is to understand *particular* actions and events and thoughts within particular, if not peculiar, situations and circumstances and contexts. The "dominant empiricist epistemology" of our age does not much appreciate this way of understanding. The concept of story or narrative as the foundation for all

5. That this convention became more standard for "false" or "fictional" stories, and especially for fairy tales, does not thereby nullify their appeal, however unserious, to some past reality which was no longer real and to a "make believe" that things related were once real.

historical knowledge is a special form of human understanding which is uniquely distinct (or *sui generis*) in its own right. There is a sense in which, as W. B. Gallie argued, "as in the sciences there is always a theory, so in history there is always a story."[6] Carrying the analogy further, he pointed out that just as in any science a phenomenon selected for study is a starting point for discovering more comprehensive explanations and systematic general theories, so an event (action, incident, or episode) is a starting point for historical study.[7] This is so precisely because the event is so memorable or noteworthy — so "story-worthy" — in what it tells us that we are compelled to know more. We want to know more, whether about a success or tragedy, so that we can know, in more intimate circumstance, in total context and fuller detail, either for its own sake, perhaps to satisfy curiosity, or for its comparability to concerns which are our very own.

Any action, being, or event worth a story, in a broad and comprehensive sense, is an "adventure" — meaning that it contains clearly detectable elements that are accidental, contingent, surprising, unforeseen, and/or unpredictable. It is this element in history as story that makes it worth following. History as story is something worth following, following stage by stage, and following until it brings us to some sort of conclusion or ending point. This is so because, ultimately, it is through the story itself, and through its telling, that the essentials of historical understanding are produced and transmitted. It is with these essentials — the ingredients that make up such a story and, at the same time, the conditions that are necessary to make such a story into genuine history — that we are especially concerned here.

## I. Individuality and Institutionality: The Dialectics of Identity

The attractions of the past in the form of story begin not with a consideration of *all* that has ever happened and *all* that is past — nor even

---

6. Gallie, *Philosophy and the Historical Understanding*, 2nd ed., 2.

7. Ibid. Or, in Gallie's words, "just as an investigation becomes scientific only as a result of critical dissatisfaction with received theories and the consequent desire to find an agreed method for testing and selecting among these, so an investigation becomes historical only when critical minds are impelled to devise tests for the vague and often inconsistent claims to truth which most traditional stories contain."

all that has happened to human beings, nor even all that has happened to them in one place or at one time. Rather, history as story begins with focusing attention on that most human element at the diametrically opposite pole of existence — namely, the individual, the particular, and the unique. The primary attraction of stories lies in the worth of the individual person and in the various adventures and contingencies of experience which happen to *one single* personality in relationships to other persons, entities, and forces in the world. It is individuality and uniqueness that is important, which ever strives for recognition and success or which suffers from want of sufficient sustenance, satisfaction, or security. It is the individual person who, however much that person holds in common with others, possesses a face, and a name — and, above all, uniqueness. Persons who are faceless and nameless do not count, or are counted as less than fully human. Deep within each person, it is possible to suggest, are stirrings of self-awareness and self-con-sciousness — in a word, stirrings of self-identity. These stirrings call for answers to basic and profound questions about that identity, about life and about destiny. What or who am I? How did I get here? When? From where? What has made me what I now am? What did I do — or what did others do — to make me what I now am? How much do I deserve what I have gotten? What has happened (to me and those around me) to make all of this possible? Where have I been? When did that happen to me? Why did things happen to turn out the way they did? Questions such as these, and many more like them, are so primordial that they hardly need elaboration or justification. They are intrinsic to whatever it is that is "human" in each of us.

It is precisely at this point, however, that a curious and remarkably enduring feature of human action requires closer examination. This feature is that propensity of human beings to create, construct, imagine, or invent: the propensity by which they develop abstractions and, above all, the propensity to establish institutions. This concerns the way institu-tions are constructed and the close relationship, even in terms of identity, between individuality and institutionality. "Institution" is the name we give to anything that is done or thought over and over again. It includes anything built, or made to stand, anything so regularized or routinized as to become established (in custom, tradition, or continuous usage). Some-thing instituted is that which has come into existence and remained in existence as a continuing presence *by means of human agency.* Anything abstract or concrete, material or immaterial, intellectual or emotional, important or trivial; anything established or set up so that it becomes recognized as regular, customary, conventional, patterned, or traditional in usage; any appeal to "the way things are done" or "the way of doing things": any such phenomenon we call an "institution." But what is especially interesting and peculiar, in this regard, is the way in which — over time and in place — individual identities can become institutional-, ized and the way in which qualities of human individuality, if not personality, can be ascribed or attributed to institutions. Nowhere is this dialectical interplay of identity between individuality and institutionality more evident than in the functioning of stories within history.

## A. Identity and Individuality: The Primary Focus of History

Before an infant has passed many months in this world, almost from its earliest moments of intelligent eye contact and audible utterance, it sees faces and hears names. Names attached to persons, as also to things and to actions or events, give a primal sense of personal identity and primal importance — a compelling interest. Amidst personal bonding, in hugs and kisses, smiles and sounds of approval, words like "mama" and "dada"[8] are first pronounced and first heard. A child's own name brings it identity, approval, and recognition. Names of persons in intimate proximity do the same. And very quickly names of actions and events, each designating a new experience, proliferate in all directions. As actions and events in the surrounding world increasingly impinge upon and intersect within the arena of rapidly widening varieties of experiences, it does not take very long before questions multiply more rapidly than experiences themselves. Rapidly learned lessons quickly pile up within memories. Immediate biological parents and siblings are surrounded by other "family" members, friends and community — some younger and some older and some much, much older. Some of the much older kin members and friends are no longer even actually visible or audible — except in pictures, recordings, letters, and artifacts. Yet the "presence" of many who are actually

8. These are but the European and American equivalents of similar sounds pronounced wherever there are primordial bondings in the world. Elsewhere the sounds are "ama" or "ana"; "baba" or "aba" or "papa" or "apa" — everywhere remarkably similar.

"absent" is still felt. While presence is no longer so audible or visible "in the flesh," it is felt nonetheless. Indeed, the influence of those long departed can remain so strong that they are considered to be actually present "in spirit." Vivid memories are evoked and fascinating stories told about them can be entrancing in their fascination — even though what each person hears or understands in the same set of words may be quite different. These old stories, told and retold, become deeply ingrained and become parts of domestic lore and legend. The typically American idiom, "I remember when she [Grandma, etc.] took me with her . . . "; or "My dad used to take me along"; or "You should have been here when our men came back from the war"[9] is replicated, with variations, in every clime and culture. With such phrases many a standard anecdote has begun. The storehouse of lore within every household is part of its very identity and part of its most intimate history.

Separation from one's immediate past is always deemed a personal tragedy. It is called amnesia. Anyone without memory of his or her own personal past suffers from loss of human identity and, therewith, loss of recognition. It is hard to imagine a more vital element in human relationships. Such loss is like death itself. To have no common connections, no common roots to share with persons of common background and heritage, is to suffer a kind of death. To know where one belongs and to whom one is related by a common past, in more than a casual way, is crucial to life itself. Some of the very strongest bonds of solidarity within intimate circles of community and locality, as also of clan or nation or larger society, consist of the commonalities of shared experiences. Common legacies of enjoyment and sorrow, along with handed-down artifacts and implements, but especially items of common heritage in shared memories, legends, lore, and records — all of those things that have been passed down from generation to generation — are the very stuff of both personal and communal identity and of existence itself. Any person or community without such common understandings of a common past suffers loss, and is weakened and thereby impoverished. Any community (or nation, for that matter) without such knowledge suffers from a debilitating "collective

9. Most cultures are far more specific in nomenclatures pertaining to family members. Outside the English-speaking world, in Africa and Asia and Europe, separate terms for "mother's mother," "mother's father," "mother's brother," and so forth — as distinct from our rather simple terms for aunt, uncle, cousin, or grandparents — emphasize the specificities of individual identity and of emotions which they evoke.

amnesia"; and, by that very fact, also suffers from both debilitating social anemia and chronic weakness. And if a genuine identity cannot be found and possessed then something very much like it, in both personal and collective memory, must be fabricated or invented, or even stolen, to fit in its place, so essential a part of us is the relationship between our history and our identity.

Stories and folklore still continue to serve, as they have far back into the most obscure antiquity, as the vehicles for preserving domestic and community strength. They are among the oldest forms of domestic and local history known. They are also, interestingly, among the youngest; and, as such, in fact, are ever being fashioned, preserved, and refashioned so as to meet needs both of persons as individuals and of individual communities. Strong families are constantly producing, storing, preserving, and restoring stories about themselves, often going to considerable lengths to make sure that "all the facts" are accurate, authentic, captivating, and well preserved. For this reason, not surprisingly, the strongest families may tend also to be the oldest. In any age and in every clime, it has been such families which, after all, have possessed both the greatest resources for holding onto the past and the largest stakes in making sure that heritages are preserved. These families have left no stone unturned, not only to make sure that power and wealth are passed on to their children (and children's children) but also to make certain that their children's children will be able to trace themselves back to hallowed roots of the family from which they have sprung and to that past that is their common communal possession. Instances of families that, from their own oral traditions or records, have made claims to a long antiquity, into which they trace themselves back one or two thousand years, are not uncommon. Such longevity has been particularly evident among clerical, priestly, or ruling lineages. Such families have often woven details of kinship and chronology, interlacing important events and episodes of achievement or adventure, calamity or tragedy into incredible and even wonderfully marvelous tapestries of "historical" belief about themselves.[10] Such understandings about themselves, however much they may mix fact with

---

10. Such claims are not just pre-Homeric. Nor are they merely the "king-lists" of ancient Egyptian or Chinese dynasties. Brahmanical or rajput succession *(vamsa)* lineages in India, and Jewish genealogies rising out of Hebrew Scriptures, not to mention comparable remains in Africa, are but a few examples of survivals of this sort.

fancy, become treasures. Yet, one can discover that neither the grounds nor the strengths of belief in such histories have ever been even or uniform. How accurately and well such stories serve to represent the past can itself be seen, nevertheless, as having been of crucial importance to the strength and survival of those families and the communities that produced them. This was so, one may venture to suggest, whatever the size of a particular community may have been, whether simply a partnership of two persons or a large multinational corporation, and whether it was a tiny nation-state or an enormous, worldwide empire.

## B. Institutionality in Individuals: The Magnifying Lens of History

Human limitations and constraints, emphasizing individuality and uniqueness, within wider contexts enable each story to retain a clear focus and to return to beginnings and origins. It is from within the matrix of kinship (family, community, etc.) lore, which we have just discussed, that the focus upon one, single, individual person, in relationships with other persons, can be seen as first arising; and it is here that such concentrated attention seems eventually to achieve epic proportions. This narrowing of focus seems to begin, in any age, long before more disciplined historical inquiries emerge from the mists. It is also here, from out of this kind of context, that autobiography and biography, taken together, can be seen as acquiring a special place and as possessing special features which have made them *the* quintessential art form. This is true, both for storytelling as an art and also, therewith, for historical narrative as a form of enlightenment.

"Autobiography," Wilhelm Dilthey suggested, "is the highest and most instructive form in which the understanding of life confronts us."[11] Here, the phenomenal (or outward) course (or sequences) of one person's life, within one certain and definite environment, intersects the philosophical or reflective (or inward) sequences of that same life. Here, a platform exists for the learning of one person's experiences and for the understanding of past events. Here, the person who has striven to

---

11. Wilhelm Dilthey, *Pattern and Meaning in History: Thoughts on History and Society*, edited and introduced by H. P. Rickman (London: George Allen & Unwin, 1961), 85.

understand certain specific past events is the same as the person who has experienced some of the vicissitudes of those same events. Here, the same person who has been seeking to understand the connecting threads of events in the course of her or his own life has already sought to construct, perhaps from several different perspectives, a coherence for the sequences in one life's story and to select a rhetoric with which to represent that life as it is (or was) first put into words. Past plans and bygone purposes, things once (and perhaps that still remain) valued most, are thrown into sharp relief against a background of those experiences that have actually both shaped and have been shaped by the same sequential flow of events. One person's memory, in this way, has to manage the task of singling out those things (actions, episodes, events) considered to be most significant and worthy of being told and has, by the same decisions, to allow other things to sink out of sight and be forgotten. Illusions once held in the past are modified and corrected by the onward and stern and unrelenting march of events. Elementary problems in the selecting of "story-worthy" facts, as well as problems of grasping and describing the subtle and not so subtle connections between those facts, are faced. Conceptions of sequentiality, terms describing the flow of past and present events that have been experienced, are now held together and linked to ways of conceptualizing anticipated future events that have yet to be experienced. Amidst a world of contingencies, surprises, and uncertainties, past and present and future are thus held together by a common thread and are imbued with importance and meaning. Here, in a single oral or literary form of narrative expression, in one single person's reflections upon the ever onward moving course of life, one can "approach the root of all historical comprehension."[12]

But what is true for autobiography is perhaps just as true, if not more true, for biography. Only here there is one crucial difference. Biography, by its very nature, possesses an inherent capacity for acquiring greater objectivity and balance. The biographer, simply by virtue of

---

12. Ibid. In some cultures, however, autobiographical remains and stories have been retained only in oral form or have only rarely been preserved and handed down in written form. (In India, for example, an extreme paucity of premodern autobiographical writings — e.g., *Archakatanaka* by Banarasi — is counterbalanced by very rich oral traditions. This is even more true for sub-Saharan Africa. [See later chapters for more on this subject.]

being another person than the person being described, has the advantage of being able to achieve a greater critical detachment and distance. The "outer events" of the one life being described, right up to the time of death, can be seen. These actions can also be scrutinized within a wider context of events in the world at large. Biography, for this reason, has a dual capacity — capable not only of giving a better balance between the central point of focus and the wider horizons, but also, like someone with two eyes, capable of providing stereoscopic depths to what is seen by the beholder, whether as biographer or as someone to whom the biography is addressed.

It is perhaps for this reason that Barbara Tuchman described biography as a veritable "prism of history"[13] — as the focal point for the intersecting and interconnecting and contextualizing of a wide variety of other events as these impinge upon and surround the sequences and contingencies in the life of one single person. Every human life, whatever its larger significance, has a story that can be told. Every human life can serve as a document — of flesh and blood and spirit. As such, it can inform us of what happened in one out of a potentially infinite number of different instances of human experience and existence. The story of every human life, with all its sequences and its surprising and unexpected turns, can serve as a lens through which to see and understand the larger world. For the most part, the stories of most individual human lives lie in relative obscurity and darkness, except to their immediate possessors and their near friends and relations. What little historical light can be refracted through the stories of such individuals remains dim. Some of the most obscure refract so little light that they hardly show much of the ground immediately around and beneath them; and even this is soon lost from memory and swallowed into oblivion. But here and there, and every once in a while, some story about an individual emerges and we learn about actions, circumstances, and events that are more than ordinary. Placed in a position of special worth or advantage, with special recognition or significance, the story of the life of such a personality serves to illuminate many things around it, both near and far. Or, to apply the metaphor of theater, such a figure occupies the

13. Barbara Tuchman, "Biography as a Prism of History," address to the Symposium on the Art of Biography, National Portrait Gallery, Washington, D.C., 14 November 1978, published in *Practicing History* (New York: Alfred A. Knopf, 1981), 80-90.

center of the stage and has a place of central attention precisely because the story that surrounds it intersects and interacts with a much larger world. Events of great moment in the lives of many people can be seen to meet in the life of one such person.

Precisely this duality of perspective,[14] this combination of attachment and detachment, of subjectivity and objectivity, of individuality and universality — as seen by looking at the world or an age through the prism of one person's life — can make biography, especially biography combined with or built upon autobiographical materials, one of the very finest and potentially most enlightening forms of historical craftsmanship. Such craftsmanship calls forth art and science of the highest order. Such craftsmanship puts a special kind of storytelling — the telling of "true stories" — in a class by itself. As a vehicle for historical understanding of larger subjects, it is a form of productive artistry which not only has a peculiarly powerful way of attracting and holding attention but, more remarkably, for actually constructing historical knowledge. The capacity to produce new historical understanding lies in the very *telling*, as also in the actual *following*, of the story itself. History without biography, in short, is like an art gallery without portraits or like a symphony concert without musical sounds.

## C. Individuality in Institutions: The Widening Focus of History

Just as individual persons can be institutionalized, whether as heroes or villains, so also faceless, inconsequential functionaries, or ideas and doctrines, such as dialectical materialism or divine predestination as institutions themselves, can take on the attributes of individual identity, if not attributes of personality. Institutions can acquire "faces" and can be made to appropriate to themselves pseudo-human traits of character development. What makes this possible is not just their very continuity and durability over time but also, perhaps more importantly, those "character" traits which come to them, either from their own stories or from how these are understood. This process of individualizing (if not personalizing) institutionality occurs especially, and whenever, a narrative focuses upon the continuity of some idea or convention, some

14. Dilthey, *Pattern and Meaning in History*, 89-93.

tendency arising out of that story. When this happens, a storyteller can intervene to inform us that the narrative has some "grander" or "higher" or "larger" theme. Thus, for example, stories that sequentially detail the lives of dramatically different individual persons — from Abraham and Sarah to Joseph and from Joseph to Moses and Joshua, and from Joshua to Samuel, Saul, David, and Solomon — may also tell how, through successions of unpredictable contingencies and changing vicissitudes, and from generation to generation, some matters of larger consequence (concerning a "chosen people" and "divine purpose") worked out the way they did.

This interplay between individuality and institutionality was succinctly described by W. B. Gallie: "All history is, like saga, basically a narrative of events in which human thought and action play a predominant part. But most historical themes [which, as individual constructions become "institutionalized"] tend to run beyond the interests, plans, lives, and works of any one group or generation. . . . History seems to run past individuals, using them for a little while and dropping them without any compunction when their usefulness is exhausted."[15] While one may know that human beings "make history" and that "human actions within the world and nothing else" make up what we call historical knowledge, that kind of history that can especially interest people pertains to a flow of particular ideas, fascinating features, and/or dominant trends which once shaped the actions and aims of successive generations of people. Ideas and trends can be seen as rising up and moving; as moving toward some sort of culmination; and, even after reaching that culmination, as remaining part of a yet larger unfinished story (see "Tendency and Teleology" below). Sagas exemplify this institutional feature in history. As chronologically arranged successions of stories, believed for the most part to be true, they not only set out to link listeners to their original ancestors but they also serve to carry along certain overlapping and larger patterns which are of dominant concern (interest and worth) to their listeners. Some tendency, trend, or theme gradually discloses itself to listeners, emerging out of the sequences of events and successions of stories; some latent quality, peculiar and particular to those events, is carried over from narrative to narrative in such a way that, as a fixed point of

---

15. Gallie, *Philosophy and Historical Understanding*, 69.

reference, it can gradually become more clearly recognized. The recognition of this pattern quality in a saga is, in itself, an intellectual accomplishment. This accomplishment has required a capacity to stand back from particular sequences so as both to see the larger trends and to reflect upon those complexities, peculiarities, and subtleties within an emerging sequence of narratives and within the progression of a saga as a whole.

It is important to note that a pattern, quality, or trend such as this, like qualities inherent in any living individual or institution, is neither a general theory (or law) nor a manifestation of any theory. It is something recognized only in and through closely following one particular sequence of events. It is something of a kind which can only be expressed and followed in a story itself. It is something so intrinsic to the story that it cannot be seen as an element dragged into the story from outside the story in order to explain it. Once this feature within history as story, and story as history, is grasped, it is possible to appreciate the fact that, however vast or complex a particular institution may be and however much certain features, traits, and trends within that institution develop out of the telling of its story, it is the unique identity and individuality of that institution, as an institution, that remains the central focus for the production of historical understanding about it. (See "Tendency and Teleology" below for more on teleology.)

Actions of institutions, in other words, can be followed just as avidly, consistently, thoroughly, and unapologetically as actions of individuals. The effort of following the actions of an institution, or an institutional phenomenon — be it a doctrine, a popular movement, a technology, or a war — is in many ways comparable to the enterprise of following an individual. Only in place of those traits of human identity or character that are associated with each individual's "face" and "personality," certain "dummy" traits that are inherent within the character or "face" of faceless institutions are discovered or identified. Indeed, the story of the actions and adventures (origin, rise, expansion, influence, decline, etc.) of a particular institutionalized abstraction — such as a form of government, legal system, social doctrine, scientific theory, art form, or musical composition — can generate an historical interest which is quite as distinct as, and no less compelling than, an interest that is focused upon those individuals who might have originated, sustained, abandoned, or destroyed those institutions. In other words, the human capacity to follow a story for its own sake can be applied to institutional abstractions and structures just as well as to individuals. Established habits, skills, and structures can acquire or be invested with metaphorical faces and personalities; and "life prospects" of adventure, contingency, and surprise can be every bit as exciting or "story-worthy" as the life of any heroic artist, inventor, military genius, sports figure, dramatic performer, or industrial tycoon.[16]

## II. Sequentiality and Contingency: The Dialectics of Fascination

Another peculiarity of history as story is the way in which historical understanding, truth, and knowledge are actually produced. Truth of this sort comes *in the telling* and *in the following;* and, just as much, *in the compelling worth, or interest,* of the narrative itself. In other words, one does not simply come to historical understanding merely by applying some general theory or by leaping to the conclusion of that story. Historical understanding requires "following" it in sequential detail — understanding words and progressions of words as, in orderly continuity, they describe successions of actions and events, feelings and thoughts, of individual persons as these persons move through episode after episode, until they reach some culmination, destination, or ending point. Sequential following entails a peculiarly direct and empathetic involvement of mind and heart, so that, almost involuntarily, from some inner compulsion or curiosity, the follower (as listener, reader, or, nowadays, viewer) is pulled forward by the very flow in details of what is being described. The more skillfully a story is told, the less necessary it is for the storyteller to pause, interrupt, or intrude upon this flow in order to provide explicit explanations. Rather, each and every individual person is followed just as if one were following the actions of an actual living person who is directly in front of us and in whom we have taken a personal interest. To "follow a narrative" in history means that, in Gallie's words, "whatever under-

16. At this point, however, Gallie (*Philosophy and the Historical Understanding,* 4) reminds us that more complexities and dilemmas apply to historical understandings of this sort than can (or need) be explored here. While some spheres of human activity or thought can hardly be investigated without reifying abstractions, others end up in reductive absurdity.

standing and whatever explanations a work of history contains must be assessed in relation to the narrative from which they arise and whose development they subserve."[17]

What makes this so — what makes it possible, if not necessary, for us to follow a story — are certain other essential features of any story as such, features which are also no less essential in our coming to historical understanding. These are elements of inherent *fascination* or "interestability": the capacity to compel interest, arouse curiosity, or what Gallie calls "story-worthiness"; inherent plausibility, the capacity to provide correspondence between the story and reality, as found in common experience; and inherent unpredictability, the capacity to generate unforeseen intrusions, unexpected surprises or turns, and sudden contingencies. The first of these features, a story's inherent "story-worthiness" or capacity to compel fascination, is perhaps *the* single most essential feature in any narrative. However, because this feature is utterly dependent upon the other two, it is useful to look at them before looking at what it is that they evoke.

## A. Plausibility and Contingency: The Tensions of "Following"

In order to reach its "inevitable" conclusion, any good story moves through a sequence of episodes, incidents, interim endings, and possible final outcomes. The world through which the story moves is a familiar world. It is a world that is known, if not completely, at least to the degree that, by touching ordinary everyday experience, one can anticipate the flow of events and tentatively predict routine outcomes. Put differently, most of what constitutes any story is acceptable precisely because it speaks to things with which we are already familiar. This feature of acceptability and plausibility, together with what is somewhat predictable, is both large and essential. Virtually every episode and incident in a story, if it is to be understood, requires a contextual framework of ordinary acceptability. It must show that the events that occurred and the occasions that brought those events about were not far-fetched. Only within such context can the central flow of

17. Gallie, preface to the first edition of *Philosophy and the Historical Understanding*, xi.

events be followed. Yet, at the same time, this very familiarity and predictability, however pivotal its importance within any good story, also possesses a recessive trait. There is very little, if anything, in the routine and hum-drum predictability of almost all actions in life that is worth a story. Details of this sort are boring. They are boring precisely because the information they convey is so filled with what is expected, what is habitual and customary, and what has a repetitive sameness. What is ordinary is all too plausible — too plausible to be interesting or worth telling about.

But it is precisely within and into exactly such an acceptable, intelligible, and plausible context that unexpected contingencies intrude. A latent sense that something unexpected will happen is what gives a story its hold. Expectation of the unexpected creates suspense, tension, and a waiting. It is this sense of something impending, something yet unknown — something noncustomary and nonroutine — that brings surprise and heightens expectation. It is those breaks with continuity, those *sudden turns*, that make a good story worth telling and worth following. Moral, mental, and intellectual strengths, among other factors, are either confirmed or their flaws exposed. Contingencies, discontinuities, and disjunctions become apparent.

## B. Interest or "Story-Worthiness": The Dimensions of Concern

Once one realizes what it is that makes a story worth following, it is not difficult to discover what a story really is and what is required to "*follow a story*." A story is a venture, a new approach, an adaptation to something unforeseen. It obliges us to follow it through on its own terms. These terms are embedded within its very actions, purposes, and values. They prompt it, direct it, and sustain it within its own world. They convey something about which we want to know *more* — whether of loss or gain, failure or success. It is something which we cannot learn without involving ourselves more deeply and intimately, either for its own sake or for its comparability to concerns and situations which belong to us in our own world. Any action becomes worthy of telling when it contains clearly detectable elements of accident, adventure, surprise, and unpredictability.

Among essential features of any art, as such, and certainly of any history as a narrative art, only accuracy of information is more important than the capacity to attract and hold interest. Above all else, almost at the cost of not conveying accurate *information*, a story fails in its essential function if and when it is not of compelling *interest*.[18] If it cannot capture and hold and move minds and hearts, if it cannot attract notice, if it cannot actually be seen as possessing inherent worth, it is "still-born." It is, for all practical purposes, dead. Story, like any other art form, must have a constituency. It must have patronage. Someone must be willing, at least figuratively, to "buy" it. Someone must value it and want it enough to obtain it, to hold and keep it. Otherwise it will be thrown out as useless and consigned to oblivion.[19] A "good" story, one that is genuinely captivating, is one that is capable of amazing twists and surprising turns. It is so alive, so captivating, so creative, so energetic, so significant in its appeal, that it grips its followers (be they hearers or readers or viewers), holding them on the edge of their seats. In so doing, it enters into *their* worlds and into *their* imaginations. It reaches into what they already know in such a way that they become aroused and, in a mental and emotional sense, "catch fire." It is at this point, as soon as a story has become *inspirational*, that it becomes "story-worthy." It is no small wonder that both individuals and institutions, families and nations, build up their memories and construct their histories around those events which attract their attention and hold their interest.

## C. Tendency and Teleology: The Trajectory of Culmination

History is offended by romance and simplicity. Things that never were or that never could be as neat as they seem when first encountered are its bane. Important actions and momentous events are, invariably, both

18. Tuchman, in "Biography as a Prism of History," stresses the crucial importance of attracting *interest*. She writes, "[F]or me, the reader is the essential other half of the writer. . . . If it takes two to make love or war or tennis, it likewise takes two to complete the function of the written word." A cake is baked to be eaten. A story untold and unheard is hardly a story at all.

19. It goes without saying, of course, that one generation's junk may be another generation's treasure. But, even then and despite constant changes in style, taste, and value, old stories can and often do speak to remote generations and peoples.

more complicated and also more natural than can be told in so many words. This is so, even when Gallie maintains that "narrative is the form which expresses what is basic to and characteristic of historical understanding."[20] There are features within historical understandings, as such, that strengthen the claim that history is always a kind of story. There are also special conditions within history as story that are required in order to authenticate historicity (see "Rhetoric and Verity" below). History and story also hold another feature in common. It is that special characteristic which, for want of any single term, can be called "culmination" (or "ending").

How a story is brought to an end, how a narrative is concluded, is one of its most crucial and necessary parts. No story, and certainly no history, can be left hanging. The phrase "And so it came about that . . . ," or "At the end of it all . . ." need not be explicit. Yet, however expressed or not expressed, a need to know how things ended is as important and compelling as the interest in closely following the story was from its beginning and all the way along its narrative course. This is something expected, something waited for. Without it, suspense and tension remain unresolved. Without its being proper and plausible — acceptable, convincing, and intelligible (or logical), as distinct from contrived, far-fetched, ill-conceived, or "manufactured" — an entire story lacks coherence and comes into jeopardy. Indeed, sometimes, just as ambiguity and uncertainty can occur at various stages within a story, marking out abrupt changes or contingencies, so the climax of a story can be deliberately held in abeyance until the very end. This can be done either for artistic effect or as an epilogue. Again, for artistic purposes or for purposes of better following a narrative, a story's ending can be put at the beginning. Whatever the case, culmination is essential to story.

As with story, so with history. As already pointed out, understanding a historical event, as found in a genuine work of history, requires a sequential *following* or *tracking* of details, taking them one by one through successions of accidents and contingencies, down to its very end. Systematic sciences, whether natural or social, are not as interested in following the details of what happens as they are with learning whether or not predicted results occur or whether or not theories are

20. Tuchman, "Biography as a Prism of History," 66.

correct. Historical understandings, on the other hand, occur as much within the very details of approach as in the results of arrival and conclusion. It is in the particularities of detail, as embodied within actions and events, that historical understandings of a final ending or culmination are to be found. These details themselves seem to possess as much intrinsic worth to human life (and affairs) as even the most deeply entrenched principles, whether philosophical or scientific. Somehow, people come to conduct themselves humanely (or morally) and think about other people only insofar as they can find common identity with them or common interest in others.

Indeed, it is in the details of real life situations, embedded within details of stories as such, that personal or social involvement (both emotional and intellectual) seems to take place. Likewise, in the details of great events, stories rise to a "transpersonal" level and to a wider institutional focus — covering broader localities, even regions and continents, and tracking events from generation to generation. In the process of doing so, previous endings become interim endings and turning points in a longer and larger flowing of events toward culminations and outcomes of greater magnitude and larger consequence. Patterns of movement, tendencies or trends, become discernable. Gradually these are disclosed, emerging from the details only to disappear while other tendencies become evident. Any tendency or trend, any pattern recognized in and through the development of particular sequences of events, is no more than just that: it is not a law, nor is it a principle or theory. It is merely a set of facts showing what philosophically might be called a "future tense" (or "teleological") claim to verity. Through sequences of markers, interim endings, traces, and turning points within any particular narrative episode, often depending upon the particular viewpoints of individual observers, a flow of events can be seen as a tendency or trend; and this flow can indicate a possible, or even probable, direction which may be followable if and when further events occur in the future. Again, depending upon the stance one takes, the *final* culmination of a historical story may never have taken place. One generation's ending may have only been another generation's beginning in a saga of human affairs.

## III. Rhetoric and Verity: The Dialectics of Truth and Falsehood

Storytelling, as we have already noted, is one of the highest and oldest of art forms. As such, it calls for a capacity to enter into the very essence of human life in all its verity. Stories so imitate life that they enlarge our understandings of it and are able, as it were, to re-create or re-enact it in the minds of persons who either convey or receive them. Good stories, in fact, are usually founded upon very selective and very special perceptions, upon remarkable depths of insight, upon a certain extraperceptual clairvoyance or inner vision of the way things really are, were, or ought to be. Good stories, hence, draw upon more than ordinary powers of imagination. Nor are even these qualities enough. Good stories usually reflect a wonderful genius in verbal expression. Every artist must be able to express depths of insight, understanding, and vision by working with some sort of materials. But instead of working through the medium of clay, stone, and wood as a sculptor or with the tempos, tones, and tunes of sound as a musician, the storyteller and storywriter must be wonderfully adroit and exquisitely skillful in working with words — with symbolic instruments beyond sound and sight.[21]

One of the most ancient names for this art is "rhetoric." Rhetoric is that special expertise in the use of words that enables them to achieve the specific purpose for which they have been designed. It is that system of disciplines, skills, and theories, whether oratory or literary, by which correctness in the crafting and putting together of words brings its own rewards. It is also that elegance and style by which the deployment of powerful words is not only achieved but also done in such a way that those words persuade, win arguments, and gain support for some particular goal. That the term has sometimes come to mean something close to its opposite — something artificial, declamatory, empty, false, gilded, inflated, insincere, overdone, or just showy — in no way nullifies the essentials of the original meaning of the concept.[22] As is so often

21. C. S. Lewis, *Studies in Words* (Cambridge: Cambridge University Press, 1967), shows just how fascinating this kind of artistry can be.

22. *Lexicon on Difficult Words,* part 2 of *Reader's Digest Reverse Dictionary* (London and New York: Reader's Digest, Inc., 1989), 724, defines the term "rhetoric" as literary, political, or oratorical language; or the study of its structure and effects; speech or writing that is impressively high-flown — but that may also be empty of real meaning.

the case with concepts, such twistings themselves reflect inner conflicts and contradictions which have so often, if not constantly, raged within human beings as individuals and within their institutions.

## A. *Representation and Misrepresentation:* *The Affinities of Fact and Fiction*

Stories — not to mention those who produce them — can be deliberately and purposely true or false. Whether or not stories are deliberately false or deliberately true, they invariably strive to accomplish at least two things: first, they strive to attract attention or, by some means, to awaken interest; and, second, they strive to convey information or intelligence. Having already dealt, in some measure, with the first of these two essentials (in the immediately preceding portion of this chapter), the second is examined here. Stories that cannot convey information that is accurate, reliable, and trustworthy, however entertaining or fascinating they may be, cease to possess direct utility as history. Yet, conversely, the very depth, extent, and frequency of false information, sometimes disguised under such euphemisms as "disinformation," are sufficient to warrant closer investigation. Deceptions, as fabrications and fictions or as lies and untruths of whatever color and by whatever name, are too common and too deeply embedded in the very grain of human actions — in so much of what people have actually done in the past, to themselves and to others — for such things to be either ignored or brushed aside casually.

Stories created for the express purpose of deceiving come in many shapes and sizes.[23] Lying is so endemic in human relationships that it is difficult to find circumstances or situations in which this kind of activity does not occur or purposes, both high and low, for which it is not or has not been assiduously employed.[24] A tiny child, often to our

---

23. One common or colloquial meaning for "story" or "stories" pertains to the deliberate telling of falsehoods. Thus, for example, to say that "stories" about someone are being carried or told is a way of indicating that falsehoods are being peddled.

24. Sissela Bok, *Lying: Moral Choice in Public and Private Life* (New York: Pantheon Books, 1978), is a serious contemporary study from a philosophical standpoint. Patrick Collinson's "Laudable Lying in the Age of Dissimulation," review of *Ways of Lying: Dissimulation, Persecution and Conformity in Early Modern Europe,* by Perez Zagorin,

amazement (if not dismay), often tries to hide some unpleasant truth, or its consequences, at a very early age. A "con" artist sets out to win the confidence of one person or a group of persons, attempting to convince those who listen that something which is actually false is true, doing so in order to achieve some special advantage, so as to mislead or swindle. One person (or group) "libels" another, spreading false stories that serve no other purpose than to damage reputation and undermine relationships.[25] A spy (or members of an espionage net-work) fabricates a partially false history and identity in order to gain access to valuable secrets. A nation concocts false stories about itself or other nations with which it is at odds (even doing both together) and then spreads such stories — as something we now call "propaganda."[26] A regime at odds (or at war) with its own people and with those over whom it rules covers up true facts and puts out smoke screens of false stories in order to protect itself or to carry out some institutional pur-pose (which it dignifies under the guise of "policy").

All stories that are deliberately constructed so as to deceive strive to create a sense of confidence in the authenticity of facts that they convey — or, if they are concerned with commerce and finance, to establish a line of credit — where none is deserved. For this very reason, in the long run, false accuracy is often self-defeating, especially since confidence (or reputation inspiring confidence) is difficult to rebuild and reputation slow to repair. False stories and deceptions often betray shortsightedness, tending to undermine and to destroy the very confi-dence being sought, and leaving behind a legacy of distrust, fear, and suspicion (both within and among persons and peoples). Perhaps the most insidious and dangerous of all forms of deception and falseness are those by which people — whether as individuals, families, or nations — somehow manage to deceive even themselves. False stories, in other words, are the very antithesis of historical veracity; and yet, at the same time, because of their manifold abundance in human affairs, they con-

---

*Times Literary Supplement,* 1 March 1991, 23, also provides a sample of recent work. See also Philip Kerr, ed., *The Penguin Book of Lies* (New York: Viking, 1990); and Eric Berne, *Games People Play* (New York: Grove Press, 1964).

25. For such stories, however they may be explained, there can be little if any excuse — they diminish quality of life and are inherently anti-human in character.

26. Of course, for some groups, propaganda is nothing more than the spreading of perceived truths. This is what missionaries try to do when they "propagate" a gospel.

stitute an important substance of that past which historians strive to understand. If anything, undetected falsehoods serve to undermine and destroy historical knowledge, leaving behind deepening shadows of fear, ignorance and insecurity.

Certain kinds of admittedly deliberate false stories, on the other hand, are created solely for the purpose of entertaining or teaching lessons, even historical lessons. Such stories, whether called "fiction," "fable," or something else, come in many shapes and sizes — so many, in fact, that any attempt to categorize or label them all would be futile. In their most realistic forms, however, these kinds of stories also set out to imitate life. As such they strive for plausibility by constructing real-life situations; and they contain abrupt or surprising turns, contingencies very similar to those which most people have experienced in their own lives. Stories of this sort, if they are effective, also strive to allay boredom and do so by stirring emotion and arousing thought. When successful, they evoke laughter and tears and sober reflection. Comedy and tragedy, as the very stuff of life, are their frequent themes. In fiction, as in history itself, plausible "realities" and unpredictable turning points are the substances portrayed. In novels, plays, poems, and other forms of artful fabrication, it is the world we all know which they strive to fashion. And even where less "realistic" settings are created, stories cannot wander too far from human experience before they seem too far-fetched and are seen as ridiculous.

Among the best of those fantasies which remain popular — such, for example, as the *Narnia Tales* of C. S. Lewis or the *Lord of the Rings* by J. R. R. Tolkien — wholly new and imaginary worlds, together with their own entirely plausible and internally consistent histories, have been fabricated. In such stories as these, stories which seem ubiquitous in every age and clime and culture, we gain a new appreciation for that wonderful creativity of which the human being is capable. Marvelous effects are achieved, with words of such transparent beauty and elegance that listeners and readers are held in thrall. Words transport listeners and readers into other worlds and into new dimensions of possible life, existence, and reality. Works of this kind are important because they appeal to some of the highest aspirations and deepest longings within what is best and most human in all of us. Conversely, when so designed, they can also produce baneful dread and stark terror. In other words, the finest of such stories, by touching timeless and deep affinities within each individual, are capable of uplifting the spirit and of inspiring responses perhaps undreamed, unknown, or unpredictable.[27]

Qualities of indescribable or inexplicable ecstacy and enchantment, not to mention deepening conviction, are among the experiences that well-made and well-told stories can evoke. That element within each of us that seems to rouse a human need for such experiences was carefully explored over a half century ago by J. R. R. Tolkien. In "Beowulf: The Monsters and the Critics"[28] and "On Fairie Stories"[29] he dealt with the relative merits of epic and myth in history, exploring the inner values of fantasy, recovery, escape, and consolation. "On Fairie Stories" suggests exactly how and why stories that possess no historical veracity are, nevertheless, capable of conveying deep truths which are, in themselves, timeless. Any experience that is felt as a close escape from death, for example, can lead to an emotional and mental experience which is its polar opposite. This dialectically, or diametrically, opposite experience Tolkien calls "eucatastrophe." It is such an exquisite experience, he argues, that it evokes what can only be described as a deeply redemptive impulse — an aspiration that lifts the human spirit to the very thresholds of life beyond life and to a sense of immortality.

## B. Perspicacity and Veracity:
## The Ambiguities of Reality and Illusion

As already noted, rhetorical skills expressly developed for the purpose of communicating unique insights and for narrating events, skills for representing beauty or ugliness or truth, are skills that just as easily have been applied to the production of fiction, fantasy, or falsehood ("disinformation"). As also noted, this feature in mankind, this propensity to deceive

27. Or, conversely, of degrading the quality of life.

28. J. R. R. Tolkien, Sir Israel Gollancz Lecture, presented 25 November 1936, published in *Proceedings of the British Academy*.

29. Originally composed and delivered as an Andrew Lang Lecture (University of St. Andrews, 1938) and published in *Essays Presented to Charles Williams* (London and New York: Oxford University Press, 1947), republished in *Tree and Leaf* (Boston: Houghton Mifflin Company, 1964) and in *The Tolkien Reader* (New York: Ballantine Books, 1966).

and falsify, has played no small part in the story of past human events. Indeed, if the examination of past experience and evidence of past events conveys any sense of continuity in recurring patterns of human behavior, it is surely this: the capacity for deception, including self-deception, can have significant, even tragic, consequences. This capacity to deceive seems to be limited only by the powers of imagination and inventiveness that people possess. Those devices of craft and cunning used in the conjuring of falsehood are often, in themselves, facts in the stories about which the historian seeks understanding and which, as storyteller, he or she may feel need to be revealed. It is no small wonder that this feature in storytelling has produced a strong inclination among many scholars to look at any and all forms of storytelling with suspicion.

Yet this very tendency toward suspicion, this critical, even skeptical inclination, is itself one of the most important capacities that a historian can possess. A disciplined willingness to question the veracity of every element in any story is an attitude or inclination that is certainly no less necessary for historical narrative — for stories as history — than is the testing knowledge in any other discipline. Antonyms of "fiction" are, after all, "fact," "truth," and "reality."[30] Yet, as noted, great fiction like any other form of art rises to its fullest potential, its ultimate heights of human worth, only when it demonstrates a capacity to reflect deeper truths and probe more profound realities of the human condition. Those very qualities required of a good novelist are very much the same as those essential for a good historian. Each must exercise a deep capacity for human empathy, sympathy, and insight, whether in understanding individuals as persons or in understanding institutions as reflections of both personal and impersonal activity. Each exhibits extraordinary gifts and powers of imagination. Each is able to exploit a sensitive capacity for discernment and discrimination in the selection (or exclusion) of facts. In so doing, each can discover the significance of key items buried under masses of otherwise shapeless and meaningless historical detail and then put emphasis upon what is genuinely important.[31]

30. As pointed out by Barbara Tuchman in her essay "The Historian as Artist," in *Practicing History* (New York: Alfred A. Knopf, 1981), 46. A writer who tries to portray historical reality rather than fiction could just as well be called a "realtor" (were not this term already applied to sellers of "real" or "permanent" property).

31. Louis Gottschalk, *Understanding History: A Primer of Historical Method* (New York: Alfred A. Knopf, 1950), 45, 195ff.

When the historian is so equipped, able to employ critical imagination with discipline and skill, and when the historian consciously
strives for fidelity in telling the story about past events by employing
those facts that are most crucial — facts revealed through perceptions
drawn from experience and evidence — there can then be little doubt
that the historian stands in a position of special privilege. The very
decisions a historian is obliged to make will make this so. Selecting facts
with care and showing discernment in coaxing facts that "fit" requires
a rational sifting and testing of evidence. This evidence itself must, at
the very least, answer some "inner sense" of what rings true. Out of the
many more facts than can possibly ever be used, even though those facts
may also be parts of the story, it is only the "special" or "select" facts
that are chosen. And these facts are chosen precisely because they are
what the historian as narrator believes to be those facts best suited for
representing the truest story. The very task of making the right choices,
however agonizing, confusing, or difficult and however painful or slow,
is what rhetoric is all about. The greatest challenge the historian as
storyteller faces is that of maintaining human interest and excitement.
It is in the story-worthiness of a particular line of narrative that this
must be done, yet without departing from any of the essential facts
(actions, events, episodes, incidents, etc.), without leaving out any important facts, and without twisting any significant facts out of context.
This task is never simple or easy. Nevertheless, as often as not, the very
flow of essentials in any historical narrative has a way of generating its
own kind of inner logic. Once a person becomes caught up in *following*
the details of every unexpected twist and turn in the story, and once it
is possible to see with clarity how the whole story fits together, the very
curiosity generated with each surprising turn, insight, or discovery and
the excitement of pursuing it becomes memorable in itself.[32]

It is then, precisely at the moment of final achievement, that the
historian faces special dangers. It is then that the historian, as artist and

---

32. The experience and excitement of "following" history as story is very comparable to the action of "following" some sports event — whether tennis, baseball,
basketball, football, or ice hockey. Even when one expects to know much of what will
happen — serving, returning serve, volleying, lobbing, slamming, and so forth — each
single play has a unique quality and each unexpected turn can lift the level of tension,
even when one knows that only one side will win and even if one knows which side
that will be.

storyteller, is called upon to exercise a measure of restraint, checking to make sure that the excitement of creative achievement does not carry the narrative beyond what is warranted by evidence. This occurs in the very way history is told, retold, and written. History becomes, by this very process, not just a literary craft but, in the best sense, an important member within that ancient and venerable discipline called rhetoric. And, as such, historical writing calls for all of those consummate skills by which artistry and science are combined to achieve some determined purpose. That combination of artistry and science called "rhetoric" falls within a literary tradition which dates back to the dawn of intellectual life. Every culture and clime, in every age, has possessed special remnants, scraps, and traces of such understanding. Few modern European historians — even English historians from Gibbon to Macaulay, Churchill, and Trevelyan — have not been well acquainted with the classic works of Homer, Herodotus, Thucydides, or Tacitus.

Yet, even so, what Suzanne Gearhart has called the "open boundary between fiction and history"[33] is confusing. This is so because, quite clearly, both fiction and history are capable of undermining each other. History as story is very much like — as performed and as witnessed — theater. What is written on the page by a historian/narrator and what is done on the stage by a dramatist are comparable "as the best means of articulating the continual transgression of the boundary between the literary and the historical, the fictional and the real."[34] "Theater," in this sense, is not simply a metaphor. It is a model of perception — a way, albeit severe, of simultaneously focusing upon both textual and contextual elements. A stage, like a page, is a point where elements being "represented" intersect: "Perception is always framed by interest or attention; the clearest perception occurs when the consciousness of the process of framing is most acute — or when the spectator in the theater of perception is most conscious of the other attentive spectators, whose presence reminds each spectator that he is indeed in a theater."[35] This being so, the old boundaries between history and literature or between history and fiction, as also between philosophy and history or between

33. Suzanne Gearhart, *The Open Boundary of History and Fiction: A Critical Approach to the French Enlightenment* (Princeton: Princeton University Press, 1984), 285-92.

34. Ibid., 291.

35. Ibid., 190-91.

science and literature, if not even those between other disciplines, are brought into question: "The theater signifies the eruption of what is posited as the nontextual in the textual while, at the same time, it reveals the fictive, theatrical characteristics of the historical event."[36] Of course one can easily carry this comparison too far. Still, the argument that good history, like good fiction, literature, or theater, must possess the capacity to catch and hold perceptions of events in this way is insightful.

In the final analysis, however, both the veracity of story as history and the validity of history as story depends and is conditioned, like historical understanding of any kind, by certain other factors. Among such factors, R. G. Collingwood identified three that he felt are altogether essential and W. B. Gallie added a fourth: A story that is "as true as possible," as a historical account "of what really happened" is, first of all, something *located in time and space* (something with a date and a place — something not required in art works, such as novels, paintings, songs, etc.). Second, to be historical, a story is consistent both with itself and with the world around it — something that is not necessary in purely imaginary worlds — and yet is interconnected with actions and events of a particular (and actual) people, place, or time.[37] Third, a story constructed as history "stands in a peculiar relation to something called evidence" — something not simply made up or swallowed but something existing here and now, which anyone can check out.[38] Finally, a historical narrative demonstrates its "emphatically public character" — something received out of a common past involving both continuous critical revision and continuous interpretation of that past, something that is not necessary for artistic works as such.[39]

---

36. Ibid., 292.

37. Any assumption that history consists of *the whole* human past, or even a large piece of one spacial/temporal world, and that such a history is a whole made out of combinable bits and pieces of historical understanding is dangerous. Rather, in the end, history is "our" history and, as such, is something about what has happened which historians have succeeded in making understandable to "us," whoever "we" may happen to be.

38. R. G. Collingwood, *The Idea of History* (Oxford: Clarendon Press, 1946), 246-47: "The whole perceptible world, then, is potentially and in principle evidence to the historian."

39. Gallie, *Philosophy and the Historical Understanding*, 62-64. A novelist or poet is not obliged to "improve upon his or her received material" in order to make a "truer"

## C. Epistemology and Theory: The Revolutions of Credibility

The foundations for history as story are both deep and strong; moreover, in the eyes of some thinkers, they are becoming stronger. As defined by Gallie, "Historical understanding is the exercise of the capacity to follow a story, where the story is known to be based on evidence and is put forward as a sincere effort to get at *the* story so far as the evidence and the writer's general knowledge and intelligence allow."[40] It seems clear, from this line of thinking, that historical understanding itself is produced in the very acts of telling and following a story. This kind of understanding, moreover, possesses both dialectical and dialogical features:[41] polarities of natural and historical events, objectivity and subjectivity, knowledge and faith, things impersonal and personal, storytelling and story-receiving, are brought together and become intimately related in the very making of narrative history.

Moreover, however ambiguous or incomplete understandings of any particular past may sometimes be, what can be known about that past occurs and is formed by a kind of participatory interaction, emotional or moral involvement, and by some sort of intellectual synthesis of elements within the narrative itself. This requires each participant to closely follow details in the sequence of events, through various and unexpected contingencies, until those details bring the participant to an expected culmination. This seems to be just that sort of understanding that comes to each individual person from experiencing the varying vicissitudes of actions and events in real life. Events

---

or "more acceptable" version; nor to fully master previous literature and previous judgments on a subject. Utilizing what is authoritative in records from the past involves more than simple "scissors and paste" acceptance and more than merely unmasking errors, fakes, falsehoods, forgeries, or superstitions.

40. Gallie, *Philosophy and the Historical Understanding*, 105. He continues: "But to follow an historical narrative always requires the acceptance, from time to time, of explanations which have the effect of enabling one to follow further when one's vision was becoming blurred or one's credulity taxed beyond patience."

41. While it is fashionable among some deconstructionist and/or postmodern thinkers not only to deny *any* such thing as objectivity but also to relativize, subjectivize, and tamper with, if not even to trivialize, both past events and evidences of past events, such outcomes are not necessary to the dialogical and/or dialectical approaches which they espouse. (For more on this, see chapter 10.)

in a historical narrative are followable and/or intelligible only in the same general way, and to the same general degree, that they are in actual life experiences. Of course, unlike any other kind of story, a historical narrative rests upon evidence: evidence showing that the events related actually happened and that they happened in some time and place (however roughly assigned these are). Finally, a historical narrative is better able to make its content intelligible by showing interconnections between that content and other relevant historical events and by placing that content within a larger historical context.

Beyond appreciation, renewed intellectual commitment to the importance of history as story is one of the important intellectual revolutions of our time.[42] The long dominance of Enlightenment epistemology and positivist models of verity over the natural and social sciences, a dominance which did not assign much significance to narrative's cognitive role, now seems to be in decline, if not ending. The claims made by contemporary deconstructionists, notwithstanding, that the storyteller's own "story" (position) or the listener/reader's own "story" prevents access to any correct assessment of evidence (as found in a text or anywhere else) are also under serious attack. Yet, even as proponents of the importance of narrative face Enlightenment, positivist, and deconstructionist critiques, arguments in favor of narrative understandings seem to be rapidly gaining strength. The close relationship between narrative and human understanding has now become recognized as salient to many academic disciplines. This recognition, in reaction to neopositivism, began with analytical philosophers over thirty years ago. Following N. R. Hanson's *Patterns of Discovery: An Inquiry into the Conceptual Foundations of Science* (1958), Thomas S. Kuhn's *The Structure of Scientific Revolutions* (1962) showed the importance of narrative in the history of science and transformed the philosophy of science. Arthur C. Danto's *Analytical Philosophy of History* (1968), revised and called *Narration and Knowledge* (1985), and W. B. Gallie's *Philosophy and the Historical Understanding* (1967) carried these same transformative changes into the philosophy of history. As a result, to quote Danto, "all of science was brought under history rather than, as before, history having been brought under science

---

42. Richard A. Rhem, "Sleeping through a Revolution," *Perspectives* 6, no. 4 (April 1991): 8-14.

construed on the model of physics."[43] Much more recently, Alasdair MacIntyre's *After Virtue: A Study in Moral Theory* (1981) has tied narrative to a resurgence of virtue ethics; and Alvin Plantinga's "Reformed Epistemology," in *Religion and Rationality* (1983, edited with N. Wolterstorff), has appealed to biographical factors in justifications for belief. Narrative theology has become a dominant force in contemporary theological reflection. Recent psychology of counseling stresses the importance, in the possession of mental health, of a person's possessing an acceptable narrative construction of her or his own life that includes its misfortunes. If one assesses the value of narrative for clearer understandings on the basis of these and similar developments in each important discipline, that value seems to be not only high, but also increasing. Indeed, the epistemological foundations of each separate discipline now seem to show a growth of closer relationships with narrative.

Meanwhile, for historical theory itself, Hayden White has led the way. In *The Content of the Form: Narrative Discourse and Historical Representation* (1987), he has explored some ramifications of defining history as a genus within the species of story and of establishing the "epistemic status of narrativity." In so doing, he has identified several categories, positions, or schools of thought: (1) Anglo-American analytical philosophers mentioned above (including Dray, Gardiner, Mink, Walsh, and Morton White) who defend narrative as "especially appropriate to the explication of historical, as against natural, events and processes"; (2) "social-scientifically oriented historians" (Braudel, Furet, Le Goff, Le Roy-Laduri, and others of the French *Annales* group) who consider narrative to be a nonscientific, even ideological strategy which must be extirpated if history is to become a genuine science; (3) "semiologically oriented literary theorists and philosophers" (Barthes, Derrida, Eco, Foucault) who regard narrative as just one more "discursive code" among many which might or might not be useful in attempting to represent reality; (4) certain "hermeneutically oriented philosophers" (Gadamer, Ricouer, etc.) who see narrative as manifesting "a specific kind of time-consciousness" or structuring of time; and finally, (5) practicing historians, defending no

43. Arthur C. Danto, *Narration and Knowledge* (New York: Columbia University Press, 1985), xi.

particular doctrine or theory to the exclusion of others, who "do" history eclectically without regarding "narrative representations" as a serious theoretical problem.[44]

\*     \*     \*

To recapitulate and conclude, a narrative or story that deliberately strives for historical truth usually possesses a different and, some would say, a profoundly deeper purpose than pure fiction. A story as pure fiction is devoid of genuine relations between real actors, actions, or events. The purpose of historical narrative, its essential requirement, is not only to inform but to inform as accurately as possible. To do less is to fail. And the degree to which a "true" story does less is the degree to which it fails. While it may and, indeed, must excite interest — that is, command attention and bring notice — and while just as certainly it may entertain, enthrall, or even inspire — these elements are secondary, albeit important, embellishments of the main purpose by which narrative serves as a vehicle for conveying information about past events, information that is accurate, reliable, and trustworthy. Perhaps the only possible exception to this principle — at least one that might be debated — pertains to stories that need never have been (nor could be) told and that, if and when told, were capable of doing damage and harm, whether to individuals or to institutions. Such stories, even when historically true, are employed for nonhistorical purposes. Whether as malicious gossip or tattling or as propaganda to gain some political end, historical understandings are then being employed to some partisan end. However true they may be in a historical sense — in telling about things that really have happened — such stories and such histories, when used to change human or institutional relationships, achieve a "rhetorical" purpose, sometimes at costs too great to be reckoned. Such stories, like tools or weapons of war, become subjects of narrative history. Like fables, their dialogical antithesis, the issue of their historicity as such becomes subordinate to their utility (e.g., as propaganda or whatever it may be). This may be so whether or not such stories also uncover falsehood, ignorance, and prejudice.

44. Hayden White, "Narrative in Contemporary Historical Theory," in *The Content of the Form* (Baltimore: Johns Hopkins University Press, 1987), 31.

But whatever the case, stories that are accurate and true in relation to real events of the past are but another name for *history*.

Yet, two basic and crucial requirements, above all, distinguish historical narratives as stories. Stories essential to history in this form possess (1) fidelity and genuineness of information about real and significant events; and (2) genuineness in qualities that enable them to attract and hold attention. The degree that history as story falls short of either one or both of these criteria is the degree to which it also ceases to be *effective*. The old saw that a good story should never be allowed to suffer for not being entirely true is, in like measure, simply false — it is a flawed maxim. In any successful story, historical or not, distracting embellishments and exaggerations are avoided.[45]

45. This principle must hold even if one must admit, at the same time, that the very acts of selecting some facts over other facts lead unavoidably to distortion, exaggeration, and oversimplification. Even such selection, as an artistic prerogative, needs to be faithful to what is essential in past events.

*Chapter 4*

# History as Anecdote:
# A Vital Essence

*Ideally, history itself should be rewritten entirely in terms of anecdote, for these alone assert their authenticity above the prejudice and conformism of the professional historian.*
Richard N. Coe[1]

*A necdote* is not just a "small story." It is a special kind of small story, one that "documents" an event. Its importance lies in the peculiar and even unique capacity it possesses to convey the very essence of truth (or understanding) about particular "happenings" in the past: it illuminates human events and human experiences. Coming out of the mists of earliest consciousness and remnants of memory, linking it to origins of folklore and oral tradition, in times (and places) when facticity, historicity, and mythic verity were not yet separated into distinct categories or concepts, anecdote continues to retain a very powerful kind of authenticity and potentiality in human discourse and understanding.

The classical Greek *anekdota* (ανεκδῶτα) — literally "[something]-not-given-out," "not-published" or, as yet, "unpublished"[2] — is a "small

---

1. Richard N. Coe, "The Anecdote and the Novel: A Brief Enquiry into the Origins of Stendhal's Narrative Technique," *Australian Journal of French Studies* 20, no. 1 (January-April 1985): 7.
2. Any standard reference, such as *Chambers Twentieth Century Dictionary*, ed.

hard truth."[3] It is commonly understood to be a "brief account," or a "short narrative" of a "memorable event." It is the relating of a "remarkable experience" or a "striking incident" imbued with memorable significance and truth. Detailing some event or experience "as it happened," it graphically tells "how it really was"; and, in doing so, it draws upon some "hitherto unknown" or "unpublished" sources.

Often related out of someone's memory,[4] the really good anecdote, in its classic mold, requires formal structure, consummate artistry, rhetorical skill, and polished technique. It must have a beginning, a middle, and an ending. Properly constructed, its facts must not contradict deeper substructures of historically verifiable truths. Used to give emphasis or make some point within the context of a larger (or longer) work; employed for highlighting interest or for throwing new light upon life; or presented simply for its own sake: anecdote is betimes amusing, curious, gossipy, pungent, revealing, or even risqué; it is sometimes crude, grotesque, or vicious; and, at times, it is inspiring or even sublime. Yet, it always retains some of its deeper nature as an insightful recital of essential "small hard truths." This is so even as it makes a point, illuminates or illustrates "how it really was," and drives home a particular idea. Artfully "done," a good anecdote is not just delivered: it is "performed." By means of explicit detail; implicit omission; captivating dialogue; wonderful mimicry; plays upon words; turns of phrase; spirited appeals (which can be droll, humorous, or pathetic); exquisite timing; and climactic endings: an anecdote can combine all sorts of captivating devices so as to give listeners a "deeper glimpse of life," showing how "it really was" within a particular situation. A strong imagination and a powerful memory, when harnessed to those narrative gifts displayed in the form of anecdote, can throw graphic light upon *the* "large picture." By such means, many a heavier

---

A. M. MacDonald (Edinburgh, 1972), 46, informs us that it comes from a conjunction of the Greek roots *an-*, "privative" [consisting of the absence or removal of something: absence or negation], and *ekdotos-*, "published" [from *ek-*, "out"; and *didonai-*, "to give"], so adding up to the word *anékdota-*, "something given out but not published."

    3. It is what Stendhal described as the *petit fait vrai* of narrative — the "little actual happening," "little factual verity," "little hard truth," or "little true fact." Coe, "The Anecdote and the Novel," 7.

    4. An "insider's" perspective or "private" knowledge, something which often, if not usually, puts a different spin on previously held understandings.

subject becomes "humanized," and less bloodless.[5] Whatever its form — whether autobiographical, biographical, or nonbiographical — anecdote serves as an ideal vehicle for conveying factual details about an actual event.[6]

I

It is rather surprising to discover how little attention has been given to the inner nature and structure of the anecdote as such. While my own searchings may undoubtedly yet uncover something more valuable, the best analysis of anecdote that I have found so far is found in an article by Richard N. Coe. In an inquiry into the origins of Stendhal's narrative technique, he has explored the inner structure of the anecdote, in both its classic and nonclassic forms. The classic anecdote, as epitomized by Stendhal, must possess at least five, if not six, distinguishing features.

First and foremost, an anecdote is effective or genuine only to the degree that it conveys something true. In other words: "No truth, no anecdote!!" Without truth, a "little story" or "funny story" or "joke" is merely and simply and nothing but that. Without story, on the other hand, a pithy insight or observation is no more than a maxim, or an assertion with "truth-bearing" potentialities. A *maxim* is in no way similar, whether couched as aphorism, paradigm, proverb, theory, or "wise" truism — such as Lord Acton's famous statement that "Absolute power corrupts absolutely!" A maxim states some general principle which serves as a guide or rule. An anecdote narrates facts and circumstances, giving details in sequence. An anecdote, even if and when it points to some conclusion or some general observation, will not do so explicitly. The anecdotist who really "knows his [or her] stuff" studiously refrains from drawing any general conclusion. This is left entirely up to the audience. It is the audience (or reader) who draws

<hr>

5. For variant comments, definitions, and expositions, see P. Kirk King, ed., *Writing from A to Z* (Cincinnati, 1990), 18-19; Raymond Berry, ed., *Literary Terms* (San Francisco, 1966), 6; A. F. Scott, ed., *Current Literary Terms* (New York: St. Martin's Press, 1965), 14; Northrop Frye, ed., *The Harper Handbook to Literature* (New York: Harper & Row, 1985).

6. At the same time, when used as a means of highlighting that event, it is often accompanied by parenthetical commentary or observations.

inferences and connects the particular to the general. In any case, whether anecdote or maxim, the form of one is the other form inside out, back-to-front, or upside down: one gives a general conclusion or theory without supplying evidence; and the other does just the reverse, narrating details and providing evidence without drawing general conclusions or principles. The empirical and the theoretical, by nature, work in opposite ways.

Second, anecdote is what Stendhal called *petit fait vrai* — that is, it carries within itself a truth of such significance, exceptionality, and veracity that it is, for that very reason, memorable. The contrast between the "hard little truth" of anecdote and the softness (even "falseness" or "shallowness") of sweeping generalization highlights this feature in anecdote. Here there is a basic conflict: between the banality of composite averages and the insightfulness of startling exceptions — exceptions that make the rule. Attempts to gain historical understanding, when devoid of anecdotal elements, all too quickly cease to assert truths that transcend the conforming restraints of general or theoretical explanation. Generalization, or theoretical explanation, in history by itself, is likely, more often than not, to degenerate into or be driven by ossifying doctrines; and these themselves are often merely agendas or covers for dogma, doctrine, and ideology.

Third, anecdote is extremely personal, if not private. As a mode of expression, it calls for consummate skill and developed techniques. Accent, gesture, voice, and personality play crucial roles. The same anecdote, told by different persons, can convey different understandings. Anecdotal truth, embodied in dramatized intimacy and enhanced by theatrical technique, is narrated in proximity, bringing anecdotist and audience into a closer, more confidential and familiar relationship.

Next, as with any form of theater, anecdote creates illusion. The very impression of spontaneity and simplicity, even naiveté, which anecdote conveys is, in fact, anything but that. Anecdote, at its best, is nothing if not artful. Its cunning devices are ingeniously contrived, neatly balanced, carefully crafted, and shrewdly wrought. Its rhythm, timing, and tone are subtlety personified. Slyly lulling senses into comfortable conformity and a familiar mundanity, the anecdotist suddenly transforms soporific and deliberately murky shapelessness into something sharply edged. As the performance approaches its finale, tension builds, and then, with startling speed and flashing wit, a thunderous revelation breaks upon the listener. Nothing, one must repeat and stress, can be less spontaneous than a really good anecdote.

Fifth, at its very epicenter, the good anecdote captures and captivates the human spirit. Any artistic masterpiece has this quality. It touches the heart. It plumbs the very depths of despair and reaches the heights of ecstasy. It plucks at the strings and strums the chords of emotion. It breathes and echoes with sobs and hysterics. Gusts of humor or pathos reverberate from those who hear and listen. Alternately soft and tender, biting and bitter, grotesque and risqué, piquant and satirical, or even sublime, this kind of tale is driven home with force and verve. No anecdote is worth the name if it does not "breathe" wind and wit and *hwyl*.[7]

Sixth, and finally, anecdote conveys and possesses historical authenticity *as* anecdote only if, when, and to the degree that it demonstrates detachment. Between teller and thing told, between anecdotist and anecdote, distance is required. Objectivity separates the creator from the thing created. Self-effacing genius is not confused with what it has made. The performing Self is not the Story. No amount of personal brilliance or wit can be permitted to inflate the narrator. Narrator, as actor, can play, and be excused, any part but that of hero — witness, victim, simpleton, or butt — anything so long as anecdotist is out of the spotlight. Let any teller take the slightest personal merit or glory and both he as teller and his anecdote look ridiculous. Worse still, both teller and tale then become guilty of the inexcusable crime of boredom.[8]

7. This old yet common Welch expression traces its ancestry from old Anglo-Saxon *(segl)* and Latin *(vailum)*, the root from which we get our word "sail." It has many meanings and overlapping connotations. But at its center, like wind catching sail, is the sense of an infectious, even overpowering conviviality: an ecstatic or fervent hilarity and mirth, or zest, alternately dampened by desolation or lamentation. All this and more marks the progress or journey of this concept from one place and time to another. *A Dictionary of the Welch Language,* Volume G-L (Cardiff: University of Wales Press, 1968-87), 137-38.

8. Here, interestingly, a gender distinction arises: namely, a claim, or at least a hint, that anecdote is a peculiarly masculine prerogative, a genre in which "no woman has truly left her mark." The feminine equivalent, as Coe sees it ("The Anecdote and the Novel," 6), is the diary or the letter. Even this, when filled with anecdotal material, offers less room for the dynamics of anecdotal drama. "By contrast," Coe suggests, "no male writer since Saint Paul has achieved immortality exclusively through his Correspondence."

## II

It is in this last feature that the structure of the classic anecdote confronts us with a strange paradox. The very activity that produces something so supremely synthetic, sophisticated, and artificial is the activity that also establishes the facticity and veracity of a genuine historical event. Historical events which, by themselves, obviously occur within an otherwise shapeless context and a seemingly unstructured environment require structured narration to document and establish authenticity. In other words, *a* truth is established at the expense of *the* truth. What is it that lies behind this apparent contradiction, raising questions and insinuating suspicions?

It is facts that make a genuine anecdote. It is facts that make it good and that establish its power. Details of the most improbable character are able, by their very improbability, to make themselves convincing. No mere imagination, the audience is made to feel, could invent facts so amazing. And hence, they must be true. The very exceptionality of the details and facts becomes the bond and seal of authenticity. In comparison, claims that are vague or general, propositions seemingly platitudinous or hypocritical, if not clearly clichés or stereotypes, become suspect. Worse yet, they need but one exception to be proved false, or untrue. Many an axiom or maxim, as explanation or generalization, especially when too inflated or sweeping, looks banal. It sounds like so much "cant" or "dogma" in the presence of "hard little facts." Just as factual authenticity and historicity "reside in" and "rest upon" *evidence* found in *documents*, resulting in calls for historiographic resorts to ever more rigorous documentation, so also, for the anecdote, details serve "to document" the facticity of the particular episodes which are being recounted. This has been so, since the time of the ancients, long before Herodotus and Thucydides employed them with such skill. It is this quality of intrinsic detachment, objectivity, and documentation within anecdotal description that poses a problem for the historian: namely, the dilemma of preserving the inherent "truth-bearing" authority of the anecdote while, at the same time, controlling, or at least somehow downplaying (muting or disguising) the contrived character of its narration. Anecdotal artificiality and sophistication, in short, are at odds with authenticity and detached documentation.

No clear or entirely satisfying answer or solution to this dilemma seems to have been found. How, in other words, does artificiality in narrative authenticate life in experiences and events? How are apparently unstructured and shapeless contexts of real events made understandable? The answers to such questions seem to lie in different kinds of artifices, ruses, and stratagems. One can, for example, downplay or disguise the artificiality of an anecdote by producing evidence of events and experiences contained within an anecdote without actually producing the anecdote itself, thereby leaving others to draw their own conclusions about the historicity of what is related. Resorts to this kind of device, and others too many to examine at length here, lead to the production, in turn, of nonclassical forms of anecdote. Some anecdotes, as a consequence, have been deliberately personalized and given unstructured form. That is, they have been "deconstructed" and, thereby, left without their usual beginnings, middles, and endings. Sometimes even the punch line, finale, or point has been omitted. Thus "syncopated," formal linking elements within a sentence have been cut and left entirely to the imagination of the listener. One is given, as it were, a "neighbor's-eye-view." Or, when extended, anecdotes have been made into "*nouvelles*": an art form in which dialogue has replaced narrative and smaller anecdotes have been incorporated. Literary devices for fusing together many forms of anecdotes — classic, personal, extended, etc. — within longer short stories have made possible the retention of all the classic qualities of the true anecdote while, at the same time, also serving to satisfy that reluctance to draw conclusions, to erect formal structures, or to spell out a truth that the anecdotist may feel.

## III

Extended anecdotes which contain other anecdotes and which have been lengthened into increasingly longer episodes have eventually, in turn, been extended into full histories (or novels). These have then become, with each addition, more and more complex. During this process of extension, distinction between history and novel, between "faction" and "fiction," can be made clear or can remain murky. Much depends upon degrees of detachment or personal involvement, in each kind and size of anecdote. Personal responses to the historical events which cannot be expressed directly or in simplistic terms, merely by inclusion in an anecdote or a maxim, can be shifted into the realms of fiction and allegory. The shifting of anecdotes from historical works into novels and short stories, whereby a fictitious narrative presents a picture of "real life events," especially focusing upon crises in the lives or life histories of men and women, has in no way altered the essential historical character of the genuine and true anecdote.

Nevertheless, due to its many uses, in its generic form the anecdote remains ubiquitous. Its purposes in human affairs, in all places and all times, have been manifold — whether historical, literary, pedagogical, political, rhetorical, or theatrical. Sometimes used as "filler," or as added "sauce" or "spice" in public discourse, anecdotes have been "manufactured" synthetically, mass-produced, and marketed. Once made saleable as a synthetic product, certain anecdotes have been mixed with aphorisms and jokes, for use at banquets or on speaker circuits. Some anecdotes have become so famous and popular, traveling so far and wide, that their shadows have become bywords and metaphors. Removed from original context of historical circumstance, carcasses or ghosts of powerful anecdotes become enshrined in timeless shells — in fables and parables as much as in metaphorical allusions, phrases, or proverbs. Whatever their long journeys, whether in factual or in fictional forms, short accounts of "hard little truths" about single, isolated events, experiences, or incidents taking place at crucial turning points within larger courses of events have become the very essence of most genuine historical understandings. Within larger frameworks of narrative, where *history-as-story*, even when accompanied and surrounded by interpretative analysis, is still the most ideal and the most preferred vehicle for conveying the very essence of particular historical understandings, the place of anecdote remains unchallenged. No amount of secondary analysis, interpretative theorizing, or building of models and paradigms by professional scholars, among whom academic historians have been conspicuous during the past two decades, has yet been able to eradicate or undermine the paramount supremacy enjoyed by anecdotes.

Examples of anecdotes, of course, abound, both in history and in literature. So ubiquitous and so universal has been their presence in human affairs and in history, so vast their numbers, that they have become "like the sands of the sea and the stars of the sky, beyond counting." Whether genuine or false, whether good or bad, comic or tragic, somber or jovial, effective or ineffective, famous or obscure, alive or dead: anecdotes in every shape, size, and form have abounded. Anecdotes, in one form or another, still give meaning to many of the most classic of our metaphors and myths. They even ornament some the most tired platitudes, trite stereotypes, and banal clichés. Often, one phrase, or even one, two, or three words, within a particular cultural tradition encapsulates, encodes, or symbolizes a famous or popular anecdote. Virtually everyone in the Judeo-Christian world, for example, knows and even understands (down to tiny details) what certain biblical allusions mean. Simple terms from Hebrew Scripture can immediately evoke anecdotal meaning. Such expressions as "curse of Cain" ("Am I my brother's keeper?"), "Babel," "Potiphar's wife," "Passover," "Jericho," "Goliath," "rivers of Babylon," "fiery chariot," "fiery furnace," and "handwriting on the wall" are codes that conjure up underlying anecdotes in an instant. Likewise, in the Christian Gospels (including the Acts of the Apostles), words like "Bethlehem" or "manger," "wise men" or "magi," "Cana," "Prodigal Son," "Great Temptation," "driving out the money-changers," "Last Supper," "thirty pieces of silver," "Golgotha," "Damascus Road," and hosts of other expressions do the same thing. All the classical cultures, whether of Greece, India, China, or of the Islamic world, are thick with the threads, woven networks, and metaphorical allusions to anecdotal material.

However much one may value any particular or any exemplary anecdote, the role played by anecdotes within larger frameworks of historical narrative — "history as story" — is all-pervasive. The pivotal and persuasive importance that many a "true-little-tale" gives is just that essential flash of insight, that revealing essence within the framework of a larger story. In that very moment of truth, light is thrown upon the whole of a larger episode. Thereafter, the mythic and the historic are repeatedly subject to exegetical and hermeneutical examination and revision. At the same time, anecdote as history, by its very nature, also depends upon the framework of the larger historical narrative for its veracity. Its energy comes from those critical turning points, those times of crisis, when all history (meaning all events in a crucial period) seems to stand still or hang in the balance. No one, for example, can quote Wellington's memorable comment that Waterloo was "a near run thing" without somehow appreciating how desperate was that fathomless panoply of emotions, deeds, and suspense-filled events, that sense of miraculous deliverance from destruction, that lies behind one word or phrase. Any action of private memory, making a nonpublic assessment public, can transform a previously obscure "little hard fact" into something contemplative, critical, cautionary, and timeless: insomuch that all who read remember, reflect, and take to heart the larger framework of "master" narrative concerning what happened. In cryptic, marvelously terse words (of wonderful economy and efficiency), a common understanding of "what really happened" is engendered and a commitment to historical understanding occurs.

While many anecdotal traditions might be examined more closely here, undoubtedly some of the most famous and striking concentrations of anecdotes anywhere to be found are those collections and sequences contained within the historical parts of Hebrew and Christian Scriptures. Virtually every larger event recorded therein, indeed, consists of a carefully selected and highly structured distillation of anecdotes, each a document put in place to carry forward the essentials of a narrative. Taken from oral traditions about happenings, "small hard truths" carefully remembered, handed down from generation to generation for some time before ultimately being recorded in writing, they represent facts, tightly packed, concentrated, and reduced to barest essentials. The very concentration, density, or economy of words, and precision of meanings in facts contained in these strings of anecdotes, is truly astonishing. So also are these essences of historical truth. As essences of mythic and theological verity, they have been transmitted down through many passing centuries, if not millennia. Moreover, having survived ravages of time and turbulence, both natural and political, the credibility of these texts has withstood nearly three centuries of critical assault from scholars.

The rejection of these texts as a reliable record of events, starting in the time of Spinoza, gained momentum and speed during the Enlightenment. These texts were subjected to severe scrutiny, driven by critical doubts that sometimes verged on fanaticism. Their composition, dating, content, and form were questioned, and they were pronounced unreliable, records that were more didactic than historical, vehicles for falsehoods ("myths") rather than facts. The events and personalities they described, from Abraham down to Jesus, were seen as fabrications. Not until the death and destruction of two worldwide wars and the horrors of holocaust exposed the possible depths of human depravity and wickedness as never before did the tide begin to turn. Gradually, respect for the dependability of these records returned, restored by archeological findings and by recovery of ancient texts which established the veracity of dates, events, and persons described in the Torah. Those denying the historicity of events have, in recent years, been put on the defensive, as detail after detail has been corroborated. Indeed, with the exact datings now being made, it is possible to conclude that, in terms of reliability, historical anecdotes found in the narrative books of Samuel, Kings, and Chronicles are on a par with the finest works written by such Greeks as Herodotus and Thucydides. Better history was not produced in ancient times.

Anecdotes in many forms, either standing alone or as parts of larger stories, lie at the heart of historical understandings found in Hebrew Scripture. They are, indeed, the very essence of those understandings. The records of ancient Israel and of Jewish peoples abound with them. Covering a period of nearly four thousand years, the historical understandings contained within them come in many shapes and sizes. On the level of human relationships alone, much of what we can learn is often filled with horror, pathos, and tragedy. Exactly how horrible and how tragic cannot be appreciated without taking the whole of that history into account. All sorts of conclusions can be drawn from this history. Yet nothing is more marked than the capacity for evil and folly, corruption and wickedness, by which mankind has brought pain and sorrow and suffering upon itself. It is difficult not to see that the only constraints upon propensities for wrongdoing among Jewish peoples seem to have come out of the central importance of their experiences and of events behind those experiences within their history. Religious faith generated out of experiences of events made it possible for countless generations, despite many failures and oppressions, misfortunes and sufferings, to establish foundations on which they were able to build lives and attain remarkable achievements and no small measures of satisfaction, if not security. Certainly, if these records have any veracity at all, they tell us — anecdote by anecdote — how it was that, but for events in their lives, this small people could never have survived and how many, especially those who lost their faith, were hounded and hunted down until they all but vanished from the earth.

The story of Christians also begins with anecdotes and is, to a remarkable degree, quite similar. A condensed corpus of these anecdotes, passed down from year to year, was written down and canonized.

This happened only after the more highly complex, intellectually dense, and tightly packed phrases found in the Epistles (of Paul and Peter, if not John) had been in circulation for some time. Built upon under-standings which assumed and presupposed knowledge of the historical events written in the Hebrew Scriptures, these new records are filled with allusions to events related in previous anecdotes. Whether or not the Epistles, filled with all their profound theology, were written first, one of the Gospels may have been among the *last* elements of biblical literature to find an established place within the canon. With this last entry, the records were closed and sacred remembrance, as memory-in-history, became complete. That the anecdotes and longer stories might have come after the most complex treatises, given what we now know about the construction of anecdotes, can hardly be a matter for wonder.

# Sample Anecdotes

## Sample 1: A Self-Authenticating Personal "Document"

### *"Get Rid of Him! He's a Thief!"*

His name was Kaniyapa. He stood beneath a slowly moving fan hanging from the eighteen-foot ceiling in the grand dining room of "Red Craig." This stately "garden house" in Nungambakkam, Madras, had been built two centuries earlier, by a sepoy general of the Honourable East India Company. It now belonged to the State Bank of India and served as the residence for its chief accountant, Stephen Chase. Stephen, a Madras native from an old Anglo-Indian family, had already helped us to find and rent a nice house; and now, in September 1965, he was helping us to staff it with servants. We needed a cook.

Kaniyapa's "chits" — letters of reference — were glowing. One declared that his Swedish meatballs were "out of this world." Another extolled his delicious lemon pies. Our mouths watered: these were among our favorite dishes. With minds nearly made up, we were ready to make our decision. The salary request seemed reasonable — only one hundred rupees a month.

Our host turned to Kaniyapa and, looking him over closely, remarked, "I can see that you are a thief!" Visibly shaken, Kaniyapa's face darkened. We were shocked! How could anyone say such things to a complete stranger? To someone never before seen? Unpleasantness of this sort was not something to which we were accustomed. Something was wrong. In the face of this apparent insult, we kept silent. Kaniyapa, his eyes flashing with indignation, abruptly withdrew and left the house.

Turning to Stephen, we asked, "How could you make such an accusation? You have never seen this fellow before!" Smiling, he replied, "Did you not notice? Not one of those chits says that Kaniyapa is honest!! That omission alone is significant! But worse still, the fellow is insolent and surly. Did you not notice that he came into this room wearing shoes? Old tennis shoes at that? In India, no servant, certainly no person seeking employment as a family servant, will wear shoes within the house. These should have been left at the door."

The matter did not end there. New and inexperienced, acutely conscious of the slight Kaniyapa had suffered, we brought him to our house for further consideration. Our mouths were still watering at the thought of the succulent dishes which he could put before us. Perhaps, as Americans, unaccustomed to unpleasant, seemingly unprovoked confrontations, we were too naive. Whatever the case, a few days after interviewing other candidates whose chits could not compare with those of Kaniyapa, we hired him.

The meatballs *were* delicious, and the lemon pies *were* beyond compare. Guests at our table in Nungambakkam remarked upon the excellence of our cuisine. But one problem soon became apparent. However full we kept our refrigerator and larder, food disappeared, inexplicably and mysteriously. Moreover, butter and cheese and milk seemed to vanish at an ever more alarming speed. More food was disappearing than could possibly have been eaten by ourselves and our houseguests. How could any one family, we asked, consume so much food? It was enough to run a small restaurant. But, without evidence, it was difficult to resolve this problem. We did not wish to be unjust — to presume guilt. Moreover, we did not wish to be without a cook, especially one whose dishes were so delicious.

One day, when the Swedish meatballs were especially tasty, I asked, casually and appreciatively, where in the world Kaniyapa had learned to make such a wonderful dish.

"Kodaikanal!" he replied. "Amrikan missionary lady teaching me."

"Is that so?" I pressed. "Where in Kodaikanal?"

"Very steep hill. Baptisht Hill. Kodaikanal, my native place."

"When was this?"

"Long, long ago! Maybe pforty-one, or pforty-two."

"Where did this lady live on Baptist Hill?"

"Verrry top house."

"What was its name?"

"House name 'Eureta,' I think."

"What was missionary lady's name?"

"Lady name 'Prikinberg.'"

Amazed, I suddenly realized that up to this point Kaniyapa had never learned my name, or that of my family. Being literate *only* in Tamil, he had not been able to make out the roman letters spelling F-R-Y-K-E-N-B-E-R-G on the gatepost of our house at 2/A College Lane, Nungambakkam. Nor, as far as I knew, had he yet ever heard anyone pronounce the name "Frykenberg" since taking employment with us. In short, there had been no way for him to know that Kodaikanal was the place where, from 1937 to 1942, I had gone to school — at the now famous Kodai International School. Moreover, it had been during 1941 and 1942, precisely in those years, that my mother had come to spend months in Kodai — out of a mother's wish to give more loving attention to her children. The house in which we had lived during those years had been at the top of Baptist Hill. Its name had been "Eureta"!!

"Kaniyapa," I exclaimed, "do you not know my name? My *inti peru* (Telugu for 'home name') is 'Prikinberg!' That person, that American missionary lady who taught you how to make Swedish meatballs and lemon pie, was my mother!"

A look of shock and wonder crossed Kaniyapa's face. His amazement was truly as great as my own. I told him that I was going to write my mother about this marvelous coincidence. This I immediately did. In those days an air letter took over a fortnight to reach America. Two weeks later, Kaniyapa suddenly came to us at breakfast waving a telegram. His mother was seriously ill and he was urgently needed in Kodaikanal. He was very sorry, but it would be necessary for him to go immediately to Kodai. He asked for a leave of absence, promised to return as soon as possible, and introduced us to his "brother," Muttu. Muttu, he assured us, was an excellent cook — almost as good as Kaniyapa himself.

Kaniyapa disappeared. We never saw him again. Muttu was a fine, if sloppy, cook — he tended to throw food about with reckless abandon, so that flies and other insects constantly endangered our health.

Two weeks later, a letter arrived from my mother. Her words were memorable indeed: "Yes," she wrote, "I well remember Kaniyapa! He is a fine cook. But get rid of him! He is a thief!"

## Sample 2: Two Churchillian Anecdotes

### Churchill Bathed

*Churchill contrived to meet nearly all the great wartime leaders while bathing himself, Stalin being the only notable exception; the CIGS, Sir Alan Brooke (later, Lord), described the procedure:*

26 March 1943. The PM sent for me. By the time I . . . reached him in the Annexe he was in his bath. However, he received me as soon as he came out, looking like a Roman centurion with nothing on except a large bath-towel draped round him. He shook me warmly by the hand in this get-up and told me to sit down while he dressed. A most interesting procedure. First he stepped into a white silk vest, then white silk drawers. Then a white shirt which refused to join comfortably round his neck and so was left open with a bow-tie to keep it together. Then the hair (what there was of it) took much attention, a handkerchief was sprayed with scent and then rubbed on his head. The few hairs were then brushed and finally sprayed direct. Finally, trousers, waistcoat and coat, and meanwhile he rippled on the whole time about Monty's baffle and our proposed visit to North Africa.

Bryant, *The Turn of the Tide* (London, 1957)[9]

### Churchill in Twilight

The last years were sad, but not as sad as some make out. He knew very well that his place in history was secure. The few friends he had were gone. The only person he ever loved, his wife, didn't like the Riviera, and liked Lord Beaverbrook still less; so he often went there alone. Once

9. As found in *The Oxford Book of Political Anecdotes*, ed. Paul Johnson (Oxford: Oxford University Press, 1986), 221.

he rang up a friend of mine, who had a villa in Monte Carlo, and said that he would like to come to lunch. My friend was rather apprehensive, and invited Mrs (Daisy) Fellowes, the Singer sewing-machine heiress, who had known him for many years, to help him out. Soon after lunch began, he closed his eyes and appeared to pass out. Mrs Fellowes then said to her host: 'What a pity that so great a man should end his life in the company of Onassis and Wendy Reves.' Suddenly, to their horror, one eye opened and Churchill said: 'Daisy, Wendy Reves is something that you will never be. She is young, she is beautiful and she is kind.' Then the eye closed again.

Lord Boothby, *Recollections of a Rebel*[10]


## Sample 3: A Wellington Anecdote

### The Iron Duke

*Many anecdotes are recorded concerning Arthur Wellesley, the Duke of Wellington. Among the most famous is his remark that the Battle of Waterloo had been "a near run thing!" Another is as follows:*

Lady Salisbury asked which was the greatest military genius, Marlborough or Napoleon?

'Why, I don't know — it is very difficult to tell. I can hardly conceive anything greater than Napoleon at the head of an army — especially a French army. Then he had one prodigious advantage — he had no responsibility — he could do whatever he pleased; and no man ever lost more armies than he did. Now with me the loss of every man told. I could not risk so much; I knew that if I ever lost five hundred men without the clearest necessity, I should be brought upon my knees to the bar of the House of Commons.'

Earl of Stanhope, *Notes of Conversations with Wellington, 1831-1851* (London, 1888)[11]

---

10. As found in *The Oxford Book of Political Anecdotes*, 222.
11. Ibid., 111.

## Sample 4: A Famous Charge of Impeachment

### *Warren Hastings's Trial*

> *In 1788, Edmund Burke and other leading Whigs succeeded in bringing an impeachment charge against Warren Hastings, who had been Governor-General of India. The trial opened before the House of Lords on 13 February 1788 and lasted until 1795, when Hastings was acquitted. Fanny Burney, one of the Queen's ladies, was present the first day.*

The business did not begin till near 12 o'clock. The opening of the whole then took place, by the entrance of the *Managers of the Prosecution;* all the company were already long in their boxes or galleries. I shuddered and drew involuntarily back when, as the doors were flung open, I saw Mr Burke, as Head of the Committee, make his solemn entry. He held a scroll in his hand and walked alone, his brow knit with corroding care and deep labouring thought — a brow how different to that which had proved so alluring to my warmest admiration when first I met him! so highly as he had been my favourite, so captivating as I had found his manners and conversation in our first acquaintance, and so much as I owed to his zeal and kindness to me and my affairs in its progress! How did I grieve to behold him now the cruel Prosecutor (such to me he appeared) of an injured and innocent man! Mr Fox followed next, Mr Sheridan, Mr Windham, Messrs Anstruther, Grey, Adam, Michaelangelo Taylor, Pelham, Colonel North, etc. . . . When the Committee Box was filled, the House of Commons at large took their seats on the green benches. . . . Then began the procession, the Clerks entering first, then the lawyers according to their rank, and the peers, bishops and officers, all in their coronation robes; concluding with the Princes of the Blood — Prince William, son to the Duke of Gloucester coming first, then the Dukes of Cumberland, Gloucester and York, then the Prince of Wales; and the whole ending by the Chancellor, with his train borne.

Then they all took their seats. A Serjeant-at-Arms arose and commanded silence in the court on pain of imprisonment. Then some other officer, in a loud voice, called out as well as I can recollect words to this purpose: 'Warren Hastings, Esquire, come forth! Answer to the

charges brought against you; save your bail or forfeit your recogni-
zance!' Indeed I trembled at these words, and hardly could keep my
place when I found Mr Hastings was being brought to the bar. He
came forth from some place immediately under the Great Chamber-
lain's box and was preceded by Sir Francis Molyneux, Gentleman Usher
of the Black Rod; and at each side of him walked his bails, Messrs
Sullivan and Sumner. The moment he came in sight, which was not
for full ten minutes after his awful summons, he made a low bow to
the Chancellor and court facing him. I saw not his face, as he was
directly under me. He moved on slowly and, I think, supported between his two bails, to the opening of his own box; there, lower still,
he bowed again; and then advancing to the bar he leant his hands upon
it and dropped on his knees; but a voice in the same moment pro-
claiming he had leave to rise, he stood up almost instantaneously, and
a third time profoundly bowed to the court.

What an awful moment this for such a man! A man fallen from
such height of power to a situation so humiliating, from the almost
unlimited command of so large a part of the Eastern World to be cast
at the feet of his enemies, of the great tribunal of his country, and of
the nation at large, assembled thus in a body to try and to judge him!
Could even his prosecutors at that moment look on and not shudder
at least, if they did not blush?

The cryer, I think it was, made in a loud and hollow voice, a
public proclamation: 'That Warren Hastings, Esquire, late Governor
General of Bengal, was now on his trial for high crimes and mis-
demeanours, with which he was charged by the Commons of Great
Britain; and that all persons whatsoever who had sought to allege
against him were now to stand forth.' A general silence followed and
the Chancellor, Lord Thurlow, now made his speech. . . . 'Warren Hastings, you are now brought into this court to answer the charges brought
against you by the Knights, Esquires, Burgesses and Commons of Great
Britain — Charges now standing only as allegations, by them to be
legally proved, or by you to be disproved. Bring forth your answers
and your defence, with that seriousness, respect and truth due to
accusers so respectable. Time has been allowed you for preparation,
proportioned to the intricacies in which the transactions are involved,
and to the remote distances whence your documents may have been
searched and required. You will still be allowed bail, for the better

forwarding your defence and whatever you can require will still be yours, of time, witnesses and all things else you may hold necessary. This is not granted you as any indulgence: it is entirely your due: it is the privilege which every British subject has a right to claim and which is due to every one who is brought before this high Tribunal.'

This speech, uttered in a calm, equal, solemn manner, and in a voice mellow and penetrating, with eyes keen and black, yet softened into some degree of tenderness while fastened full upon the prisoner — this speech, its occasion, its portent and its object, had an effect upon every hearer of producing the most respectful attention and, out of the Committee Box at least, the strongest emotions in the cause of Mr Hastings. Again, Mr Hastings made the lowest reverence to the court and leaning over the bar answered, with much agitation, through evident efforts to suppress it: 'My Lords — impressed — deeply impressed — I come before your Lordships, equally confident in my own integrity, and in the justice of the court before which I am to clear it.' . . .

A general silence again ensued, and then one of the lawyers opened the cause. He began by reading from an immense roll of parchment the general charges against Mr Hastings, but he read in so monotonous a chant that nothing could I hear or understand, than now and then the name of Warren Hastings. During this reading, to which I vainly lent all my attention, Mr Hastings, finding it I presume equally impossible to hear a word, began to cast his eyes around the House, and having taken a survey of all in front and at the sides, he turned about and looked up; pale looked his face — pale, ill and altered. I was much affected by the sight of that dreadful harass which was written on his countenance. Had I looked at him without restraint, it could not have been without tears. I felt shocked too, shocked and ashamed to be seen by him in that place. I had wished to be present from an earnest interest in the business, joined to firm confidence in his powers of defence; but *his* eyes were not those I wished to meet in Westminster Hall. . . .

I hope Mr Hastings did not see us; but in a few minutes more, while this reading was still continued, I perceived Sir Joshua Reynolds in the midst of the Committee. He, at the same moment, saw me also and not only bowed but smiled and nodded with his usual good humour and intimacy, making at the same time a sign to his ear, by which I understood he had no trumpet. [She was joined in her box by

one of the prosecutors, William Windham MP.] After the first com-
pliments he looked around him and exclaimed: 'What an assembly is
this! How striking a *spectacle!* I had not seen half its splendour down
there. You have it here to great advantage; you lose some of the Lords
but you gain all the Ladies. You have a very good place here.'

'Yes; and I may safely say I make a very impartial use of it: for
since here I have sat, I have never discovered to which side I have been
listening.'

He laughed, but told me they were then running through the
charges.

'And is it essential', cried I, 'that they should so run them through
that nobody can understand them? Is that a form of law?'

He agreed to the absurdity; and then, looking still at the spectacle,
which indeed is the most splendid I ever saw, arrested his eyes upon
the Chancellor. 'He looks very well from hence,' cried he, 'and how well
he acquits himself on these solemn occasions! With what dignity, what
loftiness, what high propriety he comports himself!' Looking still on,
he next noticed the two Archbishops. 'And see', cried he, 'the Archbishop of York, Markham — see how he affects to read the articles of
impeachment, as if he was still open to either side! My good Lord
Archbishop, your Grace might, with perfect safety, spare your eyes, for
your mind has been made up upon this subject before ever it was
investigated. He holds Hastings to be the greatest man in the world
for Hastings promoted his son in the East Indies!' . . .

In the midst of the opening of a trial such as this, so important
to the country as well as to the individual who is tried, what will you
say to a man — a Member of the House of Commons — who kept
exclaiming almost perpetually, just at my side: 'What a bore! When will
it be over? Must one come any more? I had a great mind not to come
at all. What's that? — Lady Hawkesbury and the Copes? — Yes. A pretty
girl, Kitty. Well, when will they have done? I wish they'd call the question.
I should vote it a bore at once!'

*The Diary of Fanny Burney,* 13 February 1788[12]

12. As found in *The Oxford Book of Political Anecdotes*, 80-84.

## Sample 5: A Famous Regicide

*Charles I's Execution*

On the day of his execution, he dressed with special care, telling his servant Herbert, in combing his hair: 'Prithee, though it be not too long to stand upon my shoulders, take the same pains with it as you were wont to do: I am to be a bridegroom today and must be trimmed.' He added: 'Let me have a shirt on more than ordinary, by reason the season is so sharp as probably may make me shake, which some observers may imagine proceeds from fear. I fear not death. It is not terrible to me. I bless my God I am prepared.' He was kept waiting four hours, between ten and two, before being taken to the scaffold. There, he 'looked very earnestly upon the block and asked if it could be no higher'; but this was refused. After his last speech and his profession of faith, he handed his 'George' [garter] to Bishop Juxon to give to the Prince of Wales, with the word: 'Remember!' To Colonel Hacker, in charge of the guard, he said 'Take care that they do not put me in pain'. Then, to Juxon: 'I go from a corruptible to an incorruptible crown, where no disturbance can be, no disturbance at all.' Then, looking again at the block: 'Is it fast?' 'It is fast, Sir.' To the headsman, Young Gregory Brandon, disguised with false hair and a beard. 'Strike when I put my arms out this way' (stretching them). Then 'immediately stooping down, he laid his head on the block'. But his hair came loose, and Brandon put it back again; the King, thinking he was going to strike, said 'Stay for the sign.' Brandon: 'Yes I will, and it please Your Majesty.' Then the King gave the sign. Philip Henry, a 17-year-old Christ Church student, testified: 'At the instant when the blow was given there was such a dismal groan among the thousands of people that were within sight of it (as it were with ONE CONSENT) as he had *never heard before;* and desired he might never hear the like again, nor see such a cause of it.' Then, 'immediately after the stroke was struck . . . according to order, one troop [began] marching from Charing Cross towards King Street, purposely to disperse and scatter the people'. Nevertheless, many crowded round the scaffold to 'dip their handkerchiefs' in the King's blood and were 'admitted for moneys'. The soldiers sold pieces of the blood-stained scaffold boarding, from a shilling to half a crown each, 'according to the quality of the persons that sought them'. Payment was also charged to see Charles in his coffin at St James's Palace, 'by which means the soldiers got store of moneys, insomuch as one was heard to say, "I would we could have two or three such majesties to behead, if we could but make such use of them"'.

S. R. Gardiner, *History of the Commonwealth and Protectorate* (London, 1903).[13]

## Sample 6: Two Anecdotes from the Gospel According to John

### The Samaritan Woman

A report now reached the Pharisees: 'Jesus is winning and baptizing more disciples than John'. In fact, it was only the disciples who were baptizing and not Jesus himself. When Jesus learned this, he left Judaea and set out once more for Galilee. He had to pass through Samaria, and on his way he came to a Samaritan town called Sychar, near the plot of ground which Jacob gave to his son Joseph and the spring called Jacob's Well. It was about noon, and Jesus, tired after his journey, sat down by the well.

The disciples had gone away to the town to buy food. Meanwhile, a Samaritan woman came to draw water. Jesus said to her, 'Give me a drink.' The Samaritan woman said, 'What! You, a Jew, ask a drink of me, a Samaritan woman?' (Jews and Samaritans, it should be noted, did not use vessels in common.)

Jesus answered her, 'If only you knew what God gives, and who it is that is asking you for a drink, you would have asked him and he would have given you living water.'

'Sir,' the woman said, 'you have no bucket and this well is deep. How can you give me "living water"? Are you a greater man than Jacob our ancestor, who gave us the well, and drank from it himself, he and his sons, and his cattle too?'

Jesus said, 'Everyone who drinks this water will be thirsty again, but whoever drinks the water that I shall give him will never suffer thirst

---

13. As found in *The Oxford Book of Political Anecdotes*, 36-37.

any more. The water that I shall give him will be an inner spring, always welling up for eternal life.'

'Sir,' said the woman, 'give me that water, and then I shall not be thirsty, nor have to come all this way to draw.'

Jesus replied, 'Go home, call your husband and come back.'

She answered, 'I have no husband.'

'You are right,' said Jesus, 'in saying that you have no husband, for, although you have had five husbands, the man with whom you are now living is not your husband. You told me the truth there.'

'Sir,' she replied, 'I can see that you are a prophet. Our fathers worshipped on this mountain, but you Jews say that the temple where God should be worshipped is in Jerusalem.'

'Believe me,' said Jesus, 'the time is coming when you will worship the Father neither on this mountain, nor in Jerusalem. You Samaritans worship without knowing what you worship, while we worship what we know. It is from the Jews that salvation comes. But the time approaches, indeed it is already here, when those who are real worshippers will worship the Father in spirit and in truth. Such are the worshippers whom the Father wants. God is spirit, and those who worship him must worship in spirit and in truth.'

The woman answered, 'I know that Messiah' (that is Christ) 'is coming. When he comes he will tell us everything.'

Jesus said, 'I am he, I who am speaking to you now.'

At that moment his disciples returned, and were astonished to find him talking with a woman. But none of them said, 'What do you want?' or 'Why are you talking with her?'

The woman put down her water jar and went away to the town, where she said to the people, 'Come and see a man who has told me everything I ever did. Could this be the Messiah?' They came out of the town and made their way towards him.

Meanwhile, the disciples were urging him, 'Rabbi, have something to eat.'

But he said, 'I have food to eat of which you know nothing.'

At this the disciples said to one another, 'Can someone have brought him food?'

But Jesus said, 'It is meat and drink for me to do the will of him who sent me until I have finished his work.

'Do you not say, "Four months more and then comes the harvest"? But look, I tell you, look around on the fields. They are already white, ripe for harvest. The reaper is drawing his pay and gathering a crop for eternal life, so that the sower and reaper may rejoice together. That is how the saying comes to be true: "One sows, and another reaps." I sent you to reap a crop for which you have not toiled. Others toiled and you have come in for the harvest of their toil.'

Many Samaritans of that town came to believe in him because of the woman's testimony: 'He told me everything I ever did.' So when these Samaritans had come to him, they pressed him to stay with them; and he stayed there two days. Many more became believers because of what they heard from his own lips. They told the woman, 'It is no longer because of what you said that we believe, for we have heard him ourselves; and we know that this is in truth the Saviour of the world.'

Chapter 4:1-42, *New English Bible* (Oxford, 1971 edition)

## Lazarus, Mary, and Martha[14]

There was a man named Lazarus who had fallen ill. His home was at Bethany, the village of Mary and her sister Martha. (This Mary, whose brother Lazarus had fallen ill, was the woman who anointed the Lord with ointment and wiped his feet with her hair.)

The sisters sent a message to him: 'Sir, you should know that your friend lies ill.'

When Jesus heard this he said, 'This illness will not end in death; it has come for the glory of God, to bring glory to the Son of God.' And therefore, though he loved Martha and her sister and Lazarus, after hearing of his illness Jesus waited for two days in the place where he was. After this, he said to his disciples, 'Let us go back to Judaea.'

---

14. If the context (10:40-41 and 11:47-54) is included, the historical meaning of the narrative is changed, so that it is linked to the plotting of Jesus' death. What prompts this selection is a penetrating paper by Eleanor Stump entitled "Betrayal of Trust: Philosophical Biblical Exegesis" (paper presented in a conference called "Narrative and Human Understanding" held at the Library of Congress (Washington, D.C., 11-13 June 1992).

'Rabbi,' his disciples said, 'it is not long since the Jews there were wanting to stone you. Are you going there again?'

Jesus replied, 'Are there not twelve hours of daylight? Anyone can walk in daytime without stumbling, because he sees the light of this world. But if he walks after nightfall he stumbles, because the light fails him.'

After this, he added, 'Our friend Lazarus has fallen asleep, but I shall go and wake him.' The disciples said, 'Master, if he has fallen asleep he will recover.' Jesus, however, had been speaking of his death, but they thought he meant natural sleep.

Then Jesus spoke out plainly: 'Lazarus is dead. I am glad not to have been there; it will be for your good and for the good of your faith. But let us go to him.'

Thomas, called 'The Twin', said to his fellow-disciples, 'Let us also go, that we may die with him.'

On his arrival, Jesus found that Lazarus had already been four days in the tomb. Bethany was just under two miles from Jerusalem, and many of the people had come from the city to Martha and Mary to condole with them on their brother's death. As soon as she heard that Jesus was on his way, Martha went to meet him, while Mary stayed at home.

Martha said to Jesus, 'If you had been here, sir, my brother would not have died. Even now I know that whatever you ask of God, God will grant you.'

Jesus said, 'Your brother will rise again.'

'I know that he will rise again', said Martha, 'at the resurrection on the last day.'

Jesus said, 'I am the resurrection and I am life. If any man has faith in me, even though he die, he shall come to life; and no one who is alive and has faith shall ever die. Do you believe this?'

'Lord, I do,' she answered. 'I now believe that you are the Messiah, the Son of God who was to come into the world.'

With these words she went to call her sister Mary, and taking her aside, she said, 'The Master is here; he is asking for you.'

When Mary heard this she rose up quickly and went to him. Jesus had not yet reached the village, but was still at the place where Martha had met him. The Jews who were in the house condoling with Mary, when they saw her start up and leave the house, went after her, for they supposed that she was going to the tomb to weep there.

So Mary came to the place where Jesus was. As soon as she caught sight of him, she fell at his feet and said, 'O sir, if you had only been here, my brother would not have died.'

When Jesus saw her weeping and the Jews her companions weeping, he sighed heavily and was deeply moved.

'Where have you laid him?' he asked.

They replied, 'Come and see, sir.'

Jesus wept.

The Jews said, 'How dearly he must have loved him!'

But some of them said, 'Could not this man, who opened the blind man's eyes, have done something to keep Lazarus from dying?'

Jesus again sighed deeply. Then he went over to the tomb. It was a cave, with a stone placed against it. Jesus said, 'Take away the stone.'

Martha, the dead man's sister, said to him, 'Sir, by now there will be a stench. He has been there four days.'

Jesus said, 'Did I not tell you that if you have faith you will see the glory of God?'

So they removed the stone.

Then Jesus looked upwards and said, 'Father, I thank thee! Thou hast heard me. I knew already that thou always hearest me, but I spoke for the sake of the people standing round, that they might believe that thou didst send me.'

Then he raised his voice in a great cry: 'Lazarus, come forth.'

The dead man came out, his hands and feet swathed in linen, his face wrapped in a cloth.

Jesus said, 'Loose him! Let him go.'


Now many of the Jews who had come to visit Mary and had seen what Jesus did, put their faith in him. But some of them went off to the Pharisees and reported what he had done.

Chapter 11:1-46, *New English Bible* (Oxford, 1971 edition)

## Chapter 5

# History as Antiquity:
# A Mythic Legacy

There is within all of us a primal need to know who we are, and from what or whom we are descended. This is a search for beginnings and origins. Some need within compels us to search for things particularly and peculiarly unique in our own pasts. We want to know where we came from. We also want to know about things that distinguish us as individuals and as families, not only from other living beings but also from other human beings. This search for what is distinct about us and about our own special past is a search for affirmation of dignity and worth. It is a curiosity about our own identity. Beyond our primal need for security and for satisfaction of basic wants, a sense of immortality links us to the past (as also to the future). It is, above all, a primal search for roots. History as antiquity lies at the heart of that consciousness within each of us which gives us a link with the remotest past, even striving to link us with eternal verities. We probe dusty artifacts, ruins, and writings to uncover the character and genesis of peoples. We search out the faintest traces of thoughts rising out of the mists of earliest antiquity.

And yet, strange as it may seem in our day of high literacy and revolutionary information handling, "the oldest thoughts . . . that have anywhere come down to us in written form,"[1] were produced only *after* cultures and languages and technologies had been highly advanced for a very long time.[2] They come to us from rulers who had already long

1. Herbert Butterfield, *The Origins of History* (London: Methuen, 1981), 47.
2. This is a point on which there is still considerable argument. V. Gordon Childe,

possessed the technologies of surplus agriculture, enabling then to store grain and amass wealth. These rulers had already long held those instruments of coercion which enabled them to enforce their power and to control resources. These rulers had already long ago managed to build complex organizations, construct elaborate cities, develop advanced cultures and steeply differentiated social structures. In the deltas, valleys, and flood plains of the Nile, the Tigris and Euphrates, the Indus and Ganga, and the Huang Ho rivers, rich civilizations had developed long before the first appearance of writing. It is futile to speculate, therefore, about which of these civilizations might have come first or which might have been more advanced. Each perhaps could have developed autonomously. Yet, however distinctive each civilization was, the pictographic character of earliest writings in all four regions and the similarities between their agrarian systems suggest that, at the very least, these cultures might have been in touch with each other.

Whatever the case, collections of artifacts and writings have been uncovered, enabling much scholarly attention to be focused upon these areas. It is easy to begin, even if quite arbitrarily,[3] with records of misty antiquity produced in the Nile and Mesopotamian deltas, emerging out of the already rich cultures of Egypt and Babylonia. The historical remains of earliest China and India, along with those of Greece, if not quite so old, remain especially noteworthy for the remarkable levels of cultural achievement they attained and the "classical" standards they set (cf. chapter 6). No less old than these and no less "classical" were those structures of historical understanding that emerged out of the "Semitic" roots from which emerged the great monotheistic traditions (chapter 7).

The order of treatment assigned for this analysis of the structures of historical understanding, therefore, suggests no clear or definitive answer to questions of priority or to questions about relative antiquity. Each of these particular historical traditions can validly lay some claim to being very old, if not the oldest. The question of which is the oldest

*What Happened in History* (Harmondsworth, Middlesex: Pelican Books, 1942), 93ff., took what may be seen as an archaic but reasonable view — that elaborate blueprints and measurements required some form(s) of writing.

3. This approach is unequivocally Western and Eurocentric. It is the place identified with earliest antiquity in Western minds, even though cultures within their own homelands were already well advanced.

is avoided, if for no other reason than that there is no satisfactory way to give a definitive or final answer. We are not entirely sure where formal historical understandings first originated or which people first began to construct "better" understandings of past events. Attempts to make such a determination, while fraught with difficulties, need not be avoided entirely. But for purposes of this study, there is no need to link issues of relative antiquity with those peculiarities which any particular tradition of historical understanding more clearly represents.

## I. Antiquity of the Nile Valley and Watershed

Earliest written perceptions of the past that have survived, often nothing more than the scraps that recorded something about contemporary events, were produced by prominent persons. It is the great and the powerful of antiquity whose thoughts have come down to us. Very powerful persons, individuals coming from powerful families or representing ruling dynasties, had the means to order the making of these records. As far as one can tell from what has survived, royal lineages (or "families") had been ruling over Egypt for untold centuries before they seriously attempted to make sure that what they had done and what they thought should be written down. They had held sway over many lands and peoples for so long and had already accomplished such enormous (even incredible) feats of engineering that they apparently wanted all of posterity to know what they had achieved. Huge dams and canal networks for purposes of irrigation, gigantic dwelling places (palace-temples) for themselves and their deities, colossal funerary monuments (pyramids and tombs), and "wonders" of manifold variety attested to their prowess and served to reflect the sophistication of their culture.

They seem to have found it important, if not crucial, to assert themselves by showing off this latest advance in technology. Perhaps to celebrate their own importance and to emphasize their superiority over all other peoples in yet one more way, they displayed the latest and newest invention to come out of their "research and development" departments — namely, this remarkable new capacity to record and separate thoughts and words used to express thoughts from those who did the thinking. The detaching of thoughts from their thinkers and words from their speakers by putting them down in a durable written form was an event of truly wondrous significance. "The disembodied word," no longer context-bound and no longer requiring rituals or prescriptive rigidities in order to gain weighty solemnity, became transcendent. The event could almost be seen as miraculous or magical. Cognitive content and meaning, freed from context of speaker or listener, gained a new distinctiveness and power.[4]

Whether or not the pronouncements which such rulers ordered put down in written form were essential to their continued possession of power is difficult to ascertain. Even if that had actually been the case, the documents they left to posterity would probably never have been used to make such admissions. Yet, for all the words dedicated to the memory of themselves — words of conceit, self-congratulation, and self-praise difficult to equal — one thing seems quite clear: monarchs of Egypt were not without means to celebrate their huge claims.

Whatever the circumstances, the words that have survived lead us to surmise that they were used as a means of further strengthening control, either in defense of existing claims or in attempts to expand those claims. Priestly scribes compiled and drew up simple lists. These, later expanded, became annals; and annals, in turn, became more and more elaborate. Chronicles, as such, do not seem to have come into use in Egypt until much later, perhaps only after rulers and their critics in other parts of the world had already begun to bring new forms of writing into use. We can suspect that, at least in some measure, there were practical reasons for making these lists. Among needs and problems of immediate concern, some may have been the very same as those that had led to the production of those grand and huge works of monumental construction which have survived to this day and which still bear mute witness to some of the wonders of antiquity.

Quite clearly, beyond immediate and utilitarian needs of daily business, the earliest records of Egypt also show anxiety about longterm issues: they seem concerned with problems of controlling and preserving a high quality of life already attained. Even more obviously, they seem obsessed with the quality of life *after* death. This preoccupation with death and with afterlife, if only to escape torments in some

---

4. Ernest Gellner, *Plough, Sword and Book: The Structure of Human History* (London: Collins Harvill, 1988; Chicago: University of Chicago Press, 1989), 70-75.

netherworld or if not, perhaps also, to enforce a prescriptive code for the preservation of a steeply hierarchical agrarian order, seems so obsessive that its motivation is itself an important factor.[5] Whether or not this need to demonstrate power over life after death was related to current and immediate problems of political survival or whether or not the need to preserve bodies from whatever it was that man or nature might do to them after death seems to have arisen out of some very definite and real fears. These are matters about which one can only speculate.

Nevertheless, one thing seems obvious when looking at what has been left for us to interpret: that relatively small number of persons of antiquity who could order the production of writings such as those that we possess also had, above all things, a need to record if not also to demonstrate their ability to exercise supreme *control* over everyone and everything, over all existence. It seems to have been exceedingly important for anyone who sat upon the throne of Egypt to be able to show how completely all power was held and to what extent the monarch was in charge. Moreover, this control had to be shown in very precise and vivid detail. Control over each and every person, over all supporters and subordinates, had to be so total that none would ever dare to think otherwise. These earliest of Egyptian writings provided, for all who might read them in coming generations, the exact details about every aspect in the totality of this control. They seem to be telling the reader in no uncertain terms that nothing in existence, neither in this world nor the next, could be exempt from that authority and power that the Great Ruler Himself could exercise.

Control and predictability, in all relationships, had to be made plain and clear. This had to be true both in life and in death. As seen in constantly recurring forms of life and death around them all the time, so also in details of life *after* death, control had to be emphasized. Control had to be totally and utterly inevitable and predictable: control over all forces, natural or supernatural; control over regularly recurring times and seasons of the year; control over all living things; control

5. E. A. Wallis Budge, *Egyptian Magic* (1899; reprint, London and New York: Routledge, 1988). Also see his *Book of the Dead, an English translation of chapters, hymns, &c. of the Theban recension, with intro., notes, &c.; with twenty-two plates and four hundred and twenty vignettes,* 2nd edition, revised and enlarged, 11th impression (London: Routledge & Kegan Paul, 1923; reprint, 1977).

especially over all domesticated forms of life, over every kind of cattle
and every kind of people. The need to "show and tell," with details about
exactly how all kinds of control operated, seems to have been urgent.
The records seem to scream this need. It is as if the very survival of a
ruler, both in this world and the next, depended upon a general pervasiveness in perceptions of total control. Enjoyment of secure tenure as
a ruler, and continued exercise of awesome authority, would seem, by
such reckoning, to have been closely linked. All people, all possessions,
all lands, and all things upon earth demanded such control. An assured
and orderly succession of one's own progeny required it. Then, and only
then, when one could clearly demonstrate the ground upon which all
claims to rulership rested, could rulership be secure. Only a super god
— a god-king — could ever be expected to harness so much cosmic
power and to exercise so much earthly authority.[6]

The term *pharaoh* appears in the earliest records. It refers to the
"dwelling place" of the "majesty" of that individual person who, at any
given time, possessed the total combination of all the supreme powers
necessary for complete and absolute rule over all of Egypt. It was *the*
title used to show that he was not just *the only* man who ruled over all
mankind but also *the only* god who ruled over all gods and all other
beings. Even among gods and demons and supernatural forces, there
could be no equal to such a being. No other being could exercise more
total and ultimate control than the pharaoh.[7] Were such authority and
power ever to come into question, then the ability to retain supreme
authority would also come into question; and then, order itself could
not be expected to last. The very foundations of dynastic rulership rested
upon cosmic verities.[8]

To the end of affirming total authority and power, therefore, lists
of items that were actually "controlled" were compiled. Each list looks
to us (and may have been), in fact, little more than a "brag sheet." Each

6. What happened to a supreme ruler of Egypt who failed to establish such claims,
especially when he tried to convert his subjects from the prevailing royal cult of Amon
in Thebes (Karnak) to the more abstract and monotheistic and universalistic worship
of Ra-Horakhti Aton, is suggested in an old work by Arthur Weigall, *The Life and Times
of Akhnaton: Pharaoh of Egypt* (1910; revised, London: Thornton Butterworth, Ltd.,
1934).

7. Budge, *Egyptian Magic*, 177.
8. Ibid., 192-227, 228-45.

list enumerated those things, one and all, over which the particular king — reigning as "Horus, son of Osirus" (or "son of the Sun," *Ra*) — claimed actual and total control. Under pharaoh himself and his ruling dynasty ("family") were all personal servants, priests, officials, and sub-ordinate functionaries. Also under the same ruler were all lowlier subject and slave peoples, those who were as dust beneath his feet. Each list looks to us as if it were meant to impress upon all, in very clear and detailed terms, exactly how truly awesome and how truly wonderful the monarch actually was. Lest any detail be forgotten, it seems to have been imperative, both for power in this world and for power in the next, that a full record be made, showing exactly what the king possessed and exactly what he had done.

Moreover, because it was important to show that the pharaoh's deeds were altogether imperishable, each record had to be made per-manent. For that reason, each record had to be inscribed in stone or clay (either in hieroglyphic or, later, in demotic script).[9] In case any person in a future generation be tempted to tamper with the divine and eternal words being put on record, special curses were prescribed and dire consequences predicted for any who would dare to do so. These stone inscriptions then stood as mute reminders to one and all, in all succeeding generations, exactly what penalties were in store for those who tried to violate what these words had declared to be inviolable. Later on, papyrus scrolls made the same kinds of threats. Especially for those not yet born, future functionaries who would serve before the throne, if not also all lowlier peoples, words told exactly and explicitly how vast had been the things controlled by the once and future divine-ruler and how dire would be the consequences of those who violated his will. Among things listed under divine-royal control were the days and months and seasons of each year: the years and the cycles of years, the risings and fallings of the Great River (Nile), the plantings and harvestings of food crops, the comings and goings of all events, and the holdings and the losings of goods, animals, and slaves. Specified and numbered in detail, so that the very cosmic universality of divine-royal possessions and domains might be proclaimed, things beyond the grave were also listed. So that all persons might forever know and that none might ever doubt that such a divinity sat upon the Throne of the

9. Albertine Gaur, *A History of Writing* (London: The British Library, 1984), 60-65.

Universe, this instrument was graven in stone so that it could last forever.[10]

One is tempted to ask how much of what was written was believed by those who produced such lists. Yet, for any who have lived in the twentieth century and beheld the capacity for self-deception among both individuals and voting populations, one need not be entirely skeptical about possible limits of credulity in the past. However accurate the inventories on these lists might have been, there must have been kings and subjects in early antiquity who actually believed that these words represented truth and who accepted the assumptions underlying them. Why else, one might ask, would they have gone to such trouble to record these words so indelibly in stone? At the same time, one need not doubt that there were those who were skeptical and cynical about the pretensions described in royal documents.

One practical (and fascinating) legacy of such list-making in remote times is our calendar. Not only did supreme rulers of Egypt claim to represent the Sun-God and to require recognition of events in the Solar Year, as distinct from the Lunar Year, but they also required worship of the Dog-Star *(Sothis;* or, in Greek, *Sirius)*. In their extreme dependence upon the waters of the Nile for survival and prosperity, those who lived and ruled in Egypt marked the coincidence of the annual event of the "return" or rising of the river's waters by the first appearance of the Dog-Star. This dependence upon punctuality and regularity led to a religious and ritual observance of the Dog-Star Year.

Among those constant repetitions of life and death which made humans aware of natural cycles in an ordered world, by which all beings were meant to complete their ordained courses in an orderly and predictable manner, none was supposed to be more predictable than the annual flooding of the Nile. This event occurred in conjunction with the time when *Sothis* again became visible on the dawn horizon. The conjunction was seen as especially auspicious.[11] That being so, it was important that this conjunction of events mark the beginning of each new year. By careful observation and reckoning of this event over many

10. James Henry Breasted, ed. and trans., *Ancient Records of Egypt: Historical Documents from the Earliest Times to the Persian Conquest, Collected, Edited, and Translated with Commentary*, 5 vols. (1906-7; reprint, New York: Russell & Russell, 1962).

11. Siegfried Herrmann, *Time and History*, trans. James L. Blevins, Biblical Encounter Series (Nashville: Abingdon Press, 1977), 102-4.

years, Egyptians developed a system of marking times and seasons and years. Their Dog-Star Year was divided into three seasons — Flood Season, Cold Season, and Hot Season. Each season contained four months, or lunar cycles, of thirty days. In order that the calendar year coincide with the new reappearance of the Dog-Star (on our 19 July), a correction of "five lost days" was always added. Egyptians, aware that their system was by no means perfect, never worked out a system for completely correcting it. Instead, by accounting for the loss of only one day in every four years, they calculated that every regular passing cycle of 1,460 years (4 × 365) would bring the Dog-Star Year and the Solar Year back into conjunction.[12]

It is this calendar that Julius Caesar later discovered. After consulting with scholars of his day, he adopted it and ordered it taken back to Rome. His "Julian" Calendar, albeit somewhat "corrected" and then calibrated according to years since the founding of Rome, became the official calendar of the Empire. This calendar was still being used when, during the four years between A.D. 139 and 143, the next conjunction of the Sun and Dog-Star years occurred. This calendar was still being used in the sixth century (A.D.) when a Christian monk, Dionysian Exiguus or "Denis the Little," adapted the calendar to church needs. But he made an erroneous calculation for the year of Christ's birth and then mistakenly renumbered all previous and subsequent years, based upon the first of January B.C. Finally, this same calendar was further changed by Pope Gregory XIII. In 1582, 1,629 years after the action of Julius Caesar, he added ten days to the calendar in the year of 1582, by the fiat of simply calling the fifth day of October the fifteenth. By Papal Bull, he also mandated a further addition of one extra day each for the century-turning years 1600 and 2000 (but not for the years 1700, 1800, and 1900). Not until the middle of the eighteenth century, however, did Britain and the rest of the English-speaking world adopt the Gregorian Calendar.[13]

12. Breasted, "Chronology" and "Chronological Table," in *Ancient Records of Egypt*, 1:25-47, drawing heavily on the work of Eduard Meyer, *"Aegyptische Chronologie,"* *Abhandlungen der Königlichen Preussichen Akademie* (1904), gives a succinct treatment of this subject.

13. A careful exposition on this complicated subject is found in the *Macropaedia* of *The New Encyclopaedia Britannica*, 15th ed., s.v. "Calendar," with further details in *Micropaedia*, on Babylonian, Assyrian, Hittite, Egyptian, Greek, Roman, Jewish/Christian, Muslim, Hindu, Chinese, Mayan, Mexican, etc., under the same.

The very calendar now used by the entire world was originally a device by which, back in the remotest shadows of Egyptian antiquity, the dynastic power of "The Pharaoh" was sustained. This fact, by itself, serves to highlight the great importance that Egyptians put upon the principle of a fixed and cyclical regularity. What they observed as predictable in all "natural events" became a set principle of law. The principle was so centered and focused upon the throne that, with each succession (death of the old and coronation of the new) — but especially with each successive fall and rise of a new ruling lineage (dynasty or monarchy) — a full cosmic and natural cycle would be perceived as coming to a close. A new cycle, involving a new creation of the entire universe, would then begin. Each renewal of rulership by a new dynasty was a rebirth of life and a replication of creation. Each death of a king called for a fresh cosmic renewal. Each new creation coincided with new rulership, as epitomized in a new pharaoh.

Each reign, therefore, was also a ritual event. It was a marker which, once fixed, then served to mark all sub-events. Such being the case, it is no small wonder that so much stress was put upon the careful recording of such things as king-lists and date-lists. By carefully arranging long lists of successive rulers into closed dynastic cycles, social and political order could be shown as being in conjunction with cosmic regularity and with divine order. The word for god and the word for king became synonymous with the words for creation, order, prosperity, regularity, rightness, rule, security, and truth. All these events, as forces, had to be brought into conjunction and kept that way. If any single principle, any one word, expressed this cosmic order and regularity, this word was Ma'at. Ma'at was, in some sense, but another name for destiny. It was also, therewith, a name for history.[14]

Perhaps there is no more famous representation of this earliest kind of historical record than that now known as the Palermo Stone.[15] A record of royal piety and virtue, however fragmentary the information it contains, this document affirms the view that, even in times of crisis and change and even when the position of a particular pharaoh as the sole and

14. Siegfried Morenz, *Egyptian Religion,* trans. Ann E. Keep (Ithaca, N.Y.: Cornell University Press, 1973), first published in Stuttgart, 1960, under the title *Aegyptishe Religion.* This work provides a comprehensive analysis of the underpinnings and complexities of this subject.

15. Breasted, *Ancient Records of Egypt,* 1:51-72.

all-powerful god was being challenged, this primacy of the position itself would always need to be reasserted. "Worshiping Horus of Heaven" and "hacking up" foes (in this or that city) or "smiting troglodytes" who do not worship Horus are parts of a standardized litany.[16] Exact and total *correctness* of procedures and rituals are essential both in the proper piety of the supreme ruler and in the piety of his priests. The Stone, coming from the fifth dynasty, gives but a faint glimmer of an already very long past as perceived by people at that time.[17]

Only when events are arranged in chronological order and only when these are then synchronized with the calendar do annals, as such, first come into being.[18] Annals, defined quite simply, are chronological listings of deeds and events compiled by command and on behalf of a ruler. Surrounded with all of the paraphernalia of divine and magical powers, rituals, and sanctions associated with high office, annals were not to omit mention of events in which such properties had been manifested. Out of the mists of antiquity, Egyptian and Mesopotamian annals seem to emerge at approximately the same time.

The most famous records surviving from Egyptian antiquity are very late works. Now known as the "Campaign Annals," these obviously self-conscious documents give, in great detail, continuity, and precision, reports of victory in battle and success in restoring tranquillity to the realm. One report by a scribe of Thutmose III named Thaneni hails the outcome of a great battle at Megiddo: "His Majesty [Pharaoh] commanded that a record of the victories which his Father Amon gave him be placed in the Temple. . . . I followed the Good God, Sovereign of Truth, King of Upper and Lower Egypt. . . . I recorded the victories."[19] After a march against the prince of Kadesh and other rebels, the account vividly details the numbers of prisoners, chariots, horses, cattle, and armor captured: "champions lay stretched out like fishes on the ground."[20] Another account, about the

16. Ibid., 104, 125.

17. Burr C. Brundage, "The Birth of Clio: A Resume and Interpretation of Ancient Near Eastern Historiography," in *Teachers of History: Essays in Honour of L. B. Packard*, ed. Henry Stuart Hughes (Ithaca, N.Y.: Cornell University Press, 1954), 226. Chronology: fifth dynasty = 2500-2350 B.C.; eighteenth dynasty = 1570-1320 B.C. (Thutmose III, 1490-1436); nineteenth dynasty = 1320-1205 B.C.

18. Brundage, "The Birth of Clio," 200.

19. Breasted, *Ancient Records of Egypt*, 2:438-43.

20. Ibid.

deeds performed by Rameses II at the Battle of Kadesh (c. 1280 B.C.) during his struggle against the Hittites, tells how the Pharaoh, after marching his army into a trap, not only escaped destruction but single-handedly destroyed 2,500 enemy chariots.[21] As a feat in "historical" bragging, this annal is almost without parallel. Finally, a more gentle claim is made by Rameses III: the Pharaoh, having restored order and peace and having made temple endowments to Amon in Thebes, to Ra in Heliopolis, and to Ptah in Memphis, boasted: "I planted the whole land with trees. . . . I made people to dwell in the shade. . . . I enabled women of Egypt to go . . . wherever they desired [without being molested]."[22]

Not until much later, when records *about* kings rather than records *by* kings were kept and when such records were produced by those who had some reason to look at what the king did from a more detached and critical perspective, did chronicles begin to appear. This appearance, wherever it occurred, seems to reflect occasions in which some functionary, whether ecclesiastical or priestly, managed to gain a kind of control over record-keeping which was independent of the monarch. Often this could be only in the name of some power other than that of the king and his family. Changes in circumstance brought changes in emphasis; and these, in turn, brought new interpretations of the past. Such changes coincided with changing notions about the nature of the world and, therewith, changes in the nature of institutional relationships within Egypt. As the nature of society and the functions of rulership changed and as new functionaries arose whose control of resources became, even if ever so slightly, separated from that total control which had previously been claimed by the monarch, new kinds of records reflected new ways of perceiving the past. References to the divine status of rulers, previously seen as fixed and determined by fate, begin to reflect some awareness of uniqueness in attributes of individual rulers and particular events. Records reveal that, in times of transition, when events were turbulent and rulership broken or limited, divine failure was declared and the monarch himself was blamed for having brought upheaval and uproar upon the land. When such things happened, one writer could lament, "Look! One strikes another! And another violates what you have commanded!"[23]

21. Breasted, *Ancient Records of Egypt*, 1:298-327.
22. Breasted, "Papyrus Harris," in *Ancient Records of Egypt*, 4:405.
23. Herrmann, *Time and History*, 108-9, quoting *Words of Admonition by an*

Egyptians of antiquity had difficulty explaining times of chaos. Once the cycle of cosmic order broke, both god and god-king were seen as worthy of blame. Only the god-king could restore Order *(Ma'at)* to its rightful place, so as to bring back predictability, regularity, and control. During later stages of early Egyptian antiquity, when the empire seems to have reached its greatest extension under some of the most powerful of its rulers, one can see a gradual realization that, sometimes, even a single event might have held a particular and especially fateful significance. Cyclical understandings of the past are not abandoned; but new concepts indicate new ways of looking at events. One such concept, coming late in the irregular reign of Amenhotep IV, is *Sha-it (s.it)*. This seems, when translated, to have meant something like that span of each person's life between birth and death that is "determined" or "fixed" and numbered.[24]

A further distinction between happenings seen as regular or cyclical and happenings seen as irregular or unique — between events decisively momentous and those merely or simply recurrent — begins to emerge. A unique event, significant moment, or turning point, applied to a given situation, was described by the word *at ('.t)*, while a recurrent or regular event (season or time) might be described by the word *ter (tr)*. The expression "[God] cuts down the rebel in his *at*" became distinct from words about "dissolution of '*ter*' [world order]."[25] In other words, that *kind* of time which occurs in repeated or cyclical happenings which might be described in geometrical metaphors (circular lines or cycles) was no longer seen as being the same as that *amount* of time which is seen as the set bounds of one man's life and which is peculiar to his own particular destiny. Now, as perhaps never before, time in Egypt begins to look like a linear progression of unique events. In the words of Siegfried Herrmann, "It is certain that the Egyptians thought in terms of a cyclical course of time, that the ruler experienced and expressed the time of his rule in ritual form, and that the order of life was consummated in present courses in connection with *Maat*. The

---

*Egyptian Wise Man,* as translated from D. Otto, *Der Verwurf an Gott: Zur Entstehung der ägyptishen Auseinandersetzsliterature* (Hildesheim, 1951).

24. Herrmann, *Time and History,* 110, comparing this concept with the Greek *heimarmene* and with the Latin *fatum,* indicates that Egyptian deities had more power over fate than did Greek and Latin deities.

25. Herrmann, *Time and History,* 111.

determination of the individual destiny is just as certain in terms of a
firmly set period of life, the right moment, the uniqueness of the personal and 'historical' hour. Such insights were adopted only gradually
in the long course of their history. . . ."[26]

## II. Antiquity of the Mesopotamian Valley and Watershed[27]

Conditions of severe insecurity seem, at least initially, to have pervaded
cultures which arose in the vicinity of the Tigris and Euphrates. Life for
those from families important, powerful, or resourceful enough to make
records of their memories and thoughts seems to have been far less
predictable than for those who ruled in the vicinity of the Nile. Circumstances seem to have been less certain or secure, more prone to calamity
or capricious turns of fortune; and recorded memories take on a brooding or haunting quality. So much strife, such struggles for survival, such
competition over resources, and so many encounters between good and
evil make for melancholy perspectives. Against terrible malevolence and
injustice, there is a cry of outrage: "You dole out suffering ever anew!
. . . If a man of deceit conspires, you, my god do not stop him! On the
day shares were allotted to all, my share was suffering. . . . Suffering
overwhelms me!! . . . Never has a sinless child been born to its mother!
. . . A sinless youth no longer exists as of old!"[28]

To struggle for survival in a land so barren and marshy, where rivers
were so unreliable and unruly, was difficult enough. There either was not
enough water or floods swept everything away. It took enormous effort,
massive amounts of forced labor and sophisticated technology, to bring
such waters under control. It took continuous effort and vigilance to keep
that precarious control from slipping or disintegrating. Some natural

26. Ibid., 113.

27. Included within this category are the cultures of Sumer, Akkad, Babylonia,
Assyria, and various peoples, such as the Hittites, Elamites, Amorites, and others who
were at one time or another dominant in the land "between the two rivers," the Tigris
and Euphrates.

28. Translation found in Butterfield, *The Origins of History*, 39. For context and
greater detail, see Thorkild Jacobsen, *Treasures of Darkness: A History of Mesopotamian
Religion* (New Haven: Yale University Press, 1976), ix; and his *Literary and Religious
Texts* (London: British Museum, 1963).

disaster or some human predator could so easily take away everything one had achieved. Yet, despite such risks, returns could also be enormous. It took elaborate and extensive drainage and irrigation systems — networks of canals sometimes fed by trunk canals as wide as twenty-five feet — for crops planted in silt-enriched soil to receive just the right amount of water just when it was most needed. But harvests could be huge. It took a remarkable kind of local infrastructure to make the whole system work — a very highly organized economy, a steeply stratified society, and a centralized local polity. Yet structures of this sort could not be achieved nor maintained without incessant struggle. Even so, since they were no stronger than their weakest components, such structures were delicately balanced and life was precarious. Against malevolent forces undermining them from within or assaulting them from without, there was little room for maneuver or free play.

Memories of calamity and conflict loom large in the earliest records of Mesopotamia.[29] Dire events, leaving legacies of brooding ambivalence and doubt, are described in the materials that have been unearthed. Mingled among epic poems and prayers, hymns and incantations, lamentations and legends, myths and proverbs, are fragmentary details about precarious business enterprises, dealings with treacherous allies, and negotiations with predatory foes.[30] What emerge from these records are stories. These tell about the existence, as early as 4000 B.C., of numerous tightly organized urban localities. Each had its own autonomous system of power; each, its own central citadel raised upon a man-made platform above the floodplain; each, its own "god-house" or temple for its own local deity; each, its own storehouse or treasury for grain surpluses and manufactured goods; and each, under the management of its own bureaucratic priesthood, engaged in commerce and striving for mastery over other urban centers. Yet, no single one of these

29. Samuel N. Kramer, *Lamentations over the Destruction of Ur* (Chicago: University of Chicago Press, 1940).

30. Sumerian records of early rulers of Lagash are among the better understood of available remains: inscribed upon clay tablets in cuneiform script, these consist of administrative, business, legal, and votive documents, together with incantations and letters. For a thumbnail sketch see the *Encyclopaedia Britannica*, 1976 ed., both *Micropaedia*, s.v. "Sumerian language" and *Macropaedia*, s.v. "Languages of the World." For a classic general overview, see A. Leo Oppenheim, *Ancient Mesopotamia: Portrait of a Dead Civilization* (Chicago: University of Chicago Press, 1964; revised 1977 by Eric Reiner).

earliest "city-states," as they might be described, nor even any single combination of them, seems to have ever been able to remain predominant, at least for very long. Some new threat, whether from a new people or a new technology, seems to have been constantly rising which could upset the carefully constructed balance of power or the precariously prosperous equilibrium.

Thus, from earliest antiquity in this area, we learn that cultural advancement or economic development occurred within a context of ceaseless competition, conflict, and rivalry. Where the territorial sway of local domains seems always much more limited than in Egypt, minds also seem much more preoccupied with the demands of immediate survival — with the incessant demands of conflict, diplomacy, and war. No one power can feel secure by itself or expect to survive for long without alliances; and yet, no one alliance can remain secure for very long. Each year, it seems, brings new change, new situations, and new threats, with occasions for hard choices and tough decisions. Under such circumstances, where few can remain unaware of the wretchedness of the human condition or where constraints seem to hedge it about from every side, one can begin to appreciate the nature and depths of despair.

It is within the context of this juxtaposition of unpredictable circumstances, this mingling of potential prosperity with impending disaster, this "uneasy equilibrium between chaos and order" that one can begin to search for answers to basic questions of how peoples of early Mesopotamia viewed their own antiquity. When all is said and done — after draining marshes and building canals, after developing hydraulic technologies, after establishing industries (textile production, leatherwork, metalwork, masonry, and pottery), after extending trade networks both far and near in all directions, and after concentrating power within a dozen or more increasingly advanced "city-state" systems, each with its own central citadel combining its "god-house" and storehouse, and each surrounded by fortified walls — records show that local power was ever tottering on the brink of some destruction, including self-destruction.[31]

This picture of ceaseless struggle and heroic resistance in the face

31. Samuel N. Kramer, *History Begins at Sumer* (1956; reprint, Philadelphia: University of Pennsylvania Press, 1988).

of tragedy is the material from which epic narratives are made.[32] This sense of tragedy lying close to the surface can explain the nature of the impulses of historical understanding that we find coming out of Babylonia's remote past. Heroic deeds were required. Leaders had to face overwhelming difficulties and, in so doing, were not always victorious. Nice people did not always win. Within the hostile environment surrounding Sumer and Akkad, some heroic person had ever to meet and surmount challenge after challenge — doing so again and again until, at last, he too was overwhelmed. The pathos in the words of such figures as Gilgamesh and Enmerkar[33] and Sargon and Narim-Sin is palpable. Here, where folk-memory and folk-tale seem to be writ large, deeds are expanded — and eventually exaggerated out of all proportion to the original events that they purport to represent.

The list of people succeeding each other in the control and development of lower Mesopotamia is long. Among the earliest, perhaps between 4500 and 3500 B.C., are a non-Semitic or pre-Sumerian people, called Ubaidians (named after the village where their remains were first found). After them came various Semitic peoples, each adding something to the cultures and technologies which had been there before them. This process seems to have continued until a high level of civilization was established. Then came the Sumerians, called so because of the rich language and literature which they developed. Sumerian records tell us about what was happening in the twelve or more walled cities over which they ruled (c. 3300 B.C.).[34] Each city, surrounded by its own irrigated lands and agricultural villages and "ruled" by its own deity and its own priestly "gentry," required a close collaboration between its agrarian, commercial, industrial, and warrior constituents. Each city's deity, with its own temple citadel, bureaucratic center, storehouses, and treasury, held sway — not only over peoples within its own domains, but over all other deities commanding worship and ruling over similar city-states in surrounding domains. With

32. Samuel N. Kramer, *Mythologies of the Ancient World* (New York: Doubleday, 1961).

33. Samuel N. Kramer, *Enmerkar and the Land of Aratta: A Sumerian Epic Tale of Iraq and Iran* (Philadelphia: University Museum, University of Pennsylvania Press, 1952).

34. Kish, Ur, Adab, Akshak, Bad-itbira, Erech, Lagash, Larak, Larsa, Nippur, Sippar, and Umma.

the increasing rivalry came a greater need for centralizing military power. Warlords, originally rising to power out of necessity, then became increasingly dictatorial. As demands of centralizing power continued, first one and then another small principality was obliged by the demands of security to adopt some form of kingship.[35] Thus, within a context where all local deities and/or all local kings seem to have constantly made claims to sway over the domains of neighboring city-states, little lasting security could be enjoyed. Not until some truly superior king finally came to power and was able to acquire more strength than all the rest and not until, by virtue of his superior skills, he was able to negotiate the construction of some sort of a more encompassing contractual or legal framework, did prospects for a more durable peace over the whole area seem to have become possible. However fragile such an arrangement, the prospect of this sort of arrangement was the sort of stuff out of which legends and epics are made. And so, indeed, did the epics come into being. These show us how events were explained and understood.[36]

However, it is the listings of local rulers and their dates, initially quite simple and somewhat spasmodic, which give us starting points. Such records apparently served several purposes. They seem to have provided a legal framework for transactions in business and commerce; and they seem also to have provided data essential both for divination (telling the future) and "history" (telling the past). A steady progression of such documents, each of them becoming more elaborate and sophisticated, indicates an increasing importance of record-keeping. Then, suddenly, some documents appear. These are not only much larger but amazingly more detailed in the information they contain. Four sets of such records are especially noteworthy. Now known by the technical names assigned to them by scholars upon their discovery, they are (1) the *Sumerian King List;* (2) the *Narim-Sin Text;* (3) the *Weidner Chronicle;* and (4) the *Neo-Babylonian Chronicle.*

Among the earliest documents, the Sumerian King List stands out.

35. Cyril John Gadd, *The Early Dynasties of Sumer and Akkad* (London: Luzak, 1921).

36. One of the most famous, the *Epic of Gilgamesh,* recently translated again, is readily available: John Gardner and John Maier, *Gilgamesh: Translated from the* Sîn-Leqi-Unninnī *Version* (New York: Alfred A. Knopf, 1984). See Kramer, *Mythologies of the Ancient World.*

A clear departure from the simple rosters which merely gave regnal names and years, it looks like a "crisis document"[37] and, as such, has a political agenda. Its purpose seems designed to show that down through ages from remotest times, even before Utuhegal came to the throne, kingship had always been a stabilizing factor and that it was an important and necessary institution. Casting its network of listings over the whole Tigris and Euphrates valley, the text provides terse and unembellished chronologies of political institutions, tracing the wanderings of kingship from city to city — moving from Akshak to Kish; and thence, to Uruk. From this we learn that Etana, king of Kish (c. 2800 B.C.), was the first to unite the separate "city-state" principalities;[38] that "seven kings then reigned for 491 years"; after which "kingship to Uruk was carried."[39] As the text gradually thickens with information, more and more borrowings from epic, folklore, legend, and myth appear. These reveal, for example, that Entmerkar was the king who built Uruk, that Gilgamesh was the son of a high priest, and that Sargon of Akkad grew dates before he became cupbearer of the king of Kish (Ur-Zababa). Clearly the most remarkable feature about this list is the way in which, by using the Flood as a historical pivot, the writer was able to add an antediluvian section to his already completed list. Thus, with a remarkable backward "stretching of historical imagination,"[40] he could inform his readers that, "When kingship was first lowered from heaven, kingship was in Eridu."[41] At the same time, the compiler of this list did something else noteworthy. With all candor, he specified which of his sources (tablets) had been damaged or destroyed; and he readily admitted that some supposed kings had never really been kings at all. At the same time, lest too much credit be given, it is necessary to also notice that this same scribe was not above trying "to force correct evidence into a mold" so that it might better conform to his own preconceptions about what had happened in the past.

The next document, recorded later, takes a very different perspec-

37. Brundage, "The Birth of Clio," 205-6.
38. Thorkild Jacobsen, *The Sumerian King List* (Chicago: University of Chicago Press, 1939, 1964), xvi, 216.
39. Jacobsen, *The Sumerian King List,* 109-64.
40. Brundage, "The Birth of Clio," 206.
41. Jacobsen, *The Sumerian King List,* 144; and Gadd, *The Early Dynasties of Sumer and Akkad.*

tive. Instead of dwelling upon the royal origins of orderly rule, the Narim-Sin Text stresses the role of divinity.[42] It is the gods who set up and throw down thrones. Once again, as each local power began to strive with other local powers for ascendancy, so that all people again became vulnerable to external forces, a great god had to intervene. After the decline of Elamite rule (c. 2530-2450 B.C.), it was the heroic Sargon (c. 2334-2279 B.C.) who united the city-states. But this he could never have done had not the goddess Inanna arranged for heaven's highest god, Enlil, to enable him to create a lasting system of government.[43] This system, serving as a model for later rulers, lasted for a century; and Akkad enjoyed great power and prosperity. But then, during the reign of Narim-Sin, barbaric Gutians invaded the land. In the chaos and devastation that followed, city-states once again fought against each other. Quite obviously, those priests who wrote about these events felt no obligation to gloss over past failings, whether of personality or of policy. Without fear of reprisal, they could brood upon cosmic forces which brought such calamity and dwell upon questions of human destiny. Consequences could be related to causes; and, perhaps as never before, ethical and human and moral factors could be considered. Attempts to interpret the meaning of past events in antiquity grew more interesting.

This capacity for "critical" reflection becomes much more pronounced in documents related to the first Babylonian dynasty. In what is now known as the Weidner Chronicle, a cosmogony serves as a prelude to understanding the past. The high gods, Anu and Enlil, are reported as having allowed predominant kingship to pass from city to city because the god Marduk had not been properly honored. Only as long as Marduk and his temple of Esagila were respected could any city be allowed to acquire or to retain great power and prosperity. On that account, when Ur-Nammu, first king of Ur's third dynasty, devised a code of laws and brought that city to unprecedented heights, this was due to his worship of Marduk. When Amorites conquered the land,

---

42. Brundage, "The Birth of Clio," 207, quotes the extended translation of this text by H. G. Guterbock published as an article in *Zeitschrift fur Assyriologie* 42 (1934) and 44 (1938); and on pp. 224-25, adds a translation of *The Weidner Chronicle* (made from Guterbock's rendition).

43. Diane Wolkstein, *Inanna, Queen of Heaven and Earth . . .* (London: Rider Press, 1983).

ruling over it so that Sumerians could never again recover their separate identities, this too was due to the power of Marduk in Babylon.[44]

Babylon's first dynasty brought the city to true imperial ascendancy. Hammurabi, the sixth and greatest monarch of this dynasty, ruled for forty-three years. After enlarging his empire by means of conciliation and conquest, he too set about amalgamating and integrating all of the older Sumerian and Akkadian codes, some of them hundreds of years old. His great Code, methodical down to the finest detail and containing nearly three hundred items, covered many matters, such as false accusation, business practice, family dispute, land holding, debts, loans, wages, and military service. But all his laws sought to reinforce one underlying principle: namely, that the strong should not injure the weak. Rule of law as the foundation for civil society and the bulwark of political stability became enshrined, perhaps as never before. Only by such means could the rights of individuals and of separate communities hope for protection or redress.[45]

The rule of kings and governments and laws had by now become matters for inquiry which could call for better and more systematic understandings of the past. Nor were those who wrote about such things in antiquity any longer quite so dependent upon rulers for their positions and so subject to royal pleasure for their very lives. Instead, the priests as authors of such inquiries were able to indulge in speculation — or, at least, to express the results of such speculation. Their writings show evidence of a need (and a wish) to know more. By looking at the oral and written legacies that survived (whether annals, epics, lamentations, myths, or bureaucratic reports), they could ponder details about what made one system work better than another. Even when they reached conclusions that indicated that past failure to heed Marduk had resulted in chaos, loss, and suffering, they could, nonetheless, set in motion a new kind of use for historical knowledge. History could be employed for more than didactic and polemical purposes. Using archives of tablets kept within the temple of Marduk, priestly scribes of Babylon could begin to compose a history of the entire world and try

44. Cyril John Gadd, *History and Monuments of Ur* (London: Chatto & Windus, 1929). See Brundage's interpretation in "The Birth of Clio," 208.

45. H. W. F. Saggs, *The Greatness That Was Babylon*, rev. ed. (London: Sidgwick & Jackson, 1988).

to construct a coherent understanding of its past. What they produced, now known as the Neo-Babylonian Chronicle, was a remarkable achievement.[46]

Yet, before this remarkable work could be composed, devotees and priests of Marduk had themselves to suffer many centuries of impotence, loss, and subjugation. Between the early and later Babylonian dynasties, there were long interludes of non-Babylonian rule. Assyrians, Elamites, Kassites, and Hittites, at one time or another, held sway over Mesopotamia. When the second dynasty of Babylonian monarchs arose, its most outstanding ruler, Nebuchadrezzar I (c. 1124-1103 B.C.), restored Marduk to a place of power and worship. Then, after more centuries of struggles for supremacy between Chaldeans, Arameans, and Assyrians, the Assyrian empire, with its great city of Nineveh, came to dominance. Not until after the death of Ashurbanipal did yet another dynasty arise in the city of Marduk. Nabopolassar and his son Nebuchadrezzar II (c. 605-562 B.C.) restored the supremacy of Babylon once again.[47]

Since the Neo-Babylonian Chronicle was not produced until after these interludes, however, we need to consider the nature of contributions to historical understanding left by some of those dynasties that interrupted Babylonian ascendancy in Mesopotamia. Annals and chronicles left by the Hittites and Assyrians are especially noteworthy.

Little in the way of new insight or understanding can be found in what was left by Assyrian monarchs. Their campaign annals trace a development of over six hundred years. Their great rulers — Shalmaneser I (c. 1280), Tiglath-Peleser I (c. 1100), Ashurnasirpal, Sennacherib,[48] and his son, Ashurbanipal — excelled in bombastic self-exaltation and exulting over victories. Their annals merely show off, in detail, what deeds of conquest were performed and what great spoils were taken. Only occasionally, as when Ashurbanipal tells about a

---

46. Cyril John Gadd, *The Fall of Nineveh: A Newly Discovered Babylon Chronicle* (London: Oxford University Press, 1923), is based upon a huge series of tablets which are thought to have comprised the corpus of the official history of Babylon. Some of the main tablets in this series, now catalogued and preserved in the British Museum, are described by catalogue number in Brundage, "The Birth of Clio," 288 nn. 27, 28.

47. *New Encyclopaedia Britannica*, 15th ed., s.v. "Babylon."

48. D. D. Luckenbill, *The Annals of Sennacharib* (Chicago: University of Chicago Press, 1924), xii, 196.

mountain campaign, does one find some confessions of human frailty, hardship, lamentation, or weakness. Even then, it is difficult to feel very sympathetic over the unhappiness of a monarch who could gloat about running a rope through the jaw or rubbing salt into the wounds of his vanquished foe.[49] All in all, Assyrian annals are full and bold and stereotyped. They reveal a boring sameness, as if having read one, one has read all: "I destroyed, I devastated, I burned with fire!" Sheer power and swift violence are standard themes.[50]

About Hittites, little was known until this century. But as thousands of tablet inscriptions have been uncovered and deciphered, the remarkable achievements of this people have begun to be appreciated. The "Land of Hatti" was ruled from Hattusas, a city located in the remoteness of the Taurus Mountains of Anatolia (near the present Turkish town of Boghazkoy). The name, coming from peoples who originally lived in the country, was appropriated and applied to the culture and language of their Indo-European conquerors (c. 2000 B.C.). Hittite kings ruled and created ever larger states, even an empire, at different times during the next millennium. At the height of their power (c. 1600 onwards), the greatest of the Hittite kings, such as Mursilis (c. 1340), became known to Egyptian pharaohs against whom they fought. Egyptian records referred to this monarch as the "Great Kheta" (or Great Hittite).[51]

What makes the Hittites so remarkable to us today is evidence of their astonishingly human, if not humane, sensitivity. In their own understandings of past events, as seen in their writings, a lofty moral tone can be discerned. This was almost unprecedented for much of the world of their day. In their annals, in their legal codes, in their treaties, and even in their prayers, Hittite rulers and scribes convey profound moral insights, linking ethical behavior with social and political consequences. Their annals convey a clear-sighted power of analysis, examining data and explaining actions to a degree hardly found in any other historical under-

---

49. D. D. Luckenbill, *Ancient Records of Assyria and Babylonia,* Cuneiform Series (Chicago: University of Chicago, 1926), 2:73-99, 312, 378.

50. A. T. Olmstead, *Assyrian Historiography* (Columbia, Mo.: University of Missouri Press, 1916).

51. O. R. Gurney, *The Hittites: A Summary of the Art, Achievements and Social Organization of a Great People of Asia Minor during the Second Millennium B.C., as Discovered by Modern Excavations* (London: Penguin Books, 1952, 1975).

standings of antiquity. While they may constantly invoke or refer to one deity or another, they devote much care to describing each situation in detailed and exact human terms. Their military narratives are perfunctory reports which are sober and terse, giving more space to social conditions and to political implications of events than to vainglorious pomp. It is as if each annal were a "working paper" or a "business report" addressed to a council of notables whose knowledge and understanding of real situations was such that it was necessary to argue and persuade — like a hardworking and bedraggled modern city mayor trying to persuade bureaucrats and councilors and pressure groups.[52]

In their laws, Hittite rulers seem to have been milder and more humane, especially in their treatment of offenders, than were most rulers of the realms that surrounded them. In their penalties, neither the Code of Hammurabi nor the Hebrew Torah was so generous.[53] In their treaties, Hittites applied the same humane principles to other peoples as they applied to their own. They sought relationships of full reciprocity, "covenantal" or "contractual" obligations based upon ideals of mutual benefit and mutual respect.[54] Finally, in their prayers, one can discern a spirit of anguish, self-examination, confession of sin, and repentance for evil found in virtually no other records of antiquity (with the exception of the Hebrews).[55] Hittite kings — Mursilis II, Hattusilis II, etc. — seem to have been capable of showing public contrition: they could admit that all people, "being only human," were prone to evil and wrongdoing; and they could beg for pardon, either for themselves or for others weaker than themselves.[56]

It seems clear, therefore, that the Neo-Babylonian Chronicle cannot be seen in isolation. It cannot be properly understood outside the context of the development of Hittite and Assyrian, not to mention Egyptian, historical writings during previous centuries. Indeed, as we shall see in the

52. Gurney, *The Hittites*, 63-79, 104-16.

53. Gurney, *The Hittites*, 88-101.

54. J. A. Thompson, *Deuteronomy: An Introduction and Commentary* (Leicester: Inter-Varsity Press, 1974; Downers Grove, Ill.: InterVarsity Press, 1976), indicates a consensus in recent biblical scholarship concerning the role of Hittite treaties as prototypes of the "covenant" relationships claimed as being forged between peoples of Israel and Yahweh.

55. James B. Pritchard, ed., *Ancient Near Eastern Texts Relating to the Old Testament*, 2 vols. (Princeton: Princeton University Press, 1950).

56. Ibid., 132-77; and Butterfield, *The Origin of History*, 69-71.

two chapters on classical and monotheistic historical traditions, many of these ways of understanding the past ran along parallel and sometimes intersecting (or interwinding) lines of development. While evidence of cross-cultural borrowings and influences may not be altogether certain, many if not all of these comparable developments were occurring, at least in some measure, during the same centuries. Like the Hittite records, the Neo-Babylonian Chronicle also consists of a huge collection of clay (cuneiform) tablets. Yet while the Hittite materials are archival documents which served as tools of government, law, diplomacy, and religion in their own day, the Neo-Babylonian Chronicle seems, more than likely, to have been a deliberate attempt to reconstruct the past by drawing upon any and all documents as its source materials.

Written during the periods of later Babylonian and Persian rule and kept in the temple of Marduk in the city of Babylon,[57] the tablets of the Neo-Babylonian Chronicle seek to trace the history of the world from its beginning. Except when asserting Marduk's sovereignty over all of destiny, both in the past or future, the chronicle shows that degree of open curiosity and intellectual detachment in treating details, that kind of sophistication in assessing unique events, without which the writing of a genuine history would not be possible in any age. From these tablets, one can get many fascinating details: descriptions concerning the fall of Nineveh in 612 B.C.;[58] or about the day in 539 B.C. when Cyrus entered Babylon and "Green branches were spread in front of him," a "state of 'peace' was imposed upon the city; and Cyrus sent greetings to all Babylon."[59] These historical understandings, according to Brundage, "deserve to rank in importance with such milestones as the histories of Thucydides . . . and Ranke."[60]

\* \* \*

When one considers the enormous span of years that is generally thought to make up the ages of early antiquity in Egypt and Mesopotamia, the development of any cogent kind of historical understand-

---

57. Many of these, for most of this century, have been kept in the British Museum. For an early description, see C. J. Gadd, *The Fall of Nineveh*.

58. Pritchard, *Ancient Near Eastern Texts*, 302; and C. J. Gadd, *The Fall of Nineveh*.

59. Pritchard, *Ancient Near Eastern Texts*, 306.

60. Brundage, "The Birth of Clio," 221.

ings in written form seems, at least on its face, to have been very, very slow. Moreover, as with most records in our own day, those matters touched upon in the records seem to have been almost exclusively concerned with contemporary events. Even the king lists and the annals are concerned not so much with the past as with the present. Concern with portraying the past seems to have been important only insofar as it touched upon some immediate, if not an urgent, set of interests. And these interests, insofar as we are able to discover what they were, were those of individual persons or families who possessed enormous power and wealth, individuals and comparatively small groups who ruled over large numbers of people or who fought over issues of wealth and power and people. Finally, so as to command the authority that they needed and in order to command their families and their servants, all of these early manifestations of understanding of the past appealed to belief structures and values. They appealed to God, to gods or to cosmic forces, and to events of the past to help them control circumstances of the present, if not of the future. What they wanted was success and succession for themselves and their heirs, together.[61]

61. For further consideration of this subject, see W. F. Albright, *From the Stone Age to Christianity* (Baltimore: Johns Hopkins University Press, 1941); R. C. Dentan, ed., *The Idea of History in the Ancient Near East* (New Haven: Yale University Press, 1955); L. W. King, *Chronicles Concerning Early Babylonian Kings* (London: Luzac and Co., 1907), 1:2; H. A. Frankfort et al., *The Intellectual Adventure of Ancient Man* (Chicago: University of Chicago Press, 1946); and John A. Wilson, *The Burden of Egypt* (Chicago: University of Chicago Press, 1951).

## Chapter 6

# History as Classicity:
# A Critical Criterion

How historical understandings first arose and how they became identified with antiquity is the story of four, not just two, of the great earliest valley civilizations. The antiquity of India and China was no less impressive than that of Egypt and Mesopotamia. Each of these other two civilizations was as huge and as different from the other as each of them was different from the Ancient Near East.[1] More to the point, India and China, like Greece and Rome, can be seen as being "classical."[2] This distinction can be made because, beyond unbroken continuity of identity and essential uniqueness of character, these cultures have been seen and are still seen as classical. "Classical" is the designation used to signify standards of achievement and critical judgment set so high that subsequent ages and cultures measured themselves against those standards. In some respects, the standards set so long ago still serve as starting points or as criteria for critical judgments.

For purposes of this study, what is meant by "classical" has been expanded. The concept as defined and elaborated upon here pertains to those levels or peaks of cultural perfection and intellectual sophistication once reached in the past which set standards for subsequent times. These standards were such that, ever since, they have remained as criteria against

---

1. No convenient and precise label has yet been invented for this area: the "Fertile Crescent" covers only the whole area of the Mesopotamian and Nile valleys and watersheds; "Middle East" or "Near East" is too elastic and vague.

2. Indeed, some claim the Indian continent alone has always contained not one but two classical cultures — one rooted in Sanskrit and the other in Tamil.

149

which subsequent achievements have been measured. Application of the term, originally and often normally confined, at least in the West, to Greek (and Roman) models, is here expanded so as to include other cultures where standards of high achievement attained comparable levels: most notably those set by the "classical" civilizations of India and China. Of course, high standards were also attained both in ancient and later times by other civilizations. These occurrences can be identified and so designated especially where a peak of cultural achievement can be seen as having reached a "crowning culmination of what had preceded [it] rather than as the beginning of what followed."[3] The three especially distinctive and separate worlds that are seen as easily meeting the standards of classicity as it has been defined here — the Greco-Roman (extended to Byzantium high culture), the Indic (including both Sanskritic and Dravidian high cultures), and Sinitic (including Japanese high culture) — all arose out of the mists of high civilization in earliest antiquity.[4] Since those civilizations were, as has been made increasingly apparent, already advanced, only an arbitrary decision is being used to draw upon conventional usages of the label "classical." Moreover, all of these classical civilizations, in that sense, were derivative (or secondary) civilizations. That is to say, they all emerged from, or were superimposed upon, high cultures that had previously developed within one of the four great river valley civilizations, or in reasonably close proximity to them.[5] Interestingly,

3. John Ellison Kahn et al., eds., *The Right Word at the Right Time: A Guide to the English Language and How to Use It* (London: Reader's Digest Association of Great Britain, Ltd., 1985), 131-32. There is danger of confusion in contexts between uses of "classic" or "classical" in their respective senses. One common mistake is to use "classical" when one means "classic." A classical poem is one composed in Greco-Roman times; a classic poem could be any fine poem falling into a "class" of poems. Also, "classical" sometimes refers to a pinnacle of achievement which, while seen so for its time, is now outmoded. In that sense, while Newtonian physics has been superseded by that of Einstein, it is still seen as classical rather than as classic. Something "classic," on the other hand, is typical (or archetypical) of a "class" (or "category") of things, which set a standard or tradition and is well known for qualities it possesses.

4. Also classical, by our definition, are traditions of Israel and Judah (Hebrew high culture); some forms of Christianity (at least Greek, Latin, Coptic, and Syriac, but perhaps other forms); and of Islam (as manifest both in Arab and Persian standards of high culture). Monotheistic forms and traditions of classicity, however, as a class by themselves, are examined in chapter 8.

5. Greek (or Hellenic) and Roman culture, after all, also came out of the eastern Mediterranean matrix of the Nile and Mesopotamian worlds.

however, all of those civilizations defined as classical for purposes of this study also reached their highest pinnacles of achievement during approximately the same centuries. Moreover, all paralleled or resembled each other in many other important ways. (However, only two of these models are examined within the compass of this study: the ancient Hellenic and ancient Indic forms of classicity.)

At the same time, it is useful to remember that in addition to the Hellenic there also arose yet another set of traditions (or family of cultures) which meets the definition of "classical" described above. This set of traditions, arising out of the same cradle of civilizations (considered in chapter 3), also achieved unprecedented standards of accomplishment and sophistication — standards so high, especially in historical and theological understandings, that they too set standards for critical inquiry that were never surpassed. This set or "family" of traditions, in its genesis, harks back to the "seed of Abraham" — to events remembered and experiences reflected upon in the Hebrew Torah, the Chronicles, Prophets, Epic Poems, and Songs. In Hebrew Scripture (as also in later Christian Scripture), a comparable but different spirit of critical detachment and precise understanding about events gained strength. (This stream of historical understandings, together with its own "classical" features, is examined in chapter 7.)

It is also important to be reminded that no classical high culture simply sprang into being, full-blown and mature. Each rested upon slowly built-up residues of earlier "high cultures" which had been developing for many centuries, if not for millennia. In each instance, a long-term catalytic reaction had occurred between earlier host cultures which already combined surplus agrarian economies with urban sophistications. In each instance also, an intrusive newer culture, with perhaps a more advanced technology but also perhaps culturally less sophisticated, had overrun the older civilization. Societies in each of these classical worlds managed not only to preserve large vestiges of their original cultures but also, in some measure, to retain a largely continuous and unbroken line of contact with previous cultures. Moreover, they then became "models" for cultures in subsequent ages. Subsequent cultures then tried to emulate and to claim, often with some justice, that they had maintained direct contact with and lineal descent from a cultural heritage that was thought to be "classical."

Thus, to recapitulate, from "classical" beginnings to more recent times, each classical tradition has managed, in some way, to pass down a considerable measure of its original essence, basic roots, and critical standards. Ever since, successive peoples have looked back upon the ancient standards and have given them that designation which we today still, quite properly, describe as classical. The concept, applied to the high cultures of India and China[6] in the same sense that it was long applied to the high cultures of Greece and Rome, denotes both unbroken continuity in identity and high standards of achievement which were models for emulation in subsequent ages.[7] Perhaps the one salient feature that all of these cultures acquired and then transmitted, which was most characteristic of them all, is something that, for want of a better single description, can be called "intellectuality." This common element, together with a distinctive language which could serve as its vehicle, can be found in all classical worlds. A power of abstraction, power to detach the mind and the person from concrete events and particular objects, enabled thinkers in each of the classical worlds to strive for and to formulate general principles and therewith to produce sophisticated works of art and logic, poetry and philosophy, and science. Such developments set into motion creatively different and more dynamic ways of conceptualizing the universe and relations among entities within it.

## I. Classical India[8]

One stereotype about India keeps cropping up. Over and over again, the rhetorical question is bluntly, even crudely asked: Why is it that

---

6. And, from thence also, to Japanese high culture.

7. While the term "classical" can, however, also be applied to other cultures — e.g., Hebrew, Persian, Arabic, etc. — consideration of these two classical worlds is sufficient for the purposes of this study. Moreover, there is considerable overlapping between different categories of analysis in this study.

8. "India" or "Indian," as used here, denotes anything lying within the continent (more commonly referred to as subcontinent), the area that today would include what are now the more recently constructed countries ("nation-states") of India, Pakistan, Bangladesh, Nepal, Sri Lanka, and Afghanistan: everything south of the Himalayas, south and east of the Hindu Kush, and west of the jungled mountains which separate Assam from Burma. "India" and "Indian" are about as precise as the concepts "Europe" and "European." "Indic" might serve, except it is usually confined to Indo-Aryan languages or cultures. The concept "Asia" is so imprecise that it is a useless semantic conundrum.

peoples of India have never developed any advanced or sophisticated understandings of historical events? Why is it that, in India, even concepts of events themselves — history both in immediate and in ultimate senses — never evolved very far? In fact, why have peoples in India never developed histories that were their own? Put yet another way: Why is it that Indians have never been "historically minded" and have never possessed much historical consciousness? How is it (or why is it) that "they" never developed much curiosity about events, as such, at least about events in their own past; or developed ability to produce much in the way of clear, precise, or sound knowledge about what has happened within India down through many ages?[9]

In dealing with this issue, we need again to erase some misconceptions and confront semantic problems. Since neither the term *history* nor any comparable term from outside India (whether *geschichte, istoria,* or even the term *science* for that matter) has any exact analogue or counterpart in India, we must search for Indic concepts which convey something as close as possible to the meanings we are seeking. Even those indigenous concepts found in India that come closest to "understanding the past" or "knowing the past" need to be understood, as much as possible, as they may have been used within their own, most immediate, "natural" and cultural contexts. The very idea of "event" or of "past," for example, can lead us into trouble. These terms too, as such, have had no direct or exact parallels in India. Thus, when something about an event or about the past is spoken about, something which modern minds may consider to have already happened or passed, listeners in India are just as apt to consider that such a thing has just been "breathed" or "sounded" aloud orally and therefore "heard," and that such a thing is, in fact, both "present" and "represented" by virtue of its having just been expressed (in breath and sound). The ontology and epistemology of the "things" which have happened suggest that, when "things" are written about as things that have already happened, those things "come into being" again, at least in the mind of the hearer (or reader).

9. Apart from the implied condescension or insult, even if unintended, one needs to be aware of the tendency of every dominant ideology to declare to others who came before or which are now superseded or subservient, "You have no history!" meaning either "You have no past," "You know nothing about your past," or, worst of all, "Your past does not matter." However one may wish to put it, this is an ideological issue.

To make matters yet more complicated, even within the continent, profound differences have existed between what today are called the classical or high conceptualizations, as systems or traditions of thought, and those which, while perhaps even older, have remained locked within local folk cultures. The older traditions, while often relegated to lesser positions of importance if not to outright oblivion by those who possessed more power, have nevertheless exerted ceaseless and persistent pressures "from below." No attempt to impose a classical order, dominant system, or universal culture has ever entirely succeeded. Always rising from below have been various forms of "corrupting" local influence: the working out of something that, in my other work, I have called the "white ant principle." And yet, without wishing to either denigrate or ignore powerful undercurrents in folk understandings of the past which are still very much alive in India and which may perhaps yet be preserved (even though growing weaker under the impact of modernizing and secularizing institutions), in this study we are confining ourselves only to those understandings of the past arising out of what today might be called the "great" or "high" (Aryan, Brahmanical, Indic, Sanskritic, and/or Tamil) traditions.[10]

Among various terms arising out of classical Sanskrit which have long conveyed kinds of understanding about the past, two are of particular relevance. But even before these can be examined, it is important to be aware of one fundamental and all-pervasive attitude towards all events (History), however minute or cosmic, and towards any and all forms of existence (History), however microscopic or universal. This perspective is best perceived in the classical understandings of mortality. Within Indic traditions going back to early Vedic times, life and death, in all their manifold forms, are viewed as completely and profoundly ephemeral. They are only bits and pieces of illusion *(māya)*. Even space and time, however conceived, whether particular or pervasive, are but manifestations of passing illusion. This being so, the only things that truly exist and the only things, therefore, that truly happen or can be

10. Of course, even the "great traditions," as expressed in classical Sanskrit and Tamil, have had continually dynamic interactions with those traditions that are local, both incorporating local elements and contributing elements to them. This interplay comes in many forms and under many names: among recent efforts to describe this interactive process, one by M. N. Srinivas which gained some intellectual currency is the concept of "Sanskritization."

events worth noticing are those things that are intrinsic and essential within each and all of those things that are ephemeral. It is only the particular self or soul *(ātma)* that is truly real and that possesses truly spaceless and timeless properties. Only the universal All *(Brāhman)* into which every soul is eventually and ultimately merged can be as real or possess such properties. This is that which encompasses *all* cosmic and eternal existence. This is that Force that moves all other forces. It is best understood, in metaphorical terms, by reference to the root meaning of *Brahman* which, technically, means "breath" and, by extension, "sound." All things that are or have ever been, according to such thinking, are merely echoes of primordial sound.[11]

The two Sanskritic concepts that most appropriately serve as starting points, particularly when used in conjunction with each other, are *itihāsa* and *purāna*. *Itihāsa (it-i-hāsa)* literally means "it thus was," "thus it was," or "this is what happened." *Purāna (pūrāna)* means "ancient" or "old" ("withered or worn"); "an event of the past," "happenings" or "something remembered." It is only *smriti* as distinct from *sruti*. Things more directly "heard" are more sacred than things gained secondhand. Hence, an ancient legend or tale or any old traditional history is merely *smriti*. Finally, as *smriti*, *purānas* fall into that category of sacred works covering fifteen hundred years in post-Vedic times, which treat five topics *(pancha-lakshana)* supposedly compiled by the poet Vyasa.[12] More specifically, it is a category of texts based upon a canonical model which combines history and legend, mythology and narrative stories of relations between deities, demons, and humankind.[13] In short, *purāna*, as a term, can mean any or all of the above.

11. I am personally indebted to my colleague, Dr. V. Narayana Rao, professor of Telugu Sanskrit literature and an authority in both Sanskrit and folklore, for many insights on this subject.

12. Sir Monier-Williams et al., eds., *Sanskrit-English Dictionary* (Oxford: Clarendon Press, 1899), 635, col. 1.

13. J. Duncan M. Derrett, *Religion, Law and the State in India* (London: Faber & Faber, 1968), 16, defines *purāna* as "history" and myth. In am indebted to the Conference on the Puranas, held at the University of Wisconsin August 1-4, 1985, for a rich trove of recent research. Aside from what is called the *Mahā-Purāna* (or Great Purana) and the eighteen chief or High Puranas, usually divided into three groups (1. *Rajasa Purāna* [which exalts Brahma]; 2. *Stattvika Purāna* [which exalts Vishnu]; and 3. *Tamāsha Purāna* [exalting Shiva]) of six puranas each, there are hundreds of *Sthala-Purānas*, each of which pertains to events related to one locality or place (especially to a temple).

The renowned historian of ancient India, Romila Thapar, has suggested that many understandings of events that actually occurred are embedded within different kinds of textual materials. These kinds of materials she likens to so many layers, or geological stratas, of the earth's crust. Such stratified layers, consisting of varying mixtures of rock and shale and minerals, must first be penetrated, then mined for ores, and the ores then smelted, so that valuable metals may be extracted. From this analogy, Thapar goes on to demonstrate how layer after layer of textual residues from the past, with varying quantities and qualities of valid information, can be extracted. Masses of materials have survived and, when extracted and refined and sifted, tell how people living in India thousands of years ago themselves looked at their past. More than that, she has shown how historical understandings from the past, which one can still extract from such materials, tended to survive within "important" families and within those extended families, clans, lineages, birth groups, or "castes" (jāti-s) out of which later elite families had arisen. Most significantly, she has stressed the importance of historical understandings found within the classical itihāsa-purāna tradition. This tradition began within the Rig-Veda itself and, over millennia, has come down into the Vamshāvali chronicles of more recent, premodern, if not modern times.[14]

## A. Birth and Cosmic Family Identity

In one respect, there is complete accord within the earliest records of India. All things began with breath and sound (Brahman). From this sound and breath, ultimately, came each and every kind of living being, whatever its "birth" (jat) and whatever its family.[15] It is the family, more than any other institution, that has always known where it came from,

14. Romila Thapar, "Society and Historical Consciousness: The Itihasa-Purana Tradition," in Situating Indian History, ed. Subysachi Bhattacharya and Romila Thapar (New Delhi: Oxford University Press, 1986), 353-83.

15. Jāt: Too often limited to differentiations of birth or caste (jāti meaning "birth groups") within the larger category of mankind, this same concept actually applies to each and every form of biological life. Missing from it is any meaning or connotation that might either indicate a concept of humanity as such, or any sense that jāti was in any way limited to mankind.

how it came to be where it is, and how to trace its roots back to cosmic origins. Political systems (regimes or states) and other institutions of whatever size, whether small or great, could come and go as they were ever wont to do. But the family went on and on. It was the only thing from the past worth remembering. It was, or wished to be, very nearly eternal and timeless. If a family were "pure" or well-born — and if it remained so — it could go on, one generation succeeding another, forever. Thus, it is of utmost importance to understand the nature and quality of its intrinsic worth and to learn how anyone could gain greatest benefit therefrom. Quite obviously, this kind of knowledge *(veda)* could be nothing less than sacred — a matter of profoundest "religious" significance.[16]

Bound up in myths of origin, as in the *Matsya Purana* (or Fish-Purana), was the story of Manu and the Flood. Manu, perhaps suggestive of primeval, archetypal man *(manava:* "mankind"), was the primary ancestor of all the "pure" families and of all "respectable" lineages. Informed by a fish he had caught that his world would be swept away by a great deluge and that he would have to build a boat, both to save himself and the seven primordial sages *(rishis)* who were the repositories of all knowledge, Manu did what he was told.[17] Landing his boat safely on a mountain top and staying there until the flood subsided, he begot (or created) offspring — several sons and one daughter. The eldest son of Manu was Iksvaku. Iksvaku was the original ancestor of the Suryavamsha, the Solar Lineage of all who were of high and proper *kshatriya* birth — of kings, nobles, and warriors. The other great line of *kshatriya* families, the Chandravamsha or Lunar Lineage, came from Illa. She too, as the androgynous daughter of Manu, became known as the original ancestral begetter of kings and nobles and warriors.

As can thus be seen, obsession with genealogies of birth and descent lies at the very heart of all historical understandings in India. Moreover, even today the primacy of such understanding can be seen in almost any family *(jāt-parivār)* that claims "purity" of descent (often tracing this to roots in cosmogony). This preoccupation has never

16. Attaching or prefixing the adjective "religious" to such significance would find its Indian equivalents in the terms *dharma* (duty, order, religion) and *karma* (cause and consequence), two sides of the same reality.

17. In some texts, there are seven Manus (and even seven creations and floods).

weakened. Indeed, if anything, the preoccupation seems to have grown ever stronger and more sophisticated with every passing century.[18] As a result, historical knowledge about the genesis of the ranking and structuring of all species of birth (*jāti*-s), branches of descent (*vamsha [vamsa]:* Sanskrit; or *vamca:* Tamil), and categories *(varna)* of mankind became the central theme into which virtually all other stories had to be woven.

At its very root, therefore, the business of remembering or understanding past events served the purpose of validating biogenetic or biosocietal *division* and of applying procedures for careful social *discrimination*. First, all of mankind proper — excluding monkeys, untouchables, and other four-limbed creatures[19] — had to be carefully divided and then subdivided. By birth and descent, there was a line drawn between those who were noble *(aryas)* and those who were ignoble and servile *(dāsyas)*. It seems clear that later, stemming directly from accretions both to the *Rig-Veda* itself and also to the social system, there came a further rationalizing and refracturing of the Cosmic Order *(Dharma)*. This was reflected in the anecdotal song-story of Purusha: Prajapati, Lord of People (society), made a sacrifice *(yajna)* out of parts of his own body. Organically distinct and separate categories (*varnas:* colors) came out of different parts of his body: from his mouth came the all-knowing, word-sounding *brahmanas* (*varna* [color]: white); from his arms came the brave and valiant *kshatriyas* (*varna:* red); from his thighs came the calculating and productive *vaisiyas* (*varna:* yellow/gold); and from his feet came the hard-laboring and servile *shudras* (*varna:* black). These symbols, whether anatomical or abstract, represented ranks of ritual purity and biological origins, each with its own

18. Thus, just as Egyptians perfected sciences and arts of necrology, as seen in the Book of the Dead and in techniques of mummification and preservation, so in India it was "purity of breath" (life itself) and "purity of birth" (origins) that were traced back to earliest cosmic beginnings.

19. A large proportion, perhaps a fourth or fifth of what would today be considered to qualify as having any part within humankind, seem to have been excluded. These were all those within the "fifth" (or *panchama*) *varna* (or color-code/category). Elements born into that level were seen as so impure, so polluting, that they could not be included. These were the ancestors of what are now "*dalit*" (broken/smashed) or "untouchable" castes. Also originally excluded were those of the servile fourth category, the *shudras*. A. L. Basham, *The Wonder That Was India* (London: Sidgwick & Jackson, 1955), 143-46.

fixed and set hereditary functions. Brahmans produced this fourfold structuring of mankind into a "color-coded" system *(varnāshram-ādharma)* of ranked birth groups *(jati-s)*. Peoples of the top three categories were considered "pure" and/or "twice-born" *(dvija)*. Peoples in lower categories (either black or "colorless") were polluting and "once-born" or worse.[20]

Birth *(jāti:* caste) and descent *(vamsa)* determined all. Each "color" defined a separate class, a separate strata. Within each strata there were many other separate, altogether distinct birth groups *(jatis:* or ethnic communities) — what we now know as castes[21] — each of which sought to preserve its own intrinsic identity by resorting to increasingly strict rules. Over centuries beyond counting, rules gradually became so strict and tight that, eventually, members from families within one "pure" or "respectable" caste could neither intermarry nor even interdine with members of families from any other caste. To violate family and caste rules was to invite the most dire of consequences (e.g., expulsion or death). Moreover, since each of these castes was completely distinct from all others, at least in legends, stories, and theories about its birth and lineage, it can hardly have been strange that each viewed itself and was viewed by others as a completely distinct biological life-form (or species). (Nobody today really knows how many birth groups or castes there are that will neither intermarry nor interdine. Rough estimates put the number as high as three thousand.)

The highest category or *varna* of castes, being an expression of the very breath of "God" *(Brahman)*, possessed those godlike qualities most closely associated with divine and wondrous powers of cosmic breath: powers of language and rationality, magic and spirituality, ritual fire and sacrifice. The next highest strata, having also descended from divine ancestry — tracing lineages back to the Sun or the Moon — possessed such purity of blood and such virtues of valor, including courage and

---

20. This, probably stemming out of the original twofold division mentioned above, may originally have been less than fourfold. Thus, for example, only Aryan rulers *(rajanyas,* as forerunners of *kshatriyas)* and *brahmans* may have been the original "twice-born," while all other peoples over whom they ruled were beyond the pale. Another or third "twice-born" class could have been added later.

21. This, coming from *casta* and meaning "breed," is a legacy of the Portuguese. It reflects their being the earliest Europeans *(Farāngis)* to have made their presence felt along the coasts, and in the courts of rulers.

skill in martial arts and political sciences, that there could be no dis-
puting their divinely ordained role upon earth. For both of these highest
*varnas*, rules of marriage and descent and succession *(vamsa)* were so
important that violation was unthinkable.[22] The third *varna*, being
"gold" *(varna:* yellow), consisted of all those whose "birth" *(jat)* made
them exceptionally well qualified for banking, commercial, and industrial enterprise. Birth qualified people of this *varna*, called *vaishiyas*,
to be the entrepreneurs who produced the material goods and services
of the world. Below them, in the "black" *varna*, were all those castes
whose genetic coding qualified them for physical labor, manual service,
and toil. Finally, beyond the pale and altogether outside the *varna* system
were those who were so low, so polluting, and so untouchable that they
did not qualify to be or do anything. This "colorless" *varna*, usually
consisting of backward aboriginals *(ādivāsis)* and savage forest peoples,
was fit for nothing more than carrying out "night soil," sweeping up
dirt, and scavenging in rubbish.

Yet, however pervasive idealized and stereotyped *varnāshramadharma* became, it is important to remember that this was a Brahmanical
construction and a Brahmanical vision of social realities. Moreover, the
influence of this vision, powerful as it undoubtedly seems to have been,
was far from total. There is plenty of evidence to show that, however much
fear their magic might inspire, Brahmans were constrained by and subject
to the power of ruling families in each locality. Kings, nobles, and warriors,
notwithstanding awesome cultural power held by Brahmans, normally
maintained positions of material, political, and military superiority. While
Brahmans quite understandably put themselves at the top of the ranking
system which they themselves had created, the two categories of elite
power were mutually interdependent. One could not function without
benefits provided by the other. Moreover, especially in South India, where

---

22. Basham, *The Wonder That Was India.* Philip Woodruff, in *Call the Next Witness*
(London: Jonathan Cape, 1945), describes the *kshatriya* ethos prevailing in Rajasthan.
See also Lawrence Babb, *The Divine Hierarchy* (New York: Columbia University Press,
1975); Louis Dumont, *Homo Hierarchicus: The Caste System and Its Implications* (Chi-
cago: University of Chicago, 1970; rev. ed., 1980 [from French original edition in 1966]);
Morris G. Carstairs, *The Twice Born* (Bloomington: Indiana University Press, 1961), and
critique by D. F. Pocock in vol. 5 of *Contributions to Indian Sociology*, ed. Veena Das
(New Delhi: Sage, 1961); and Adrian Mayer, *Caste and Kinship in Central India* (London:
Routledge, 1960).

attribution of proper *kshatriya* status was much more scarce and thinly spread, restricted mainly to a few great imperial dynasties (e.g., Cheras, Cholas, Pandiyas, Pallavas, and such), ruling families had little doubt about their own intrinsic worth or about the sacred heritage of their lineages which entitled them to their legacies of political lordship, whether over village or kingdom. This was true even though Brahmans attributed to most of the warrior peoples and lords no more than fourth *varna* status within their ranking system. Even in the north, when the cultural power and social status eventually fell, at least outside of the great pilgrimage centers, so that some were seen to be of much lower purity and quality than Brahmans of the south, the ruling families themselves continued to know how to maintain those historical understandings about themselves which were vital to the maintenance of their elite status as nobles, rulers, and warriors.

Whatever the case, rules of proper order *(dharma)*, were absolute and of crucial importance to the positions of any dominant elite. And these were, on the whole, the special preserve of the Brahmans. Brahmans, as the great interpreters of events out of the past, told about how things had gone very wrong and how damages beyond calculation had come from violations of *dharma*. Neither Cosmic Order (*Dharma:* i.e., Religion) itself, nor that individual or family duty *(dharma)* to which one was uniquely born, could ever be tampered with — certainly not with impunity. Therefore, rules of exclusion were meant to make sure that damage-control measures went into operation at the slightest sign of danger. One's family *karma* was inextricably linked to one's own *dharma*.[23]

Lessons about what had happened (or could have happened) came out of a profusion of anecdotes and story cycles *(akhyānas)*. Vena, the mythic king, had to be killed because of his wicked rule and his failure to perform the proper ritual (family) sacrifice. His successor, Nisada, was too incompetent and had to be removed from the throne. The sages (*rīshis*) had finally been obliged to bring another *raja* to power who was righteous. This ruler, Prithu, had done so well that the earth, personified in the goddess Prithvi, had given him her name.[24] Through such anec-

---

23. These could be seen as two sides of the same coin.
24. Louis Dumont, "Origin Myths and Theories of Kingship," in *Religion, Politics and History in India: Collected Papers in Indian Sociology* (Paris and The Hague: Mouton Publishers, 1970), 70-88, esp. 72-73.

dotes, the origins of political differentiation, generating extreme skills of discrimination and exclusivity between high-born lineages, could be explained by one generation to the next, for generations beyond counting. Historical details were embedded in *puranic* texts. Containing anecdotes of all sorts, embodied in legend, myth, saga, and story, these texts not only conveyed information of "how things happened" *(itihasa)* during generations long gone, but also provided materials with which later generations could question and challenge earlier understandings. If later versions went so far as to replace earlier versions with "better" views of the past, such revisions served to mirror earlier institutions and to reflect the character of contemporary institutions which were being "corrected" (even if this may not have been the aim of such revisions).

Myths seem to have served as major devices by which, out of necessity, families or groups of families (lineages) of disparate origin could legitimize new kinds of relationships with each other. It was a way to "fabricate" facts so that historical understandings could be made to match political realities. However fabricated, such devices enabled a fusion or integration of hitherto only vaguely related elite families. In this way distant "twigs and branches" might also be drawn together and then linked to the branches and trunks and roots of common origin. Anecdotes about common origins, with ritual formulas of recitation, served to weld common assumptions about the realities and verities of the world. They served, gradually, to broaden and strengthen the frameworks of power by which local families (dynasties) could cement a mosaic of domination across the vast Indo-Gangetic plains of North India.

The senior Iksvāku Lineage — known as the Suryavamsa or Solar-Line-of-Succession — traced itself back to mythical origins in this way. By such means, a tightly knit pattern of sibling-linked marriages among various *kshatriya* families seems to have occurred. Many of these seem to have been local *rajas* who had prevailed and thrived during the earliest times. Yet, it also seems doubtful, because of what later would certainly have been seen to have incestuous implications, that such arrangements as this could originally have been done by means of proper performances of brahmanical ritual. Whatever the case, the earliest (mythic) marriages of these lineages were seen to have led to the birth of sixteen pairs of twins. A ritualized number of royal families seems to have been produced through mathematical sets of ritual doublings ($2 \times 2 = 4$; $2 \times 4 = 8$; $2 \times 8 = 16$; $2 \times 16 = 32$ — or 16 pairs of children). Lineages stemming from these sixteen original "branches" then served, forever after, as markers for the outer boundaries of purity by which the legitimacy of marriages and rituals within the lineage could be determined. Whatever the historicity of this origin, the story itself became the mode of proper *itihasa*. It served to validate a timeless, cosmic identity and understanding, which then served the purpose of legitimatizing later Iksvāku successions. Purity of blood is what seems to have become crucial.

Similar kinds of mythic "memory" about the past became *the* carefully preserved legacy, not only for the Suryavamsha and the Chandravamsha lineages, but also of any family having dynastic aspirations or pretensions. The same kind of formula was repeated, with variations, throughout the subcontinent. Indeed, such formulas were also used by any and all successions to rightful leadership within sectarian institutions, whether large or small. Both leader/teacher *(guru)* and disciple/student *(chela, sishya)* would continually, often daily, recite the institutionalized "lineage" *(vamsa)* and "tradition" *(parambaram)* of the ideology *(sampradāya)* held by the corporate "body" or "society" *(sangham)* of the "family" *(jat-paravan)* to which a person belonged and into which that person would become a properly initiated and properly legitimized member. History and "cosmic order" (religion: both as *dharma* and as *yajna* or "sacrifice"), in this as in all kinds of situations, became so mutually interdependent that one was embedded within the other.

## B. Eulogies and Epics

From the earliest of times, out of the mists of antiquity from whence the Aryan presence in India emerged, rituals *(puja-s)* and sacrifices *(yajna-s)* had always been — and indeed, long continued to be — the focal points of historical rememberings and understandings. It was during such events that occasions occurred for songs *(stuti)* and eulogies *(prasashti* or *gathā)*, for presentations of endowments and gifts *(dana)*, for story cycles *(akhyāna)*, and for great epics *(kathā-s)* to be recited. Heroic deeds by larger-than-life beings, long-dead legendary figures, forbearers, sages, or "gods" had to be "breathed," in narrated and recited and sung forms. Over and over again, as one generation succeeded another, these would be repeated and expanded upon, with embellishments, interpolations, and accretions. Anecdotes, with fables and proverbs used to point out some immediately needed lessons of wisdom, remained central within this kind of historical tradition.

"Thus it was" *(itihāsa)* that the primordial moral man, whose name was Pururava, and the originally celestial woman, Urvasi, were brought together in marriage. They were the beings who became the ancestors of the Chandravamsa, or "Moon Lineage." From this lineage came the royal and noble *(rajanya)* dynasties and the related warrior families. No genealogy of a properly self-respecting elite family could be given which did not hark back to the ritual sounds, as made by chanting brahmans, by which they linked themselves to the Bharatas, Purus, Kurus, or to some other hoary family whose name might be found in the most ancient texts, if not within the *Rig-Veda,* at least in the *Sathapatha Brahmana.* From these texts, each family might then trace itself, through interpolations, into the great epics: the *Rāma-Kathā* or the *Bharat-Kathā.* Successors of these epics, in turn, eventually turned into those mammoth epics, those ritualized monuments, always consisting of eighteen volumes, which are now known almost universally as the *Ramāyana* and the *Mahabharata.*

All past events found in these great epics had originally been centered in great sacrifices. Whether centered in the great Fire Sacrifice or the Horse Sacrifice, or some other sacrifice, the stories that emerged out of these epics themselves became sacred objects; and, hence, the preservation of their magic power as epitomized in "breathed" utterances was crucial. The smallest detail of poetic syllable and sound — in every tiniest hint of tone, tune, and tempo, especially within poetic *(kāvya)* form — not only became a matter of cosmic significance but also contained elements of cosmic and sacred power.[25] Stress was upon exactness. This, in and of itself, was a sufficient inducement. "Embedding" details reflecting every absolute essential of accuracy and continuity in historical un-

25. Indeed, since cosmic and magic power was attached to sound, the slightest, smallest mispronunciation could have dire consequences of an adverse nature, both for the ritualist as well as for the family for whom a ritual was being celebrated. It was for this reason that ritual specialists (*brahamanas,* as the very breath and essence of cosmic and divine power) were required.

derstanding could hardly be avoided. Because descent and lineage were so all-important and exactitude so crucial for proper performance of ritual sacrifices, it was necessary for the sounds themselves to be pronounced and made explicit in no uncertain terms and with utmost care. A prescribed pattern of strict differentiation, and of even stricter exclusion, prevailed. Any family that did not measure up to prescribed standards of blood purity found itself expelled and shunned. The whole ranking order *(varnashramadharma)* had to be stated and restated, over and over again. To make sure it was right, this had to be done with exactly arranged mnemonic and rhythmic patterns of repetition. The slightest variation could lead to disaster — namely to exclusion and expulsion from rank and status. This would come not through any centralized political or ecclesiastical institutions, but through every conceivable form of ostracizing, or shunning, in the form of anti-polluting socioritual apartheid.

The events out of which the greatest epics arose are about tragedy. They are about what happened when *dharmic* rules were violated. In the case of the *Mahabharata,* a chain of dire events occurred which ultimately led to a huge "world" war. What had taken place on the great northern plains, near Kurukshetra (not far from modern Delhi), was an enormous struggle. It had all begun with avoidable and silly quarrels. The Pandava brothers and the Kaurava brothers had slowly and inexorably turned their petty disagreements into a bloodbath of unprecedented and vast proportions. Cousins and relatives from common family lineages, anyone and everyone who could be mustered, had joined the battle. As the numbers of casualties mounted, with the heaps of dead and mournful wailing of women rising above the clash of arms, the heroic Arjun and his charioteer, later identified as the divine Lord Krishna, had a momentous dialogue. They discussed how or why it was that such a terrible thing could ever have come about and what steps might yet be taken to restore peace, justice, and order *(dharma).* It is this talk, this smallest of portions within the huge epic, which is known today as the *Bhagavad Gita* (or "Song of the Lord"). For many people, the *Bhagavad Gita* still represents both history and sacred writ; moreover, its lessons serve as a guide both to piety and to purity.[26]

26. Not to be confused with the *Bhāgavad Purana,* which is much more exclusively concerned with the deeds of the god Krishna, the *Bhagavad Gita* is readily available, in English translation, in almost any bookshop.

The *Ramāyana*, on the other hand, concerns usurpation — and fidelity. Rāma, the legitimate and proper and righteous successor to the throne of Ayodhya, was deprived of his birthright and driven from his rightful domain by an evil usurper. He suffered many hardships during many years of wandering. In dark forests he encountered demonic and evil forces. His ever faithful wife Sita was abducted and taken off by Ravana, the ruler of Sri Lanka. With "monkey people" (or folk of the *bandar-lok jati*) and their king, Hanuman, as his allies, Rāma was able to conquer Sri Lanka. Ravana was defeated and Sita rescued. Eventually restored to his rightful place as king of Ayodhya, Rāma's reign remains one epitomizing a utopian "reign of righteousness" *(rājadharma)*. This epic, despite all its fanciful and moralistic, even sentimental and "soap-opera" features and interpolations, has been perceived in India as providing "historical" understandings about the past. However, many have believed that it rests upon a bedrock of understandings about events that actually took place. As with many epics, the question of where to draw a line between fact and fancy has remained. Few in India do not know something about the *Ramāyana* and fewer still doubt the historicity of its core. Its emotive appeal, moreover, can hardly be underestimated, as recent events in Ayodhya show.

## C. Family Succession: Lists or Genealogies

Falling along a gradient between what we today perceive as facts about the past that are "internalized" (or "embedded") and what we today consider elements of "externalized" (or "empirical") historicity, as also between strong oral traditions and written texts, were the *itihāsa-purānas*. These gradually acquired a status comparable to that of a "fifth Veda."[27] That is, even as oral (and bardic) traditions were evolving over

27. *Veda,* meaning "knowledge" or "understanding," is the name given to the most ancient body of what in the West might have been canonized as "sacred writ," which the Aryans brought with them into India, or developed after their arrival. From the Vedas came the Brahmanas (Commentaries), Aranyakas (Forest Sayings), and Upanishads (Contemplations: philosophical or theosophic interpretations). These, together, constitute *Smriti,* or Received Sound (comparative to Revelation). The first, or original, Veda is the *Rig-Veda*. Springing from this, in successive streams, are the *Sāma-Veda,* the *Arthava-Veda,* and the *Yājur-Veda*.

many centuries and before they were finally compiled and much later, in some measure, "fixed" in written form, *puranic* texts came to be looked upon as forms of hallowed (or quasi-sacred: *srūti*) text.

Genealogies or succession lists within *puranic* texts, which had previously been used merely to formalize older materials, were manipulated. They were used to perform new functions and to do so in different ways. The appropriating of bardic materials, putting oral information about the past into fresh literary forms, was, by itself, nothing new. Similar kinds of appropriation had previously occurred within the textual codifications of all the Vedic traditions. Nor could the Brahmans *(brahmanas)*, as priests and ritualists, have been blind to the controlling possibilities of turning oral information about the past to new uses (within literary forms which were exclusively their own). Virtually each and every *purana* contained at least one succession list or genealogy, known as a *vamśānu-ćarita*. Such lists traced the lineages of various kinds of political, religious, or social elites as corporate entities — dynastic rulers, important families, teachers of texts, disciples of learned or sectarian traditions, leaders of religious movements and organizations (*sangha*-s), newly rising ancestral groups, and virtually any other family, caste, or group seeking to legitimize its claims by linking itself to the hoariest and most exalted or famous events of the past. Less obvious, but still evident within each formal genealogy, would be information about ceremonials, marriages, kinship networks, landholding arrangements, migrations, and much more.

Romila Thapar argues that "The historical epicentre of the *itihāsa* tradition was the *vamśānucarita* which, as the name suggests, was the genealogy of all the known lineages and dynasties up to the mid-first millennium A.D."[28] Each "succession history" *(vamśānu-ćarita)* section within a *puranic* text contained two or three parts: first, a mythical part which went back to the rule of Manu (or, perhaps, to the seven Manus) which had been swept away by the Flood; second, another (one or two) parts detailing the generations of descent from Iksvāku and Aila into the Suryavamsa and the Chandravamsa. The senior or Suryavamśa line was recorded only from eldest son to eldest son and seems, by its resort to primogeniture, to suggest more tightly controlled systems of monarchical succession. The junior line, being more segmented and assimila-

---

28. Thapar, "Society and Historical Consciousness," 365-66.

tive, branched off in different directions from its root, thereby seeming
to suggest the possibility of more innovative interactions and alliances
with entrenched families in various localities. Since the assimilative
features of these succession lists covered many centuries, with both
invasions and migrations occurring and recurring, these lists would
seem to indicate processes of intermittent political, ritual, and social
accommodation.

By means of such lists as these, newer ruling families were apparently assimilated and legitimized within older lineages: some ruling
families from among the Shāka (Sythian), Yāvana (Bactrian or Indo-
Greek), Kushāna, Hūna (Hun), and other powerful invaders who had
entered the continent; and some families of ruling chieftains from
among powerful forest peoples (now often lumped together under a
single category called *adivasi* (or aboriginal peoples) with whom it was
sometimes necessary to come to terms. Both kinds of assimilation, while
often interrupted, seem never to have stopped, whatever claims to the
contrary were being made. The *vamśānu-carita* portions of puranic
literature, therefore, served as a device for preserving a record of social
and political relations among important local families. However, even
in serving as a method of legitimizing "outsiders" who had recently
entered an area and acquired local power, this section of each *purana*
recorded the names of rising newcomers and their families only when
proper performances of sacrifices had been made by Brahman ritualists
and only if ceremonies were described. Without such actions being
entered into the historical record, no new family could expect to find
its name entered into the sacred text.

In all of this, just as the great Flood served as *the* great marker for
the genesis of family roots, so too the Mahabharata War served as
another great marker. Each event marked the ending of one epoch and
the beginning of another. Family purity could never again be quite the
same as it had been before. As each new layer of assimilation and
legitimation was recorded and reflected in the texts, there could be no
absolute or fool-proof way of telling how or where processes of adul-
teration and lineal corruption would end. Indeed, as each category,
subcategory, and sub-subcategory of lineage reflected layers of dominant and subordinate political, ritual, and social status, layer by layer,
there seems to be no doubt that some tainting and tampering took place.
Even certain *shūdra* families of great power and strength, having ac-

quired power and rulership, could manage to creep into the record. This was especially possible in South India. Here Brahman functionaries of one sort or another, whether as administrative officials or as priestly ritualists or as learned scholars, had long ago denied those warrior and ruling castes which dominated the agrarian countryside in each area any *vārna* rank higher than that of *śhūdra*. Here there had rarely, if ever, been any rulers of genuinely *kshatriya* status, meaning that, being Aryan, they could trace their lineage to a *vamća* of the sun or moon. It was in the south, after all, that one found demon-kings, such as Ravana, and monkey-kings, such as Hanuman, neither having legitimate claims to succession within an Aryan lineage. From a South Indian perspective, or from a perspective of rulers in Sri Lanka or across the seas in Java, Rāvanna becomes the tragic and heroic king whose realm was con-quered by a cruel northern invader, Rama. This "upside-down" *Ramāyana* could, in the eyes of southerners or island rulers, be cele-brated as the *Rāvannāyana*. But all such corrupting and downward developments could only remind Aryans that this age was, after all, the Darkening Age *(Kali Yuga)*.

## D. Family Chronicles and Family Biographies

As if there could never be enough validation of understandings from the past to satisfy those who ruled, an even newer set (or category) of texts began to develop in the post-Gupta period (perhaps from about A.D. 600 onwards). This consisted of two complementary forms of historical understandings: the *ćarita* (or *chāritra*) and the *vamśāvali*.

The first was a form of biographical writing. Drawing upon an earlier form of eulogy known as *praśāsti*, the *ćarita* was unashamedly panegyric in its content. Even so, it described understandings of the life of an individual in considerable and exact detail. Such detail served to explain how one person's family had risen to new positions of power and rulership over some particular territorial domain and how this could not have occurred had not that one person made some crucial contributions to bring that power and rulership into being. The impor-tance of taking great pains to remember the special role and status of such a person in the establishment of a family's high position of power, rank, and status seems to have provided, in and of itself, sufficient justification for the producing of a written record. The best-known and perhaps the earliest example of such writing is the *Harshacharitra,* by Banabhatta. But Bana's work, whether it set a pattern or followed a pattern already well worn about which we have no evidence, was certainly followed by many similar kinds of work. As a genre of writing about understandings of the past, works of this kind reached their highest expression between the eighth and twelfth centuries. But, even thereafter, works of this kind continued to be produced.

The second new form was the *vaṃśāvali.* This, as its name implies, was a chronicle. But it was not just a chronicle about an individual, nor a chronicle just about a family, nor even a chronicle of noble birth (succession purity and/or descent within lineage), although it was all of that. Rather, it was a chronicle concerning all of the things that controlled a family. Expressed in somewhat different terms, this was a chronicle of understandings about the domains, territories, or possessions which had been controlled by one particular family or dynasty. However large or small that domain or kingdom or empire might be, in all of its parts and particles, the function of the *vaṃśāvali* was to make such matters clear. For its source materials, this kind of chronicle drew upon all sorts of varied oral traditions and all sorts of local (*sthala,* or "place") histories (*purānas*). These kinds of records could be found within the areas controlled by the family (*vāmsa*) in question. These local records provided a rich profusion of source materials out of the past, of those kinds just described above. The very existence of such materials made a great difference to perceptions of the past.[29] A much different quality of understandings about the past emerges from such materials. Yet, in virtually all such chronicles, it is the eternal and timeless purity, the verity and worth of the family itself, and relations between that worth and the legitimizing of its authority

---

29. "The sources drawn upon by the authors of the *vamćāvalis* included the *sthala-puranas, upa-puranas, tirtha-puranas,* caste or *jāti-puranas,* and *mahātmyas,* all of which were texts recording the past and the evolution of places, sects and deities, locations of pilgrimage, dominant castes and local history. Such texts were part of the larger Puranic tradition and, although conforming to the major *puranas,* in spirit if not in form, included a large amount of local and regional data. The oral sources consisted of bardic fragments and ballads on local heroes and events of significance, not to mention the genealogies and marriage-alliances of land-owning families, for the bardic tradition was still alive, and remains to this day." Thapar, "Society and Historical Consciousness," 380, n. 48.

and power over a particular territorial domain that was always of central concern to those whose names (and lineages) were to be found within these materials.

## E. Classicity and the Standard of Timeless Order

Recent scholarship has tended to challenge the view commonly held among modern historians that the *Rajatarangini* by Kalhana,[30] now sometimes known as the Kashmir Chronicle, is the only example of a "genuine" historical understanding that India ever produced, or that the only other work in South Asia which modern scholars could consider as having comparable quality was the *Mahavamsha* of Sri Lanka.[31] Revisions of older judgments and questions about the appropriateness of what we know about how understandings of the past were handled in classical India — that is, of historical understandings anywhere within the subcontinent before the arrivals of Islam and the West — are coming increasingly into vogue.[32] Scholars in the past generation have attempted to show that the conclusions drawn from achievements of previous scholarship were erroneous and that older views can now be discounted, if not altogether discredited. The uncovering of numbers of chronicles written about the Chalukya rulers of Gujarat during the period from A.D. 940 to 1305 and disclosures of similar chronicle traditions in other parts of the subcontinent have served to reinforce changing views of how understandings of the past developed before the com-

30. Edited by M. A. Troyer (Calcutta, 1840; Paris, 1890); English translation by J. C. Dutt (Calcutta, 1887; reprinted 1979); by M. A. Stein (Bombay, 1892), with English translation (Westminster: A. Constable, 1900; reprinted 1960); and English translation by R. S. Pandit (Allahabad, 1935). In addition, mention can be made of the *Dvitiya Rajatarangini* by Jonaraja (c. 1434); the *Tritiya Rajatarangini* by Srivara Pandita (c. 1489); and the *Chaturthi Rajatarangini* by Prajyabhatta and Suka. First, second, third, and fourth versions are described in some detail by A. K. Majumdar, "Sanskrit Historical Literature and Historians," *Journal of World History* 6, no. 2 (1992): 288-92.

31. A. L. Basham, "The Kashmir Chronicle," in *Historians of India, Pakistan and Ceylon,* ed. C. H. Philips (Oxford: Oxford University Press, 1961), 57ff.

32. Arrivals which, in some parts, have yet to occur. What is involved in this kind of formulation is a tacit recognition that spacial and temporal differentials need to be recognized when looking at the impacts of the "arrivals" of different cultural understandings about the nature of events and historical understandings.

ing of Islam.[33] These more recent findings about the nature of earlier kinds of historical understanding are now being used to argue that classical understandings of the past in India came closer to, or even ran parallel with, those of other classical traditions. This is seen as being especially so, for example, with respect to preoccupation with the politics of cities and kingdoms, as these developed within other classical civilizations. Since such views of historiographic revision were produced over twenty years ago, however, much more radical revisions have occurred.[34] (These newest perspectives and arguments are more fully examined in chapter 10.)

Nevertheless, the central question under consideration here needs to be answered: namely, in what way did historical understandings in ancient (or pre-Islamic) India reflect and respond to standards embedded within the classical tradition(s) of India? How, in other words, did classical standards serve as the criteria by which understandings of the past were acquired, preserved, recorded, and shaped? Answers to this question are neither simple nor straightforward. Two approaches, as possible answers, are suggestive or insightful.

One of these approaches, made by a historian over thirty years ago, argues for the presence of a critical "scientific spirit in Ancient India," without answering the question directly. In describing, in some detail, exactly how a rational spirit of free inquiry in India triumphed over mythology, theological belief, and popular superstition, R. C. Majumdar concludes that "[t]his spirit at first took the form of philosophic speculations into the origin of the universe, but soon led to the growth of sciences by observation of natural phenomena, collection and classification of data, practical experiments and formulation of general laws."[35]

More recently, another approach has been made by a Sanskritist. Sheldon Pollock argues for the application of the classical discipline of critical interpretation or investigation (*Mīmāmsa*) to descriptions

---

33. A. K. Majumdar, "Sanskrit Historical Literature and Historians," 293-301; and *Chalukyas of Gujarat* (Bombay: Bhavatiya Vidya Bhavan, 1956).

34. A. K. Warder, *Introduction to Indian Historiography* (Bombay: Popular Prakasham, 1972); J. P. de Souza and C. M. Kulkarni, eds., *Historiography in Indian Languages* (Delhi: Vikas, 1972). See also works by D. D. Kosambi and Harbans Mukhya.

35. R. C. Majumdar, "Scientific Spirit in Ancient India," *Journal of World History* 6, no. 2 (1992): 265-73.

of past events *(Itīhāsa)*.[36] But having done so, he answers the question in a rather oblique way, redefining both the ontology and the epistemology of past events so that historical understandings can be viewed in different ways. By suggesting an obliteration of the distance between historical narrative and literary narrative, as also between fact and fiction, and by questioning the sense of historicity in all classical cultures but especially in Greco-Roman antiquity, he argues that "the historicity of human existence was cognized, appropriated, and processed in traditional India as elsewhere," but that this was done by means of "a special modality, and subject to categories, ideas, and constraints peculiar to traditional India, the result being that the 'historiographical' end-products often differ from what we encounter elsewhere in antiquity."[37]

Here is where the critical standard that comes into play as a criterion for judging past events is classical discipline *(Mīmāmsā)*. This is that which makes the authority and verity of any and all *knowledge* (Veda) "dependent on its timelessness."[38] Particular events among families and persons, in other words, must be linked to their relationships with "beginninglessness" and "endinglessness," where matters of ultimate purity and worth lie. The logic of events and their linkage with *dharma/karma* becomes crucial to understandings of events. Thus, if "*dharma* is stipulatively defined, or rather posited without argument, as a transcendent entity, and so is unknowable by any form of knowledge not itself transcendent" and if "all cognitions must be accepted as true unless and until they are falsified by other cognitions," then grounds for knowing *dharma* by means of "any cognitive act based upon perception" are eliminated.[39] Pollock's argument is that, since the "Vedas were emptied of 'referential intention,'" other sorts of Brahmanical effort had "to suppress the evidence

36. Sheldon Pollock, "*Mīmāmsā* and the Problem of History in Traditional India," *Journal of the American Oriental Society* 109 (1988): 603-10. Also, "Problems of Historicity in South Asian Thought," unpublished paper prepared for SSRC/ACLS, Iowa City, September 1988.

37. Pollock, "*Mīmāmsā* and the Problem of History," 606.

38. Gerald Larson, "Karma as a 'Sociology of Knowledge' or 'Social Psychology of Process/Praxis,'" in *Karma and Rebirth*, ed. Wendy O'Flaherty [Doniger] (Berkeley: University of California Press, 1980), 305.

39. Pollock, "*Mīmāmsā* and the Problem of History," 607.

of their own historical existence — a suppression that took place in
the case of *itihāsa*, 'history,' itself."[40] In short, Pollock feels that the
classical discipline using critical standard or measurement was really
a highly intricate and complex ideological outlook. This outlook in
classical India "privileged system over process — the structures of the
social order over the creative role of man in history — and that, by
denying the historical transformations of the past, den[ied] for the
future and thus served[d] to naturalize the present and its asymmetri-
cal relations of power."[41]

In other words, mental constructions and representations of illusion *(Māya)*, when viewed in the light of the Timelessness of Cosmic
Order *(Dharma/Karma)*, necessarily constrained both history as events
within time, or *Itihāsa* as events occurring within any one *Yuga:* each
*Yuga* having four parts, each consisting of exactly so many hundreds
of thousands of years; one hundred *Yugas* making one *Maha-Yuga;* one
hundred *Maha-Yugas* making one *Kalpa;* and one hundred *Mahā-Kal-
pas* in turn making something else, in a never-ending structure, a
context within which historical understandings of events *(itihāsa)* become all but insignificant and meaningless. How this standard of
classicity may be compared to other standards, such as that of Greece
(or China), is a question that we can pursue next.

## II: Classical Greece[42]

Ironically, even though our word *history* meaning "inquiry" (ιστορια:
*istoria*) together with much of our intellectual apparatus is inherited
from the ancient Greeks, the question about whether or not they
actually had much of a sense of history or even much appreciation for

---

40. Ibid., 609.

41. Ibid., 610.

42. The label "Greek" is not what they would have called themselves. Both
Herodotus and Thucydides wrote about "Hellas" and "Hellenes" as "our countrymen,"
"our common brotherhood," sharing a "common culture," "being of the same stock and
the same speech," and "our common shrines of the gods and rituals, our similar customs." *Herodotus* 1:1; 8:144. *Thucydides* 1:1-22. *Graeci* was the Roman name for them:
see M. I. Finley, *The Ancient Greeks* (1963; reprint, Harmondsworth, Middlesex: Penguin, 1981), 17.

the past is still a matter of debate.[43] From classical times to the present, scholars have been divided on this question. On one side are those who, throughout the centuries, have argued that ancient Greeks were the world's first historians. These call Herodotus the father of history and Thucydides the founder of scientific discipline and investigation. On the other side are those who, down through the ages, have emphasized the "a-historical" or "anti-historical tendencies" in Greek culture. They debunk the historical quality of works written by ancient Greeks. They call Herodotus the "Master of Liars."[44] There is enough substance in evidence and in the logic of arguments based thereon to support either of these points of view. Indeed, because both arguments carry weight, it is perhaps just as useful to suggest that they talk past each other and that, since both deserve some credence, the two positions need not be seen as inherently contradictory. We simply do not have enough information to resolve this apparent paradox.

The story of how the past was understood or how such understandings were generated in ancient Greece is, at best, confusing and complex. Moreover, since the earliest traces of such understandings have disappeared, our conclusions rest upon extremely fragmentary evidence. Yet, enough material has survived from the classical times that despite the huge destructions and losses that came in subsequent ages, scholars have been able to piece fragments together so as to make some reasonably significant and valid judgments.[45] For purposes of this analysis, moreover, one need not deal with or solve all of the many intricate technical problems related to fragments in order to gain insights into ways that ancient Greeks looked at the past.

43. Herbert Butterfield, *The Origins of History* (London: Methuen, 1981), 118-21.

44. M. I. Finley, introduction to *The Greek Historians* (New York: Viking Press, 1959); "Against Apion," in *Josephus* (Cambridge and London: Harvard University Press, 1926), 1:163-71; R. G. Collingwood, *The Idea of History* (London: Oxford University Press, 1946), 20-21.

45. Over the past century and a half, two series have been published: C. and T. Müller, *Fragmenta Historicum Faecorum,* 5 vols. (Paris: Didot, 1841-75); and Felix Jacoby, *De Fragmente der Griechischen Historiker,* 16 vols. (Leiden: E. J. Brill, 1923-58), seven volumes of text on some 856 fragments; nine of commentary on 607 more fragments, still in progress.

## A. *Catastrophe, Destiny, and Unpredictability*

To appreciate how Greeks in classical times might have looked at events, both in their own age or in previous ages, it is important for us to try to comprehend, in some small measure, those peculiar circumstances in their physical environment which might have affected them. Certain contextual features that might have been distinctive or even exceptional and that might have given a special texture to the cultural life of Greeks, whether as individuals or as communities, need to be investigated. But among those circumstances and developments which over many centuries might have influenced Greek ways of thinking, perhaps the most difficult to explain, at least with much satisfaction, are the combinations of factors that might have coincided with or "conspired" to bring about the rise of that most peculiarly complicated and most fascinating of all Greek achievements — namely, the growth of what we now call "intellectuality." At the heart of this intellectuality, perhaps the single most distinctive legacy of classical Greece was the growth of a special capacity for abstract, detached (or objective), and rational inquiry, a capacity that characterized all of the classical cultures (of China, India, and tiny Israel) in ancient times.

Appreciation of the influence of physical environment — of the geography of place, space, and climate — is a useful starting point, however cautiously one makes inferences.[46] Among these, perhaps the most obvious feature is the pervasiveness and ubiquity of shorelines. Scattered along and around thousands of miles of the ever-turning and twisting shorelines of the Aegean Sea, both along its peninsular mainlands and along its many islands, are countless inlets and coves. Behind these coastal pockets and ribbons of beach, the entire region abounds with sharply escarped mountain ridges and deep valleys; beyond these are occasional inland plains, usually not far from some seashore. Climates in each place varied greatly, depending upon altitude and latitude, proximity to water, or season of the year. Weather could also be unpredictable. Barriers of land and sea, mountain ranges to cross, and sea lanes to navigate made casual travel difficult and at times hazardous.

46. R. J. Hopper, "The Geographical Background," in *The Early Greeks* (New York: Barnes & Noble, 1976), 1-8; H. D. F. Kitto, "The Country," in *The Greeks*, rev. ed. (Harmondsworth, Middlesex: Penguin, 1979), 28-43.

The whole area, with its essential ruggedness of environment, could be a challenge. Here, indeed, was a ready-made nursery for seafaring and a laboratory for adventure and survival.

Going to sea, taken by itself, has always required some extra measure of daring, dexterity, and energy — not to mention some minimum of imagination, invention, and technology. And, while seafaring enterprises have offered excitements and rewards, this kind of activity could hardly take place without arousing a commensurable sense of considerable risk and uncertainty.[47] Available evidence seems to indicate that small and semi-isolated settlements developed in coves and inlets along the coasts; moreover, it also seems to show that, while some peoples penetrated inland and settled upon richer agricultural lands, "it was on the edge of the sea, not in the hinterland, that Greek civilization flourished."[48] Each of these settlements, it would seem, generated its own distinctive economy, culture, and historical legacy. Each, developing out of its own richly unique set of experiences, apparently preserved its own distinctive lore — customs and memories of important past deeds and events. Later, with increasing colonization of still more coves, inlets, and islands, contacts and conflicts between communities already inhabiting other coves and inlets, islands, and strong-points provided a context for ever-broadening cultural comparison, discovery, and exploration.

With increasing encounters, rising levels of conflict and strife also seem to have increased in frequency and complexity. And sometimes, with a rising incidence of adventure on land and sea accompanied by mounting levels of violence in various forms of brigandage and piracy, it is not unreasonable for us to imagine how a climate of insecurity and uncertainty may have grown more pervasive. Among peoples at all levels of society, whether they were noble or low-born, a tradition of periodic cataclysm and sudden destruction engendered such feelings. Skeletal remains of past settlements or relics and ruins of former glories, such as the oldest palace-fortresses and temples of Minoa and Mycenae show-

47. The poet Hesiod, in his *Works and Days*, mentions this while describing the basic institutions of the world, using animal fables and maxims to stress alternative costs of idleness or labor. M. P. Nilsson, *A History of Greek Religion* (Oxford: Clarendon Press, 1925), 181-87.

48. M. I. Finley, *The Ancient Greeks* (New York: Penguin, 1981), 17.

ing clear traces of violent destruction, may well have served to give
substance to this kind of uneasiness.[49]

But most important of all in Hellenic minds were the ruins at Troy
and the legends they evoked. Whatever had happened there was cloaked
in darkness and shrouded in mystery. It was the stuff of epic poem and
folk tale, telling of heroes and gods who once fought. Whatever had
happened to end the "Golden Age" of Minoan and Mycenaean over-
lordship, and whatever had happened to peoples of the whole area
before the fall of Troy, became a matter sharply demarcated from what
came after. In the minds of those who lived in later times, the "Golden
Age" could be distinguished from what happened just before and during
the "Dark Age," with its decline and obscurity.[50] A time of catastrophe
and chaos (c. 1200-1100 B.C.) might even have brought about the disappearance of literacy itself.[51]

What had happened in Greece at the fall of Troy and what happened long thereafter, dire as it apparently must have been, became an
abiding obsession. Preoccupation with this specific event remained
strong ever after. At deeper levels of feeling and thought, some sense of
the profound unpredictability of events seems to emerge from within
some of the oldest words that have survived out of the Greek past.
Unpredictability, so evident when one looks at the ruins left over from
past catastrophes, seems to have generated attitudes of profound pessi-
mism about life and uncertainty about the future. The pervasive sense
of a dark destiny and of foreboding, as also of tragedy, is found in much
of the epic and mythic literature. Nor can one forget, in this connection,

49. Nowhere is this sense of brooding, of impending catastrophe, or of disaster
more evident than in the epic myth about Oedipus, a tale arising out of blended folk
tales of Thebes and eventually set into the dramatic tragedy produced by Sophocles.
See M. P. Nilsson, *The Mycenaean Origin of Greek Mythology* (Berkeley and Los Angeles:
University of California Press, 1932; New York: W. W. Norton, 1963), 104-8.

50. Interestingly, while both Indic and Greek forms of classicity dwell upon the
"Dark Age" or *Kala Yuga*, their approaches and responses seem be quite opposite from
each other: one putting this firmly in the past, before which there had been a bright or
"Golden Age," the other putting emphasis upon a deepening of darkness and illusion
in the present and, logically, into the future, until total dissolution occurs and the whole
cycle repeats itself, doing so a hundred times to make up a *Kalpa*. Although I am open
to persuasion, entropy seems to be a stronger perspective in classical India than in
classical Greece.

51. R. J. Hopper, "Obscurity and Recovery," chap. 4 in *The Early Greeks*, 52-82.

that many of our words describing anxiety, doubt, and dark uncertainty — e.g., skepticism, stoicism, cynicism, despair, and other terms — are, in themselves, a continuing legacy of an outlook coming down to us out of Greek ideas and influences. Another possible consequence of brooding uncertainty may have been a consciousness of the individuality of each single soul. Each individual soul, attempting to reflect upon the meaning and purpose of inner doubt and pain, suffering and turmoil, could hardly avoid searching for less than obvious clues.

Whatever the case, we cannot explain how systems of abstract thinking began to develop during the classical age. Fear, pain, and suffering, as one is ever reminded (whether by the words of Job or of Samuel Johnson), can "wonderfully concentrate" the mind. Reactions to cataclysm and uncertainty can bring about, in minds of gifted individuals, inexplicable consequences. What caused minds in ancient Greece to generate such combinations of mental discipline, insight, reflection, and speculation we do not know. Centuries later (c. A.D. 94), a scornful Flavius Josephus remarked, "The land of the Greeks . . . has experienced countless catastrophes, which have obliterated the memory of the past; and as one civilization succeeded another, men of each epoch believed that the world began with them. They were late in learning the alphabet and found the lesson difficult."[52]

## B. Contradiction, Conceptualization, and Critique

Apparent contradictions and inherent uncertainties of life in ancient Greece, seldom facilitating neat or ready answers and often accompanied by agitation and anguish, seem to have prompted more than ordinary probings for answers. These seem to have led to elaborations and refinements in mental reconstruction. Out of the old anecdotes and fables about events came legends and myths, tales and stories — about mortals who were like gods and gods who were like mortals. Scholars, combining the mythical with the metaphorical, made various kinds of distinctions: between power and servility, tragedy and comedy, pathos and frivolity,

52. Ibid., 167. Thackeray's translation of William Whiston, *The Life and Works of Flavius Josephus* (Philadelphia: J. C. Winston, n.d.): "ten thousand destructions . . . blotted out memory of former actions. . . ."

fact and fancy, justice and injustice, liberty and bondage, free choice and destiny, things physical and things metaphysical, real and unreal, and forces seen and unseen. These are but a few of the intellectual polarities that began to emerge. Long after the Trojan War, critical comparisons and distinctions were made between specific events that had passed, as events in themselves, and understandings of past events, together with limitations in understandings of past events. In other words, critical "history," as an intellectual "inquiry" into the details of events, seems to have begun to come into being.

Intellectual developments, apparently begun during the age when the brilliant Minoan-Mycenaean cultures were at their zenith, do not seem to have entirely disappeared during the dark ages that followed. Even during successive and seemingly endless periods of darkness and strife, when counter-intrusions followed intrusions and when local communities inflicted violence upon each other, a capacity for combining abstract and concrete thinking seems already to have started. Great thinkers of classical times did not, after all, suddenly appear, as if out of nowhere. Rather, it seems reasonable to presume that this propensity for acute observation and reflection and speculation, producing some of the most intellectual thinkers of all time, had been slowly developing. Such developments would seem to have started long before the eighth century B.C., when Homer and Hesiod are thought to have put together their own compilations of accumulated lore and when they rendered the feelings and ideas of previous ages into verse.

Thinking about times of periodic cataclysm, about events that had destroyed mankind, certainly became fixed within Greek tradition. They can be found at least from the time of Homer and Hesiod onwards. Not surprisingly, we find such thinking fully developed in Plato and Aristotle. In retracing steps by which, over and over again, survivors and their descendants had previously rebuilt civilizations, Aristotle could write, "they invented laws and all the bonds that link the parts of a city together; and this invention they called Wisdom. Such was the wisdom (in advance of physical science, *physika theoria,* and of the supreme Wisdom that is concerned with divine realities) that was given to the Seven Sages who invented the virtues suitable to a citizen."[53]

53. From a fragment of a now lost dialogue, *On Philosophy,* found in Jean-Pierre Vernant, "The Crises of the City: The Earliest Sages," chap. 5 of *The Origins of Greek*

Observable repetitions in the course of events, while not seen as possessing that steady regularity that marked the ebb and flow of the great river of Egypt, could still be envisaged in cyclical terms. Time, symbolized metaphorically as a serpent biting its own tail, was seen as linking cosmic processes of creation and destruction. So seen, each cycle of time ended with a catastrophe. In Orphic thought, time as *chronos* (or Chronos the deity),[54] as basic and elemental as earth and water, could "never grow old." Quite distinct from either Chaos or Ether, Time originated all things and it ended all things, including all things that live and think. Thereby, time also implied its opposite — timelessness: as an ultimate destiny, as a fulfillment of better things, as immortality, and as eternity.[55]

Perhaps as elusive as *chronos*, if not more so, was the Eleusian concept of *aeon*. Time as expressed in this concept (also previously conceived as a deity) seems to have been conceived as being both a force acting upon the cosmos from outside it and a regulating device acting upon the cosmos from within it. "Aeon in his divine nature remains always the same . . . and always keeps the order of the world the same — which is and was and will be — the beginning, the middle and has no end, having no part in change. He is the creator of eternal divine nature in all."[56] These and many other concepts, some mythical and others mystical or religious in origin, eventually found their way both into Greek philosophy and, as we shall see, into Greek history. Thus, for example, Plato could distinguish between real time *(chronos)* and ideal time *(aeon)*, one reflecting the other; and Aristotle could compare time

---

*Thought* (Ithaca, N.Y.: Cornell University Press, 1982; Presses Universitaires de France, 1962), 69. The seven sages, and famous aphorisms attached to their names, according to *Brewer's Dictionary of Phrase and Fable* (1985 edition), were (1) *Bias:* "Most men are bad"; (2) *Chilo of Sparta:* "Consider the end"; (3) *Cleobulus of Lindos:* "Avoid extremes" ("The Golden Mean"); (4) *Periander of Corinth:* "Nothing is impossible to industry"; (5) *Pitticus of Mitylene:* "Seize time by the forelock"; (6) *Solon of Athens:* "Know thyself!"; (7) *Thales of Miletus:* "Who hateth suretyship is sure."

54. Originally a god who, with the Titans, fought Zeus, but sometimes confused with Kronos, the father of Zeus. See Martin P. Nilsson, *A History of Greek Religion*, 2nd ed. (Oxford: Clarendon Press, 1949), 24.

55. Ibid., 215-16. See also G. J. Whitrow, *Time in History* (Oxford: Oxford University Press, 1988), 40.

56. Siegfried Herrmann, *Time and History* (Nashville: Abingdon Press, 1977), 116. Nilsson, *A History of Greek Religion*, 210-15.

*(chronos)* used for measuring change, movement, and variability with eternity, immutability, and timelessness *(aeon)*.[57] But how these two conceptions could be logically related to each other remained inscrutable, something difficult to fathom or to agree upon.

Quite obviously, a great gap lay between high peaks of cosmic or universal abstraction and lower-level, more earthbound descriptions of isolated phenomena or unique events. What ran counter to the natural order of things or what took place outside the normal pattern of expectations produced uncertainty and anxiety. All imponderables of existence were determined and fixed by *moira*. Moira, the blessed divine mother of all earthly order, held life and death in her hands. Even the anthropomorphic gods who might foresee future events and who might wish to strive against her could not alter the natural order. *Moira* made and unmade. She both established and fixed or destroyed and overturned. Each soul's time on earth (or fate) was set by her. Each person's destiny (fortune, fate, etc.), a seeming riddle of conflicting elements and forces as it was, was already beyond escape. Odysseus could never have escaped the dark forces that were ranged against him had not Athena come to his rescue.[58] Thus, Solon, one of the Seven Sages of Athens, declared, "Destiny *(moira)* brings both good and evil, so that even the tricks of immortal gods cannot be escaped."[59] Mortality was so certain, so inescapable, that morbidity and tragedy became fixations. Not until much later, in the Hellenistic period, did a brighter and more hopeful concept make its appearance and overturn the dark-haired *moira*.

Yet another concept for time, *kairos*, was much more limited, and eventually, linear. Meaning something like "point in time," "right moment," "segment [or set] of events," or "decisive turn," the concept seems to have signaled a clear break with bonded cycles of nature and a certain consciousness of particularity, peculiarity or uniqueness in specific events. *Kairos* was the Greek term that would later be constantly used by Jewish scholars in their translations. It was the word they would use for that most famous soliloquy on time, in Ecclesiastes (chapter 3). But in this text, quite clearly, time was no longer seen as any kind of pro-

57. *Timaeus*, by Plato; and *Physica*, by Aristotle. Whitrow, *Time in History*, 41-42, 46. Herrmann, *Time and History*, 117.

58. A. T. Murray, *Odyssey* (Cambridge: Harvard University Press, 1919), 2:436.

59. W. F. Otto, *The Homeric Gods* (New York: Octagon Books, 1954).

gression, whether cyclical or linear, so much as it was being recognized as a distinct and immediate moment or turning point; moreover, by then, *kairos* as such was being seen as a conjunction of earthly happenings with divine will. "Where there is no God," this definition indicated, "there also could be no kairos." It was only a simple, further step of logic before someone would begin to posit a concept of time completely free of any kind of fatalistic or deterministic superimposition.

It was Greek sages and thinkers themselves who, after the long recovery from another great dark age, began a new age of enlightenment. As expanding colonies and city-states again became powerful and wealthy, the penchant for hard and careful reflection about the uncertainties of life was awakened. The Greek diaspora spread far and wide across land and sea. Thinking it important to learn something about those with whom they dealt or those who were their overlords, they brought back ideas, information, and technological skills borrowed from older civilizations, especially from the great empires of Egypt, Babylon, and Persia. Significantly, nothing like this had ever been done before, at least in a systematic and thorough way. Under inspired Ionian leadership, a remarkably critical spirit of rational inquiry began to develop. Accepted assumptions were questioned and conventional answers doubted. Attention was focused not just upon the eternal and the timeless, but upon the most immediate and most particular of entities and events: details of earth and sky, human relations, and past events. A new and remarkable script, adapted from the Phoenician alphabet, became wonderfully adept, powerful, and even subtle — the ideal instrument for conveying precise ideas.[60] Ways of thinking also became more analytical, more intellectual, and systematic.

Rising seapower and wealth in turn led to the development of new technologies. Technologies of war, especially the deployment of heavily armed foot soldiers *(hoplites)* arranged in tightly locked formations *(phalanxes)* and of heavily armed, triple-decked warships *(triremes)*, were matched by technologies of peace. Systematic study in arts and sciences led to the making of laws and to the constructing of govern-

---

60. The same could also have been said for the *deva-nāgari* script of Sanskrit: its emphasis upon exactness of sound (tone, tempo, tune, etc.) being so demanding that, once developed, misspelling became impossible; and Panini, in consequence, is now seen as the inventor of the science of linguistics.

ments (and of diplomacy). These, in turn, enabled the "citizens" of
Athens and Sparta to react against tyranny and instability. In response
to times of violent turbulence, for so long the bane of Greek communities, structures of power were devised so as to make them more durable
and effective. To reduce uncertainties provoked by injustice and to maximize long-term security, each polity designed its own uniquely "abnor-
mal" structure.[61] A new and experimental kind of city-state *(polis)* came
into being, one in which rule of law rested upon carefully devised
constitutional and democratic principles and procedures.[62] At the same
time, Greeks of Ionia studied the manners and institutions of "alien"
peoples with whom they dealt, especially those, like the Lydians and
Persians, who might become dangerous. For that very reason, first serious attempts to write carefully and critically about past events, about
what had actually happened, were not so much about Greeks themselves
as about other peoples. As explained by Moses I. Finley, "It was the
Ionians, again, who first thought to ask questions in a systematic way
about the supposedly known facts, in particular about their meaning in
rational, human terms."[63]

## C. Classical and Critical Inquiries about Events

One need not grope too deeply to find a few historians who might have
come before Herodotus. Anaximander of Miletus, perhaps the first
writer in Greek prose, dared to examine the origins of events, studied
geography, and perhaps drew the earliest maps. Through critical analysis, he sought and stressed natural causes, attempting to do so by
rigorous observation and speculation. Hecataeus of Miletus, living
under the rule of Darius, produced a genealogy and a geography. In-

---

61. Hopper, *The Early Greeks,* 160-87. Dorian villages *(obai)* of Sparta's territory
answered, in times of war, to two kings; and in times of peace, to an assembly *(gerousia)*
of twenty-eight old men (age sixty or older), chosen by acclamation from a body of
citizens *(homoioi),* with five annual magistrates (*ephors* or "overseers") also elected each
year. Soldier-citizens became so through conduct and through membership in a common club or mess. The full-time citizen army, with its complex organization, depended
upon cultivation of their land, something which was done by slave-laborers *(helots).*

62. Cynthia Farrar, *The Origins of Democratic Thinking* (Cambridge: Cambridge
University Press, 1988), 300.

63. Finley, *The Greek Historians,* 2.

troducing the former as an attempt to rationalize myths, he wrote, "I write what I believe to be the truth, for what the Greeks have to say strikes me as both inconsistent and ridiculous."[64] In the latter, perhaps inspired by Persian expeditions and explorations, describing the world as made of Europe, Asia, and Libya, he also drew a map (based on that of Anaximander). Indeed there is a sense in which the geography of Hecataeus inspired the fashion of "modern" or "contemporary" history which attained such excellence.[65] Among other earlier figures, Xanathus and Hellanicus may be mentioned: the one perhaps for producing a chronology using the fall of Troy as a fixed point of reference, and the other, who outlived Herodotus, for being the prolific author of a series of local histories and chronographies, along with a history of Athens *(Atthis)*. Hellanicus, falling among hosts of "mythographers," attempted to construct a plausible understanding of that murky zone that fell between contemporary events and the "age of heroes."[66]

The two greatest historians of Greece, Herodotus and Thucydides, like the two most famous philosophers, followed each other in successive generations. So much has been written about each of them that it would be impossible within the compass of this study to do more than briefly summarize their significance.

Herodotus of Halicarnassus (b. 484 B.C.), came from a city on the eastern shore of the Aegean. His "Researches" *(Histories)* about human events, with special reference to the Persian Wars, were "undertaken so that the achievements of men should not be obliterated by time and the great and marvelous works of both Greeks and Barbarians should not be without fame, and not least, the reason why they fought one another."[67] To extend understandings beyond the horizons of what was then known, he personally conducted investigations, gathering facts, examining evidence, questioning and cross-questioning expert witnesses, checking testimony: distinguishing between primary and secondary evidence, between plausible and implausible stories, between

64. T. S. Brown, *The Greek Historians* (Lexington, Mass.: D. C. Heath, 1973), 9-12.

65. J. B. Bury, *The Ancient Greek Historians* (London: Macmillan, 1909; New York: Dover Publications, 1958), 11-18.

66. Ibid., 16-18.

67. De Sélincourt, trans., *The Histories* (Harmondsworth: Penguin, 1971); A. D. Godley, trans., *Herodotus*, 4 vols. (Cambridge: Harvard University Press; London: Wm. Heinemann Ltd., Loeb Classical Library, 1920-24).

what was more certain and what was less valid. Even when faithfully relating less than probable items of information, he pointed out how far-fetched they were. He clearly marked allusions to deterministic elements, fates, and forces beyond explanation, so that one could tell the difference between one kind of interpretation and the other. Most of his material came from oral tradition, as preserved in the great houses of notables, kings, priests, or participants.

The purpose of Herodotus was to capture the story of how an enormous army (of some 1.75 million) and navy (1,200 ships) was ultimately defeated by fragmented forces of Greeks who could hardly muster 40,000 men and 378 ships for any given battle; and to justify the role of Athenian dominance in the Persian Wars. Both skeptical and pious, he wove a complex narrative of subtle shadings, surprises, and turns: "His great discovery was that one could uncover moral problems and moral truths in history [events], in the concrete data of experience, in a discourse which was neither freely imaginative like that of the poets nor abstract like that of the philosophers. That is what history [historical understanding] meant to Herodotus. . . ."[68] Athenians, of course, appreciated him. Other Greeks, no less understandably, labeled him the "Father of Lies." The new discipline, if one could yet call it that, remained problematic. Honest thinkers could still doubt whether one could ever truly understand events, even those of the recent past, while others could wonder whether trying to do so was even worth the effort.[69]

Thucydides was probably a young man in his late twenties when the decisive war broke out between Athens and Sparta (431 B.C.).[70] In deciding to write the definitive history of the war, he embarked upon something quite remarkable: he would make an analysis of something that had yet to happen, an event not yet even over, events lying in the future. For the rest of his life, he toiled on this huge enterprise. The war lasted twenty-seven years; but Thucydides, who survived it by perhaps five years, never finished his great work. Such were the standards of perfection which he set up for himself that he was never able to accom-

68. Finley, The Greek Historians, 6.

69. Brown, The Greek Historians, 25-45; Finley, The Greek Historians, 27-216. For further recent interpretation, see John Gould, Herodotus (London: Weidenfeld and Nicolson, 1989), with notes on further readings.

70. G. B. Gundy, Thucydides and the History of His Age, 2 vols., 2nd ed. (Oxford: Basil Blackwell, 1948).

plish what he had set out to do, at least to his own satisfaction. For this very reason, much of what Thucydides wrote became, in some respects, less interesting to read than Herodotus but at the same time more thought provoking.[71]

Thucydides can be seen, even today, as a historian's historian. He is fascinating for advances in the science and technology that he brought to historical craftsmanship.[72] Obsessed with methodology, he was ever collecting material, sifting evidence, cross-checking sources, revising, and rethinking the war, both in its causes and in its consequences. He self-consciously set out to do better than Herodotus. Herodotus, in his view, had been careless, slipshod, and slovenly, in his handling of data. To remedy such weakness, Thucydides took pains to check and doublecheck each eyewitness testimony, to reexamine chronology, and to construct a completely rational analysis. He wanted his work to be free of "emotive" or "romantic" allusions to oracles and divine portents. In each detail, he took great pains to tell of things exactly as they had happened, even down to the smallest details of art, medicine, or science. One cannot, moreover, but be impressed by his transparent sincerity. Yet, for all of that, Thucydides was, at least in some respects, more like a newspaper correspondent who, both during and at the end of his career, kept writing up summations of all his findings about events that were really very much part of his own age. He wrote of things his ears had heard and his eyes had seen, and accounts of things which he knew others had closely examined and witnessed.[73]

In many ways Thucydides tackled more than he could manage. What was supposed to be a "possession for all time," both a detailed narrative description of a war and a deeper probing into fundamental political questions, never quite attained the right balance. In his search for understanding events, as in any rational inquiry, he needed clear

71. F. M. Cornford, *Thucydides Mythhistoricus* (London: Arnold, 1907; New York: Greenwood Press, 1969). John H. Finley, Jr., *Thucydides* (Cambridge: Harvard University Press, 1942).

72. C. N. Cochrane, *Thucydides and the Science of History* (Oxford: Oxford University Press, 1929).

73. Charles Forster Smith, trans., *Thucydides*, 4 vols., rev. ed. (1919; reprint, Cambridge: Harvard University Press; London: William Heinemann Ltd., Loeb Classical Library, 1980).

criteria of selection. What was relevant and what had to be discarded required such criteria. Yet, in his methods or principles of selection, Thucydides tended to oscillate between including too much or too little detail and explanation, often not defining his criteria for a particular course of action. In his search for general archetypical causes or stereotypical patterns, he tended to describe a single specimen and let that serve his purposes so as to avoid repetition. In putting together two different kinds of writing within his work — one giving precise and almost impersonal details in strict chronology and another probing beneath and behind events to discover secrets of political behavior — he never resolved the tensions inherent to the conflicting kinds of investigation that he conducted. As again explained by Moses I. Finley, "The paradox is that to give meaning to history he tended to abandon history. If the historian, by definition, concentrates on the concrete event, then Thucydides, for all his advance over his predecessor in techniques of investigation and checking, was a poorer historian, or at least less a historian, than Herodotus. It is plain that he could have been a greater one."[74]

In the centuries that followed Herodotus and Thucydides, subsequent attempts to understand events failed to possess quite the same standards of investigation or analytical rigor. Xenophon's *Hellenica* was a lone survivor among a spate of local histories of city-states in conflict. His best work, *Anabasis,* gave a detailed and fresh account of how a military officer, while on the march with an expedition of ten thousand mercenaries into the heart of the Persian Empire, saw the world through which he was passing. Among "lost" historians of the fourth century, Ephorus produced thirty books in which he tried to separate historic from mythic events; but his effort was spoiled by playing solid understandings against rhetorical effects (a game that keeps coming back into vogue). Between Xenophon and Polybius, two hundred years later, nothing survived. The career of Alexander the Great failed to produce anything more impressive than memoirs of those who accompanied him and added to the legends about him. Later, when Polybius began to write, political concerns compelled him to ask questions about how it was that Rome had succeeded in conquering the world and in doing so within such a short time.

74. Finley, *Thucydides*, 12-13.

Among Greek historians who continued to write history in later centuries some stood out: Diodorus Siculus composed a universal or world history in the first century; Dionysius of Halicarnassus, at the end of first century (B.C.) wrote a massive *Roman Antiquities;* Arrian and Dio Cassius also focused upon Rome. Plutarch, in his biographical portraits, showed creativity and originality. Yet, over all, judgments of historical understandings are severe: "Herodotus and Thucydides, however, led nowhere. What came after them was less systematic, less accurate, less serious, less professional. The fathers of history produced a stunted, sickly stock, weaker in each successive generation apart from a rare sport like Polybius."[75]

\* \* \*

In considering classicity as a critical standard for understanding events, many questions remain: Why did not other giants take up where Herodotus and Thucydides left off? What can explain the lack of further progress in attempts to understand human events? Can one conclude that either Greeks or Indians, as such, were more interested in general principles than in detailed descriptions and explanations of concrete particularities, even when trying to understand some particular event, such as a war or a succession? Perhaps for this very reason, Thucydides' efforts were bound to end in frustration. Neither Greek nor Indian thinkers seem to have wanted to remember only or precisely *what* had happened in any particular event. They wanted to know *why.* They wanted to understand exactly what happened in particular human events in the same way they sought to understand exactly what had happened in particular events perceived as phenomena of nature or of the cosmos: namely, by general theories and fixed principles. Poetry and philosophy seem to have given them more of what they were seeking. If so, changeless and universal qualities in events, rather than particular and transient qualities, gave them more of what they really wanted. If so, one can also find resemblances between the classicity of Greece and the classicity of India. For all we know, the clas-

75. I am greatly indebted to the work of my colleague, Kenneth S. Sacks, *Diodorus Siculus and the First Century* (Princeton: Princeton University Press, 1990), 242, 17. His insights continue to inform and inspire me.

sicity of China may not have been all that different. "Of all the lines of inquiry which the Greeks initiated," Finley concludes, "history was the most abortive. The wonder is not so much that it was, as that, in its short and fruitless life, its two best exponents still stand as the greatest the world has seen."[76]

76. Finley, *Thucydides*, 20.

# Chapter 7

# History as Theodicy:
# A Redemptive Event[1]

*Search now into the days gone by, long before your time,*
*beginning with the day that God created mankind upon the*
*earth; search from one end of heaven to the other, and ask*
*whether any such thing as this great thing is has ever been*
*seen or heard? Did any people ever hear the voice of God*
*speaking out of the fire, as you heard it, and remain alive?*

Deuteronomy 4:32

Until now, all of the forms of historical understanding that have been examined have on the whole tended to be "presentist." That is to say, they have reflected how different persons thought, and thought differently, about contemporary events (current and recent history), upon "what happened" *within their own time.* Even those most thorough and thoughtful of classical Greek historians, Herodotus and Thucydides, were intent on giving a more complete and correct account of their own contemporary world: they wanted to accurately "record" what had recently happened before it could be forgotten. Herodotus did not go to the

1. For matters of critical expertise outside my own discipline which are found in this chapter, I am profoundly grateful for information and insights provided by colleagues, especially Professor D. A. Carson, biblical scholar at Trinity International University, Deerfield, Illinois, and Keith E. Yandell, University of Wisconsin-Madison.

Egyptians simply out of idle curiosity. While he discovered from them more about the Greek past than Greeks themselves knew, his main purpose was to explain what had happened within his own time and within recent memory. Thucydides sifted evidence and tested facts with critical detachment, digging beneath contradictory accounts to make sure of the accuracy of his descriptions of events. But what both Herodotus and Thucydides wrote, by the very fact of its being so carefully selected, preserved and protected against loss, only became "history" of remote events for later generations, becoming so merely by the lapse of time. Rarely did later generations become so intent on preserving, rediscovering, or critically reexamining events long past that they strove to constantly refine their knowledge so as to produce ever "better" or newer redactions, reconstructions, or revisions of previous understandings.[2]

Of course, as already indicated in the previous chapter, Greeks both "constructed" and "researched" the past. Among Greek historians, moreover, a distinction developed between those who followed a more "literary" (or didactical, ideological, polemical, and theoretical) tradition, taking more liberties and feeling more free to create speeches out of thin air when citing sources, and those who followed a more "empirical" (or critical and "scientific") tradition, showing more concern to see that their "facts" were well founded and supported by evidence. In the latter tradition, Greeks exercised a degree of critical detachment and scientific thoroughness which established standards of investigation for all subsequent generations. Yet, as this chapter will attempt to show, standards as rigorous as those set by the Greeks had also already long been operative among ancient Hebrew historians. Thus the question of whether or not the Greeks, alone and by themselves, "invented" history is not all that conclusive or easy to answer in any definitive or final sense. Moreover, there are grounds for believing that the earliest Christian writers, as historians, drew upon and benefited from both Greek and Hebrew historical traditions in nearly equal measure.[3]

---

2. Moses I. Finley, introduction to *The Greek Historians* (New York: Viking Press, 1959), 1-21; and Herbert Butterfield, *The Origins of History* (London: Methuen, 1981), 80.

3. Lovelace Alexander, *The Preface to Luke's Gospel: Literary Convention and Social Context in Luke 1:1-4 and Acts 1:1* (Cambridge: Cambridge University Press, 1993), indicates that, as far as the two Greek traditions are concerned, Luke followed the forms of the "scientific" tradition.

What developed within ancient Israel, therefore, is all the more remarkable, if not unique.[4] Here, in the words of Baruch Halpern, was "a people not only supremely conscious of the past but possibly more obsessed with history than any other nation that has ever existed."[5] Among various forms of historical understanding that have emerged from the mists of antiquity, none has ever quite compared with what came out of the monotheistic traditions. All of them can be seen as stemming from the "seed of Abraham." The very existence of these monotheisms, as well as the antitheistic and atheistic ideologies of their much later or more recent progeny, has rested upon events and understandings of specific events. From the people of ancient Israel down to the present came a line of thinking, a perspective in which cycles of time, inner states of mind, or reliance on myths and symbols alone could never, of themselves, be enough. Obsessed with remembering and reflecting upon concrete events with facts about the real world, this was a perspective which looked across the entire broad sweep of *human* events: from first beginnings in a most remote and irrecoverable past to final endings in a remote and unprecedented future. The totality of all events in History was seen as a linear progression. What had occurred was viewed as neither haphazard nor random: certain specific events had occurred and certain other events would continue to occur in a straightforward, if irregular, progression. This would continue until, in the fullness of time, all of History (and human affairs) would reach a final consummation. In short, from their very beginnings, Abrahamic understandings of History, one and all, have been historicist.

But this view of human events was also obsessed with historicity, with the reality of what had actually happened. Obsession with reconstructing details, explanations, and interpretations of certain specific events became foundational for all Abrahamic monotheisms (if not also for later nontheistic ideologies which those monotheisms engendered). Neither Judaism, nor Christianity which sprang from Judaism, nor Islam which sprang from both Judaism and Christianity (nor even forms of Marxism which sprang from these monotheistic faiths), could afford to reject the historicity of certain specific or singular events and still remain

4. Baruch Halpern, *The First Historians: The Hebrew Bible and History* (San Francisco: Harper & Row, 1988).
    5. Ibid., 81.

viable. Not one of these belief systems could continue to exist without a very characteristic and defining certainty about historical understandings of certain *particular* events. These understandings were not just some vague or general or mythic feelings about things gone by. Rather, they called forth a tenacious clinging onto some one single event, or one set of events, which none would ever be allowed to forget.

Each member within this lineage, this "family" of Abrahamic descendants, harked directly back to its own peculiar, particularistic, personalistic sense of the historicity of some one event, as basic to its own self-understanding (or identity), its survival, and its vision. While each tradition traced itself — in cultural, intellectual, or spiritual terms — from the "seed of Abraham," it also traced itself from the concrete and definite experiences of individuals as persons. The experiences of these individuals were embodied within remembered and reflected descriptions and foundational narratives. Each tradition, in its own way, looked back to the historicity of its own remembrances and its own texts. These were founded upon facts, sometimes of "mythic" dimension and importance, contained in even more ancient memories and writings.

Among all the most ancient and original of such hallowed memories, as embodied in texts stretching back over millennia, none were more foundational than those of the Law (Torah), the Chronicles, the Prophecies, the Poems, and the Songs of ancient Israel. These Hebrew texts recorded, in abbreviated but careful detail, the pivotal events of a whole people as experienced by particular individuals. Other persons, building upon the understandings of these events and experiences, later expressed further insights within the Greek texts of the Christian canon. Experiences of events by persons of yet another branch of the same stem were later recorded and fixed within the Arabic texts of the Quran by Muhammad. In "modern" and more recent times, nontheistic (if not antitheistic) understandings of the human experience have been expressed in the various forms of post-Enlightenment ideology, such as nationalism, socialism, and Marxism. For sheer restlessness, critical questing, and constant reappraisal, revision, or research arising out of ceaseless compulsions to improve previous understandings, all these traditions have reflected the ideological and intellectual impetus arising out of their original roots.

Intrinsic to all monotheistic traditions themselves has been a particular perspective which juxtaposes human nature and divine grace. This perspective has always stressed, in varying degrees, the reality of human depravity, human evil, and self-destructive human failings. But this perspective, at the same time, has also refused to accept as inevitable the logical and fatal consequences of depravity as irreversible or final. Rather, in one form or another, it has recognized a need for redemption. This redemption has served at once as both the ground of true history and the hope of true History (in its eschato-logical sense). Perceptions of this redemptive feature within human (Judeo-Christian) experience have then placed human events within an enlarging context of "revelations." These revelations have also been seen as themselves a manifesting of divine interventions within human affairs. No more dramatic demonstration of the dominant place of both History and historical understanding among the monotheistic peoples of the world could be imagined than this fundamental and overriding fact: the most basic, most accurate, and most important kinds of knowledge came to mankind only as and when God revealed Himself and, even then, only in human events and experiences. All of History, in the largest sense, could also be viewed (and often was) as a gigantic Super Event. Moreover, certain specific events within that History have also been seen as redemptive, and hence, as something worth knowing more about.

To repeat, the self-disclosures of God by God were always seen, first and foremost, as historical. ("It *did* happen!" "It *has* happened!" "It *does* happen!" "It *is* happening!" "It *will* happen!" Such terms testified to Revelation as Event.) Revelation itself was seen as consisting of multiple events.[6] Conveyed through generations, both through narrative testimonies about experiences, about certain unforgettable events themselves, and through interpretive reasonings and speculative reflections upon those events, Revelation was never seen as coming merely out of some extraordinary innate human capacity. No amount

---

6. H. D. Schmidt's view, expressed in "Jewish Philosophy of History and Its Contemporary Opponents," *Judaism* 9, no. 2 (Spring 1960): 129-40, can be seen as going two ways. If "Jewish interpretation of historical events is derived from the central concept of God" and if, therefore, "a Jewish philosophy of history will always remain a branch of theology," it is no less true that theology has also been, at the same time, a branch of history. In short, theology itself, as it gradually became refined, emerged out of critical reflections about historical events.

of rational brilliance, no combination of powerful intellectual insights, no profound philosophical speculation, scientific theory, or logical analysis, nor deeply intuitive and mystical feelings could ever be, either of and by itself (or even taken together), sufficient. Moreover, insights and understandings that have counted have often come in critical moments. Thus, the most unforgettable experiences and the most wonderful, even miraculous encounters had sometimes come in moments of direst despair. Altogether amazing escapes from certain catastrophe or inevitable disaster and miraculous rescues from terrible calamity had occurred. Light had suddenly shone in depths of darkest night. Amid details of circumstances surrounding such moments had come sudden, unexpected, never-to-be-forgotten "surprises" — *turning points* of History.

Such interventions or intrusions into the course of human events were almost invariably seen as events that "turned things around." Intrinsic to such momentous happenings, there had invariably been contingencies and uncertainties: tensions fraught with elements unforeseen and circumstances unanticipated. Paths tortured by the human capacity of free choice in particular situations had always, it seemed, been delicately balanced against the larger course of events. Unprecedented developments could be seen as having led, in the end, to some even larger, grander, and more final "fulfillment."

However, ideas about this larger course of events, when properly understood, could never be allowed by those of proper understandings to fly in the face of hard facts. Dogmas (or theories) about History could not be used to escape from the reality of events. What happened had happened. Facts about the past, however inconvenient or unpleasant, could not be avoided. Facts had to be confronted. Truth, in this sense, became an expression of facts, gained from the school of experiences and events. However much some might feel that "the heavens declare[d] the glory of the Lord" (Ps. 19:1), it was always *on earth* and *in time* — within the playing out of events and within understandings of events — that God and History could be understood. In events God had chosen to reveal Himself, His designs, His purpose, and His will. In God's Revelation, as celebrated in rituals or recitals of remembering, in poetic or narrative or artistic expression about events, and in truths derived therefrom, historicity and historicism were closely intermingled and often merged.

## I. The Remembrance of Redemption: The Exodus

*Remember* that you were slaves in the land of Egypt, and that the LORD your God brought you out with a mighty hand and an outstretched arm.

Deuteronomy 5:15

*Remember* that you were a slave in the land of Egypt, and the LORD your God redeemed you.

Deuteronomy 15:15

*Remember* the day when you came forth out of the land of Egypt *all the days of your life.*

Deuteronomy 16:3

*Remember* the days of old, consider the years and ages that are past; ask your father to recount them and your elders to tell you the tales.

Deuteronomy 32:7

Over and over and over again, the clarion call "Remember!" *(Zakhor!)* rings out.[7] It is not an option. It is a command. Altogether essential, ever critical, and desperately urgent, its imperatives are absolute. Its exercises are unequivocal, unconditional, and unqualified. It is also a promise. Indeed, it is part of a compact or contract, a sacred and ever-lasting covenant. It defines a dramatic, vital, ongoing, and often tense relationship. Between a single, all-knowing and all-powerful Creator and a single, free-wheeling and often errant creature, whether man or

---

7. Yosef Hayim Yerushalmi, *Zakhor: Jewish History and Jewish Memory* (Seattle and London: University of Washington Press, 1982), indicates that the term occurs at least 169 times in Scripture, with God and his people constantly enjoining and remind-ing each other to "remember" and "forget not"! Moreover, just as significant are many other passages where the idea is as central even though the verb itself does not appear. Thus, for example, when the Ten Commandments are introduced (Exod. 20), there is an affirmation that the God who delivers his law is none other than the one who has redeemed his people. Again, Deut. 6 sets forth the importance of passing the memories of singular redemptive events, one by one, from generation to generation, in perpetuity.

woman, communication is possible. But such communication often broke down. Viewed in retrospect, this relationship, emerging out of crucial encounters, was always marked by profound, even revolutionary, shifts in human understandings. Such understandings, however gradually refined through deeply felt, sometimes traumatic and sometimes sublime human experiences, had always become manifest in the course of events. Out of events themselves had come the personal and corporate experiences by which and in which ultimate understandings of God developed.

Despite constantly oscillating dialectics of encounters between — mankind and God, between the human and the divine, between faith and doubt, between obedience and obstinacy, between rebellion and submission — certain select events themselves had become catalytic. Dramatic confrontations had taken place. Between God's personal acts of intervention in the affairs of individual persons and/or groups of people and those actions by which certain persons and peoples responded to such interventions, there had always been constant, even if uneven, sets of tension. It is for this reason that relationships between living and breathing beings required *remembrance* on both sides. This was always viewed by the people of ancient Israel as a two-way street. Remembrance was "not-forgetting." It was enjoined upon both parties in any contractual relationship.

## A. The Terms of Remembrance

Over and over again, the same phrases are repeated: "Remember when. . . ." Such phrases were vital to the survival of the "seed of Abraham, Isaac, and Jacob." Injunctions that kept declaring, "Remember you were a slave," "Remember what Amalak did," "Remember how Balak plotted," "Remember how I redeemed you and rescued you," "Remember these things, O Jacob!" "O Israel! Never forget," were set against divine assurance: "I will remember the covenant . . . between myself and living things," "I will remember my covenant with Jacob . . . ," "I have heard the groaning of the children of Israel . . . and I have remembered my covenant," "I have surely not forgotten my people," and "I have surely remembered you." The key to the story of one small person's struggle in the midst of overwhelming danger and hopelessness, and of the survival of one small people, so few in number in the midst of so many powerful peoples, was seen to lie in adherence to this double imperative of "two-way" remembrances. The most incredible fact to be remembered was that, despite many past achievements and triumphs, as well as defeats and failures, through nearly four thousand years of colossal disasters, horrific oppressions, and unmitigated tragedies, a single people had somehow never quite disappeared from the face of the earth. They had even managed to thrive.

Historical understanding, like memory itself, is always selective, always partial. No human capacity, on its face, could be more fragile, frail, or fickle, more treacherous or liable to playing tricks, than memory. Yet, ironically, it was just this facility that was harnessed for purposes of preserving understandings of most important events. By careful drilling and exercise, one delicate aptitude was made the tool of choice, the instrument for generating momentous historical insights. If not all that was remembered was recorded and if not all that was recorded was then remembered, nevertheless, various combinations and permutations of what *was* remembered *and* recorded became a foundation for reflection. Ultimately, to know God, to learn about what God was really like, to study all of Creation, and to see all existence and time as redemptive events, required careful specificity and selectivity. Exactly what had happened, in the details of one particular life, had to be carefully remembered and recorded. From reflection upon particular sequences of remembered and recorded events came convictions about the uniqueness and linearity of nonrepeatable events.

Human events went forward, not backward, or around in circles. There could be no going back to Eden. One and only one "fiery, flashing and ever-whirling sword" barred the way. Once distinctions between good and evil produced standards of judgment, an evocative litany of unique events, each one and only one, each memorable and even "mythic" in its symbolism, marked the record: only one Cain was marked for retribution; only one Babel brought descent into linguistic confusion; only one post-deluge rainbow promised ecological preservation; only one Abraham, redeemed from offering his only son, became the "Father of Faith"; only one Joseph was sold into only one bondage in Egypt; only one Passover (Paschal of Redemption) bought only one escape or Exodus from Egypt and only one Red Sea crossing; only one Mount Horeb (Sinai) encounter established the everlasting covenant;

only one people was chosen; only one tabernacle, only one ark of the covenant, only one wilderness sojourn of over forty years, only one Jordan crossing (marked with stones of remembrance), and only one land of promise ("flowing with milk and honey") marked the chain of events by which ancient Israel came into existence. And yet, later, after the destruction of the first temple (and Jerusalem), and after yet another redemption from another bondage, another captivity, another dispersion, and another exile, the children of Judah suffered the destruction of their second temple (and Jerusalem), leading to the suffering of yet another dispersion and exile. But none of these events were seen as cyclical repetitions of older events, nor as some descent from a golden age. They were events which, each in its own turn, were seen as unique — events each of which could have turned out differently. *If only* different decisions had been made by individuals or peoples who were responsible, both to God and to themselves, for their own behavior, things could have been different. Each dispersal, in turn followed by yet another redemption and by yet another returning remnant, could have been different. Without remembrance, both of blessing and of bane, none of these things could be understood.

By means of rituals, recitals of powerful but terse anecdotes, and metaphors, poems, and songs, the early descendants of Israel and then the early descendants of Judah transmitted historical understandings from generation to generation. The disciplined energy and force of words used to convey their history, in turn, served to reinforce their corporate identity as a people. Repeating basic facts, over and over again (turning each fact this way and that, so as to let it catch many facets of light and many reflections of meaning), history was employed in the service of truth. History aided efforts to preserve a community. No better model of abbreviated or "abstracted" history, at its very best and in its very essence, can be found. In their liturgies of bare essentials, for example, one can hardly surpass the creed which early peoples of Israel used to regularly and solemnly celebrate the first fruits of each year's harvest:

> A wandering Aramean was my father; he went down into Egypt; and sojourned there, few in number; and became there a nation great, mighty, and populous.
>
> But the Egyptians dealt ill with us, afflicted us, and imposed cruel slavery upon us.

> Then we cried unto the Lord, the God of our fathers; and the Lord heard our voice, and saw our humiliation, our hardship, and our distress.
>
> And the Lord brought us forth out of Egypt with a mighty hand, and with an outstretched arm, with great terribleness, and with signs and wonders.
>
> And He has brought us into this place, and has given us this land, a land flowing with milk and honey. . . .

> Deuteronomy 26:5-9

Here is everything in a nutshell: humble origin, national growth, oppressive slavery, divine deliverance, endowed land, surplus abundance, and recognition of a divine intervention in human events. Here is history that is both personal and communal. Here is something each subsequent generation appropriates; and here members speak of these particular events as "my" and "our" events, as being about "us."

## B. The Event as Revelation and Revelation as Event

One can find nothing to compare with the impact of the Exodus upon the outlook and identity of any other single people. The fall of Troy certainly left its impact upon early and classical Greek thought; but no people today celebrate their convictions about that past by annual recitations of passages from the *Iliad* or the *Odyssey*. Indeed, only recently has the historicity of that event, long doubted, been reconfirmed. More analogous perhaps might be the impact of the Magna Carta upon the consciousness of England's people. But neither the American Pledge of Allegiance, the Constitution, nor the Declaration of Independence is quite comparable. Lincoln's Gettysburg Address may also be pondered. These may be seen perhaps as having had a comparable impact, as slogans of the French, Russian, or Chinese Revolutions. Hitler's appeal to the Aryan Volk sought to evoke such a consciousness. So also, in our day, have the clarions of Islamic revival and the slokas of *Hindutva*. But these events are too recent, and their consequences too uncertain, for the events they mark to be considered comparable. Besides, their ritual recitations have not and are not seen as "historical documents" in the same sense. Historical understandings, in other words, made early Hebrews into the chosen people, the nation of Israel.

The focal point of this history, however, was God Himself. All events were, in one sense, God's events. Not only were noteworthy events seen as being about God and by God, as seen in specific events that showed His dealings with mankind, but they were also about all things that came from His hand. With God as "true hero," as the awesome Person beside whom there could be no other, elements of humanity became defined and described by events in relation to this most ultimate of all realities. The standard of objectivity, for the handling of all human events, became nothing less than the throne of God. All human events had to be set against this absolute standard. While that standard could never be fully met, or even as perfectly known as might be desirable, since all human knowers were only and always less than perfect, enough had been made known about God by God, in the events through which self-disclosures of God had occurred, that there could be no doubt about what that standard required. The revelation of God in events was, in itself, more than sufficient. The source of mankind's problems came not in what was not known, not even with ambiguities in what was known, but with what was already known. For this reason, there could be no excuse, no hiding from dreadful or unpalatable facts, however terrible or ugly these might be.

Thus, since the center of History could never be either humanity in general, nor even Israel in particular, a platform of historical judgment was raised which became almost unassailable. That a standard so high as this was raised in the ancient world can be recognized as an astonishing event in itself. Moreover, in the face of all odds, this has been the standard for assessing, numbering, and weighing events ever since. Seen in so severe a light, no attempted whitewashing of human behavior could work: no human being and no event could escape scrutiny; no person or community could be exempt from judgment. The curse of Adam and Eve, and of Cain, extended to all generations. The blessings of Abraham, Isaac, and Jacob came not from deeds nor from any inherent dignity and virtue on their part, but from dependence upon divine mercy. Blessings of the promise, extended to the children of Israel, and to their children's children, were conditional: they were incumbent upon God's mercy and grace and upon both faith and faithfulness to that grace. Deeds alone could not suffice. Deeds and events had to be constantly examined to see whether, in fact, any residue of faith and faithfulness could still be found.

Yet, if divine interventions were seen as central, as *the* really significant events, one might well ask why the accounts of biblical historians were not limited to descriptions of such interventions. No compelling reason, from one perspective, would necessarily have prompted anything but narratives restricted exclusively to God and his miracles. This argument can be made, except for one thing: namely, that certain events themselves revealed how enormously God had always been concerned with the actions of men and women as individual persons and with the deeds of peoples as corporate communities. This concern is seen as arising not out of any pettiness or vindictiveness, but out of a fathomless compassion for the human predicament.

Embodied in the carefully constrained details of each narrative of events, therefore, were concrete and vivid descriptions which, in the last analysis, not only showed how extremely human — meaning how often faithless, frail, or weak — *all* persons and *all* peoples have been, but also how compassionate and gracious was their Maker and their Redeemer. Hard facts about events, depicted with great chronological and locational consistency and precision, showed exactly where, and when, and how no one had ever quite measured up; exactly how and where none were worthy or deserving of even the blessings that they had enjoyed. All alike, it was clear, had fallen short of proper standards for human behavior. All, in one way or another, were tainted. In anecdote after anecdote, and episode after episode, narrative accounts provided the graphic details: faces and names, places and times, personalities and occasions, all in proper context and sequence, went into the telling of "how it really was." The original gods of Abraham, Isaac, and Jacob were not Yahweh. The propensity to turn to other gods was ever present. Abraham lied about his pretty wife to save his skin. Sarah laughed about becoming pregnant at her age. Lot settled in Sodom. Jacob was a devious trickster. Judah failed his daughter and violated her. Moses lost his temper and, in consequence, was not allowed to enter the land of promise. Ehud's resort to assassination, Jephthah's terrible vow costing him his daughter, and Samson's falling for the wiles of a temptress: each event spoke.

Yet, at the same time, evil alone, however overwhelming, is never more than part of the human story. Redemption is the major theme of history. The focus of historical attention consistently "zooms in" upon the forlorn, helpless, and hopeless "little" person, someone whose plight seems doomed and beyond all hope of rescue: the youth sold into slavery by perfidious elder brothers, falsely accused and thrown into prison; the harlot of Jericho risking her life for strangers; the young Moabite widow pledging herself to her mother-in-law, and many more. Each tells of redemption from dire surroundings and certain destruction. The very human quality of each narrative is itself astonishing. No less astonishing is the scale of critical detachment. Here, in short, is a truly amazing achievement. By any standard of measurement, but especially if seen within the context of the ancient world, the standards of historical narrative produced by the people of early Israel are without precedent, and have never been surpassed.

## C. The Messages within Events

Interestingly, historical understandings were too important to be entrusted just to historians. While "a succession of anonymous authors created the most distinguished corpus of historical writing in the ancient Near East,"[8] responsibility for probing into events and fathoming meanings seems to have gone to prophets. No single historian, as such, is known to us by name. Names of prominent prophets, however, are not only known but what they wrote eventually went to make up a large proportion of the entire biblical canon. While historical and prophetic writings seem to have been produced on a vast scale, only a fraction of these writings, mainly what went into the canon, survived. Parts of this canon, compiled over centuries, eventually contained a coherent and connected narrative of events, covering the whole span of human history from its genesis down to the fifth century B.C.

Moreover, the focus of that history was constantly and continually being narrowed. While the names of Moses and Joshua are attached to certain sequences of narrative, while the name of Samuel is linked to another phase of narrative, little is known about actual authorship. This is especially true concerning narratives found in Judges (that long period in which "every man did what was right in his own sight"). The court-

8. Yerushalmi, *Zakhor*, 12.

history of King David's reign found in 2 Samuel, following comparable details in 1 Samuel of how the throne was established and how David succeeded Saul, is about as replete with analysis, contextualization, detailed description, and explanation about exactly how and why things worked the way they did as any narrative history could be. The high costs of David's treachery in acquiring Bathsheba followed him to his grave: the taking of another man's wife and arranging that man's death did not go unnoticed; domestic grief, incest, rape, or violence humiliated the king in his old age and brought strife, tension, and usurpation to the entire kingdom.

In a later time, parallel narratives of the divided monarchy, the royal history of the Kings of Judah and the Chronicles of Israel, lead to even deeper kinds of historical interpretation. These books seem to reflect a new spirit. Deuteronomy, perhaps that "book of the law" discovered in the temple during the reign of Josiah (in 612 B.C.), may have provided the stimulus for critical refinements found in these new histories. The "Second Torah" consisted mainly of three huge sermons attributed to Moses. The fresh spirit of prophetic insight and inspiration it breathed, with its renewed emphasis upon redemptive choice and promise, almost certainly facilitated great religious reforms during Josiah's reign. Moreover, the new spirit and standards of critical assessment as set in Deuteronomy enabled historians to explain a further narrowing of historical focus. The North, Israel, had chosen to break away from the South, Judah, separating itself from the house of David, from the temple, and from Jerusalem, preferring instead its own high altars. Since not one of its kings had conformed to standards, since none had done what was "pleasing in the sight of the Lord their God," reasons for their doom and disappearance were clear. As summed in the closing lines of 2 Kings 17:7-18:

> the people of Israel sinned against the Lord their God, who had brought them up out the land of Egypt. . . . And the people of Israel did secretly against the Lord their God things that were not right . . . they built high places . . . they burned incense on all the high places, as the nations did whom the Lord carried away before them. And they did wicked things, provoking the Lord to anger, and they served idols, of which the Lord had said to them, "You shall not do this." Yet the Lord warned Israel and Judah by every prophet and every seer,

saying, "turn from your evil ways." . . . And they burned their sons and daughters as offerings, and used divination and sorcery, and sold themselves to do evil in the sight of the Lord, provoking the Lord to anger. Therefore the Lord was very angry with Israel, and removed them out of his sight; none was left but the tribe of Judah only.

With the Assyrian captivity, the ten "lost tribes" of northern Israel vanish from History. With that event, the focus of historical narrative narrows even further. Henceforth, only Judah (with parts of Levi and Benjamin) figures in historical events. But again, as before, the sifting and winnowing of events brought about still another narrowing of focus. Even Judah itself is seen as inconsistent: spared "for David's sake," it could not escape ruin which it brought upon itself. Since even Judah, despite repentance and reforms under Josiah, also "did evil" and "forsook" God, it eventually suffered the same consequences. The writer or compiler of narratives found in 2 Kings, in the midst of describing Nebuchadnezzar's destruction of Jerusalem, added, "Notwithstanding, the Lord turned not from the fierceness of his wrath, with which his anger was kindled against Judah. . . . And the Lord said, 'I will remove Judah also out of my sight, as I removed Israel, and will cast off this city, Jerusalem, which I have chosen, and the house of which I said, My name shall be there'" (23:27); and, "Surely this came upon Judah at the commandment of the Lord, remove them out of his sight, for the sins of Manasseh, according to all that he did, and also for the innocent blood that he shed; for he filled Jerusalem with innocent blood, which the Lord would not pardon" (24:4).

In describing these events, the writer invites his readers to check the facts. Over and over again, after each reign, he indicates that verification, with more details, can be found in archives and in standard sources. In the Books of the Chronicles of the Kings of Israel or the Books of the Chronicles of the Kings of Judah, not to be confused with biblical books with the same name, those who were interested could find more information: that Ahab built an ivory palace (and many cities); that Jeroboam II reconquered Damascus; that Hezekiah constructed an aqueduct in order to convey water into the city; and other details. Details also known from other sources are not mentioned. Clearly other accounts, archival resources, official records, narratives, and biographical works, including works by prophets, were available to readers of that day.

The Exile, like the Exodus and later catastrophes that befell Jewish peoples, was an altogether overwhelming and hence unforgettable event. Those who survived perpetually reflected upon what had happened. More than that, such an event was not obscure. Jews remembered! They had their histories and their prophetic writings to tell them what had gone wrong. Here was another promise that had been fulfilled, a promise running directly opposite to that of the promised land. Here was a fulfillment of promised destruction. For those who returned from Babylon and began to rebuild their city, some lessons were clear. First, survival as a chosen people had occurred: without the promised land, without either the city, the temple, or the kingdom. Thrown back upon other resources "by the Rivers of Babylon where [they] sat down and wept" over their plight, they had found inner depths of spiritual strength which were as yet hardly imagined, much less fathomed. Such strengths, seemingly more individualized (one is almost tempted to say "democratized"), called each person, not just each people, to accountability.

The result, like that seeming to arise out of the discoveries of the "Second Torah" (Deuteronomy), can be seen as a fresh outburst of historical revisions. Only now, historical thinking not only rummaged the past but the future. In one of those remarkable flights from the concrete and the real here-and-now, such as have often happened within dungeons of dire despair and doom, historical understandings became mingled with mythic and mythopoeic visions, and apocalyptic dreams about eschatological fulfillment. After the destruction of Babylon, Judah of the Return, with Jerusalem rebuilt, now became part of a world empire. The nation of chosen people, both gathered and scattered, was now led by compatriots, both clerical and nonclerical. These were officials of a large imperial bureaucracy. Whether or not there actually was a holy city and a holy temple or even a land of promise in an immediate or literal sense became much less important, at least for some. What mattered were the means by which distinctness and purity as chosen people were to be maintained and preserved from contamination. It is at this point that a more scrupulous attention to details of the law, as interpreted by priests, scholarly scribes, and teachers, as much as by prophets, came into prominence. For the children of Judah, increasingly known as Jews, what was coming into being was a particular religious system. This would eventually become known as Judaism.

In keeping with the new visions came a new reconstruction of the past, showing that this was something God had intended all along. The results of these revisions, embodied in the two books of Chronicles, to which were added the books of Ezra and Nehemiah, laid fresh emphasis upon the dialectical logic of divine judgment and divine redemption. These works attempted to show that, from Adam onwards, consequences for failure to measure up to standards of purity and righteousness that had been given to mankind, and then specifically to Moses, had always been certain. Moreover, after the Exile as described by Nehemiah and Ezra, descriptions of historical events could never again be the same. While some descriptions remained narrowly focused upon that remnant that had returned to rebuild Jerusalem, others focused attention upon the place and role of the Diaspora. Some of the Jews, as exemplified in the history of Esther, remained "chosen people" *outside* the land of promise. Indeed, from that time onwards, there were always Babylonian Jews and other thriving communities of Jews scattered across the world. Some of these Jews, as chosen people, never vanished, like the "lost tribes" of Israel. Some even went so far as to "internalize" or "spiritualize" the land of promise, reducing it to a metaphor for inner blessing and fulfillment.

But historical sources, as well as writings, especially those that survived and certainly those that later could be entered into the canon, seem to have dwindled markedly just before, during, and after the Exile. Those dire events had been so traumatic, and circumstances of destruction so terrible, that the focus of the later prophets turned to History as seen in cosmic and eschatological terms. The later prophets — the "major" writings that came down under the names of Isaiah, Jeremiah, Ezekiel, and Daniel, not to mention the twelve shorter ("minor") works under names of other prophets — were much more heavily didactic and much less historical. Nevertheless, all of these later works reveal how profoundly the emphasis had changed. The writings for remembrance now focused upon interpretations concerning the entire course of human events (History). The latter half of the book of Daniel, next to that of Ezra among the last of the prophets, after detailing events within Babylon during the whole period of Exile, concludes with a sweeping apocalyptic panorama of world history, which looked to an apocalyptic future and foretold its final end.

## D. The Eschatology of Events

The final form of remembrance to emerge from Hebrew biblical understandings of historical events looked not to redemption (or redemptions) in the past but to an ultimate climacteric of redemption in the future. The corpus of biblical understandings, as the final court of appeal for each interpretation of historical events, seemed capable of throwing light upon every new event and each historical contingency. The renewed process set in motion by the catastrophe of 586 B.C. (B.C.E.), if not by the earlier destruction of Israel in 732 B.C., had continued until it came to final fruition in the catastrophe of A.D. (C.E.) 70. No empire, whether of Assyria, Babylon, Persia, Greece, or Rome, could or would last forever. The decline and fall of each, as Daniel's prophecy had suggested and as the destruction of Jerusalem had shown, had been due to sin. Failure to live up to divinely ordained standards of human behavior, which had been set by God for all mankind and which could be known, had led to inevitable consequences.

Yosef Hayim Yerushalmi repeats a saying, so common as to need no citation, that seems both to explain and to epitomize the renewed messianic expectations: "On the day the Temple was destroyed the Messiah was born."[9] This perspective, interpreted broadly, provoked a continual searching of Scriptures, together with a continual examining and comparing of past and current events, to discover historical clues as to when, where, and how the Messiah would become manifest. Whether or not the messianic advent would be contingent upon human behavior (repentance, obedience, etc.) or upon some more inscrutable divine initiative, there could be no question but that the interim was to be spent in becoming purer and holier. However clear one's remembrance or understanding of the historical (biblical) past and however certain one's confidence and hope for the eschatological (messianic) future, events in the present remained obscure. It was no longer possible, in the words of Yerushalmi, for "the meaning of specific historical events [to be] laid bare by the inner eye of prophecy."[10]

But in the midst of dark uncertainties, it was this messianic hope that evoked a sense of the promise and remained a shining beacon.

9. Ibid., 23.
10. Ibid., 24.

Events had a purpose. Events were moving inexorably toward the eventual establishment of the kingdom of God on earth. Events would show that God's chosen people would be an important part of this process, however much they rebelled and suffered the consequences. The covenant was eternal. The true heartbeat of History, throbbing beneath the surface of events, was much more real than were more noisy rhythms of the world. Behind all the might and pomp of empires, and all the conventional wisdom of sages, stood a solitary figure. This symbol of silent rebuke against all earthly triumphs was the Suffering Servant (described by Isaiah). This was the light that would never go out. This was the true Hanukkah that alone would be celebrated during the dark postbiblical centuries — as a continuing reaffirmation of faith and as an undying hope for redemption and rescue by God. Such hope continued to burn even after the heroic efforts of the Maccabees were no longer so well remembered. It persisted despite the failures of three tremendous efforts to "hasten the end" by rising against Rome. Human efforts ended in calamity and bitter disillusion. Hope in the future coming of the Messiah survived skeptics and visionaries throughout the centuries. It certainly seems to have been considered central, at least by some, in the Judaism of the second temple period, if not in later "rabbinic Judaism."[11]

Of all the prophets and all the writers of the Hebrew Bible, however, Isaiah was undoubtedly the greatest, the most remarkable, and perhaps even the most popular.[12] His entire work exists intact. Preserved in a leather scroll, twenty-three feet long, found at Qumran after World War II, it is the longest and best ancient manuscript of the Bible known to have survived: fifty columns of Hebrew text. His words, sparkling with brilliant imagery, are embedded within the literary canons of many

11. The expression "rabbinic Judaism" is slippery in contemporary debate. It has been used to refer to the Jewish literature and its sources crystallized in *Mishnah* (codified c. A.D. 200) and later related works. But by that time such a strong reaction against apocalyptic expectations had grown that it, together with the two Talmuds and related *midrashim*, reflected a negative attitude toward messianic expectations. While, of course, such sources continued to preserve messianic hope, that became more muted and less thoroughly central or fiery. The Judaism of the second temple period (i.e., around the time of Jesus) seems to have been much more complex and diverse than what is represented in these later sources.

12. Paul Johnson, "Israelites," in *A History of the Jews* (London: Weidenfeld & Nicolson, 1987), 74-77.

cultures. Most important of all, his conceptions of humanity reach levels of moral vision hitherto unscaled. He warned Judah of catastrophe: an event that would be brought on by heedless pursuit of wealth, "joining house to house" while "beating people to pieces" and "grinding the faces of the poor." He called people to repentance, to a change of heart, and to forgiveness: "Come now, let us reason together, saith the Lord; though your sins be as scarlet, they shall be as white as snow." He extolled holiness and peace over wealth and power, looking for the day "when nation would not lift sword against nation, neither would they learn war any more."

Isaiah looked forward to the coming of a universal savior, some messianic personage sent from heaven whose name would be called Immanuel, someone who would be the Prince of Peace. This person appears again in part two of Isaiah: the Suffering Servant, already mentioned above, personifies the ultimate redemptive event, the person who carries the sins of the entire community and personally atones for the sins of many. Isaiah's appeal, beyond the claims of kingdom, nation, or tribe, was to individuals as persons of conscience and faith. Finally, Isaiah declared that no other gods exist: God is "the first, and the last; beside whom there is no God" — universal and ubiquitous and all-powerful, the sole motivating force who directs all events and will do so to the end.[13]

\*          \*          \*

Exactly how all of this entire repository of inherited and handed-down sacred writings — history, law, wisdom, song, and prophetic writings — survived; exactly how it was brought together and compiled into a single whole, is still far from clear. But in later ages, during and after the Exile, readings from the five books of Moses, narrating events up to the conquest of Canaan, together with portions from the prophets,

---

13. While many may concur with these views on Isaiah, it would also be churlish not to acknowledge that the vast majority of biblical critics in our day think of the canonical book of Isaiah as the product of an entire school of thought that flowed out of work done by Isaiah of Jerusalem. Without even attempting to enter into such problems at all, certainly not here, I would simply make reference to the importance of the recent commentary on Isaiah by J. Alec Motyer (brought to my attention by D. A. Carson).

were apparently recited aloud within each congregation. Learned
scholars gave detailed expositions and embarked upon intense discussions on interpretations of these readings. Texts were carefully copied
and no less carefully transmitted from generation to generation. What
is now sometimes referred to as a "democratization of learning" (if not
of literacy itself) seems to have occurred. This was a process by which
a significant proportion of the entire Jewish community in each place
became involved in the preservation of their own legacy. Such efforts
involved them directly in efforts to understand the works of historians
and prophets who had long been dead. But, such efforts notwithstanding, those portions of Scripture destined to survive as part of the authoritative corpus of sacred writings had already long been part of a
sealed canon. This canon, while ratified again at Yabneh, some thirty
years after the destruction of Jerusalem and the second temple by the
Romans, remained fixed, secure, and intact. Historical narratives found
in Scripture had by that time long ago acquired, among Jews and Christians alike and everywhere, what Yerushalmi describes as an "immortality to which no subsequent historian could aspire and that was denied
to certain historical works which already existed."[14]

A profound shift seems to have occurred after the destruction of
Jerusalem and the second temple. Thereafter, both the writing of history
and, therewith, the writing of prophecy seem to have virtually ceased.[15]
The rituals of remembrance continued, contributing a strong sense of
identity for the Jewish community and fortifying it against all onslaughts
for the next fifteen hundred or more years. As far as can be known,
virtually all works produced by the last Jewish historians, all efforts to
make detailed narrative contributions to the understanding of events,

14. Yerushalmi, *Zakhor,* 15. Three books of the Maccabees, preserved among
Christians, continued to remain unavailable to Jews themselves until modern times.
M. Dagut, *The Biblical Account of the Conquest of Palestine* (Jerusalem, 1954), n. 13. The
view that the Hebrew canon was "finally sealed" at Yabneh, long current in liberal circles
(and still prevailing among some) — because it fit late-dating on canonical sources that
reflected popular scholarly agendas — is now almost certainly considered to be wrong.
Most recent writing on the subject argues convincingly from primary sources that
Yabneh in no way "sealed" the canon. Just as Martin Luther raised questions about New
Testament books over a millennium after the New Testament canon had been closed in
any meaningful sense, so it is possible to see Yabneh as raising and settling questions
about the canon long after the fact of its earlier closure.
15. Yerushalmi, *Zakhor,* 16.

disappeared. While we know the names of some of these historians and the titles of the works which were produced, mainly through the works of contemporaries or through hints, attributions, or snippets found in later works, little of substance survived the successive holocausts which Jews suffered. We know, for example, of the 144-volume history of the world produced by Nicholas of Damascus, the friend of Herod whose writing was done in Jerusalem.[16] We also know about Justus of Tiberias, whose works also vanished (albeit centuries later). But what we know of such historians and their works comes from the relatively modest number of volumes written by Josephus Flavius, all of which seem to have survived. Josephus is the one noteworthy exception to this disappearance of works written by Jewish historians. His *Jewish War,* written immediately after the destruction of A.D. 70, and his *Jewish Antiquities,* published twenty years later, within a decade of the Rabbinic Council at Yabneh was largely ignored by Jewish peoples. Josephus was viewed as a traitor. He was seen as one guilty of betraying his own people. As a commander of Jewish forces which were besieged, he had been forced to surrender his garrison, an act for which he was never forgiven. The remainder of the war, the agony and trauma of destruction and utter devastation, he witnessed from the sidelines. Yet, without Josephus, little would be known about Jewish history during the Hellenistic period, from the conquest of Alexander the Great down to the destruction of Jerusalem and the temple.

The story of the Jews and their survival for nearly four thousand years is, however interpreted, a story of successive tragedies and triumphs. It is a story of a never-ending and ongoing predicament. It is a predicament in which struggles for survival and amazing triumphs have often been followed by devastating disaster and horrific suffering. This predicament has made it possible for one small and seemingly insignificant people to find grounds for faith and reasons for hope in particular events, events which for them have possessed redemptive qualities. The events that have made their historical understandings especially acute were seen as theodicy. For ancient Israel, and for the countless generations of Jews who, as the children of Judah, continued to observe the

---

16. Martin Hengel, "The Sources of the History of Earliest Christianity," in *Earliest Christianity* (London: SCM Press, 1974), 3-34, esp. 7, speaks of Nicholas of Damascus as the one whose work provided much of the data used by Josephus. Also, cf. F. F. Bruce.

remembrance of events experienced by their ancestors, ancestors who began as downtrodden slaves, the history that matters is theology and the theology that matters comes out of events. Yerushalmi, in his penetrating and powerful *Zakhor: Jewish History and Jewish Memory*, provides some of our most informed understandings. His words aptly summarize the place of history as theodicy: "It was ancient Israel that first assigned a decisive significance to history [both the past and representations of that past] and thus forged a new world-view whose essential premises were eventually appropriated by Christianity and Islam as well."[17]

## II. The Remembrance of Redemption: The Resurrection

For I have received of the Lord that which I also delivered to you, that the Lord Jesus, the same night in which he was betrayed, took bread; and when he had given thanks, he broke it, and said, "Take, eat! This is my body which is broken for you: this do in *remembrance* of me." After the same manner also he took the cup, saying, "This is the New Testament in my Blood: this do, as often as you drink it, in *remembrance* of me."

1 Corinthians 11:23-25, italics added

But the Comforter, who is the Holy Spirit, whom the Father will send in my name, he shall teach you all things, and bring all things to your *remembrance*, whatsoever I have said to you.

John 14:26, italics added

For Christians, from their beginnings through every age since, the Resurrection has held both personal and universal significance. Quite quintessentially, this event remains *the* Christian event. That is to say, along with the Incarnation[18] and Atonement,[19] the Resurrection is

17. Yerushalmi, *Zakhor*, 8.

18. Among the strongest recent works on this subject are Brian Hebblethwaite, *The Incarnation: Collected Essays in Christology* (Cambridge: Cambridge University Press, 1987), and Richard Starch, *The Word and the Christ: An Essay in Analytic Christology* (Oxford: Clarendon Press, 1991). I am especially grateful to my colleagues,

pivotal to Christian belief.[20] It is the event of *remembrance,* the event observed, witnessed, remembered, contemplated, and recorded, and handed down by Christians ever after. The earliest Christians, from what we know, seem not to have been particularly interested in looking at the course of other immediate or mundane events. Their hearts were where their treasure was. What they called their "Blessed Hope" was in heaven. They expected to see the world, with all its injustice, misery, and sorrow, soon come to an end. They wanted to make sure they were ready for *that* event; and they strove to prepare all of humanity, as many as possible, for the same event. For that very reason, Christians practiced the disciplines, exercises, and rituals of *remembrance.* They wanted to recapture and hold in remembrance every exact detail, to understand exactly what had happened — to Jesus the Messiah, to themselves as his Church, and to many of those who surrounded them. Attempts to appreciate how early Christians developed this remembrance and how they understood their own views of the Resurrection, whatever the cultural environment within which they lived, can be compared to attempts to appreciate how early descendants of Israel maintained their remembrance of the Exodus. For Christians, the Eucharist itself, as a regular and supreme act of *remembrance* in "joyful grace," could have no meaning or worth apart from the Resurrection.

Human thinking about death, quite obviously, is both ubiquitous and unceasing. That being so, thinking about the relationship between death and life, and the prospects or possibilities of life after death and thinking

---

Keith E. Yandell and D. A. Carson, for helpful insights and suggestions. See Yandell's "The Logic of God Incarnate," a paper later published as "Some Problems for Tomistic Incarnationists," *International Journal for Philosophy of Religion* 30, no. 3 (December 1991): 169-82. See also Ronald J. Feenstra and Cornelius Plantinga, Jr., eds., *Trinity, Incarnation, and Atonement: Philosophical and Theological Essays* (Notre Dame: University of Notre Dame Press, 1989); David Brown, *The Divine Trinity* (La Salle, Ill.: Open Court Publishers, 1985).

19. Alister E. McGrath, *Iustitia Dei: A History of the Christian Doctrine of Justice,* 2 vols. (Cambridge: Cambridge University Press, 1986); and Thomas V. Morris, "Divine Necessity and Divine Goodness," in *Divine and Human Action: Essays in the Metaphysics of Theism* (Ithaca, N.Y.: Cornell University Press, 1988), 313-44.

20. Thomas F. Torrance, *Space, Time and Resurrection* (Grand Rapids: Wm. B. Eerdmans, 1976), 61-105: "If the resurrection is not an event in history, a happening within the same order of physical existence to which we belong, then atonement and redemption are empty vanities, for they achieve nothing for historical men and women in the world" (87).

about what a life after death might be is also timeless and ubiquitous. Such Indic concepts as transmigration *(samsāra)* and reincarnation *(avatāra)*, not to mention "absorption" or "release" *(moksha)* and "annihilation" or "extinction" *(nirvāna)*, are but small samples of this category of imaginative, philosophical, speculative, or theological thinking. Conceptualizations concerning the resurrection from the dead, in the most general sense, have also been timeless and ubiquitous. Speculations and suppositions about this possibility can be found in virtually all religious systems. But more specifically, within the great traditions arising out of Abrahamic monotheism, the doctrine has become more pronounced. It is found in the most ancient of Hebrew Scriptures: from the time when Job first declared his conviction that "Though after my skin worms destroy this body, yet in my flesh shall I see God" (19:26); down to the time of Daniel's declaration that "those who sleep in the dust of the earth will wake, some to everlasting life and some to . . . eternal abhorrence" and that "the righteous would shine forth like the stars in their heavenly Father's realm" (12:1-3). Before the advent of the Christian era, Jewish thinkers, notably the Pharisees, had made belief in a future resurrection one of their fundamental doctrines. Most specifically of all, we know that, from earliest times, Christians have viewed the resurrection of Jesus from the dead as, quite absolutely, the single most pivotal event of their faith. It has been seen not only as *the* event which assures life after death, as a set of everlasting relationships (with God: in "eternal salvation"), but also as the single most pivotal event upon which virtually all other beliefs in Christian faith must, of necessity, hang.

The evidence required for rational assent to the actual occurrence of this event, as well as its nature, is far from simple or easy. Just trying to discover exactly what that event was and what it entailed for those who first accepted it (if not what it has entailed ever since) is a formidable undertaking. There has never been a time, ever since the days when the event is first reported to have occurred, when there have not been those who doubted that the event took place and when some have not doubted that such an event was possible. The historian's task, when acting within the canons of history as a modern discipline, is to deal critically with what is known, with what is not known, and with how to tell the difference. The task is to make critical assessments in such a way as to construct a coherent understanding of what actually did happen and, at the same time, to understand the entire context within which that event and other related events took place so as to find grounds for making a rational assessment of what actually did happen. Such a task is made all the more daunting, in our age, as indeed in any age, by the massive clouds of doubt and hostility, sometimes accompanied by violence, which have assailed Christian assent to the historicity of the event. In modern times, especially since the dawn of the Enlightenment and scientific positivism, emphasis upon critical assessment, careful observation, exact methods, weighing data, correct reporting, physical evidence, and hard facts has been combined with various forms of "secular" humanism, in common efforts to reject any conclusion that might seem to smack of dependence upon "the unexplained" or "the unknown," the miraculous or the supernatural.

It is interesting that, with few exceptions, historians themselves have carefully avoided attempts to reach conclusions regarding the historicity of the Resurrection. Why this should be so is not altogether clear. Perhaps practitioners of this craft have done so out of that combination of caution, skepticism, and humility which are the congenital hallmarks of any sound historian. Historical conclusions, for "critical" historians after all, must always be contingent and always devoid of finality. A historian's final judgment is always and forever suspended. It is suggestive, barring the uncovering of further evidence. Perhaps historians as such have felt that their "theater of operations" should consist, more properly, of an examination of the deeds and thoughts, however heroic or sordid, of the living, of peoples, and of institutions, especially of states, societies, and cultures, not to mention the contexts within which events take place. Perhaps historians have felt that study of this subject should be left to other thinkers, especially theologians. However much that may or may not be so, it is nevertheless interesting that the most critical, solid, and properly critical work on this subject has been done by theologians. By way of comparison, just as the crucial historical understandings of ancient Israel (and Judah) as "chosen people" were too important to be left to historians and became the special responsibility of prophets, so too the crucial historical understandings of the Christian Church (and churches) as "chosen people" were also too important to be left to historians and, in consequence, became the special responsibility of theologians.[21]

21. Perhaps this is nowhere made more explicit than in Harvey Van Austin, *The Historian and the Believer: The Morality of Historical Knowledge and Christian Belief* (New York: Macmillan, 1966): "I wished to make it clear that the basic intention behind the entire book was theological" (xvi).

Leading the way in erudite and thorough study of this subject is Peter Carnley. His work, entitled *The Structure of Resurrection Belief,* is a rigorous and searching analysis of major issues addressed and questions asked by virtually all of those scholars over the past two centuries who have tried to understand the event and its meaning. It makes both critical and constructive assessments. It explores various epistemological, onto- logical, metaphysical, historical, and theological difficulties and examines both the historicity *and* the mystery of the Resurrection as an event in itself. Carnley focuses particular attention upon transcendental dimen- sions, probing into the implications within "what was seen" and the "appearances" and/or "presences" of Jesus immediately after the Resur- rection. He especially scrutinizes those claims that, from the beginning, have raised doubts and uncertainties among Christians and non-Chris- tians alike. He critically ponders items of "evidence" taken from witnesses and handed down in oral tradition, as later recorded in earliest written accounts. And he weighs views of scholars who have reflected upon the historicity of the Resurrection, thinkers both early and contemporary.

## A. *The Event and the Evidence*

The task of investigating the historicity of the Resurrection can be divided neatly into two parts. For heuristic or pedagogical purposes, these can be visualized as circles. The first circle concerns evidence connected to the event itself, as understood from *inside* the most im- mediate context of the event. It concerns "what was seen" within a span of fifty-two days: from the Crucifixion and Resurrection of Jesus to the Ascension and Pentecost. The second circle concerns evidence related to the event, as understood *outside* the immediate context of the event. A widening circle, or series of concentric circles of evidence radiate outward, in time and space, from the event. These two circles can be considered as separate categories of evidence; but the second circle can itself be divided into subspheres, from which data is extracted. Taken together, these concentric-circles and subcircles embrace questions about historicity and historicism.

The demand that information concerning the occurrence of any particular event, however mysterious, should be seen for our purposes as comparable to information concerning any other ordinary historical event is an understandable demand. The same can be said for questions concerning the comparability (or the similitude) of all historical events. The Resurrection is an event that was reported. It reportedly occurred at a particular place on earth and at a particular point in time: a roughly datable instant three days after burial in a location either within or just outside Jerusalem. That believers and doubters alike down through the ages have made demands favoring such comparability is both under-standable and reasonable. Such being the case, the most appropriate approach, especially within the intellectual environment of the past two centuries among those engaging in critical-historical inquiry, has been to submit the evidence to scrutiny and testing.

While other names could be mentioned, during the last century and a half two thinkers in particular can be seen as defenders of the proposition that the Resurrection was indeed a historical event.[22] Sep-arated from each other by one hundred years, each faced remarkably similar circumstances: namely, combinations of wavering Christians and skeptical non-Christians who were questioning the historicity of the event. B. F. Westcott's *The Gospel of the Resurrection* (1866) was probably published in direct reaction to a work of German higher criticism put forth by David Strauss. It came out at a time when works by Charles Darwin, John Stuart Mill, and Auguste Comte were seen as undermining the intellectual foundations of Christian belief. Wolfhart Pannenberg's *Grundzüge der Christologie* (1966) also had to face Chris-tian and non-Christian skeptics.[23] Both Westcott and Pannenberg felt

22. Others who have done the same are Frank Morison, *Who Moved the Stone* (1930; reprint, London: Faber & Faber, 1968); Merrill C. Tenney, "The Historicity of the Resurrection," and Clark H. Pinnock, "On the Third Day," in *Jesus of Nazareth: Saviour and Lord*, ed. Carl F. H. Henry (London: Tyndale, 1966), 133-44 and 145-56; George Eldon Ladd, *I Believe in the Resurrection of Jesus* (Grand Rapids: Wm. B. Eerd-mans, 1975); and finally, William Lane Craig, in *The Historical Argument for the Resur-rection of Jesus during the Deist Controversy*, vol. 23 in Texts and Studies in Religion (Lewiston, N.Y., and Queenston, Ont.: Edwin Mellen Press, 1985), vii, and in his later *Assessing the New Testament Evidence for the Historicity of the Resurrection of Jesus* (Lewiston, N.Y., and Queenston, Ont.: Edwin Mellen Press, 1989). Craig is also extremely useful for bibliography.

23. Pannenberg was responding to doubts about the appropriateness of trying to explain the Resurrection as a historical event raised by Karl Barth and Rudolf Bult-mann. Also see Alister E. McGrath, *The Making of Modern German Christology from the Enlightenment to Pannenberg* (Oxford: Basil Blackwell, 1986), 161-85.

that the event should be handled with the same methodological tools as those used to handle any other event of the human past — namely, by examining comparable evidence with the instruments of scientific, critical-historical investigation.[24] The intensity with which they strove to establish the objectivity and reality of the event lay in their conviction that any kind of faith requires a firm foundation of historical authenticity. For them, the entire edifice of Christian doctrine, as manifest in Christ as the ultimate Revelation of God to mankind — from Incarnation to Atonement, to Resurrection, and to Final Consummation — rested upon the historicity of this single event.

## 1. The Event

But what, exactly, was this event? What were its constituent elements? It is important to point out that what actually happened was never witnessed by anyone. No one ever claimed to have personally seen the dead body of Jesus come to life. All of the evidence indicates, by inference, that what happened occurred within the solitary silence of the tomb. In this same connection, three further questions arise: First, one can ask whether it was the same body that had belonged to Jesus during his roughly thirty-three years that came back to life (or whether the body was, in some way, different). Next, if one answers the first question affirmatively, one can ask a second question, namely, whether it was God who caused the body of Jesus to come back to life. And, finally, if one answers the second question affirmatively, then one must ask the third question: whether God's causing the body of Jesus to come back to life, also, and necessarily, means that Christ's death — the death of Jesus-Messiah — was and is an atoning death (bringing redemption and salvation to all of humanity).[25] Answers to these questions are to be found within the nature of the evidence and the ways in which such evidence, including evidence drawn from wider contexts (the wider categories or circles of evidence mentioned above), actually was, has been, could have been, or is being handled.

24. Peter Carnley, *The Structure of Resurrection Belief* (Oxford: Clarendon Press, 1987), 36.

25. For details of the standard evangelical apologetic on this subject, see Frank Morison, *Who Moved the Stone.*

A further need for clarification arises out of the very complexity of the event and its implications. A distinction can be made, in fact, between elements of the event that were directly experienced and elements that were not directly experienced but were inferred from elements directly experienced. These same elements of evidence, moreover, can be divided again both chronologically and locationally: first, into consideration of what happened to the body of Jesus inside the grave and what happened to Jesus afterwards outside the grave; and secondly, again, into what happened to Jesus in his continuing life *between* the several appearances that were reported and *during* those several appearances.

## 2. The Evidence

Acceptance of the historicity of the event rests, at least to some degree, upon inferences. These, in turn, are drawn from claims of what are purported to have been clear, concrete, and direct experiences. These experiences can be separated into two strands or subcategories: first, the story of the sighting of the empty tomb; and, second, the cycle of stories that narrate appearances of the raised Christ. These two subevents, together, made up the event of the Resurrection insofar as it could be humanly experienced.[26] Some critics argue that they could have originated independently, and then been compared and combined at a later time. One story emphasizes the urban setting of Jerusalem, and Mary Magdalene as the person who first encountered Jesus, without the presence of any male followers. Another set of stories stresses Galilee as the place where Jesus was seen, and Peter as the person who saw Jesus. The two categories of subevents constitute the only available direct and immediate evidence of the event. "What was seen" by witnesses, reported, and then passed on was eventually incorporated within a single corpus of written texts. "What was seen," therefore, permits an opening of the event to further investigation and analysis.

What is impressive about the eyewitness reports regarding "what was seen" of the resurrected Christ recorded in the canon (Epistles and Gospels) is their reticent, sparse, and terse fabric. The very words suggest a certain incredulity. When the women reported that the tomb was

---

26. Carnley, *The Structure of Resurrection Belief,* 44.

empty, they were not believed, at least not initially. Their words were not taken seriously (Luke 24:11). When Jesus appeared on a mountain in Galilee, some who were there doubted that he had actually appeared (Matt. 28:17). The episode about doubts expressed by Thomas is all too well known. The consequence of this "slowness of heart to believe" (Luke 24:25) meant that at a later time these early followers of Jesus had to endure embarrassment. But if we put ourselves in their place, few of us would not, at the very least, find news of the return to life of a dead person to be so remarkable that it would be all the harder to accept if the evidence seemed, at best, to be ambiguous, contentious, incomplete, and even contradictory. The result seems to have been an amalgam of fragments, claims of historical fact mingled with defensive arguments in support of the validity of those claims.

(1) The Empty Tomb: This story, told in all four Gospels, contains some marked differences of detail. Some contemporary authorities either favor the Mark (16:1-8) rendition, explaining variances found in Matthew (28) and Luke (24) as essentially annunciatory (kerygmatic) or apologetic elaborations of the original in Mark; others are attracted to the mystical qualities in the story and subsequent incidents as told in John (20). Many writers, in non-historical arguments, emphasize the proclamatory or kerygmatic announcements (made by the angel): "He is not here!" and "He is risen!" It is interesting that Paul, the most prolific of all early Christian writers, never mentions what happened at the tomb or in Jerusalem. In fact, Paul never mentions any specific places or times when he writes about the event to the Corinthians (1 Cor. 15:3-7).

While much of this story, with all its complexities and nuances, could be examined in more detail and more exhaustively than is being done here, the basic question comes down to whether the testimony of Mary's discovery of the empty tomb is reliable and sufficient enough to serve as a foundation for an inference that might support the con-clusion either (1) that Jesus was resurrected by God inside the tomb; and/or (2) that Jesus went on from there to live a different and more exalted life "at the right hand of God" (to use the biblical metaphor). In short, is the historicity of the discovery of the empty tomb strong enough to support the inference that the event in question actually occurred? The debates over this question have been voluminous and stretch over many years. Those who doubt the historicity of this episode have tended to see the earliest version of the story as a legend, more as a product *of* faith than as a ground *for* faith. Those who argue in the opposite direction have tended to stress the reliability of the record in itself. All of the arguments, on either side. fall short of proof. What is clear and admitted on all sides, regardless of how much weight is given to the empty tomb tradition, is the general conclusion that this piece of evidence is, by itself, not enough. What is also conceded is the position that it by no means constitutes all of "what was seen."

*(2) The Appearances:* Each of the Gospels reports separate instances in which Jesus appeared to one follower or another, or to groups of followers. The earliest written record of these instances, however, is found at the end of Paul's first letter to the Corinthians (15:3-8). In this document, however, the "appearances" and/or personal "presences" of Jesus as the risen Christ are closely connected to and given in support of the central proclamation *(kerygma)* of the truth (gospel). Paul reminds his readers that the truth he had preached to them, the truth they had received, and the truth on which they now took their stand, and even the very truth that was now bringing them to salvation, rested first and foremost upon information. This information had not originated with him but had been imparted to him. This information was, as he put it, "that Christ died for our sins, *in accordance with the scriptures;* that he was buried, *in accordance with the scriptures;* and that he was raised to life on the third day, *in accordance with the scriptures;* and that he appeared to Cephas [Peter], and afterwards to the Twelve. Then he appeared to over five hundred . . . at once, most of whom are still alive, though some have died. After that he appeared to James, and then to all the apostles" (emphasis added). Only after that, "and last of all," Paul added, "he appeared to me, as one born abnormally [and/or prematurely]."

Even if one grants the possibility, as some argue, that Paul was not citing these appearances as hard evidence upon which conclusions could inferentially be based, one cannot deny that he asserted that Jesus had appeared and that he used the very same terms to describe his own experience as he did to describe the reported experiences of others. Whatever the discrepancies and discontinuities between and among later Gospel narratives and this earlier letter (e.g., whether there were eleven or twelve, etc.), Paul did pronounce, "Jesus did appear!" By this, he meant "He was seen!" This paramount fact concerning what happened three days after the death and the burial had one single, clear, and simple purpose. It was to provide an empirical foundation for one conviction: namely, belief about the event was basic to belief about the truth of the totality of the gospel proclamation *(kerygma)*. Whatever else might have been intended, a basic and conclusive position was being taken: namely, that the Jesus who had appeared and had been perceived as being alive was, in fact, the very same Jesus who had been known *before* the Crucifixion. The operative Greek term used by Paul was ὤφθη *(ophthae):* "He allowed himself to be seen!" as much as "He appeared."[27]

Clearly, both from words used in Paul's letter and from words in the Gospels, followers of Jesus were convinced that they had actually seen the risen Messiah. The question of whether they actually did in fact see Jesus cannot, in one sense, be fully certified. The exact nature of what it was that they actually saw could be interpreted in different ways. Regardless of how one assesses different reports found in the Gospel records, any historian who assembles this evidence and comes to some conclusion concerning the occurrence of the Resurrection must grapple with puzzling questions about exactly what it was that the evidence described. This question remains crucial.

In the end, all of the information drawn from this first circle of evidence, the circle of time and space closest to the actual event, brings one back to a consideration of the nature of the event itself. This requires comparison between the kind of body possessed by the risen Jesus and the kind of body possessed by Jesus of Nazareth from the time of his birth to the time of his death upon the cross. To argue that evidence consisting of appearances *after* the Resurrection are to be seen as constituting evidence of the same kind as that used for asserting the death and burial of Jesus *before* the Resurrection entails a conclusion that what happened afterwards, both as to the event (Resurrection) and as the evidence (appearances), can simply be assimilated into the events which occurred during the life of Jesus. But this entailment of an unbroken continuity in which the appearances of the risen Messiah can be treated as observable phenomena open to ordinary techniques of historical research raises some serious difficulties. As soon as evidence is seen as manifesting a transformation into a supernatural body or location, as

27. Ibid., 206ff. See Timothy C. Morgan, "The Mother of All Muddles," *Christianity Today*, 5 April 1993, 62-66, on the controversy over views found in Murray J. Harris, *Grave to Glory*; cf. views of J. I. Packer summarized in same article, 64-65.

soon as words indicate that the risen Christ is now "at God's right hand" or that Jesus has "gone to heaven from whence he will return," something substantially different has happened. What has been done exceeds the bounds of ordinary historical evidence, or of normal earthly facts. Questions remain unanswered.

The conclusion that one can draw is that what was hidden from view no longer only concerns what happened *inside* the tomb but also what happened afterwards *outside* the tomb. The continuing earthly and heavenly life of the exalted Christ remains cloaked in mystery and silence. It lies beyond the reach of merely human tools. Even if the perceptual experiences were, as reported, clear and distinct as reports, the actual nature of the risen Christ remains hidden and obscure. Despite arguments made by some (e.g., Tenney, Pinnock, etc.), there is no way to determine whether the body of the risen Christ that was reported and seen is the very *same* and identical body as the corpse that had been taken off the cross and buried in the tomb. A "re-animated" body could well tend, by its very nature, to make for an event devoid of those qualities of everlasting exaltation required to give it significance. The event then is drained of its very essential, redemptively salvific (soteriological), or theological meaning. Lack of human understanding concerning the supernatural nature of the Resurrection, the event by which Christ's mortal body was transformed into a body immortal, so that he could enter into his heavenly life — a life "glorified" and "transfigured," and more than a mere continuation of the previous life — means that human beings can still only *imagine*, rather than fully know, exactly what that life might be. No comparisons are possible. In short, when all is said and done, it is the *disappearances* of the risen Christ that are just as important as the *appearances*. By mirrors and metaphors, we only "see through a glass darkly."

## B. The Event within Remembrance

We can now turn to a consideration of the second circle of evidence. This concerns details *outside* the immediate context, details removed in time and space, by varying degrees, from those fifty-two days between the death of Jesus and the paraclete-inspired formal birth of his Church. At the outset, the most central experience which none could forget was the terrible trauma of the Crucifixion itself. The unforgettably ignominious execution of their leader, devastating as it undoubtedly was, seems to have left the followers of Jesus in a state of extreme bewilderment, confusion, and disarray. Far from clear about what it was that the words of Jesus had actually meant, too frightened to admit having known him, they were all too conscious of their own frailties and shortcomings. This much emerges from the pitiful words they left behind.

But something else had happened, altering their entire outlook even more profoundly. This had happened three days later. Here was something that entirely turned that earlier experience around. This new experience, immediately and dramatically and completely, transformed their entire outlook. Defeat was turned into victory. Catastrophe became what Tolkien would have called "eucatastrophe." It was that kind of experience or realization which C. S. Lewis described as being "Surprised by joy." This great "turn" seems to have come out of sudden and unexpected news, from startling new information: the same Jesus whom followers themselves had seen crucified, officially pronounced dead, and then placed in a grave, was no longer dead. He was alive! This information, drawn from immediate testimony and firsthand witnesses, indicated that he had actually been seen. Some who knew him intimately had actually spoken to him. Others had touched him. Two followers, one named Cleopas, had walked with him and talked with him on the road to Emmaus. He had been recognized in his way of "breaking of bread" and in his "giving a blessing." On the shores of Lake Galilee, he had cooked fish for followers, and eaten breakfast with them. A dawning conviction that this new information, sketchy as it was, was accurate and authentic also began to grow, especially as it was compared with new discoveries made in "archives of memory" and in "storehouses of scripture."

Suddenly, it seems, everything clicked. With what can only be seen as a development of startling, even amazing speed, at least to any observer of world events, those who had been so confused and uncomprehending and doubtful saw all sorts of things clearly. Minds began to recall, with ever increasing excitement and intensity, little things that Jesus had done and said, things he had taught. These things began to fit into a clear and distinct pattern. In fact, just prior to his final disappearance, the risen Christ had specifically brought such things to their *remembrance.* They remembered his chiding: how they were dull and "slow of heart." They remembered his remindings: "These are the words which I spoke to you, while I was yet with you, that all things must be fulfilled, which were written in the Law of Moses, and in the Prophets, and in the Songs, concerning me." They remembered how he "opened their understandings," showing how Scriptures had long ago foretold: "the Messiah would suffer death and rise from the dead the third day so that repentance bringing forgiveness of sins could be proclaimed to all peoples" (Luke 24:44-48). They remembered what they had heard, seen, and touched. They remembered and understood with a certainty and clarity as never before. Jesus himself had left no written words. But words he had spoken they now vividly remembered. These became the foundation for what they now believed and understood. Words he had spoken they now shared and carefully transmitted. Deeds and events, recalled and related in anecdotes, while often commonplace, were never again merely mundane.

Something else seems quite clear. Belief in the Resurrection triggered an amazing explosion of religious activity. This first erupted in Jerusalem and then sent radiating waves outwards far and wide. Many seem to have believed what they heard quite soon after news of the Resurrection reached them. Indeed, what then occurred was perhaps the most rapid, wide-ranging, and far-reaching spread of beliefs and convictions that, as far as we know, has ever happened — a movement of radical conversions into an entirely new and life-transforming set of world views and practices. For those who were convinced that they had seen the risen Christ, the fact of the Resurrection was itself *the* ultimate event. Their conviction was complete and it was unanswerable. They could not demonstrate what they had experienced. They had no hard, empirical evidence. But many believed because of *all the other things* which they had heard and seen, events that accompanied the simple words "He is Risen!" What seems to have added considerable weight to a simple belief in the Resurrection was the amazing transformation that took place among believers: the capacity and power that so many folk of humble background acquired, the speed with which their numbers increased, the courage with which they endured afflictions from entrenched interests and institutions, and the readiness with which so many gave up their lives for the sake of their convictions.

A wholly new and totalistic world view stemmed from the Resurrection. If Jesus as the Messiah was indeed risen from the dead, then he could be no ordinary mortal. Nothing less than God Incarnate (God-

Man or "Son of God") could he be.[28] Then the Crucifixion was no
ordinary event, not just another tragic event in a world filled with
tragedy and injustice, but something much more. What had happened
upon the day of Passover was a cosmic and universal Passover, an
ultimate act of Atonement. The Lamb of God, as the definitive expression of Divine Grace, had given himself for all mankind. An everlasting
personal relationship with God was now possible. It all seemed to add
up. Comprehension of the whole human predicament, in its dark, dire,
and utterly self-destructive propensity, when set against this lofty notion
of God's love, moved one to true repentance. The Resurrection, indeed,
called for nothing less than a totally transformed outlook. An entirely
new structure of beliefs and convictions stemming from the Resurrection was being ratified, day by day, by inner growth within each true
believer. A close and continual contact with the resurrected Messiah was
being nourished by the agency of God's own Spirit.

Yet there are technical difficulties. Anyone who posits the possibility
that the impact of Jesus and his followers was one of the pivotal events of
History must face tough questions. What can and what cannot be established? What, in short, is the nature of the evidence? Here we come to the
nub of the matter. There is something deeply implanted in all human
beings: a fundamental human curiosity. How could anyone who had
heard that Jesus had risen from the dead not want to know more? How
could such a person *not* wish to learn more, to get details about the person
himself? How could someone *not* ask questions, do a little checking up
and cross-questioning, about what was being told? It is important to
remember, in this regard, that most conversations in our ordinary, everyday world are never recorded. No reporter writes down what we say to
each other, what matters we have discussed. This is all the more so in
societies where few can read. But, for that very reason, nonliterate and
preliterate (and nonrecorded) conversations, especially anecdotes and
stories, can become all the more memorable. The anecdotes that are told
about great personalities have had a tendency, down through successive
ages, to become particularly memorable.

---

28. Keith E. Yandell, "Some Problems for Tomistic Incarnationists," 169-82. Also,
Yandell's "A Gross and Palpable Contradiction? Incarnation and Consistency" and "The
Most Brutal and Inexcusable Error in Counting? Trinity and Consistency" (unpublished
papers).

The Gospels consist of stories. Stories — anecdotes and narratives, small and not so small — are the very life breath of historical understanding. They are its heart and soul. Hundreds are the little tales told about and by some persons. For every people, metaphorically speaking, there is an Abraham Lincoln or a Winston Churchill, a Napoleon or a Wellington, a Mahatma Gandhi or a Mao Ze-dong. Their currency is strong, mostly scattered but sometimes gathered into anthologies. Many rest upon the word of a single person. Many are told and retold over dinner tables, often being rounded off so as to achieve some effect or make some point. Few of these can be certified, documented, or definitively established as genuine or true, even when most or almost all believe that they really are. Yet, even the less genuine or more apocryphal are accepted if and when they are seen as conforming to what, by consensus, is understood to have been typical. Indeed, it is often true that anecdotes bring us closer to understanding a person or an event than reams of well-documented data. An entire corpus of anecdotal material, in aggregate, sometimes serves to convey a sense of understandings that cannot be achieved by the contents of any particular anecdote. The aphorism that no anecdote (or story) should be allowed to suffer because perhaps every particle of it may not be entirely correct or true conveys this point.

From what we can discover, a screening process developed which probably took about twenty years. Anecdotes and sayings, stories and doctrines concerning Jesus and his followers were collected, shaped, and sifted into a fixed corpus of final, irreducible, recognized tradition. Many of the eyewitnesses still alive could provide fine-tuning and corroboration. At any rate, what was remembered became codified in four "sealed" versions of the same remembrances. These biographical works we now call the Gospels.[29] Accompanied by other carefully *remembered* events codified as Acts of the Apostles and by a select collection of the inspired and authoritative letters, specifically by the Epistles of Paul and Peter, James and John and Jude, these became fixed. Moreover, it is not difficult to see that the anecdotes that became part of the sacred text survived rigorous sifting and testing for utility and veracity, and contained no slightest hint nor discernible spirit of deception or dishonesty. Rather,

---

29. Richard A. Burridge, *What Are the Gospels? A Comparison with Graeco-Roman Biography* (Cambridge: Cambridge University Press, 1992).

they manifested, and manifest still, an attitude of simple humility.[30] In the words of Herbert Butterfield, "The authority accorded in the early Church to the accounts of the witnesses had its roots in the idea of faithfully conserving what had been handed down. It derived from the need which the successors of Jesus's contemporaries felt to keep the evidence of the actual witnesses alive and pure."[31]

## C. The Event and Hebrew Scripture

What enhanced the authority and authenticity, if not the historicity, of the Resurrection was its eventual and ultimate location within the older canon. No development was more momentous. In the genesis of Christian belief, nothing more profoundly gave Christians a sense of History as Destiny than those events, both past and future, which they found recorded and foretold in Hebrew Scripture. To better understand this further sphere of "evidence," one must look again, both at the larger background of Hebrew and Jewish history and at the ways and means by which the elements of this background culture were appropriated. By this means, one can see how, for early Christians, the Resurrection became *the ultimate, the prophetic, and the eschatological* event par excellence.

Above all, it is useful again to remember, and to bear in mind, that *all* the earliest Christians were Jewish. They were Jews both by birth and by cultural heritage. Jewish peoples, just at the time Christians came into being, were in the process of making profound changes in what they themselves believed. They, of all people, had begun to turn away from

30. In his epistle, John's letter described this as "that which was from the beginning, we have heard, which we have seen with our eyes, which we have looked upon, which we have handled, of the Word of life . . . that which we have seen and hear declare we to you" (1 John 1:1-3).

31. Butterfield, *The Origins of History,* 168. Words by C. S. Lewis, in *Miracles* (New York: Macmillan, 1947), 143-44, are no less apt: "The Resurrection is the central theme in every Christian sermon reported in the Acts. . . : what we call the 'gospels,' the narratives of Our Lord's life and death, were composed later, for the benefit of those who had already accepted the *gospel.* . . : they were written for those already converted. The [event], and the theology. . . , comes first: the biography comes later as a comment on it. Nothing could be more unhistorical than to pick out selected sayings . . . from the gospels and to regard those as the datum and the rest of the New Testament as a construction upon it. The first fact in the history. . . is a number of people who say they have seen the Resurrection."

remembering their past (history). The uniqueness of the early Hebrew people had been rooted, quite decidedly, in their unique way of under-standing that what had happened to them in the past was based upon *the* promise. Historical understanding began with theodicy: with redemptive interventions by a personal God, which had begun with Abraham (if not earlier). Remembering the event of their rescue from slavery in Egypt and their entry into the promised land, they had become more obsessed with remembering and understanding exact but special details of the past than any other people, either before or since. But since the promise had always been conditional, experience had also always taught them that their treatment by God had depended upon behavior. In short, the judgments of God, as well as redemptive rescues, had occurred. These had been embedded within the events that God had allowed to happen. Israel's greatest prophets had been able to show, quite explicitly, that the colossal disasters and sufferings had been brought down upon the heads of Israel's peoples by their own actions. Judgments of God, exceeding the sufferings of any other nation — the destruction of both Jerusalem and the temple, followed by dispersion and exile to other lands — were direct con-sequences of their own behavior, as brought upon them by God.

Perhaps the ancient Jews had learned too well. If what had happened to them was a consequence of their own actions, then the logic of survival was severe. If the remnant who had survived, who had returned to their promised land and rebuilt their city and temple, put God's commands first, trying to obey laws down to the tiniest detail, perhaps they would survive. Law, as remembrance of past events (History), became their obsession. Little did they realize that the very Judaism that resulted also generated attitudes toward events, both past and future, with implications that might bring further disasters. Rewriting their history, they argued that past sins and consequent sufferings had come from consorting with aliens, intermingling and becoming contaminated by them. Henceforth, going to the opposite extreme, many of them closed ranks, preserving them-selves from corruption, and separated themselves from the world around them. Surely, no matter what happened, God's promise would stand firm. Indeed, this understanding of events was still linked to that hope. Only now, events vindicating the promise no longer lay just in the past, but in the future. Empires — the Babylonian, the Persian, the Greek, and the Roman — might come and go. But the promise of God as the Redeemer of his people would stand firm. Faithfulness would bring about the final vindication. The hand of God still lay in events. The events of divine redemption were not yet completed. If consequences of wrongs by parents were suffered by children, even to the third and fourth generations, suffering was redemptive: it was chastening, compelling the stubborn or wicked to mend their ways. In a historic mission, the chosen were being obliged to bear a "double burden," bringing all of the world to a true and proper worship of God.

But lofty hopes could be too much to bear and sufferings could become too heavy. If the chosen had to wait so long, of what use were such long delays? It would have been better never to have been born. To think that a loving and redeeming Creator could form minds out of the dust only to bring about such affliction was intolerable: it would have been better if the dust itself had never been created. The anguish of past experiences, reflected in continual writing about even ordinary events, did not cease. In dark despair and continuous wrestling with God, Jewish descendants of Israel clung to their dreams. Such dreams looked forward to an ultimate event, a final consummation of History, an ultimate Rescue. A Redeemer, some Savior or Prince of David's lineage, would be the duly Anointed One: the Messiah. That kingdom of righteousness would cover the whole earth and that reign would have no end.

This, then, was the widest of all contexts surrounding the Resurrection. In this context, rejection of the Old Canon as Holy Writ was never, in any real sense, an option. Jesus and his followers were Jews. The Old Canon was already accepted and sacred. For Jewish Christians, the Old Testament was authoritative in every detail. This compelling fact, with all its implications, obliged the new chosen people (the Church) to look for antecedents and precedents in the Old Book. But in the process, a new emphasis emerged. The people of early Israel, from the time of Moses if not from Abraham, had emphasized the obligation of remembrance (Zakhor). God had made the promise. His own chosen people he had rescued from oblivion and perpetual thralldom. He had brought them out of Egypt, through the wilderness, and into the promised land. But if Jews of the Exile had turned remembrance into stricter legal and ritual observances of the Law (Torah, etc.), early Christians saw much of the Law as containing and foreshadowing prophecy (and theology). Jesus was the Messiah. As such, he was a powerful figure. Deeply implicated in the details of the Old Testament, the crucified Messiah of Hebrew prophecy could be discerned, as prefigured both in the Law (e.g., redemption, sacrifice, priesthood,

tabernacle/temple, etc.) and in the Suffering Servant whose atoning afflictions were so graphically depicted in the fifty-third chapter of Isaiah.

This vision — in which institutions of the Law looked forward to
something beyond, something serving an eschatological or prophetic
function within the larger stream of redemptive history, could be combined with grand and glorious depictions of even older prophecies pre-
figuring the Messiah as the Great Prince, Redeemer, and Restorer of
Righteousness. Butterfield found in this nexus "an important clue to the
almost incredible transformation that took place . . . so quickly after the
Resurrection. And it must have been quick, for their preaching that Christ
had risen after only three days would have been seriously damaged if the
announcement and the new Gospel had been long delayed."[32]

Prophetic understandings of Jesus and about Jesus, linking his iden-
tity as Messiah both with the fulfillment of the Law and with the Suffering
Servant, totally transformed Christian understandings. It was Jesus who, as
the Messiah, *was* the Suffering Servant. And, as Son of God, he was both
Son of Righteousness and Redeeming Savior. He encompassed all of
History, from before the Creation to after his Second Coming *(Parousia)*
and the Final Judgment. He was the Alpha and the Omega of time.
Analogies and parallels could be found everywhere. Both in old scriptures
and in recent events, "evidences" were self-evident. The interpretations of
these evidences were so amazing, so incomparable, that no imagination
could have dreamed them up. They wove many events into a single,
coherent, and over-arching pattern, a tapestry too wonderful for words.
Prophecy itself became the ground of factuality and true faith, "the evidence of things not seen," and even, like faith itself, "the substance of things
hoped for." Certain events had even happened simply in order to satisfy the
demands and certify the validity of prophecy. All of the Scriptures containing an account of God's dealings with mankind in the past were prophecy.

## D. The Event and Eschatology

The critical historian in the twentieth century who reflects upon the
historicity of the Resurrection while taking for granted concepts common in our day, such as progress or evolution, faces no small difficulty

32. Ibid., 169.

in trying to climb into the mental processes of the early Christians. No less impossible, indeed, are almost any attempts to compare or equate our understandings of history with those held in that remote past. For this very reason, concerns over "what was seen" in various "appearances" when the "presence" of Jesus became manifest to early Christians have engaged the attention of many scholars for centuries. In our own time, some thinkers have staunchly supported the historicity of the event. Others, just as firmly, have opposed it.

Among Christians strongly opposed to placing too much insistence upon strict or total historicity of the Resurrection, few were more pronounced in their views than the renowned theologians Karl Barth and Rudolf Bultmann. While in vehement disagreement with each other over the exact nature of the event and over the validity of evidences relating thereto, on one matter they were agreed. Both argued that the Resurrection, as an event, was more *eschatological* than historical. Barth, in his work entitled *The Resurrection of the Dead,* argued that the event itself was indifferent to time and space. The transcendent events witnessed outside Jerusalem (c. A.D. 33) could just as well have been glimpsed by someone in our own day. For Barth, each appearance was more than just another ordinary experience. Each experience of the event fell within that category of special events which were divine revelation. In the language of faith, each event was a miraculous "happening" *(Geschichte)*. It was something caused by God, not an ordinary human event *(Historie)* which could be open to scientific inquiry.[33]

For Bultmann, on the other hand, "the cross and the resurrection formed a single, indivisible cosmic event."[34] That single event connected "forgiveness of sins" with "reconciliation to God." It could not be understood apart from the redemptive act of God as revealed in the death of Christ as an event (Mark 10:45). The Jesus who had "died for all," who had been "put to death" for human transgressions, was the same Jesus who, in the words of Paul, had been "raised for our justification" (Rom. 4:25). As Paul had reminded Corinthian believers that "if Christ has not been raised, you are still in your sins" (1 Cor. 15:17-18), so the

33. Karl Barth, *The Resurrection of the Dead,* trans. H. J. Stenning (London: Hodder & Stoughton, 1933).

34. Rudolf Bultmann, *Kerygma and Myth,* ed. W. H. Bartsch (London: SPCK, 1953), 1:38; and W. Schmithals, "The Saving Event: Cross and Resurrection," chap. 6 in *Introduction to the Theology of Rudolph Bultmann,* trans. John Bowden (London: SCM, 1967).

Crucifixion could have no meaning apart from the Resurrection. Redemptive Atonement and Resurrection, in short, were parts of a single historic event. However, lest this selection of quotations convey a wrong impression and make Bultmann sound Barthian, there was an important distinction. While Bultmann obviously used similar words, what he meant by "event" was quite different. An event, for Bultmann, could only ultimately be reduced to the existential moment in the experience of the believer; and the believer could have nothing whatsoever to do within something objective or real "out there" (outside of subjective experience). In other words, while Barth and Bultmann could agree, in large measure, over what the Resurrection was not, they strongly disagreed as to what the Resurrection really was; and hence, over what it really meant. This was a difference too wide to bridge.

But what prompted this more heavily theological emphasis earlier in this century was a profound loss of confidence in the adequacy of historical inquiry. Critical and scientific methods by themselves were inherently incapable of establishing evidence that would be adequate to the task. Efforts to uncover historical evidence or to establish historical proof were merely human efforts, and hence they were bound to fail. Such efforts compromised acceptable biblical (Lutheran and Reformed) standards with respect to the doctrine of "justification by faith alone." Immanuel Kant, himself convinced of the utter inability of human reason to prove the existence of God, had long ago declared, "I have abolished reason in order to make room for faith."[35] Faith was, by its very nature, not capable of making itself beholden to historical inquiry.

This view reflected a complete withdrawal of confidence in historical methodology. Both Martin Kähler, in his *The So-Called Historical Jesus and the Historic, Biblical Christ*,[36] and Albert Schweitzer, in *The Quest of the Historical Jesus*,[37] stressed the permanently contingent, insecure, and relative character of historical inquiry. Ernst Troeltsch, deriding the "historicizing of all our thoughts about man, his culture and values," had predicted that appraisals of the past would always be open to revision and

---

35. Immanuel Kant, preface to *Critique of Pure Reason*, trans. Norman Kemp Smith, 2nd ed. (London and New York: Macmillan, 1958), 29: "I have therefore found it necessary to deny *knowledge*, in order to make room for *faith (Glaube)*."

36. Ed. and trans. Carl E. Braaten (Philadelphia: Fortress Press, 1964).

37. Albert Schweitzer, *The Quest of the Historical Jesus* (New York: Macmillan, 1968).

that this would continue to be done by those in the future whose values were ever changing and unreliable. The absurdity of man's predicament, of man's ever attempting to reach God through human efforts or by human merit alone, was clear. Attempts to reconstruct Babel merely brought greater confusion. Divine judgment upon such folly could only result, as on previous occasions, in predicaments beyond redemption or reprieve. Reaching for faith by means of historical investigation alone, where findings and results were ever changing and conclusions were never final, was an enterprise that would always be fatally flawed.

## Conclusion: The Redemption of Remembrance

Questions about linkages between understandings of events and religious experiences, or about descriptions of events that have involved claims of actions and supernatural interventions by God in human affairs, are not easy questions for any historian to answer. Any answers that a historian as a historian may make to such questions will always be couched within at least two cautionary qualifications. First, the conclusions that a historian draws are always contingent and tentative. They are always open to the possibility of new discovery — new evidence that might change current understandings about what happened in the past or that might raise new questions arising from or turning upon new insights and interpretations. In short, for the critical historian, evidence is always incomplete and inconclusive. What one can know about past events is always conditioned by and relative to available data, if not also by available mental acumen. Historical understanding is never absolute or complete. As a consequence, limitations to what can be known about events are simply parts of, or reflections of, many other limitations which act as constraints inherent to the human condition. This being so, it behooves any and every rational person, whether historian or not, to be humble about what human beings can know or understand and to be skeptical about the nature of understandings about past events which can be firmly held.

A second observation is also in order. It is amazing to realize how many of the facts and understandings that are held concerning events of the past, even those now subject to critical methods of scientific investigation, remain unaltered. Since historical understandings are so conditional and contingent, some being more so than others, one may well wonder how it is that so many convictions about the certainties we hold concerning past events are acquired and held onto so tenaciously. Reasons for this kind of "holding onto the past" in our understandings often arise out of conjunctions of circumstance and/or coincidence, each of which is taken to be evidence, or out of some partially understood bit of knowledge concerning an event that serves to reinforce what, in the end, can only be seen as a conviction founded partially upon faith. This conviction rests not on faith alone, but on faith reinforced by plausible results of rational inquiry and rational observation. Many carefully considered judgments are mingled combinations of partial knowledge and partial faith. This is as true for Jews and Christians as for all of humankind. The faith that undergirds belief and conviction, as the apostle Paul argued, "is not by human effort; but is itself the gift of God's grace, not of works lest anyone should boast" (Eph. 2:8).

In other words, the critical historian, with all sorts of scientific apparatus and discriminating methodologies, can neither definitively confirm and establish nor definitively deny and disprove many of the most cherished and deeply held understandings of events held by human beings. Whether the event in question concerns the historicity of the Exodus as an event in its entirety or the historicity of the Resurrection as an event in its entirety, there is simply no way in which the critical historian can completely and definitively make a claim, come to a decision, or reach a final and conclusive judgment that either event did or did not happen. For those who believe, the possibility of the event having taken place becomes more and more plausible; it then moves from possibility to probability, and from probability to certainty. This deepening of conviction is a process that occurs by means of a mingling of faith *and* reason. Moreover, precedents for viewing historical understanding as theodicy, as an examination of the redemptive project begun and carried on by an almighty but self-giving God who, both as Creator and as Redeemer-Savior, had graciously intervened in human events and had moved to fulfill divine purposes, can be traced in historical understandings which go back at least as far as Abraham, if not earlier.

That being said, the historian must personally try to put minds of contemporary persons into the situation (place and time) of the particular event in question and, in some measure, again try to situate or transpose personal imagination into the event itself. If you and I, or even perhaps a few dozen persons, were to tell others about what we ourselves had seen with our own eyes, heard with our own ears, and touched with our own hands; if we were then to hold seminars, listen to discourses, and hold serious discussions about our experiences; and if we were regularly and ever after to exchange information concerning what we still remembered about a particular occasion or a particular person whom all of us personally had known, then perhaps some of us can also begin to imagine how the occurrence of some astonishing or extraordinary event might have been received. The miraculous escape of a whole people from Egypt across the Red Sea, or the wondrous return from the dead of a person known to be dead: these are events which, once held with certainty, would as certainly be told and retold. In each case, the original or primary testimony may have been taken down firsthand; but much of the evidence remains obviously secondhand. Those who received such testimony had to decide what to do with it.

The written testimony of one person whom we know as Moses, or the written testimony of persons who are commonly known as Matthew, Mark, Luke, and John, together with the letters of Paul and Peter, were words that had been told and retold, words given that they themselves had put down, words that could be accepted or rejected.[38] Once

---

38. Observations contributed by D. A. Carson: Much early Christian apologetic, defense, and vindication turned upon accuracy in "retelling" history as found in the Old Testament. Indeed, arguments with Jews, as recorded in the New Testament, turned on correctly reading the Old Testament Scriptures as history.

1. Many conservative Jews of the first century elevated Torah to a position of hermeneutical control. Since one could only please God by strict adherence to Torah and since Abraham had definitely pleased God, some argued that Abraham must have had access to a pre-Mosaic revelation of Torah. Similar sorts of claims were made with respect to other "pre-Sinai" figures.
2. The speech by Stephen (Acts 7), and some of the sermons of Peter and Paul (Acts 2, 3, 7, etc.).
3. The logic of Paul, in Romans 4 and Galatians 3, turned on preserving the historical sequence of events absolutely: so that the Christian conclusions that he drew could only be sustained if that strict ordering of events — regarding faith and circumcision, Abrahamic faith and Mosaic law, etc. — remained valid.
4. Similarly, correct historical sequence is crucial to many arguments in the epistle to the Hebrews — e.g., arguments about Sabbath Rest (3-4), Melchizedek (7), and the Promise of New Covenant (8). The coming of a priest from the Order of Melchizedek, after the Levitical priesthood was established, announced both the obsolescence of Levitical priesthood and, therewith, the law in which that priesthood was embedded.

we ourselves begin to imagine this kind of situation, then perhaps we can also begin to imagine how, by applying our own rational faculties in coming to a conclusion about how information we have received, how understandings so acquired in the past, might have become embedded and ritualized in actions of perpetual remembrance.[39]

In conclusion, the perspectives of these understandings, as drawn from Scripture, rest upon a combining of theological presuppositions with historical events.[40] Any understanding of a theodicy, such as that of the Exodus[41] or of the Resurrection,[42] can only be acceptable if and when interpreted *both* theologically and historically. The understanding of such an event as being only or merely one or the other can never be deemed sufficient. To see a historical theodicy only in prophetic or theological

39. As noteworthy, at this point, is the importance of the Lord's Supper, or Eucharist. This stands in relation to the Resurrection as the Passover Seder to the Exodus. Both are parts of larger events in their entirety. Each is intrinsically linked to the redemptive purpose of the larger event. Thus, regardless of disputes amongst Christian believers as to the significance of Holy Communion, an insistence upon *remembering* the event of the cross, of celebrating that *remembrance* by partaking in the elements of the Communion (Lord's Supper), cannot be denied. On the very surface of the sacred text, Communion as historical event is the Christ-given device enjoining all followers to "look back in remembrance," again and again, to the unique event upon which their salvation depends (D. A. Carson).

40. Certain wings of biblical scholarship have tended to focus attention upon "retelling" parts of Scripture — such as Deuteronomy, or the books of Chronicles (which retell the books of Samuel and of Kings) — merely in order to detect tiny differences in historical detail concerning events, doing so for the purpose of arguing that the writers (as historians-cum-theologians) were concerned not so much with real and true events (history as detail, history as evidence, history as fact, and history as truth) as with "finding" or "constructing" events to accommodate or support their own particular and preconceived ideological or theological agendas. Such scholarship, skeptical in bent, pits history against theology, as if rational understandings of events could not possibly be both historical and theological at the same time.

41. Exodus as extended event, in its fullest sense, stands for the redemption and rescue of God's chosen people, the children of Israel, from bondage in Egypt; and includes a forty-year sojourn in the wilderness, and reaches across the River Jordan to the land of promise (if not beyond). It is, in short, much more than an escape from Pharaoh's armies (even though that also is part of the event).

42. This event means little if it does not include, at the very least, the Crucifixion as the atoning action of Jesus the Messiah who, as the Incarnate Son of God, purchased the redemption of a chosen people with his own blood. Resurrection as an event, in its broad compass, comprehends both Incarnation and Atonement, covers everything from the Advent to the first forty years of the Church, or seventy odd years.

terms would be to mythologize or etherealize (or spiritualize) it to the point that there would be no real or substantive historical event to understand. But to understand such an event only or merely in historical terms, as something known in the same way that one would understand any other event among human events, and as something understood only by reference to human agency and natural processes, would be tantamount to insisting that the event was nothing more nor less than another "human" (mundane or ordinary) happening and that, therefore, it contained no notion that a redemptive action was brought about by the agency of a supreme supernatural Being (God). To do that is to be neither open-minded nor scientific in any critical sense: that kind of an approach to an event of this kind would foreclose the issue of what kind of event it was that was experienced, what kind of event it is that is being considered, or what kind of agent it was who was acting. To do that is to refuse the testimony of those who, in the case of the Exodus, claimed to have been in communication with Yahweh or those who, in the case of the Resurrection, claimed not only to have been directly in touch with Jesus the Messiah but who also made depositions concerning his nature (as the Incarnate Son of God), and concerning his Resurrection.[43]

Any unique event, defined by the unique nature of a unique agent, calls for some response. Such a response, weighing claims to experiences of such an event, requires either assent or denial. Assent to what has been described as having happened defines a relationship or a situation and stipulates conditions by which consequences of the event are to be

43. There are those on the left wing of biblical scholarship whose presuppositions do not allow them to conceive of the Gospel writers as giving us access to real witnesses or as carefully recording or commenting upon events that actually took place. In pitting theology against history, such scholars render the historicity of any theological perspective automatically suspect. Yet in the last half century a remarkable revolution seems to have occurred: skeptical views of the Resurrection, including those associated with Barth and Bultmann, seem to have lost force, while treatments that reconnect the "Christ of faith" to the "Jesus of history" seem to have gained ground. For a full treatment of this issue, see Craig Blomberg, *The Historical Reliability of the Gospels* (Downers Grove, Ill.: Inter-Varsity Press, 1987) and the works by William Lane Craig cited above in note 22. In our own day, just as it would be obscene for an observer to report details of the Holocaust with cool and dispassionate detachment (without thereby, as a device, making the events themselves look even more horrific), so it should hardly seem strange that the facts recorded in the Gospels, and the events to which they bore witness, should be treated with less than "neutral" and "dispassionate" detachment, or that their historicity itself should be considered suspect on that account.

understood. Thus, after Solomon had completed the temple and prayed for reaffirmation, the record reads, "And the Lord appeared to Solomon by night and said to him: 'I have heard your prayer. . . . If my people, who are called by my name, shall humble themselves, and pray and seek my face, and turn from their wicked ways, then will I hear from heaven, and will forgive their sin, and will heal their land . . .'" (2 Chron. 7:12-15). Likewise, Paul wrote to Christians in Rome that those who confessed "that Jesus is Lord and concluded that God raised him from the dead" were simply assenting to prior testimony that the grave had been found empty; that Jesus had been seen both by individuals and by groups of up to five hundred, many of whom were still living; that witnesses had recognized the Jesus whom they already knew and had positively identified him, whether on the road to Emmaus or the road to Damascus or elsewhere; that while Jesus had entered a new realm of existence since his resurrection, he had appeared to his disciples in completely human form, "according to the Gospel witness."[44] Faith in the actuality of the Exodus and in the actuality of the Resurrection, on other independent grounds, is not negated by any subsequent doubts or denials. Whether God can become known to persons, whether awareness of divine presence within historical events can occur through the medium of what some might call "objective visions," is not a historical issue. Denial of evidence on other grounds can be seen as an unnecessarily obstinate, recalcitrant, or stubborn response. But it is a response that anyone is free to make.

44. Ladd, *I Believe in the Resurrection of Jesus*, 126; and Carnley, *The Structure of Resurrection Belief*, 247.

# Chapter 8

# History as Description:
# An Ambiguous Science

*There is some justice in the claim that history is a "science,"*
*but if so it is a science dominated by the fact that its partic-*
*ular kind of truth can only be attained by imaginative self-*
*giving in human sympathy.*

Herbert Butterfield, 1949

History is a discrete discipline. As such, it is distinctive, self-standing, self-sufficient, and quite separate from other disciplines. And yet, at the same time, while this may be so, history is also linked to other disciplines, especially with certain branches of science, philosophy, and art. History may, in some respects, be considered a science. Its practice certainly calls for scientific methodology — for surely there is a need for critical and systematic analysis, for detachment and objectivity, and for rules of procedure, if not also for constructive synthesis, in the doing of history. But history is also *more* than science — if not in some measure also considerably *less*. History certainly requires philosophy — and there is most surely philosophy in the practicing of history. Such philosophy can be either explicitly stated and defended or implicitly present in the language of discourse employed. But again history is both *more* and *less* than philosophy. Similarly, as we shall see, history is most certainly some form of art — and there is assuredly much creative and skillful art in the producing of good history. Yet history that has validity

242

must also be *more* than simply art, and as certainly, it is all too often too much *less.*

As we have already seen, there are some profound differences between events that are, that can be, that have been, or that might be only partially explained and events that are not, have not, cannot, and may never be explained. By far most events of the past will never be known; they will never be perceived from evidence, much less explained. Indeed, most of what has happened to human beings will never be known; and even out of those small proportions of past human events that can be perceived and recovered, little can, or ever will, be explained, much less explained perfectly. Since historical knowledge is never absolute and always tentative — sometimes more and sometimes less — and since its findings are rarely if ever entirely certain or free from doubt, the task of the historian is to maximize the plausibility (and probable certainty) of details about the events of the past which it purports to describe and explain. Even this can be a formidable task.

## I. The Limitations of Discipline

This brings us to a search for some of the essential distinctions between "scientific" knowledge and "historical" knowledge. Such a search compels us to discover the degree to which knowledge that is historical may ever be considered to be scientific, and the degree to which knowledge that is scientific can ever be historical. All scientific knowledge is historical. But not all historical knowledge is scientific. Historical understandings, as already indicated, can be accurate or valid without being scientific.[1] By this we mean that methods employed to accumulate knowledge — methods having to do with a systematic analysis of classes (or kinds) of objects; methods used for observing regularities, predictabilities, and replicabilities of unique events (which have occurred and which are therefore parts of what now exists or what once existed) — are of such a quality and reliability that it is possible to

1. The classic old work *The Limitations of Science* (New York: Viking Press, 1922), by J. W. N. Sullivan, is essentially as useful as ever in this regard. These same observations, however, can also be made of philosophy and art in the sense that all human activities are historical events.

formulate general principles or truths about the operations of general laws. Moreover, by this we mean that findings so acquired are, by their very nature, *both* historical and scientific.[2] One should perhaps emphasize, however, that the very methods and understandings of what we mean when we use the term *science* are themselves anything but unproblematical.

Quite obviously, therefore, the central issue here is methodological. What are deemed to be facts in the historical understanding of events[3] — whether or not those facts lie completely inside or outside what can be known by the narrower and tighter constraints on natural or "pure" science — can never be seen as incontrovertibly or indubitably true, certainly not in any ultimate sense. Historical knowledge also, even *as* knowledge, contains no such elements. Such being the case, questions of relative authenticity, proximity, complexity, and totality of "facts" become germane. Space gaps and time lapses between observer and event, not to mention the actual processes or "reaction times" constituting any event (or any chain of events); numbers and kinds of variables observable and the controllability of such variables; degrees of uniqueness of elements within any event or of any combinations of elements bearing upon a chain of events; and relative measures of comprehensiveness (or totality) of evidence available: these are but a few "factors" (or methodological issues) affecting historical understanding. *A complete, accurate, and authentic grasp of all data described as evidence supporting the occurrence of any event — both in its complexity and in its totality — can never be altogether certain.* Data recorded in a test-tube experiment can be such that, due to its relative simplicity and totality,

2. Perhaps the only knowledge that can be said not to be historical and yet scientific and which some, for this reason, may see as *purely* scientific (and nonhistorical) in the sense of ostensibly being altogether free of having anything to do with historical events, is that kind of logic or mathematics or metaphysics that is indeed "pure" — or free from all or any contamination by "natural" or "physical" events. This kind of pure abstraction or pure rationality is sometimes held to occur or exist, as it were, completely outside of space and time. Conversely, can one say that perhaps the only pure forms of nonscientific knowledge which may or may not also be entirely free of historical events may be seen as being "magical" or "mystical" or "supernatural"? These are questions that, for want of space, cannot be pursued here.

3. Sometimes, in the rhetoric of science, "facts" are also known as "data," while in the language of philosophy, these are such that they can be put forward as "propositions" or "statements of observation."

it is a "repeatable" event.[4] But who can even contemplate the probability of being able to regularly "rerun" even such a relatively discrete "historic" event as the Battle of Waterloo?[5]

It is important to make a distinction between controlled and uncontrolled events — as also between controlled and uncontrolled observations of events and between observed regularities or systems of regularity among certain kinds of events and events that are observed as being nonregular, nonreplicable, nonsystematic, and hence unique. "Controlled" events are man-made events in which all (or most) of the variables can be carefully measured and monitored. What is at issue here is the degree to which certain kinds of events may ever be understood as being identical or repeatable and hence seen, in some measure, as predictable.

Thus, when a controlled experiment is conducted within a laboratory — when an attempt is made to determine *exactly* what will *always* happen in a test tube when certain specific substances are put together in certain amounts, in certain ways, and under certain conditions of space, temperature, time, and so forth — certain specific reactions or sequences of reactions will so occur that they will be perceived to be predictable. Put differently, highly exact events can be predicated upon generalized axioms, conclusions, hypotheses, laws, theories, or the like. The same experiment will, if and when repeated in exactly the same way, bring about events that look as if they are (or appear to be) exactly the same or that look alike, even to the point of appearing identical. But even when such controlled events are recorded and recurring regularities are perceived as *looking* exactly the same each time the experiment is repeated so that technological and utilitarian ends may be served through taking advantage of a "closed" corpus of systemic understand-

4. My decision to identify what we mean by science with experimental replication in this instance is, of course, quite arbitrary. There are alternative definitions, especially among those who ardently wish for their disciplines to be "scientific," in which concepts of science — as a species of knowledge — are not so categorically separate or absolute. The "softer" a science seems to be, the weaker is any wish to include replication as an essential part of "scientific" understanding.

5. Of course, what is called science is obviously more than a methodology for experimental replication. There are, beyond doubt, other concepts of science — or of scientific methodology — which, as a species of knowledge, do not make this separation between replicability and nonreplicability quite so absolute. But then, what science is or how it is defined becomes a much more complicated semantic question.

ing, the repeated or replicated events are, in historical or in *real* terms, not the same events at all. The same *kind* of event, no matter how identical it may seem, is not actually the very same event.

In strictly historical terms, therefore, *each "actual" or "real" historical event, as such, is intrinsically unique and nonrepeatable.*[6] This is so even though what looks like that same event may be closely (perhaps even exactly) replicable in a subsequent event, and even though such replication is repeated so often that a continuous series (chain or process) of replication occurs. It is much easier, obviously, to observe and classify different kinds of events and exact replications of events when they are performed as experiments within completely controlled environments — especially in situations involving inanimate or physical elements and in situations where such elements are made to interact within completely closed environments and frameworks where all possible variables can be accounted for. But to do the same with complicated living organisms which move within a matrix of a highly complex living environment is another matter. And especially to do so in environments that are wide open is to posit a contextual framework in which orders of complexity are of such magnitude that even to imagine such an attempt simply boggles the mind.[7]

In such situations — where there are myriads of uncontrolled and unknown variables; in situations where these variables are compounded by factors of incomprehensible complexity; in situations where knowable events occur within a context where enormous proportions of all events to be understood have occurred only among members of that small segment of living organisms that consider themselves "human"; in situations where events among and within communities of human beings are themselves governed by intricately complicated and ordered

6. Positions on this issue are neatly summarized in William H. Dray, "Historical Understanding," in *Philosophy of History* (Englewood Cliffs, N.J.: Prentice-Hall, 1964), 4-20, esp. 8-10, where he contrasts and discusses the extreme positions of Hempel (positivist) and of Oakeshott (idealist).

7. What is not being explored here, fascinating as it may be, is that element in our observations in which we indulge ourselves in "play." Playing with events, "fun and games," is an excitement generated (or boredom escaped) when elements of chance or risk, lying somewhere between predictability and unpredictability, are ambivalently balanced and when curiosity or challenge is pursued. Game theory and probability theory (and gambling), in investigations of such events, attempt to apply scientific methods to play.

interrelationships of culture, intelligence, morality, and power; and, finally, in situations where most of all those knowable events that have ever been perceived have been lost or forgotten and are beyond recall or recovery — it is inconceivable that a thinking person or groups of thinking persons might presume to contemplate the possibility that all historical descriptions and explanations are (or ever can be) completely or perfectly "scientific." The making of an assertion such as this would mean that conclusions gained by applications of scientific methodologies possess absolute certainty (a kind of certainty rarely if ever claimed by careful scholars). Intellectual arrogance of this sort seems as contrary to the essence and spirit of historical thinking as to any kind of scientific thinking. If anything, history as a science is a discipline which, due to the degree of the very incompleteness of its findings, calls for attitudes of extreme skepticism and profound humility in the face of what is yet unknown, compared to what is known, what may perhaps never be known, or what may always remain unknowable.

Here, our inquiries may be interrupted long enough to consider what some may think are pious or even impious objections. Surely, some may say, there are forms of historical knowledge[8] that admit (or posit) the possibility that an almighty and all-knowing God possesses an altogether complete and perfect historical understanding, a knowledge that we as mere humans are quite incapable of ever grasping. This "God-as-Clio" argument, however, rises out of material sources and methodologies other than those that we, speaking in strictly human terms, are able to define as "historical" (or "Historical"). Such knowledge can only be validated as some form of historical understanding if (and only if) and when (and only when) it does not need to depend upon those constraints that are imposed by the methodologies we use and/or by our own limitations of skill, technology, and wit.

Again, others may insist that we should admit that, as scholars and thinkers, we behave in ways diametrically opposed to due humility and we continually display amazing amounts of undue arrogance, claiming not only to know and understand past events more perfectly than is, in fact, correct but also claiming to teach truths about what has happened in the past with an utter certainty that is far from justified. This kind

8. Perhaps others may argue that this is more accurately described as religious or theological knowledge.

of observation — that, far from feeling humble, we are often intoxicated by the sheer excitements of our knowledge — by the historical discoveries we make and the investigations we conduct — is really more of a confession than an argument. Without a doubt, the joys of even a little knowledge can make us giddy or "make us mad." It can even be dangerous. Yet, a little sound knowledge can also sometimes save us from calamity and grief.

It is at this point, indeed, that the historian must be willing to recognize that, while many historical inquiries into human affairs are valid and while many historical conclusions about what has really happened in past human affairs are quite accurate, most of our findings are always and quite necessarily contingent, and hence may need to be highly qualified. Moreover, while there may even be many kinds of events that befall people; and while some events may even need to be lumped together so as to be more easily classified; and while certain categories of human activities and categories of institutions can be seen as conforming to certain levels and patterns of generalization, most historical findings are still light years away from being informed by or resting upon anything that vaguely resembles those kinds of general laws sought in various natural sciences. The fact that historians make use of science and scientific technologies (just as they make full use of philosophy, arts, and other disciplines) does not, in itself, make history into a science. Or, to be more accurate, utilization of scientific methods does not mean that history is *just, merely, only,* or *nothing but* a science. Nor does this keep history from being *much more* than a science.

How, one might again ask, does one rerun or repeat something that even closely resembles or simulates the actions and circumstances and feelings and principles embodied in or underlying something even remotely comparable to the assassination of Gandhi, the Battle of Stalingrad, the Gettysburg Address, or the French Revolution? How, in fact,

9. This issue makes good sense, some may object, only if History is seen as composed of *events* and if History does not possess some other more elemental structure — such as something composed of forms, conceptions, discourses, and rhetorics. But this kind of objection confuses apples with oranges — events with ideas and understandings of events, objective History with subjective history, one kind of reality with another. Historical depictions of events are made the same as the events they depict. As such and at best, this kind of ontology is flawed by its own contradictions.

would one simulate or repeat anything so unique, in both character and implications, as the Virgin Birth or Crucifixion, not to mention the Resurrection, of Christ?[9] There have been many great revolutions, many famous public addresses, and many crucial battles that have occurred in the past. Some complex kinds of events have perhaps even resembled each other (albeit only in some measure). There have even been, for example, many other crucifixions. But who can provide explanations, much less interpretations, of such events so sufficient and so total that, as phenomena, they are entirely encompassed by reduction to general axioms or theorems? How can explanations be so complete that they are, by common consent, seen to be wholly scientific and, hence, so timelessly valid that they can stand beside laws of nature (or as general theories such as those brought about by Newton and Einstein)? How does one compare the replicating movements of a man-made machine, even enormously complex technological marvels such as computers — or, at another level, automatic and computer-controlled operations of heating and cooling systems within a huge spacecraft — with the personal inspiration by which Bach composed his monumental *B Minor Mass* or with the diabolical impulses that lay behind the implementing of the horror we now know as the Holocaust? Are differences merely chemical and quantitative, merely differences of complexity, mass, and scale?

*All* historical events, I would argue, even certain kinds and combinations of events, are unique and nonrepeatable. This is true whether or not they are controlled in a laboratory experiment, whether or not some of them actually resemble each other, and whether or not some events are, in varying measures, "scientifically" describable and even "explainable."[10]

It is useful at this point to look at the validity of what is sometimes called *historicism* (and sometimes known as *critical* or *analytical* history). This is a kind of philosophy about History and history. It is,

---

10. Unfortunately, it is all too easy, and there is even now an all too common tendency to oversimplify the problems relating to uniqueness and general laws. However, to move toward either extreme, whether toward the total exclusivity of uniqueness (idealist views) or toward the total inclusivity (whether in deterministic, physicalistic, or positivistic views) of fixed general laws, is to rapidly descend into the swamps of reductionism. Historians, at least those who are conscientious, honest with themselves, and responsible, try to avoid doing this.

indeed, a deterministic belief about the nature of events which arose during the nineteenth century and which has never ceased to attract adherents.[11] As defined by Wilhelm Dilthey, this historical method puts emphasis upon an empirical explanation of all that pertains to human life by looking at "the multiplicity of actors and their varied interrelations in history" and trying "to understand the processes of history."[12] It posits understanding, or even denies the possibility of historical understanding, as determined only by reference to manifold contexts and matrixes (of events) surrounding events.[13]

On strictly logical grounds, Karl Popper argued that historicism is a poor method which does not produce valid human knowledge, that "there can be no prediction of the course of human history by scientific or any other rational methods" and that "it is impossible for us to predict the future course of history." In his "refutation of historicism," he pointed out that (1) the course of human events has been strongly influenced by the growth of human knowledge; (2) the growth of scientific knowledge cannot be predicted by rational or scientific methods; (3) the future course of human events cannot be predicted; (4) there can be no such thing as a "theoretical history" of social science nor any "scientific theory of historical development serving as a basis of historical prediction"; and hence, (5) the fundamental aim of historicist methods has been misconceived and historicism itself is, quite simply, false.[14] In so saying, however, Popper did not deny the possibility of certain kinds of economic or social prediction — of predicting that certain events could take place under certain conditions. Rather, he denied the possibility of making predictions of events "to the extent to which they [might] be influenced by the growth of [human] knowledge." As he saw it, "no society can predict, scientifically, its own future states of knowledge" nor any future course of events based

11. As seen, for example, in proceedings of the Conference on New Historicism at the 15th Burdick-Vary Symposium, sponsored by the Institute for Research in the Humanities, held at the University of Wisconsin, Madison, 11-13 April 1991.

12. H. P. Richman, introduction to *Pattern and Meaning in History: Wilhelm Dilthey's Thoughts on History and Society* (London: George Allen & Unwin, 1961), 50-57.

13. In materialist analysis or Marxist science, for example, events among and between human beings are determined by relations of power, class struggle, and other givens within each situation.

14. Karl R. Popper, *The Poverty of Historicism* (London: Routledge & Kegan Paul Ltd., 1957), iv-viiff.

thereon. In other words, one simply cannot know today what one could only know tomorrow.[15]

Relationships between philosophy and history — between philosophical explanation and historical explanation — have tended to be very similar to relationships between science and history. Indeed, they have tended to cover the same ground. Among various kinds of questions which come within the purview of philosophical explanations of historical phenomena, one set of distinctions seems to look at the same issues that concerned Popper. This is the distinction, already alluded to, between what has been called *speculative history* and what is called *critical* (or *analytical*) *history*. The first, essentially ontological in character, has entailed philosophical speculations concerning the nature of History — events of the past — in relation to the present and the future. This kind of theoretical speculation has been teleological. However fabricated or formulated by thinkers ever since the time of Plato and Heraclitus, it has tended to gravitate toward the making of large generalizations about the nature and direction of all events. It has concerned itself with the purpose, or prospective trajectory of events. For this reason, it has tended to end by postulating some kind of historicism (or historical determinism).

The second is essentially epistemological in character and has usually entailed some sort of "critical" or "scientific" inquiry into the methods and nature and validity of perception, of experience, and of evidence with respect to past events, so as to discover whether they can be classified and, hence, whether they can then be fitted within the structural framework of general laws or theories concerning the nature of change and continuity within the natural universe. This too, with all its fascinations, has eventually tended to end up becoming some sort of historical positivism — or, in other words, to become just that kind of historicism that Popper strove to refute. Neither of these philosophical approaches to history has seriously worried practicing historians, certainly not for very long. Such efforts, whether by Hegel or Toynbee, have usually been viewed with skepticism.

---

15. Ibid. Popper sought to show that, however fascinating its intellectual form might be, any kind of historicism is fatally flawed. In his *The Open Society and Its Enemies* (1950), he traced the pernicious influence of this kind of thinking and of historical determinism from Heraclitus and Plato down to Hegel and Marx.

The choice in the last analysis, therefore, is not simply between historical explanations that are entirely or purely "scientific" and explanations that are not — or between historical explanations that are purely "philosophical" and those that are not. Nor is the choice merely between degrees to which various kinds of historical phenomena can be explained scientifically or philosophically and degrees to which historical phenomena cannot be fitted under either rubric of explanation. Rather, this is a question of the degree to which some phenomena, while not being explainable by either kinds of methodology, can be nonetheless exact and valid. Depending upon the size and complexity of an event or sequence of events — running along a spectrum from a tiny controlled experiment to a huge and uncontrolled cultural movement — there are degrees to which historical explanations may also be seen to be scientific explanations or philosophical explanations; and there are degrees to which historical explanations of events can never be seen as either scientific or philosophical and yet be historically valid. Such explanations must still be required to rest, nevertheless, upon both accuracy of description and plausibility of reasoning. Even speculations concerning possible interconnections between severely limited samples of evidence about incredibly complex events must rest upon the reliability of the evidence and upon the validity of any logic linked to it.

For all of the above reasons and for other reasons explained in other chapters, one may venture to suggest, at this point, that there is no other discipline so broad and so complex, so difficult to fully comprehend and yet so bound by constraints that are beyond human control. Our very vocabularies for describing and defining historical events can reflect myriad approaches to understanding events that have occurred. Thus, for example, what we describe as events and how we define our discipline or discourse can be expressed in language that emphasizes either *rhetorical* processes or *scientific* (mechanistic or methodological) procedures. Metaphorically described, historians can be engaged in finding, grasping, fitting, managing, or welding together what has happened; or they can engage themselves in arguing, convincing, lecturing, and teaching about what has happened. Yet, whatever the metaphors they may elect to use, so much empirical data may be lacking (because what is past is irretrievably gone and lost); so many variables inevitably may remain beyond human reach; so many levels of acting and thinking may yet need to be brought together and made to agree; and so many kinds of analytical distinction between things seen and things unseen may remain beyond what can be known, that the discipline we call *history* can be enormously complex, confusing, and difficult to practice. Its frustrations and limitations are no less and no more than the frustrations and limitations of human life itself. At the same time, its excitements and fascinations can bring satisfaction in good measure.

## II. The Elements of Description

As often as not, therefore, the discipline required for sound historical understanding seems to consist of, and be dependent upon, no more than trying to ensure accuracy and precision in efforts to *describe* events. Much if not most lasting historical explanation is of this sort. Consequently, valid historical understanding itself seems to be identical with, and to rest upon, nothing more nor less than valid historical description. If such is indeed the case, then the soundness and usefulness of any historical explanation or interpretation must almost invariably also depend upon the soundness and accuracy of the description of historical details. While good and skillful description may make use of any or all of what is found in art or philosophy or science, and may even draw from all three together, it is useful to remind ourselves again that history itself is neither just a form of art, nor simply a branch of philosophy, nor merely an extension of science. As a discipline, history still remains something quite, if not altogether, distinct. It is a free-standing and full-fledged discipline in its own right. It is a discipline of description.[16]

But what, then, one might well ask, is historical description? In simplest terms, the answer to this question might seem circular or tautological — that the historian's plain duty is to tell of things as they really are, or were. Yet the answer to this question is also more complicated than one might suppose at first glance. Complications arise out of the very extreme complexities of those actions that we call perception, language, and representation.

16. So also, some might argue, is fiction. The writing of both is, in many respects, the same. Only fiction writing is not concerned about whether or not specific events being described have ever actually happened. "A good story," the saying goes, "must not be allowed to suffer because what it tells never happened." See chapter 3, "History as Story: A Narrative Art."

Stephen Humphreys has argued that "history is the attempt to give veridical and adequate descriptions of change in human affairs."[17] But exactly what, one may ask, does he mean by the terms "veridical" and "adequate"? And what exactly does he mean by "change in human affairs"? Answers to such questions are crucial to the validity of the definition he has given us.[18] In what follows, therefore, some *rules of description* are self-consciously, perhaps even arbitrarily, laid down; and the open, even skeptical, approach employed in what has gone before is being abandoned.[19]

First of all, descriptions can be defined as verbal imitations of reality — as reconstructions or representations of events that are real and true, of what "actually happened." If this definition is granted, then it is not too far-fetched to expect descriptions to conform, as much as is possible, to accepted rules and standards of evidence. Evidence, moreover, is something external and hence accessible, at least in principle, to all investigators. Descriptions that do not conform to such criteria, descriptions that deliberately, or even inadvertently, reshape what is real in events, are not historical descriptions and, hence, can convey no historical understanding. However complete, imaginative, or superb their artistry may be, such descriptions cease to possess historical validity.[20] Such descriptions, to repeat, are not history.

Second, descriptions that are not adequate to those purposes for which they are produced, or for which they are sought, fail to accomplish what they are meant to accomplish. Descriptions that do not conform to accepted and understood concepts as forms of expression which allow them to fit that end fail. Concepts, as verbal devices, are the elementary modes of expression used to make descriptions conform to those conventions best suited for the purposes of understanding past events.[21]

17. R. Stephen Humphreys, "The Historian, His Documents, and the Elementary Modes of Historical Thought," *History and Theory* 19, no. 1 (January 1980): 2.

18. W. H. Walsh, "Truth and Fact in History," in *An Introduction to Philosophy of Religion* (London: Hutchinson, 1951), 72-93, critically examines the merits of correspondence theory and coherence theory as applied to historical knowledge.

19. Whatever may be grounds for certainty hereafter and whatever regulations or rules are set down must rest upon the logic of the arguments being made for their authority.

20. See the discussion in chapter 3, "History as Story: A Narrative Art."

21. Humphreys, "Elementary Modes of Historical Thought," 3. The issue of "whether there is one universally correct mode of description which should guide all

Third, at the same time, descriptions make altogether clear exactly what change in human affairs has occurred, and exactly what elements may constitute that change. Insofar as human actions, behaviors, and/or thoughts are related to or influenced by the nonhuman universe (whether perceived as natural or supernatural), descriptions deal with phenomena of that universe. Alterations in human affairs can thereby be seen to move in some direction or to possess some pattern or purpose, so that relationships of life in one defined period of time can be seen to apply to relationships of life in another time. Moreover, alterations indicate connections and differences between conditions in one time and another, so that continuities and discontinuities may be discerned. Yet, even then, descriptions of alterations are historical only if and when they attempt to show *what* changes have occurred and *how* these changes have influenced the course of human affairs.

Despite all such attempts to evoke some clearly defined rules of procedure, the actual practice of historical description itself is still a very ambiguous kind of activity. Indeed, it is extremely ambivalent, if not equivocal — often steeped in doubt and wrapped in contingency. On the one hand, what is being described is completely autonomous or independent of the describer. It exists completely *outside* the describer's mind, insomuch that the describer is not only obliged to conform to it but also, in a sense, is "judged" by it. On the other hand, either at the same time or at some subsequent time, actions also occur *inside* of the describer's mind. Moreover, since a description is never completely independent from or outside of the mind that has produced it, the same description somehow also goes out of that mind and enters into the minds of others. A description, after all, whether conveyed by tongue or pen, may well be seen as a conventional element of communication. These elements are shared, so that what is "constructed" or "produced" or "given" by the describer is also "generally accepted" or "generally understood" by those who have "received" the description.[22]

The vocabulary of description, in other words, consists of concepts and metaphors. Perceptions alone are not enough. Conceptions follow and these are transmitted. No sooner are perceptions verbalized than

historians . . . instead of many useful and satisfactory modes among which historians can choose at will," remains unresolved.

22. Humphreys, "Elementary Modes of Historical Thought," 4-5.

they reflect both the objects or events being perceived and the subjective constraints of the perceiver. If understandings are to be conveyed, the words used must show some correspondence to the actual thing perceived and some coherence within the whole context of attitudes, beliefs, and conditions that encompass and envelop the act of perception itself.[23] Words, therefore, convey more than perceptions. Words convey conceptions. Words convey metaphors; and, as such, words possess symbolic content. Words of description, in that sense, are very value-laden. Like it or not, they are fraught with the inner meanings that are embedded within them.

Description cannot be devoid of continual efforts to conceptualize and reconceptualize, to define and redefine. The epistemic and metaphysical elements in human events and in human relationships — those concepts that must necessarily generalize, summarize, or categorize "facts," putting them into various kinds of combinations, structures, systems, processes, and the like — are elements without which neither historical understanding nor any accumulating of historical understanding is possible. Generalizations or generalizing symbols that are conveyed through concepts and metaphors are, as such, never implicit in, nor necessary to, the evidence or the "facts" which they purport to represent. They are part of that rational enterprise carried on in the act of intelligent description. Earlier descriptions that are left over and survive as records of previous descriptive efforts within each culture are cumulative. These cumulative descriptions of descriptions of past events generate histories of historical understandings and those, in turn, generate histories of the writing of history, constituting what we now sometimes call *historiography*.[24]

Finally, the discipline of historical description requires a self-conscious awareness of the dangers and difficulties of bias. "Outlook" or "perspective" — that relative balance of objectivity and subjectivity embedded within the description itself — is crucial. In selecting facts (from evidence), in classifying and evaluating the relative significance of evidence, and in giving shape to historical description itself, what

---

23. W. H. Walsh, "Truth and Fact in History," 73-90.

24. "Historiography," as a concept, has not been introduced earlier and is introduced here because it represents a logical next stage in the development of any historical understanding which rests upon prior historical descriptions.

is seen as worthy of scrutiny and what is not seen or overlooked can have profound implications, both positive and negative, for what is to be understood. At the very least, potential dangers arising from the outlook of a historical observer-describer (as speaker or writer) pose a challenge. This challenge is not necessarily a counsel of despair or futility. The challenge is to recognize, to self-consciously assess, and to surmount or rise above those normal human limitations that are recognized. Such a challenge calls for decisiveness. If perfect scrupulousness — perfect attainment of fairness, critical and self-critical thinking, openness of mind, and willingness to subject all assumptions, biases, convictions, doctrines, ideologies, prejudices, to ruthless reexamination and review — is not attainable, then historical claims, by their very nature, are tentative. However much practicing historians continue to indulge their human vanity, such claims deserve to be avowedly humble. The suspending of final or ultimate judgments, especially those that are moral and condemnatory, can be combined with a striving for restrained judgments; and these can be made ever more critical, demanding, exacting, impartial, logical, precise, and rational. The very exercise of rational selection, whereby only some out of many facts are deemed as worthy of representation in telling us what has happened in the past, should suffice to urge caution and discretion both in what is described and in how that description is presented.

The very elements of description are themselves enough to generate attitudes that are profoundly, if not inherently, skeptical. If all of humanity's achievements, all of humanity's institutions, and even all of humanity's highest possibilities, including the accomplishments of all past historians (i.e., the residues of all previous historiographies), are taken with a grain of salt, an attitude or outlook is generated that influences the nature of questions asked, the nature of facts selected, and the nature of conclusions drawn. Even within the person who makes a historical description there are hidden impulses which, bound by contexts of time and place, are embedded within subconscious or unconscious parts of the mind and which, as such, cannot escape consideration. Indeed, the very recognition of the value of detachment, even if it is merely an abstraction or even if it is only seen as an ideal that can never be fully realized, constitutes an achievement in the production of better historical descriptions.

It seems appropriate, at this point, to use a concrete example.[25] Let us suppose that we were able to look at a copy of a personal letter enclosed with the copy of an official dispatch from Sir Arthur Wellesley (the future Duke of Wellington) to his elder brother. This brother, Richard Wellesley, Lord Mornington, is the Governor General of India. Dated Seringapatam, 4 May 1799, the letter is not only an event in and of itself. It is also, simultaneously, evidence of many other events that have happened or are about to happen: progress of the war against Tipu Sultan; announcement of victory in the final battle; details of the final assault upon Seringapatam; eyewitness accounts of the slaying of Tipu; observations concerning the customs, cultures, economic conditions, political institutions, and religious establishments found in Mysore; attitudes towards local persons of different caste, class, creed, rank, sex, and station; insights into matters of personal conscience, faith, and piety; feelings of affection or animosity between brothers and colleagues; styles of writing as seen in calligraphy, grammar, spelling, and vocabulary; and even such details as the qualities of ink, paper, and red tape used by a European servant of the East India Company to tie up his "daftars" (files), along with red sealing wax found upon military dispatches.

While a copy of such a letter can be seen, in and of itself, both as an event and as an artifact serving as evidence of an event, its meaning today must certainly, in some measure, be different from the meaning it conveyed on the day it was received. To the original recipient of the letter, it can be seen as both an event in itself and as evidence of many other events. To a historian who, in 1995, discovers this letter while working at the India Office Library and Records (in the British Library, London), this letter must represent both more and less than it did upon its being initially received in Madras. There are many important details that Lord Mornington must have known and understood which can never be known to a historian today and which bear upon his subsequent decisions. At the same time, the historian today knows many things about young Arthur Wellesley that his elder brother could not have known at the time.[26] He knows about the Peninsular Campaign

25. Out of habit, inclination, and necessity, I naturally turn to my own field of Indian (South Asian) History in order to illustrate my points.

26. C. H. [Sir Cyril] Philips, *The Young Wellington in India,* The Creighton Lecture in History 1972 (London: The Athlone Press, 1973), 1-38, is a good summary and context for such a document.

against the generals of Napoleon; he knows about the "near run thing" which happened near the village of Waterloo on 8 June 1815 when more than sixty thousand soldiers were slain; he knows about the subsequent political career of the Duke of Wellington; he knows about the young Queen Victoria's views of the "Iron Duke"; and he knows about many other events that later occurred, both in Britain and in India, events that might bear upon our appreciation of this letter.

Furthermore, the very act of focusing attention upon a copy of one single letter alters the situation. This piece of paper with scribbling on it is just a singular object. As such, it has been singled out and separated from hosts of other pieces closely resembling it which are to be found within the Wellington Papers. Furthermore, the act of singling it out and removing it from its complex matrix has, in itself, altered possible interpretations of its various meanings. This piece of paper, moreover, now serves a function in a context which is entirely different from what was originally intended. It is no longer simply being sent nor is it now just a message from one brother to another (or from one military officer to his superior). It is now an object of a different sort, something to be studied for some other purpose, something found only in the mind of the historian who now happens to be looking at it. Yet it is still effective both as an element and as a mode of description. It still tells something "objective." What it describes today may be something very different from what it described on the day it was delivered to Lord Mornington in Madras. But, even so, it gives us a description of events no less vivid which, nonetheless, actually did occur. Moreover, this description, while given prominence today, also enjoyed prominence at the time of its original delivery.

\*     \*     \*

Within constraints of proper caution, due humility, and skepticism, therefore, we may conclude that valid historical description seems possible. One document, as a verbal act, can adequately be made to convey an accurate impression of a small slice of life from one time to another. Even though this may be the smallest fraction of what may be recalled or what may be knowable in human actions; even though this may represent only the tiniest fragment among many genuine artifacts or of fairly exact copies of artifacts; and even though there may be some distortion due to the very fact that this is necessarily and inescapably but a partial rather than a total corpus of evidence, yet it is possible for a historian to give a clear and valid and useful description of at least some little aspect of events out of an external reality in the past. This in itself is considered to be of noteworthy human significance.

This may not seem like much. It may not, at least for some, be very exciting or very imaginative. It may or may not even include much evidence of profound intellectual sophistication, of warm interpersonal relations, or of penetrating political insights. But it does give us a small glimpse of what it is that historians do, what they try to do and what they can accomplish. For those who happen to be interested in what happened, however, this letter and what it describes can hold deep value, offering personal charm and wonderful excitement. For anyone who might be interested in the Wellesley family, the rise of Company rule in India, the demise of Tipu Sultan, or an array of other curiosities about India's past, this document shows that enough description is possible to make sure "that there is an independently existing and knowable reality to which historical description can be directly linked [which] gives us a true objective foundation for historical thought."[27]

Moreover, if one single piece of new evidence — whether found in some document, newspaper account, private letter, or oral tradition — can serve as a source for valid description, can the same not be said for two? Or three? Or more? Indeed, assuming that each piece of evidence is treated with the same kind of care and the same striving for critical detachment, are there any limits to the numbers of proper sources of evidence that can serve as materials from which historical descriptions can be made? And what if many "documents" serve as evidence to corroborate one another? If there are no limits, then the task of the careful and critical historian must be to determine what connections between various kinds of evidence can be made and how best to validate such connections. The quality of description, the concepts employed, and the metaphors used: such features then serve to raise what is being done, lifting it onto higher plains of descriptive discourse and generalization. We can thus see richer and poorer qualities of historical craftsmanship.

27. Humphreys, "Elementary Modes of Historical Thought," 8.

# Chapter 9

## History as Destiny:
## An Interpretative Quest

Historical understanding, as we have seen in previous chapters, comes out of a capacity to follow a story. It is a story known to be based on evidence and a story sincerely attempting to give an accurate and intelligent account of sequential details as far as is possible without violating other forms of general knowledge. But as noted in previous chapters, by far the largest number of all events that have happened or that are going on in the world, even those surrounding a story, are beyond the possibility of observation. Even most of those events which have been but fleetingly observed are lost beyond all hope of recovery. Nor do most events that are noticed, whatever they might be, deserve much consideration.[1] Yet, human beings, whether as individuals or as aggregates of individuals, are mainly concerned with *certain* events, events they consider significant. In terms of any particular story, only events that are deemed significant, or of special interest, are truly memorable. The number of events remembered as "facts" and the number selected as worth special consideration is, thereby, arbitrarily reduced only to those which the mind can manage and which it wishes to manage.

1. Louis Gottschalk, *Understanding History: A Primer of Historical Method* (New York: Alfred A. Knopf, 1950), 45, for example, estimated that one would have to multiply one's unobserved actions, thought, words, and physiological processes by two billion to get some rough idea of the amount of unobserved happenings going on in the world at any given time. How he came to this estimate is not explained; but it seems low if one simply factors in the current size of the world's population at any given moment.

What is important in such circumstances and contexts, however, are the criteria of judgment by which events deemed significant enough for a particular story are to be selected. A story is deemed to be a story, after all, because *some* events — or, more accurately, because particular perceptions of some events which have emerged from evidence (or from experience, drawn from evidence) — are noticed, remembered, and subjected to closer scrutiny than other events. This noticing happens while, at the very same time, the vast majority of other events taking place are either not being noticed or are simply being ignored. Yet, for all that, whether self-consciously known or unconsciously felt, some sort of criteria serve in the selection of "facts" which represent certain events; and these facts are then subjected to a process of interpretation.

But what are those factors that make some events of the past more important than others? What is it that compels people to count some events more memorable than others, while most pass without even casual or passing notice? What are those events, and those interests in particular events, which so move minds and hearts — what small purposes and what large purposes — so stir up minds that efforts are made to mark and ponder, to remember and to seek for more understanding about an event? The very actions taken to recall what happened, by the fact that they are taken, imply attribution of meaning and value. Those who take the trouble to do such things are not willing, at least in their own eyes, merely to waste limited resources in empty gestures, exercises of futility. Behind every historical effort, therefore, there is something to be gained — even if, at the lowest levels of significance, it is only idle curiosity that is being satisfied. But beyond minimal human needs of security, sustenance, and satisfaction, where there is nothing more to be gained from the gathering of information than things necessary for immediate survival, there are higher objectives and purposes. These, also arising out of longer, broader, deeper, and higher levels of human need — also often seen as essentials of "security" and/or "satisfaction" — can call for more than ordinary measures of intelligence, skill, or understanding. Indeed, some of the most profound human quests for *inner* or "spiritual" sustenance, satisfaction, security, and well-being are sometimes those which seem to be the most elusive. Nor does there seem to be any end to the quantity or quality of quests for things so valued. Valued "objects" of this sort are, in the final analysis, inextricably and ultimately rooted in perceptions and conceptions of destiny. They are ultimately, in their deepest sense, rooted and grounded in belief systems (or world views and ideologies).

This brings us to one of the central arguments of this entire study: namely, that any and all historical understandings, as such, are direct consequences[2] of those structures and systems of belief which some individual or some larger aggregate of persons hold dear. Put differently, each and every belief system is so manifested (or reflected) by those who hold it that it cannot but be inherent within the very character and shape, style and purposes of the history which is produced by those who hold it. Looking at the argument conversely (in negative terms), I would argue that no historical understandings, whether small or great (either in scope of coverage or in loftiness of purpose), are devoid of reflecting, in some measure, the belief systems of their producers and of the culture out of which they have arisen. By this same argument about criteria in historical judgment, some may go so far as to claim no belief systems in this world are exactly replicated or mirrored by the quality and quantity of history (or "lack of history")[3] they have produced. In another sense, therefore, this line of argument can lead to the conclusion that one person's history may be viewed by another person as myth or fiction and that what is considered as historical by some may be viewed as no more than nonfactual (or counter-factual) allegory, fable, or fiction by others.

## I. Polarities of Interpretation: Conviction and Description

Here a polarity in conceptions, perceptions, and understandings seems to emerge. Some sort of underlying ambivalence — what some may see as a dialectical or dialogical relationship — seems to exist between what is believed and what is described within all forms of human understanding. This ambivalence is no less apparent in historical understandings. There are no histories — whether produced in the past or produced

2. Call it "product," "reflection," or whatever metaphor seems appropriate or suitable to a particular taste, an assumption is implicit that there are certain things common to all human persons as beings.

3. "Lack of history" (anti-history or non-history) is also, within this context, a form of history and a reflection of the belief system and culture out of which it has arisen. Such an assessment is not necessarily judgmental in any condemnatory sense.

today — that do not reflect, in some measure, the deepest and most fundamental elements of belief held by the persons who have produced them. This feature of history is manifest in the way historians decide which particular facts out of the many they may have in hand they deem to be significant. Out of such decisions come selections of noteworthy events, noteworthy evidence, and noteworthy approaches to evidence. Out of such decisions have come their special perceptions and insights. Such decisions are reflected in the very content and quality of historical descriptions — in *what* historians describe and *how* they do their describing. Such decisions give meaning (color, drama, tone) to the historians' depictions of past events. Out of such decisions, in turn, come arguments, discourses, and explanations. And these then provide the basis for historical interpretation and narrative.

Inherent within this oscillating between belief and description are special features of particularity. Within each particular historical description are those underlying features, in both rhetoric and structure, that serve as expressions of a particular belief system. These may be conscious or unconscious (or subconscious), overt or covert. But each particular historian's belief system, as a complex structure of attitudes and convictions, lies embedded within the particularities of elements used in each description and within the particular purposes for which that description was made. This system of beliefs can be found, sometimes seen dimly and sometimes clearly, in the very words chosen for each historical description or narrative.[4] Words themselves reflect, however vaguely, a blending of particular appetites and aspirations and challenges, emotional responses and ethical standards, which are themselves related to immediate priorities and long-term goals of those who are producing (or receiving) them. Words, in turn, are themselves a blending together of more strongly held convictions, doctrines, and ideologies. All convictions, sacred or secular, pure or profane, exalted or mundane, together with long-held conventions, myths, rituals, and symbols, are bound together in that world view which is reflected within a particular historical description. On one side are the elemental modes of belief, both implicit and explicit; and on the other side are the elemen-

4. Yet, the observer of such things, whether as a listener or reader, is no less subject to conditioning attitudes and/or beliefs even while in the process of "receiving" historical understanding.

tal modes of historical description, some implicit and some explicit. Held together in a tight, inseparable embrace, both sets of elements, those of belief and those of description, are the essential ingredients of any particular understanding of any particular piece of the past. To repeat, it is "belief" — some system of values — that informs the immediate "interest" which lies behind each historical inquiry or account.[5]

Nor is this all there is to this polarity. At both poles there is extreme complexity. Neither belief systems, as such, nor descriptive systems, as such, are simple. And if this were not enough, a variety of different kinds of oscillatings — interactings, interminglings, and interplaying feedbacks — can occur between these polar "tropics,"[6] so that one kind of complexity is further compounded by another. Only within this matrix of compounded complexity, moreover, can one discern those criteria for historical selections and those grounds for historical interpretation which are the basis for understanding the significance of any one particular event, episode, or series of events.

## II. Levels of Certainty and Description

There are many levels and varieties of beliefs, from immediate interests and contingent values to grand and huge overarching world views. There are also, as noted in previous chapters, many levels and varieties of description. Both must be appreciated as they can be expressed at any of many levels and within many contexts of life and culture. Both must be seen as they are actually identified and then examined throughout the world. Each of many levels of belief and description must be looked at more closely if one is to more fully grasp the complexity of what may constitute the basis of historical interpretation.

History, as we have already seen, concerns what is of interest or worth to any individual person or any individual group of people. It is also what is of some utility. Not all interests are equal in value. Nor are

---

5. Whether there is also a "feedback" effect whereby historical inquiry informs belief is a matter for debate. Behaviorists, no doubt, would say so; and, to some small extent, this may indeed be what happens.

6. This metaphor is borrowed from Hayden White, *Tropics of Discourse: Essays in Cultural Criticism* (Baltimore: Johns Hopkins University Press, 1985), esp. chap. 9, "The Tropics of History: The Deep Structure of the *New* Science," 197-217.

all interests the same, or held in common, or with equal intensity, by
the same people. About life and death, love and marriage, kith and kin,
home and hearth, comfort and satisfaction, excellence in skills, job
security, property, ambition and attainment of wealth, family pride,
community consciousness, doctrinal orthodoxy, ecclesiastical conformity, political ascendancy, national patriotism, military power, and
countless hosts of other matters, each individual possesses a reservoir
of beliefs and interests and values. Some of these are well articulated
and some, only vague feelings, are not articulated at all. Various of these
beliefs and interests wrestle with each other for priority. Together they
comprise some sort of a complex structuring of interests and values
within each person. In some measure, whether more or less, some
interests, especially those informed by deepest and most basic beliefs
(doctrines, ideologies), compel the attention and concern of each and
every individual and institution. Wherever and whenever they have
existed, some matters have always commanded more and particular
attention. They also compel and command a more common interest in
certain events of the past and in some things that have happened. In
short, however one may put such things into words and whatever metaphors one may employ for such purposes, the space lying between
matters of interest and belief that are deemed to be of only limited
interest or utility and matters that are deemed to concern people most,
especially those seen as possessing "cosmic significance" or "timeless
verity," can be very wide indeed.

Moving from the most immediate, local, and mundane events to
those less so, something already alluded to occurs. Historical construction begins with the origins of individual persons, with the smallest
kinds of institutions, with most immediate forms of kinship and community, and with local legend and lore. At this lowest and most local
level, within the smallest units of any society, some of the most
primordial kinds of historical description are formed. This has ever been
so. Moreover, these kinds of description have tended to be informed by
some of the most practical kinds of interest; and these most basic kinds
of interests and values have, in turn, arisen out of a matrix of beliefs
about those verities of life itself which are even more fundamental. At
this very fundamental level, leaders of affinal groups (kith and kin, clan
and sept — i.e., "families") which are strong and resourceful, often those
that have become ruling dynasties, seem always to have possessed the

superior resources and technologies of *control*. And, distressing as the thought may be for many today, history in this most immediate sense has long been simply another name for *oppression*. "Historic" leaders are those who have had the means to make sure that the best legacies and the most valuable lessons and secrets of the past are handed down from one generation to another. At this level, information about important failures in the past, failures to heed legacies and secret "lessons" which then led to defeat and loss and suffering, have also been handed down from generation to generation. Such historical legacies have often been seen, by individuals and small groups, as having immediate as well as long-term value, lest direct and dire consequences of past failures should be repeated.[7]

At closest proximity and within the smallest compass of space and time, the ordering and strength of a household provides us with many examples of practical wisdom gained from repeated experience. Aphorisms and proverbs, as testaments of experience and insight, abound in every culture: "Always be in the saddle!"[8] "An enterprising spider can live in a king's palace!!"[9] And, at a much more modest level, the sagacious housewife knows that the appreciation of her food (interest) and her keeping of a recipe (historical description) can be combined so as to provide the domestic household with a legacy and that her recipe may continue to be passed down from one generation to the next.[10] This kind of legacy, even if initially of modest worth, can acquire increasing significance. Its benefits, grounded upon time-tested explanations, can also have ramifications pertaining to survival itself. What (or how much) one can safely drink or eat and what cannot be safely eaten or drunk; what foods can be blended so as to produce a sublime taste (and what tastes to avoid); how to cook a particular kind of meal:

---

7. Crises, of one sort or another, are events that have been marked and remembered with great care. As with birthdays, deathdays are marked. Both places of victory and places of defeat/death are marked, as in Hastings, Culloden Moor, Gettysburg, Auschwitz, etc.

8. Attributed to Akbar, first of the four Great Mughals, who together ruled in India from A.D. 1556 to 1707.

9. Prov. 30:28, in the Old Testament, or Hebrew portion of the Bible: this is the last of "four things upon the earth which, though little, are exceedingly wise" — the ants, conies, locusts, and spiders.

10. Here, something mundane and less crucial is used as an example of family history, something which is neither traumatic nor tragic.

such considerations can call for the handing down and preserving of a recipe which contains detailed instructions about what to do with certain combinations of food, spices, heat, and stirring, together with detailed information about what went wrong when the instructions were not followed.[11] Above and beyond the satisfying of basic appetites and needs for sustenance, a special cuisine provides comfort, enjoyment, and a greater sense of personal or communal satisfaction. Beyond aspirations for social power, recognition, and status, all of which come with respect for a job well done, a fine meal served in an appropriate and stylish manner (perhaps with candles to light eyes of those around some festive board at some annual celebration) emphasizes the closeness, cordiality, and strong bonds of mutual support holding a circle of family and friends together. One can also add those kinds of "diplomatic" benefits to be gained — through protocols observed on "state occasions" — by sharing such a rare and special domestic legacy with potential allies. A domestic document, handed down from generation to generation, can thus combine many elements of interest, utility, and belief with the value of historical description, interpretation, and preservation.

At another level, a successful merchant whose enterprises grow so wide and so complex that he has difficulty in keeping track of everything might create and maintain special accounts and records, usually confidential and secret, including charts and maps. These serve to remind him and to inform his heirs of exactly how much he possesses, how much he owes, what assets exist, exactly where they are located, and exactly what, year by year, has happened throughout his commercial empire. The more detailed and accurate his accounts, maps, or other records in the descriptions which they contained, the more useful would be the subtle insights and understandings which could inform future decisions, answering questions about how to carry on business opera-

11. What social volunteer is not warned about the dangers of drinking contaminated water? The health and welfare benefits to be gained by following injunctions on ritually "clean" and "unclean" foods and food practices laid down in the Levitical Law of the Torah come to mind. Some, like Mary Douglas, *Purity and Danger: An Analysis of the Concepts of Pollution and Taboo* (London: Arkon, 1984), may question the notion, *contra* Maimonides (a physician), that the origins of such laws in Leviticus had anything to do with hygiene. But what happens when someone carelessly eats pork or shrimp in South India is well known.

tions or how to handle difficult servants within the organization, or how to make future ventures less risky. Here, as can be noted by recounting the stories of such firms as the East India Company, the Hudson Bay Company, and many other great mercantile houses of the past, a critical understanding of past operations, not to mention an ability to correct mistakes or make reforms necessary to enable them to survive over many centuries, depended upon accurate historical descriptions and upon the meticulous procedures by which such descriptions were maintained. Without such crucial keys to continuity, longevity, and strength, these institutions could not have built such enormous empires or held them for so many centuries.

In a similar manner, modest levels of historical understanding can be found in the functioning of professional and governmental structures. Case histories in the medical records of hospitals; evidence and proceedings before courts of law (from indictment to argument, from charge to verdict, from sentence to appeal); curriculum vitae in academic institutions and personnel files in corporate and state administrations; findings of commissions of inquiry and reports of investigative tribunals; intelligence briefings of military and nonmilitary agencies: these are but a tiny listing of the countless kinds of practical and utilitarian "history." They are matters which call for historical description and historical interpretation of some sort. From earliest times down to our own day, there have always been powerful rulers who wanted to know exactly what happened in order to decide exactly what to do next. Historical descriptions of this sort, properly focused so that more can be known about what has happened within various institutions and what practices or malpractices have occurred which are mistaken, are *useful* kinds of description. Without such descriptions, it is all the more difficult either for societies or for states to be criticized, much less reformed.[12]

Normally, low-level description of this kind neither makes nor needs to make sweeping claims for special epistemic status. "Historical" descriptions of this kind, however, are no less valuable when applied to human institutions than are "scientific" findings within the "natural science" disciplines. "Empirical descriptions" can be made on pragmatic grounds;

---

12. Distinctions between states and strong states, like distinctions between weak families and strong families, together with their "estates," depend upon just how elaborately and well they can "institutionalize" such matters and procedures as these.

and empirical approaches, however subject to scathing glances from some philosophers of science, or from social theorists who follow in their train, are no less useful for studies of culture and society than they have been for helping to gain control over the physical environment.

But as historical description rises to higher levels — with broader reach and wider scope in space and time, encompassing larger and larger systems of human organization and covering longer and longer periods of time — difficulties begin to grow and multiply. Abstraction increases dramatically; and, in like measure, concrete facts based upon hard evidence decrease sharply. As one leaves the dusty plains of concrete human events and institutions and as one rises into the more rarified atmospheres of historical speculation, the very character of historical inquiries begins to change. As one reaches the upper levels, where interpretations of world history and the history of civilizations are attempted and where support from hard data becomes thinner, exactly which definition of history is being used — History as "the past" or history as "understanding the past" — becomes more ambiguous. Metaphysical mists thicken as one passes into the stratosphere of intellectual history and then into those spheres of "outer space," where intellectual history must come into direct contact and interact with various sorts of ideology, philosophy, theory, and "religious" dogma. Discussions over critical distinctions between various conceptual frames of reference become more dense. Conflicts over various metaphysical interpretations of history conjure up the ghosts of scholasticism. Those kinds of historical interpretation that require the heavier oxygen of low-level description find that it is no longer possible to breathe. The air of description becomes too thin and more mundane forms of historical understanding begin to suffocate.

Ultimately, on the highest peaks of what sometimes passes for "historical" description, attempts at historical interpretation become amazingly grand. Not surprisingly, in such attempts, something in the guise of history almost invariably, if not inevitably, becomes the handmaiden of the grandest and proudest of belief systems. At these highest levels, it is the greatest world views, and institutional support structures managed by those who hold and uphold these world views, that require and, indeed, *command* the services of "history." Whether nontheistic or theistic — whether accompanied by grand ideology or grand theology, whether buttressed by grand theory or grand teleology, or whether cemented together by all of these features — these kinds of systems demand and require interpretations of the past that are suitable to their high and lofty stations. Not surprisingly, such interpretations are also called upon, at the same time, to provide panoramic vistas of the future. *All* of the past may now be harnessed so as to foretell some or all of the future. "History" of this sort, in the guise of seer and soothsayer, can be traced all the way back to the thrones of Babylon and the pharaohs of Egypt. Indeed, just as sciences, philosophies, and arts have always been brought into the service of this or that grand belief system of the past, validating and verifying the authenticity of the verities posited by them, so history too has been made to play its part. Only now, levels of historical interpretation become so elevated and so high, so far above the ordinary plains of veridical evidence, that what still masquerades in the costume of history, in fact, seems to have turned itself into a more speculative enterprise. Whatever the name of this kind of intellectual exercise, it certainly is no longer mundane history as it is usually practiced. More accurately and properly, while in earlier times efforts of this sort were sometimes called "prophecy," perhaps such efforts may now also be called "metahistory."[13]

## III. Metaphors of Conviction and Description

Facts, whether about the past or about the present (if not about the future), are not simply "found." Nor are they simply, as so often put in the language of philosophy or science, "givens." Rather, facts are constructed of questions asked about "phenomena" and about "reality." But from whence come such questions? Do they simply arise out of the "perceptions" which come from evidences and experiences of events? Are they merely the products of the "conceptions" by which these perceptions are organized or verbalized? Or are questions also to be traced back to other roots? Do they arise, after all, out of "issues of the heart," out of emotional yearnings difficult to express? Whatever the answers to such questions may be, whether moved by interests that are immediate, short-term, and shallow or by deeper, more lasting convictions, some of the most signifi-

13. Hayden White, *Metahistory: The Historical Imagination in Nineteenth-Century Europe* (Baltimore and London: Johns Hopkins University Press, 1973), spells out perimeters of this abstract discipline and sets of fascinating paradigms.

cant questions seem to stem from profound convictions about the nature
of ultimate reality, ultimate destiny, and the great "flow of events" from
the very beginnings to the very endings of time. They can also arise from
a sense of the absurdity, futility, or tragedy of our little "time on earth"
*(stund på jorden)*.[14] Or else they can arise from some sense of the meaning
and ultimate triumph of hope (or that sense of "eucatastrophe" that
J. R. R. Tolkien describes, that sigh of relief that comes when one is rescued
or granted a reprieve).[15]

It is concern about the present — especially our predicaments in
the present — that prompts us to look at the past events to see what
they might tell us. Something immediate — some concern, problem, or
predicament — draws attention and interest. What does this is not certain. Is it free choice? Is it determined? Something inadvertent and
inevitable? Debates have gone on for so long and are so thick that this
issue cannot be fully dealt with or settled here.[16] Whatever it is that
impels us to act as we do, some concern or problem in the present
usually evokes attention to events in the past, so that we ask a specific
question and pursue a specific theme. Too often overlooked and too
seldom admitted, however, is the chain of concerns, or even aesthetic
feelings, which may link some original concern (or problem) with final
description (or product). If some concern or curiosity or feeling inspires
or determines a given line of inquiry; if some similar impulse determines criteria for a selection of particular facts; and if a particular
selection of facts inspires or determines a special mode of interpretation
and analysis; and if this mode of interpretation inspires or determines
choices of a vocabulary of description, together with metaphors and
rhetorical strategies, then all of the elements in this chain are also, in
one way or another, integral to the description itself.[17]

14. The title of Vilhelm Moberg's (1898-1973) autobiography, *A Time on Earth*
(New York: Simon and Schuster, 1965). Translation of the Swedish *Den stund på jorden*
by Naomi Walford.

15. See J. R. R. Tolkien's essay: "On Fairie Stories," found in *The Tolkien Reader*
(New York: Ballantine Books, 1966), 68.

16. Alan Donagan, "Explanation in History," in *Theories of History,* ed. (with
introduction and commentary) by Patrick Gardiner (New York: Free Press [Macmillan],
1959), pp. 428-43; Peter Van Inwagen, *An Essay on Free Will* (Oxford: Clarendon Press,
1983; New York: Oxford University Press, 1983).

17. Even so, this model of how a historian might move toward historical investigation and verbal expression is altogether too neat, too "ideal typical"; consequently,

Interpretation and description, then, are inseparable. But this is so only if this chain is followed with consistency and, even so, only if elements within it are *veridical* and only if they are *adequate*.[18] The integrity and validity of this chain of identity rests in the conformity between what is found and what was sought. No description can be valid if it is falsified by the very facts which it is supposed to interpret and by the very evidence upon which it is based. Nor can contradictory or mutually exclusive interpretations — or metaphoric representations thereof — be drawn from the same facts or based upon the same evidence. Indeed, even if two interpretations-cum-descriptions are equally plausible, so that both are valid, that which is most plausible must take precedence over that which is less so. This can be so without the less plausible thereby being necessarily invalidated.

In this respect, therefore, historical interpretations-cum-descriptions, in whatever metaphorical or representational mold they are cast, are no more or less true or false, and no more or less valid or invalid, than those of any other scholarly discipline, not excluding those of the natural or physical sciences. What makes the difference are both the objects and the criteria of assessment in relation to different kinds of description. But even then, the assessment of historical interpretations must be made in terms of their *adequacy* or *inadequacy;* and these assessments must then also be made in the light of practices and standards of judgment prevailing within a given culture and at that given time and place where the interpretations take place.[19] Consequently, historical interpretations are on their most solid ground when they are limited to the composition of accurate descriptions of those events which are of most interest and concern to those who have sought them.

But even after a valid chain of identity between original concern and final description has been constructed, the end product must have something to say to the original concern. A description of facts taken from evidence is, after all, more than some random collection or vague listing of events which must somehow be "added up" into a total sum.

---

its results carry both the weaknesses and the virtues of Weberian and other social science methodologies.

18. R. Stephen Humphreys, "The Historian, His Documents, and the Elementary Modes of Historical Thought," *History and Theory* 19, no. 1 (January 1980): 11.

19. C. Behan McCullagh, *Justifying Historical Descriptions* (Cambridge: Cambridge University Press, 1985).

Without interpretation, as we have just noted, historical description goes nowhere and says nothing. Again, a description of facts which have been selected is more than just an interpretation. It is representational. By this we mean that what is contained in the historical description "stands in the place of" something more or larger than facts themselves, some conceptual framework of a larger reality. This kind of description of facts cannot easily be conveyed without resort to metaphors.

Metaphors are models *of* and models *for* reality. They are manufactured and then used in such a way as to stand in place of that which they resemble or "represent" — as, for example, when a ferocious person is referred to as a tiger.[20] They convey images which are both powerful and elementary. Drawing an example from my own field, when a truly complex and large political structure such as India is called a "Great Wheel" (*Mahachhakra*) and its functions are explained in terms of the "logic of circles" (*mandala nyaya*) or the "logic of fish" (*matsya nyaya*), a pattern of elementary symbols is intuitively applied in such a way that it can describe some enormously complex combinations of human behavior, of human institutions, and, just as surely, of human beliefs. Thus, metaphors as symbolic models of reality, each with its own internal set of rules, can lend coherence, regularity, and structure, if not even certain kinds of predictability, to huge and complex bodies of phenomena.

Descriptions that employ metaphors are not rare; nor are they necessarily strange or weird. Rather, they are parts of the mental furniture which every person develops so as to give sense and meaning to complex clusters of events with which people are continually beset. They are routine kinds of activity and, as such, inherent within all adequate forms of social communication. Even mixed metaphors, sometimes deliberately and artfully used, can add emphasis or comic relief, if not spicy pungency, to human discourse — not counting the innumerable gaffs which inadvertently complicate communication.

Of course, many sophisticated issues arise in the application of metaphors to questions which link belief systems and historical events

---

20. Common descriptive clichés abound in simple metaphors, such as "chain of circumstances," "tide of events," "winds of change," "bastions of stability," "currents of movement," and such. For a remarkably insightful study, see Alan G. Gross, *The Rhetoric of Science* (Cambridge: Harvard University Press, 1991), and its review by John Durant, "Is Science on a Social Invention?" *Times Literary Supplement*, 15 March 1991, 16.

to questions about the future. Some scholars have gone to amazing lengths to construct metaphysical and, indeed, metaphorical models of metaphors for purposes of historical interpretation. This kind of activity can be found more often in the work done by speculative "metahistorians" and philosophers of history. One scholar who has recently devoted himself to building models of models and models of model makers, to a greater degree perhaps than any other, is Hayden White. His essay "Interpretation in History"[21] is an amazingly elaborate construction and, one may suggest, a "fantastic" system of quaternary models and paradigms. These models encompass and link together, in sets of fourfold categories, various kinds of historical thinkers[22] with various kinds of historical interpretations[23] and various kinds of historical metaphors; and all of these, in turn, are linked to various modes of emplotment, explanation, and ideological implication.[24] Defending the need for a "genuine scientization . . . of a given field of study" so as to give it "a technical terminology" and so as to free it "from the vagaries of ordinary educated speech," he declares, "Every proper history presupposes a metahistory which is nothing but the web of commitments which the historian makes in the course of his interpretation on the aesthetic, cognitive, and ethical levels. . . ."[25]

At the very heart of his argument, resting upon a "recurrence of the quaternary pattern in the various levels on which interpretation is possible,"[26] are strategies for the conveyance of meaning in the use of language. Four "tropological" modes of metaphorical expression, which White calls "master tropes," are perceived by him as dominant: *metaphor* itself, *metonymy, synecdoche,* and *irony.* The first asserts "a similarity in

21. White, *Tropics of Discourse,* 51-80.

22. Historians: Michelet, Ranke, Tocqueville, and Burckhart; historiographic theorists: Hegel, Droysen, Nietzsche, and Croce; and speculative philosophers of history: Hegel, Marx, Spengler, and Toynbee, etc.

23. For Hegel: Universal, Pragmatic, Critical, and Conceptual; for Droysen: Causal, Conditional, Psychological, and Ethical; for Nietzsche: Monumental, Antiquarian, Critical, and his own "Superhistorical"; and for Croce: Romantic, Idealist, Positivist, and Critical.

24. Mode of Emplotment: Romance, Comedy, Tragedy, Satire; Mode of Explanation: Idiographic, Organicist, Mechanistic, Contextualist; Mode of Ideological Implication: Anarchist, Conservative, Radical, Liberal.

25. White, *Tropics of Discourse,* 71.

26. Ibid.

a difference" and "a difference in a similarity" so as to provide a meaning through equivalence or identity. The second and third are secondary forms of metaphor. *Metonymy*, figuratively changing the name for something but conveying the same meaning or vice versa, is seen as reductive in what it does. Thus, when one says, "Let the baby have the bottle" when one really means "Let the baby have a drink" or "Let the baby have some milk," "bottle" and "drink" and "milk" are usages that are "metonymic" to each other. *Synecdoche*, on the other hand, figuratively substitutes a part for the whole, or the whole for a part, and thereby is seen as being representative in what it does. The last trope, *irony*, suggests usages that are ambivalent, if not ambiguous, and that might even be understood as referring to dialectical relationships. Thus, the metaphorical "He's all heart!," with the right tonal inflection, could constitute an irony within a metonymy within a synecdoche.[27]

\*          \*          \*

It follows, from all of this, that what passes for interpretation within historical description can very well convey all sorts of meanings, both overt and covert. Some meanings touch the very deepest wellsprings of human belief and pertain to matters held to be of universal significance. Metaphors can convey the meanings at various levels of conceptualization. In oscillating polarities of meaning which occur at various levels of perception and conception where events are described, metaphors convey elements corresponding to the aesthetic, cognitive, moral, and ideological content of "belief" or "destiny" and combine such content in all sorts of ways. Any description of historical events, therefore, cannot help but project and reflect, whether consciously or unconsciously, at least some of that meaning and some sense of the totality of human life and its significance as this has been experienced by the person who is producing the description. In this sense, history as belief or history as destiny is both inescapable and inevitable.

Some idea of exactly *how* different descriptions of historical events have been made in the past to convey historical understandings — projecting and reflecting belief systems within contexts of attempts to describe historically what has been learned about the past — have al-

27. Ibid., 72-73.

ready been treated in various ways in previous chapters. Having examined how history, in its most elemental sense, has always had its primordial origins in human memory and how such memory and/or records of memory have functioned; and having also examined how what was understood has, from early times, corresponded with antiquity, we then turned to how history became a legacy in which classical, theological, and scientific standards have been applied to structures of historical understanding. Next, we consider how earlier understandings of history have remained embedded in more recent ways of understanding the past.

# Chapter 10

# History as Rhetoric:
# A Disputed Discourse

*Liberationist history, like liberationist theology, is not a new and higher form of the discipline; it is the negation of the discipline. If we have survived the "death of God" and the "death of man," we will surely survive the "death of history" — and of truth, reason, morality, society, reality, and all the other verities we used to take for granted and that now seem "problematized" and "deconstructed." We will even survive the death of postmodernism.*

Gertrude Himmelfarb (1994)

Remarkable changes have occurred over the last twenty years in the words used to portray the past. Underlying these changes are profound shifts in the nature of underlying assumptions. Shifts in epistemology and ontology and ideology have led to shifts in agenda, methodology, and procedure. Categories of analysis have been altered, conceptual frameworks adjusted, and semantic boundaries moved. What one scholar perceives as "hard logic" is scorned by another as "soft sentiment" or "polemical ranting." "Facts" are either being discounted or "deconstructed," even when beyond dispute. They are being seen as nothing more than fictions, works of imagination. Evidence of factuality is no longer being accepted as sufficient or desirable, much less necessary, relevant, or valid. Dogmas, dressed up as theories and paradigms (the expression "paradigm shift" is especially favored), are being awarded the status of factuality and respectability. In short, the past has become a battleground on which contesting discourses struggle. These are struggles over texts more than contexts. The weapons of choice have been borrowed from the past, by rummaging amid the musty ruins of textual (and literary) criticism.[1] The technologies of higher criticism and hermeneutics forged over a century ago are being reforged. The purpose of those entering such struggles is to destroy "constructions" of the past that are no longer deemed to be appropriate, desirable, or "correct."

Of course there is no branch of historical understanding, no stem of learning connected with human affairs, as applied to any culture anywhere in the world — whatever, wherever, whenever, or however this has occurred or now still occurs — that has not been touched or tainted by this current of changes. This current of postmodernist deconstructions and reconstructions of human events, both past and present, is seemingly all-pervasive in our day. Wherever one looks, like a creeping miasma, its baneful influences and "cultural wars" so engendered seem to abound. Few would now deny that the postmodernism currently sweeping the world has also seeped into almost every academic disci-

---

1. The now fashionable term *hermeneutics* was once used, during the last century and first decades of this century, primarily by scholars in biblical and textual criticism. The term was then recast for different use as a tool for the "new hermeneutic" and then for "radical hermeneutics" which enabled its application to any and every conceivable so-called "text" that might come to mind — with conditions and connotations implying that "text" also came to mean much more than what had once been understood by "text"!

In terms of the history of ideas, therefore, the techniques of criticism (historical, literary, biblical, textual, etc.) came to be applied somewhat differently within different disciplines. Commenting upon this, D. A. Carson finds the seed of the postmodern dilemma in Cartesian thought, as modified by Kant, developed by Heidegger, and elaborated upon by others, far removed from biblical studies *per se* (from whence some similar forms of criticism also evolved, especially in its radical, skeptical left wing).

The greatest figures in contemporary deconstruction, from Ferdinand de Saussure onwards, have followed the discipline of linguistic criticism, and have been almost entirely divorced from biblical studies. Of course, as the wheel turns, these "new" technologies are now being applied within the framework of biblical studies; but their sophisticated application and exposition within fields of literature, art, history, politics, and even philosophy of science far antedate their systematic application within professional circles of biblical scholarship.

pline — e.g., anthropology, history, literature, philosophy, science, and the like — not just in the West, but throughout the world. And, wherever one looks, behind this movement lie the bones of disillusionment. These bones, evoking the "specters of Marxism" and the shambles of its failed eschatology and messianism, not to mention its collapsed state, communism, lie strewn across the intellectual landscape of the academy.

The legacy to which deconstructive thinking may lay some legitimate claim is nothing less than the spirit of a Marxism which, whatever the pretensions of its materialist analysis in the past, now ostensibly "takes the form of a distinctive and deliberately ethereal combination of critique and self-critique." To inherit the legacy of Marxism in this way has required attempting to preserve a "multi-critical spirit against the variety of ontological, teleological, and metaphysical systematizations . . . through which it had found expression." The inner contradictions, and resulting tensions, seem patent: Marxism is unable to survive without its essential embodiments; yet, at the same time, neither can it survive further identification with those essentials to which it has for so long been connected.[2]

But here another tension becomes unavoidable. Abstractions are not enough. Events, as such, do not describe abstractions (unless the events being described are themselves abstractions, and only abstractions — as distinct from concrete, discrete, detailed, evident, and factual happenings that have taken place). Within this chapter, the remarkable changes that have taken place over the past quarter century, while they have occurred all over the world and can be understood as a category of global phenomena, can also only be described in detail by concentrating upon one part of the world. Thus, while something has clearly been happening all over the world, closer scrutiny of one or more case studies is needed in order to understand how phenomena have been fitted into one or more particular context. For this chapter, therefore, it is only natural that the writer should concentrate and focus attention upon his own field of specialization. In recent years, the contributions of postmodernism and deconstruction to the historiography of India

2. Stephen Mulhall, "Critic and Messiah: Derrida's Inheritance from Marx," *Times Literary Supplement*, 23 June 1995, 12, review of Jacques Derrida's *Specters of Marx: The State of the Debt, the Work of Mourning, and the New International*, trans. Peggy Kamuf (London: Routledge, 1995).

(and of South Asia as a whole) have been substantial, in both negative and positive terms. While dozens of circumstances, cultures, and histories of peoples or of places might have been examined so as to highlight the profound changes in historical thinking that have been happening, only one is sufficient for the purposes of this study.

Nowhere are battles of this sort being waged more fiercely than over constructions of India's past. Old terms — such as *colony, colonial* and *colonialism, Hindu* and *Hinduism, Oriental* and *Orientalism* — have taken on special and pejorative meanings and "values." Orientalism, in particular, has become a "hate object" which, because it is now allegedly an "invention of Europe," has become the focal point for an all-out war over India's past. A whole new vocabulary of fashionable concepts and categories, often deliberately undefined, has come into vogue for the purpose of destroying previously held and hence "invented" pasts. This vocabulary combines and recombines archaic with newly invented words, something that is often done without any attempt to clarify or specify meanings. A bewildering welter of nouns has been re-minted as adjectives: words such as *aporia, canonical, constructivist, dialogic* (alongside the long suffered cliché *dialectical*), *dystopian, essentialist* (or *foundationalist*), *hegemonic, heteroglossic, monologic,* or *paradigmatic* are linked to similarly nuanced nouns such as *discourse, text, imagining* or *representing, metanarrative, praxis,* and *trope.*[3] Such terms are only a part of the new weaponry. They are being wielded, perhaps deliberately, as much to confuse and obfuscate as to clarify.

The new jargon, often undefined or undefinable, serves select circles and clusters of insiders. These, like scholastics, imitate their medieval namesakes, arguing endlessly over fine points of text and doctrine. Their exegetical and hermeneutical locutions become ever more abstract and unreal. Their metaphysical disputations are accompanied by the pious canting of liturgies and by genuflections before high altars of "theory." By whatever names these disputants are known — whether postmodernist, post-Orientalist, metastructuralist, poststructuralist, subalternist, ethnoculturalist, multiculturalist, or ethno-historicist —

---

3. For a satirical spoof on this rhetorical fashion, taken to ridiculous extremes, see Brian Morton, "JOKE: L'isle de Gilligan," *Lingua Franca* 1:2 (December 1990): 28. This a reprint of "How Not to Write for *Dissent,*" found in *Dissent* 37 (Summer 1990): 299 — prefaced: "The following study (that is, étude) was originally submitted under the title "Strategies of Subversion: Discourse, Desire, and The Other in 'Gilligan's Island.' "

their agendas are similar and often overlapping. They demand drastic alterations. They want to "deconstruct" the foundations upon which previous understandings of India's (South Asia's) past have been built. Moreover, in the name of science, if not of philosophy, they are making claims about the nature of verity and of truth itself. Empirical details of historical description and narrative have become an endangered species among the fervent; furious "discourses" are raging over the possibility of understanding past events.

The nouveau "imaginings" and "re-*presentings*" of India that are now contesting the validity of all previous historical understandings are not just radical. Many seem, in varying degrees, angry and "moralistic." Righteous indignation rings in their condemnations of previous understandings. If they have their way, previous "languages" of historical cognition, with the traditional components of empirical detachment and critical skepticism, will be abolished. Old assumptions and preconceptions about the nature of reality, if not the possibility of historical knowledge itself, are no longer valid. Old presuppositions about the nature of actions, events, and ideas, seen as resting upon "imposed" and hence dubious "canons" and "texts," must be cast aside. Old knowledge, as now perceived, was (and is still) shaped by previous and hence outmoded cultural, social, and political agendas. The entire task of seeking "reliable" understandings and verities is seen as far-fetched, if not futile. It is fatally infected by a dangerous "objectivist" or "foundationalist" virus. Conversely, since all understandings of any event, any approach to truth, interpretation, or theory resting thereon, may be equally plausible, no one method of cognition is inherently more capable, asymptomatically, of determining the truth or falsity of an event than any other. Whether something actually did or did not happen, in other words, cannot be known; or, if an event is thought to have actually happened, no one understanding of it can be allowed a more "privileged" or "re-*cognized*" place than any other. In short, historical rhetoric, as it is now exercised, is nothing more than "political practice."

The new rhetorics now marching out of semantic encampments to wage war on the past go well beyond old assertions about the contingency of human knowledge. Whatever the banners under which these regiments and their warlords march — whether under multiculturalism, new historicism, postmodernism, or post-Orientalism — they seem to share certain distinctive underlying perspectives. At root they all seem to question the notion, if not the underlying ideals, of critical detachment and objectivity. Sometimes they go so far as to doubt the possibility of rational cognition. Their vocabularies suggest that the time has come for previous claims to impartiality and previous strivings to attain "accuracy" in understandings of the past to be rejected. Previous perceptions are suspect. Their pretensions are spurious and should be cast aside. Previous notions about objective reality were merely products of political practice and instruments of dominance. All forms of knowledge, all previous knowledge about the past, were imposed upon the weak by the strong. Such knowledge was foisted upon them deliberately and deceptively. It was merely an exercise of domination and exploitation. It has enabled the rich to victimize the poor, and the powerful to rule over the powerless. Previously acquired principles of rationality and standards of critical judgment are to be seen, from this perspective, as nothing more than mechanisms of political expediency and tools of oppression. The entire metaphysical apparatus of Western civilization — its systems of logic, its so-called "sciences" and "social" sciences, including its supposedly "humanistic" or "humane" arts and disciplines — needs to be demolished. The "positivistic" rhetorics of the past are instruments by which "hegemonies" continue to rule over downtrodden peoples. These systems, including colonialism and imperialism, must be exposed for what they were and for what they are still doing.

Several streams of rhetoric are currently in vogue. Heralded as theory, they can as aptly be characterized as dogma. Flowing together into journalistic academese, such confluences emptying their verbiage into contemporary historiography are not easy to comprehend or describe. Their new terminologies are now so mingled and muddled that it is sometimes difficult to discern, much less trace, their essential properties. The confusions they create make it difficult for anyone to grasp their meanings. Nowhere is this new vogue more evident than in what is now happening to perceptions of India's past. Any attempt to describe and differentiate between these different streams of rhetoric, to find the epistemic or ontological springs from which they are flowing, risks over-reduction and over-simplification. The currents of rhetoric now disturbing historical understandings can be illustrated by looking at assaults that have been launched against the previous historiography of India (South Asia). They come in the name of the following "theories": (1) postmodernism (cognitive relativism); (2) post-Orientalism (anti-

Orientalism); (3) subalternism (cultural Marxism); and (4) multiculturalism (ethno-historicism).

## I. Postmodernism

The roots of postmodernism, and of anti-Orientalism itself, lie in contemporary currents of literary criticism, philosophy, and anthropology.
They hark back to ideas of Nietzsche and Heidegger, as found in the
thinking of Ferdinand de Saussure and Jacques Derrida. It was Saussure
who really started the development of postmodernist, poststructuralist,
and deconstructionist thinking. Reduced to simplest terms, he postulated a theory which stressed the arbitrary nature of signs. Signs, as
found in words or language, are always in dialectical relationship to
other signs, regardless of objects in the real world. Common sense, he
explained, is nothing more than a cultural construct.

    This is the kind of thinking that, for example, has led some people
in our own age to believe that, before modern times, conventional
thinking held that the sun revolved around a flat earth.[4] The postmodern "project" is to show that all systems of thought are founded
not so much on objective reality as upon ideology. It is ideology that
has "constructed" the myth of objective reality. No reality, later postmodernists have argued, can be understood apart from words; but
meanings of words only arise out of reference to relationships with
other words. Language, in short, can only describe language. It cannot
point to any objective reality outside itself. This being so, even meaning
itself, and reason also, must be seen merely as by-products of culture
rather as the causal foundations of culture. Postmodernism, in this
sense, is fierce anti-foundationalism. This being so, anything that is
merely believed to be "true" can be "deconstructed." It is nothing more
than a collection of arbitrary and artificial "constructs." By separating

---

4. See Jeffrey Russell, "Inventing the Flat Earth," *History Today* 41 (August 1991):
13-19. He decries "chronocentrism — the assumption of the superiority of 'our' views
to that of older cultures — [a]s the most stubborn remaining variety of ethnocentrism."
Contempt for the past and its thinkers in comparison to the superiority of a "more
progressive" present is exemplified in the ignorance of those who denigrate the "flat
earth" myth, not realizing that this very notion, pervasive and subtle as ever, is itself a
modern invention.

words from the world, *logos* from *cosmos*, thinking that conceives of ideas about reality or about human life is "controlled" thinking and "produced" thinking. It is thinking that can have no intrinsic meaning, no substance, no significance apart from the cultures, and especially the politics, out of which it has been constructed.

Taking this project further, Jacques Derrida saw that Saussure's noncentered universe of relationality needed something more. Something had to have existed for perceptions of "opposition" to have arisen in the first place. This something Derrida called *différance*. It is something completely outside any system of reference. It is something that, paradoxically, can never be explained or understood without thereby becoming inside of and a part of the system it is trying to explain. As variously nuanced within the disciplines of anthropology, literary criticism, and philosophy, everything is "text" and, hence, "meaning." Text, as postmodernists see it, must be deconstructed or decoded in order for meaning to be discovered.[5]

One of the strongest critiques of postmodernism came from the late Ernest Gellner. As he saw it, in postmodernism "everything is meaning and meaning is everything." Postmodernism solemnly chants its own distinctive *kalima:* "There is no meaning but meaning, and Hermeneutics is its Prophet."[6] Locating itself within world politics and world history as part and parcel of a grand switch from positivism to hermeneutics, the postmodernist agenda calls for a new revolution. This is a revolution in which "preoccupation with text, and with a vocabulary of narrativity, emplement [*sic*], ultra-commentary . . . is symptomatic."[7] Accordingly, belief in positivism, belief in the existence of objective facts, belief in the possibility of explaining facts by means of a testable hypothesis that can be understood and assessed without reference to authorship or cultural milieu, is to be equated, *ipso facto*, with evil. Two agendas of this kind of rhetoric, political liberation and cognitive subjectivity, are linked: "colonialism

5. In many ways, this kind of thinking is not at all new. It is nothing more than a rediscovery of the kind of thinking that went into the making of biblical "higher criticism" during the nineteenth century.

6. Ernest Gellner, *Postmodernism, Reason, and Religion* (London and New York: Routledge, 1992), 24.

7. Ibid., 25. Gellner is quoting R. Fardon, "Malinowski's Precedent: The Imagination of Equality," *Man* 25, no. 4 (December 1990): 569-71.

went with positivism, decolonization with hermeneutics, [so that] it eventually culminates in postmodernism." Positivism was a form of imperialism in which "lucidly presented (putatively) independent facts were the tool and expression of colonial domination; by contrast, subjectivism signifies intercultural equality and respect. The world as it truly is (if indeed it may ever truly be said to be anything) is made up of tremulous subjectivities; objective facts and generalizations are the expressions and tools of domination!!"[8] "[K]icking the dead dragon of colonialism" decades after its demise is postmodernism's special mission.[9]

What concerns Gellner most about postmodernism is its cognitive relativism — its denial of the foundations for the rational understanding of anything:

> The hermeneutic equality of all systems of meaning precludes us from even asking, let alone answering, the question concerning why the world is so very unsymmetrical, why there is such a desperate wish to emulate the success of one kind of cognition, and why there is a discrepancy between fields in which success is achieved and those in which it is absent. *The real and greatest objection to relativism is not that it proposes a false solution (though it does), but that it prevents us from seeing and formulating our problem[s].* The willful and sometimes flamboyant unwillingness to face the central fact of our time — justifying this by the facile argument that men live through cultural meanings, cultural meanings are ultimate and self-sustaining, therefore all cultures are cognitively equal, therefore the central fact of our time could not have happened, even if it did — is one of the main sins of hermeneutic symmetricism, but not the only one.[10]

This "tortuous, somewhat affected fad, practiced by, at most, some academics living fairly sheltered lives . . . intelligible only and at most (and often with difficulty) to those who are fully master of the nuances of three or four abstruse academic disciplines, and much of it . . . not intelligible to anyone at all" is, in Gellner's view, a passing phenomenon.

8. Gellner, *Postmodernism*, 26.
9. Ibid., 47.
10. Ibid., 62-63. Italics mine.

## II. Post-Orientalism

Blended into postmodernist conviction, filtered through the ideological vocabularies of Antonio Gramsci and Michel Foucault, is the anti-Orientalist rhetoric begun by Edward Said. In his *Orientalism* (1978) and in his recent *Culture and Imperialism* (1993), Said put forward the idea that, regardless of any data or evidence to the contrary, the West "discovered" and "invented" the East. It did this so that it could "conquer," "control," "dominate," and "exploit" non-Western peoples. Europeans "constructed" what they called "the Orient."[11] In defining it, they subjected vast portions of the earth's surface and the earth's peoples to their will. Peoples inherently inferior and incapable of governing themselves had to be subjected to the benefits of colonial rule; moreover this had to be done by, and on behalf of, those peoples who were advanced, civilized, enlightened, and worthy. Said's agenda has been to employ rhetoric to persuade the world that Western imagination and scholarship have always been the handmaidens of political power and that culture and knowledge can only be generated as by-products of power. Quite clearly, such ideas are close to, if not directly inspired by Michel Foucault.[12] Said marshals the eloquence of rhetoric to unveil the existence of a vast and sinister system of conspiracy against the world.

But Said's rhetoric is an angry rhetoric. For those who remain attached to the norms of conventional scholarship and its methodologies, it is a polemic blinded by its own rage. Its flaws would probably have been pointed out even if his claims had been limited only to the area of his own expertise. This, he consistently and Eurocentrically calls the "Middle East." Incapable of extending his frame of reference beyond that of Islam as manifest in the Arab World, he undermines his case by making claims on behalf of all forms of Orientalism. He has little to say about Islam in India, Pakistan, Bangladesh, Indonesia, or even Turkey.

11. See cogent reviews by Ernest Gellner, "The Mightier Pen? Edward Said and the Double Standards of Inside-Out Colonialism," with letters to the editor (April 2 and 9, 1993), *Times Literary Supplement*, 19 February 1993, 3-4; and J. B. Kelly, "Imperial Masquerade," *National Review*, 26 April 1993, 48-50.

12. For an overview, see Mark Lilla, "A Taste for Pain: Michael Foucault and the Outer Reaches of Human Experience," a review of *The Passion of Michel Foucault*, by James Miller, and *Michel Foucault*, by Didier Eribon, trans. Betsy Wing, in *Times Literary Supplement*, 26 March 1993, 3-4.

Since he is entirely Western in outlook and training, he is incapable of contrasting his own Eurocentric understandings with those understandings actually held by various indigenous peoples of the Orient, especially those in Asia. In treating Orientalism as a monolith, he fails to comprehend the Orientalism of India. He hasn't a clue of how much, or to what degree, the Orientalism of India was Indian as well as European in its construction. He does not know, nor perhaps would he give credence to, the fact that for every European scholar who worked to uncover the cultural riches of India's past, there were scores (perhaps hundreds) of Indian scholars committed to the same task. As a consequence, his blending of Marxist and postmodernist language to orchestrate a great campaign of bashing the West results in what Sadik Jalal al-'Aim calls "Orientalism in Reverse."[13]

Orientalism in India was, from its very beginnings, a collaborative enterprise. Indians shared in its intellectual achievements and excitements. In a formal sense, "Orientalists" of India were initially inspired by the vision of Warren Hastings. It is precisely because he wished to combat cultural arrogance and incompetence among the East India Company's European officials that he recruited the world's first "Orientalists." Those who enlisted themselves in this grand enterprise eventually became some of the most accomplished and acculturated and enlightened of all imperial elites. Inculcated with the ideals of learning, they mastered indigenous languages, uncovered and preserved endangered texts, and became responsive to local traditions. More importantly, they were joined in this work by hosts of Indian scholars.[14]

Nor is Said the world's first anti-Orientalist. That recognition should probably be assigned to James Mill. The influence of James Mill's *History of British India* (1818) eludes Said. Regarded by contemporaries as extreme and saturated with democratic radicalism, Mill's agenda for

13. Sadik Jalal al-'Aim, "Orientalism and Orientalism in Reverse," *Khamsin: Journal of Revolutionary Socialists of the Middle East* 8 (1981): 5-26, as pointed out in Javed Majeed, *Ungoverned Imaginings* (Oxford: Clarendon Press, 1992), 196.

14. For detailed analysis, see David Kopf, *British Orientalism and the Bengal Renaissance* (Berkeley: University of California Press, 1969); O. P. Kejarjwal, *The Asiatic Society of Bengal and the Discovery of India's Past, 1784-1838* (Calcutta: Oxford University Press, 1988); G. Cannon, *The Life and Mind of Oriental Jones: Sir William Jones, the Father of Modern Linguistics* (New York: Cambridge University Press, 1990); and R. Schwab, *The Oriental Renaissance: Europe's Rediscovery of India and the East, 1600-1880*, with a foreword by Edward Said (New York: Columbia University Press, 1984).

India was far more disturbing to India's cultures than anything ever done by India's Orientalists. Had Said noticed the "Orientalist-Anglicist" controversy, he might have discovered that, at least for India, his own anti-Orientalism has come down on the wrong side.[15] Worse yet, Said never probes the deeper ambiguities, complexities, contradictions, and contextualities surrounding India's own thinkers and writers. Ram Mohan Roy, Tagore, Gandhi, Nehru, and hosts of nationalists thought so highly of India's own Orientalists (both European and Native) that they freely relied upon Orientalist works for their reconstructions of Indian history. Unlike Said, few of India's nationalist leaders, even those who went to prison, indulged in simplistic kinds of "us or them" dichotomies. By failing to delve more deeply into the consciousness, outlook, and perspective of Indians, Said seems oblivious of those who dedicated themselves to Orientalist scholarship so as to bring the benefits of such knowledge to India's peoples. Many of these failings were pointed out by David Kopf over a dozen years ago, not long after Said's influential work first appeared.[16]

In the end, Said's rhetoric results in far more than distortion, exaggeration, and overgeneralization. The heart of his problem lies deeper. His disregard, if not contempt, for mere facts or for critical rules of evidence springs from his postmodernist scorn for any concrete objective reality. His furious political agenda springs from his own ideological commitment. This consists of his own blending of the cognitive relativism of postmodernism with the historicist certitudes of Marxism. His vision makes no concession to hard evidence, critical assessment of available sources, or investigation of contextual subtleties. His kind of vision requires its own historical perceptions, vocabulary, and trajectory. His Orientalism is, in a truly Foucaultian sense, the "practice of politics."

As a consequence, Said's own ignorant "representations" of Orientalism in India are self-defeating. Such postmodernist cant and academic-journalist polemic, with its calculated mission to bring about a radical re-cognition, re-conception, re-construction, and re-orientation of India's past, fails to tell us anything new. As a result, his impact, mostly indirect and secondhand, is to be found in a coterie of disciples. These

15. David Kopf, "Hermeneutics versus History," *Journal of Asian Studies* 39, no. 3 (May 1980): 495-505.
16. Ibid.

are mainly academics in the West: scholars whose career advancement requires them to "publish or perish," whose work rests mainly on printed and secondary sources in Western languages. Like Said himself, these scholars move in that world which George Steiner calls "the secondary city."[17] Textual criticism, being somewhat akin to journalism, encourages an academic argot where dogma can all too easily parade in the guise of theory. It fosters the writing of reviews upon reviews, articles upon articles, and books upon the subjects of other books. Such work can easily be performed without ever doing any original research, without ever having anything substantively new to say, and without contributing anything to human knowledge.

Scholars in the West who have followed in Said's footsteps are to be found mainly among savants of literary fashion, subalternists or multiculturalists, anthropologists, and ethno-historians. Among the more forceful acolytes of post-Orientalism, especially among disciples who have applied the prophet's gospel to India's past, few can compare with Gauri Viswanathan. Viswanathan's *Masks of Conquest: Literary Study and British Rule in India* (1988) is clever, eloquent, and finely crafted. Resplendent in its regalia of scholarly apparatus, its rhetoric is deceptively disguised as conventional scholarship. Viswanathan's argument is that English was deliberately imposed upon the hapless peoples of India, a device designed to deceive, dominate, and exploit. As a "most effective form of political control," it "aimed at creating a sense of distance between the native Indian and his own tradition, further allowing the British government to strengthen its hold over its colonial subjects." "The British goal was to fortify its [*sic*] own political position by means of instruction in English literature, through which Indian youth were to be persuaded of England's moral and cultural virtues." As a "vital, active instrument of Western hegemony, in concert with commercial expansionism and military action," the "English literary canon" was "put in the service of British imperialism" so that the peoples of India would permanently be held in thrall. English "enable[d] the humanistic ideals of enlightenment to coexist with and indeed even support education for social and political control." In short, "the history of education in British India shows that certain humanistic functions

17. George Steiner, *Real Presences* (Chicago: University of Chicago Press, 1989), 30-49.

traditionally associated with literature . . . were considered essential to the processes of sociopolitical control. . . ." India's imperial rulers "regard[ed] the uses to which literary works were put . . . as extraneous to the way these texts are to be read."[18]

Rhetoric as history can exhibit an astounding certainty. Viswanathan's "discourse" is not hindered by critical analysis, factual evidence, or contextual contingency. It exhibits little of that self-critical caution, humility, or modest skepticism so essential for historical inquiry. Its somber doctrine is clear: "knowledge is power" and, as such, is devoid of meaning apart from relations of power, by which and for which it is acquired. No awkward fact or context needs to stand in its way. Her discourse posits nothing but a monstrous, monolithic motivation, or collective guilt. Imaginations, intellects, and "productions" in the modern world have been shaped by massive and malevolent forms of "hegemonic" evil, whose roots lie buried in Eurocentrism. That this discourse may itself be a monocultural or Eurocentric imposition, precisely the same kind against which Said has inveighed in his attack on Orientalism, is not imagined. The ultimate irony belying Viswanathan's own Brahmanical and Sanskritic lineal heritage *(vamsa)* lies in her virtually exclusive reliance upon data supplied by the British themselves, data with which they furiously attacked each other, or debated policy. Factuality, as such, also completely eludes her. Her literary Cosmic Lord *(Nataraj)*, dancing proudly upon an inert and prostrate India, is almost wholly British. One suspects that her own proud forbearers in South India, who saw the Raj as something they themselves had done much to build, would have been shocked to read such as "history."

As with teacher *(guru)*, so with disciple *(sishiya)*. This genre of Eurocentric, postmodernist, anti-Orientalist-cum-anti-Anglicist rhetoric promoted by both Said and Viswanathan totally disregards indigenous elements that undergirded the rise of English in India. Formal English education in India actually began at least thirty years earlier than Viswanathan realizes. It actually began within the kingdom of Thanjavuru (Tanjore). English literature was taught to Maratha Brahman youths on demand by a German "Raja-Guru" who had received a royal endowment to support such efforts. Also, demands for English

18. Gauri Viswanathan, *Masks of Conquest: Literary Study and British Rule in India* (New York: Columbia University Press, 1989), dustjacket, 3, 166-67.

learning in arts and sciences was so strong in Madras that thirty-thousand notables put their signatures *(chevralu)* on a petition begging the government for English-medium colleges and asking that Pachai-yappa's Charitable Trust be applied to that end. By 1839, many scholars (both Native and European) had devoted years to comprehensive projects for the description and preservation of the entire literary corpus of a civilization. Rare collections of manuscripts which they rescued can still be consulted in the Madras Oriental Manuscript Library. Again, as recently shown in a Wisconsin thesis by Peter Schmitthenner (1991), but for the lifelong collaboration between Brahman scholars and a local English official working together in privately funded "colleges," much of the corpus of Telugu literature might not have survived.

Viswanathan allows herself to see no other literary "masks": no masks that might possibly explain facts that contradict her thesis about the colonizing role of English, no masks that might disguise the syncretistic canons blended into the construction of modern Hinduism; no masks that might hide the equally "colonizing" roles of Sanskrit, Persian, and other "classical" literary canons in India; no masks screening the integrative role of that massive, Hindu-led "Indish" (Anglo-Indian English) literary canon and its assimilation of other indigenous canons; nor any masks concealing the strenuous efforts made by official disciples of Sir Thomas Munro to support the development of vernacular education and literacy. Finally, no masks can cloak the vehement advocacy of vernacular languages and the fierce resistance to English made by missionaries. Missionaries had initially resisted official support for English precisely because it would reinforce continued dominance by the old Hindu gentry and ruling classes, thereby undermining missionary efforts to initiate more radical cultural, social, and political reforms.

Events themselves rarely fit such clear, neat, and simple perspectives. Heuristic devices and deconstructions can too easily be made to support blends of historicism and cognitive relativism. Attempts to link British rule in India with literary canons could just as well have been applied to the influence of various Brahman and other elites who linked their fortunes to the Raj. The proposition that, hidden for centuries untold, a single and faceless "conspiracy" had been slowly growing, that it was then slyly imposed upon India, and that now, at long last, this sinister ideology can be exposed, is too far-fetched. Such rhetoric fails to pass the test of being persuasive. Historical understandings of this kind cannot remain fashionable for very long. The discipline and practice of history as rhetoric requires more. A few academic historians may be seduced or tantalized by it, albeit temporarily. Then rhetoric of this kind, when little more than a scholastistic fad, fades and passes away. More solid materials and structures of historical understanding last longer. History as rhetoric, to be durable, must exhibit more critical analysis and greater command of the source materials from which evidence and facts are drawn.

## III. Subalternism

Another of the more recent structures of history as rhetoric is called "subalternism." The "subaltern" is a subordinate officer. Holding a rank below those who rule or possess high authority, a subaltern occupies the position of an official "vassal." As applied to India, the term has had two histories. The first and older usage relates to ranks of lower-level noncommissioned officers within the Indian army (such as *naiks, sardars, subadars,* and *subadar majors*). The term has sometimes been expanded, metaphorically, to include bureaucrats, civil servants, vassal princes, local rulers, landlords *(zamindars)*, and even village notables *(mahajans, pattadars, ryots, talawaru)*. These are those who held position and power under the authority of the Raj, first under the East India Company (Company Raj), and then (from 1858 to 1947) directly under the British (Crown Raj).

The second use of the term is a metaphorical derivative from the Marxist lexicon. It comes from Gramsci's use, as found in his *Selections from the Prison Notebooks.*[19] It refers to that deterministic and dialectical interplay within class-conflicts throughout "History," that trajectory of all events from the remotest past to the remotest future, wherein struggles between rulers and ruled, between dominant or "hegemonic" elites and "emergent" classes who are rising out of the "masses" of peoples are incessantly occurring. It is the oppressed, in turn, who continually resist those who rule by coercive force (whether physical,

19. Six volumes, originally published between 1948 and 1951, reprinted in 1971 by International Publishers, New York.

cultural, psychological, or whatever) and who defy those who exercise
"hegemony."

"Subalternism" is a historical perspective that exploits the ambiguities and dialectics of meanings and mismeanings. It is the name
given to the latest and most fashionable form of Marxist historiography
in India. This blend of postmodernism and post-Orientalism seeks to
altogether revise and rewrite perceptions of India's past. It seeks to do
this by deconstructing, if not destroying, previous perceptions. All previous understandings of India's past are seen, *ipso facto,* as "essentialist"
or "foundationalist." Subalternists put forth an agenda that claims to
"represent" the perspectives of *all* "non-elite" or "subaltern classes," alias
"the masses" or "the people." The "constructions" claimed are those of
"popular memory" and "oral traditions." These are drawn "from below,"
with only occasional resorts to hitherto despised or yet untouched
"colonial administrative documents" and other previously neglected
sources.[20]

The founder and guru of the subalternists is Ranajit Guha. A
Bengali and a European, Marxist both by birth and conviction, he began
his career as a radical activist. In this he followed a generational pattern
of social behavior which has long been traditional among upper-crust
elements of the Calcutta gentry *(bhadralog).* Disdaining higher academic degrees as too bourgeois, his initial published works, in typical
Marxist fashion, could not have been more Eurocentric. Anyone reading
his *A Rule of Property for Bengal: An Essay on the Idea of the Permanent
Settlement* would hardly guess that the peoples of India, high or low,
had ever been capable of thinking for themselves. He describes the
discourses about India current in Paris salons and London boardrooms
of the eighteenth century, discourses in which Enlightenment phys-
iocrats and rationalists argued over fine points of political economy.
Guha's own voice, at Sussex and Canberra, might never have been heard
had failures of Indian policy not provoked outrage. Failures to amelio-
rate conditions of India's downtrodden and poor provoked the resort
to Mao-inspired Naxalite terrorism by profoundly disillusioned leftist

---

20. Edward Said, foreword to *Selected Subaltern Studies,* ed. Ranajit Guha (New
York and Oxford: Oxford University Press, 1988), vi; and Ranajit Guha, "A note on the
terms 'elite,' 'people,' 'subaltern' . . . ," appended to "Some Aspects of the Historiography
of Colonial India," in *Selected Subaltern Studies,* 44.

students of Calcutta and, in turn, the extermination of thousands of them by the command of Indira Gandhi. It was Guha who, inspired by Gramsci, Foucault, and Said, played the pied piper to some of the Naxalite survivors. He organized a kind of intellectual "collective" (to used Burton Stein's term) of younger (and would-be young) radicals of Bengal. His manifesto and essays by his disciples, printed in six volumes, *Subaltern Studies: Writings on South Asian History and Society* and a paperback anthology, *Selected Subaltern Studies,* spread his gospel to college classrooms in the West. No targeting of history as rhetoric on India's past could have been more shrewdly or strategically inspired than the sending of his message to campuses in Europe and North America.

Among those who have joined Guha, none has achieved greater prominence than Gayatri Chakravorty Spivak. A Saidian savant of literary criticism, she has served as deputy governor *(naib subadar),* playing chief minister *(peshwa)* to the reigning lord *(chhatrapati:* lord of the parasol) of the movement. She has also served as its irritant and stimulant, rubbing sand and salt into minds of the timid and building thickets of postmodernist language so dense and thorny that few can penetrate their meanings. Edward Said's blessing, in the foreword for the anthology of selected essays, acclaims Guha's "fiercely theoretical and ideologically . . . insurrectionary" manifesto as the work of an "extraordinary brilliant Indian history and political economist."

When Bernard S. Cohn of Chicago first hesitated before enlisting as a subalternist, he hastened to explain his initial vacillation. In his essay "The Command of Language and the Language of Command," in volume 4 of *Subaltern Studies,* he "dismissed the possibility of representing 'the inarticulate', 'the deprived', 'the dispossessed', 'the exploited' . . . as 'proctological history' (i.e., 'from the bottom up')."[21] The whole subaltern enterprise, as he first saw it, had been doubtful "because of its dependence on categories like 'family' which committed it to the thraldom of 'crude social evolutionism' and which thereby precociously anticipated later post-modernist criticisms of what is denominated as 'foundationalist history'."[22]

21. Burton Stein, "A Decade of Historical Efflorescence," *South Asian Research* 10, no. 2 (November 1990): 125-28.

22. Ibid. See also B. S. Cohn, *An Anthropologist among Historians and Other Essays* (New York: Oxford University Press, 1987), 19-42. Some of the prominent members of the subalternist "collective" or "guild" whose work has followed in the footsteps of their

## IV. Ethno-historicism or Multiculturalism

Yet another manifestation of postmodernist and anti-Orientalist/post-Orientalist rhetoric can be found in the work of American cultural and social anthropologists. Humanists and social scientists at American centers of South Asian Studies, especially from the University of Chicago but also from California-Berkeley, Pennsylvania, and Wisconsin, have hitherto prided themselves in being the setters of intellectual styles and trends. Trend-setters do not easily or lightly admit, or submit, to theoretical upstaging, especially on intellectual turf they consider their own. Accommodations to the latest fashions in rhetoric of this sort can be noticed in the works of some anthropologist-historians in America[23] and Britain.[24] Such "theorists" of history have found easy admission into the "discourses" of the postmodernist, post-Orientalist, and subalternist brigades, especially those of Bengal. So also, in varying degrees, can one find acquiescence to this kind of rhetoric among all sorts of other scholars who, in some measure, have been influenced by postmodernist, post-Orientalist, and subalternist agendas. Perspectives of two scholars, both from Chicago, typify this "accommodationist" stance and serve to illustrate how pervasive the new rhetoric has become in "re-presenting" the latest in historical understandings of India.

*The Hollow Crown: Ethnohistory of an Indian Kingdom* (1987) by Nicholas Dirks is a work rich in fresh empirical detail, carefully marshalled evidence, and insightful observation. It strictly adheres to the methods, procedures, and apparatus of conventional modern scholarship. At the same time, its most valuable contributions are so mingled with the impenetrable rhetoric and convoluted circumlocutions of postmodernist verbiage that meanings become confused. A

---

guru can only be named: Shahid Amin, Gautam Bhadra, Dipesh Chakrabarty, Gyanendra Pandey, Partha Chatterjee, Veena Das, Mahasweta Devi, Dipankar Gupta, Sumit Sarkar, Rosalind O'Hanlon (in part), David Hardiman, and David Arnold. In all, nearly fifty subalternist essays and a score of books by subalternists have appeared. All of these works have been written by Western-educated, English-speaking, and English-writing scholars, European and Indian. All have been produced by true believers.

23. Arjun Appadurai, Carol Breckenridge, Bernard S. Cohn, Nicholas Dirks, Sandria Freitag, Ronald Inden, David Ludden, and Anand Yang are just a few of the more prominent scholars to don the latest fashions of history as rhetoric.

24. David Arnold, David Hardiman, Rosalind O'Hanlon, and a number of others could be mentioned.

typical sentence serves to illustrate this fact: "The Indian state is barely visible to comparative sociology. When the state is evident at all it appears as a weak form of Oriental despotism, destined to disappear as suddenly, and as casually as it emerged. It seldom possesses mechanisms — hydraulic or otherwise — that could enable it to sustain itself for long. . . . Weber, Marx, Maine, and more recently Dumont have all held that in India, in contrast to China, the state was epiphenomenal."[25]

With this invocation to grand theory, the character of this study and its main argument soon becomes apparent. Indian society, according to Dirks, was long erroneously seen as "fundamentally" religious. But its underlying "political" reality has been obscured by Western scholars. Dirks sees such distortions as accounting for what happened to the Princely State of Pudukkottai. Pudukkottai "exemplified the social and military vitality of certain marginal areas in the seventeenth and eighteenth centuries before it began its long decline under a distinctive form of colonial hegemony engineered by the British. Colonialism purposefully preserved many of the forms of the old regime, nowhere more conspicuously than in the indirectly ruled Princely State." The main conclusion drawn by Dirks is that the many crowns in India were never so "hollow," nor their kings so inferior, as "Orientalism" — as that system of "colonial and post-colonial interest in controlling the East" — made them out to be. That once proud, strong, and powerful "old regime" in India was deliberately made "hollow" by "colonialism."

Materials used to undergird this study come from data found in late medieval and early modern sources, both inscriptional and "textual"; from selected imperial records and reports; and from "oral traditions" obtained as a result of ethnographic fieldwork. But the heart of the study is the author's own free exercise in rhetorical discourse. This discourse consists of a dialectic with the grand masters of sociological and anthropological theory. Its purpose is to justify the pursuit of "ethno-history." What results is a new kind of neo-scholastic exercise. Ironically, this discourse looks more like a new kind of Orientalism, just that sort of "neo-colonial" imposition against which Said has inveighed so vehemently and in which Said himself has also inadvertently taken part. To redress the "previous emphasis on religion" in favor of the "poetics of

25. Nicholas Dirks, *The Hollow Crown: Ethnohistory of an Indian Kingdom,* South Asian Studies, no. 39 (Cambridge: Cambridge University Press, 1987).

power," Dirks declaims: "In using the term 'political,' I am of course conscious of imposing an exogenous analytical term on a situation in which, as I will argue, ritual and political forms were fundamentally the same." But for many historians, especially those who since the time of Thucydides have rarely dealt in anything but political events, this kind of introduction to things "political" can come as a surprise. For political theorists, whose roots in historical understanding go back to Plato and Aristotle, such rhetoric in the guise of history can be astounding.

What Dirks means by "state" is anything but clear. How the nature of the state in India might have been different from that of other political systems; how political entities and structures in India have been "constructed" and out of what constituent elements; how these have changed; and what elemental understandings might serve to identify, inform, and isolate political processes within the subcontinent: these issues are not addressed within the arcane rhetoric employed by Dirks. How relations between political systems of different kinds, sizes, and strengths were defined; by what devices political components could be fitted together so as to assure any regime, whether old or new, with some modicum of security, stability, or tranquillity; what indigenous forms of political logic could be utilized so as to bring smaller entities into a larger-scale or continent-wide system of governance: these too are issues that current historical rhetoric seems incapable of confronting. Yet again, how little or weak polities might manage to survive or how they might have been integrated, as local governments, into larger imperial structures, without at least some gestures of accommodation or compromise, are also questions never asked. Presumably by "the old regime" Dirks means anything that ruled in the continent before that apparently faceless monolith he calls "colonialism" came and saw and conquered. But even the term "colonialism" serves only as a rhetorical gloss for all sorts of highly intricate processes of power. Without contextual elaboration and structural specification, the concept of colonialism tells us little about how indigenous forces within India might actually have exerted power or been fitted together.

More narrowly focusing upon the "hollow crown" of Pudukkottai, we learn little about how one royal family (of Kallar caste and lineage) originally came to power at the end of the seventeenth century or how it might have been obliged to come to terms with larger and more powerful political systems scarcely fifty years after the English East India

Company had first established its station at Madras. Thus, the question of how hollow a crown had to be before it became completely empty remains unanswered. Nor can an inquisitive historian learn much about the prevalency of other hollow crowns, many of which had been hollow long before the British Raj became established in India.

Yet for all its heavy rhetoric, there are durable and exciting and useful portions in Dirks's book. Such portions convey descriptive information that is altogether new. Richly detailed accounts of what dynastic families in South India recorded about themselves in *vamcāvali* and *kathā* narratives are truly fascinating. The more clearly, directly, and fully such sources are allowed to speak to us, without let or pleading, the more valuable the contents of this book become. Fortunately, these portions are as long as the discourses in nomothetic scholasticism. However, there is also a strange contradiction. Heavy reliance upon *vamcāvali* materials found in the Colin Mackenzie Collection (Oriental Manuscripts Library, Madras) is undermined by studied efforts to discredit the reliability of these very same materials. Since the manuscripts are seen as tainted inventions of capitalistic and colonialistic agents of Orientalism — despite work done by hundreds of conscientious local pandits and vakils — and since notions of caste *(jati)* are also seen as tainted, one hardly dares to ask whether, by such logic, the hoary origins of Sanskrit or Tamil might also be similarly tainted.

A second example of postmodernist and post-Orientalist commitment to history as rhetoric is to be found in Ronald Inden's *Imagining India* (1990). This work of seemingly conventional scholarship is dense with nuanced and sophisticated jargon — based largely upon figments of imagination. Heavily conformist and trendy, its politicized vocabulary draws heavily upon Gramsci, Foucault, and Said for prophetic inspiration. In the eyes of David Kopf, Inden's "Orientalist" is a pure fiction.[26] Described by a rhetoric that mingles ideology and social theory in defiance of undeniable historical facts, Inden's Orientalist is a kind of "establishment" intellectual, a "hegemonic agent" akin to an operative working for the CIA or the IMF, someone whose research has been used to advance colonialism. Inden's rhetorical understandings consist mostly of an imaginary collection of false ideas about Hindu India which he has lumped

---

26. David Kopf, review of *Imagining India*, by Ronald Inden, *Journal of the American Oriental Society* 112, no. 4 (1992): 674-77.

together under a rubric he calls "Orientalist discourse." This discourse, which he is sure has been foisted upon India by the West, he then breaks into such chapter headings as "Caste," "Village India," "Divine Kingship," and "Hinduism: The Mind of India." These chapters are filled with conveniently simple metaphors and stereotypes. The metaphors are meant to demonstrate how a superior West has always viewed an inferior India: Christianity neat and unified in contrast to Hinduism as a jungle "with the Brahman elite serving not as gardeners but as forest officers"; Western thought as masculine, rational, scientific, and tough, and Hindu thought as feminine, spiritual, subjective, and weak.[27]

What is ignored in all this rhetoric is any consideration of those sources that contradict Inden on virtually every important point that he tries to make. Behind the distortions of "Orientalist discourse" itself, Inden blames the strivings for scientific objectivity which have dominated Western thought for so long and which have wrongfully ignored subjectivity, relativity, and human agency as worthy of intellectual consideration.

Inden accuses scholars of the West of depicting events that have happened in India as being a consequence of blind forces arising from "elemental urges" and "essences," instead of crediting peoples in India with any capacity for rational choice. Taking Collingwood's indictment of scholars who have too often treated social institutions as monolithic, mechanical entities, possessing intentionality apart from or prior to the capacities of the peoples who compose them, Inden tries to show that communities of India have been polities constructed by human agency. Caste, religion, and sacred kingship have reflected the complexity of interactions between peoples and institutions, not just the dynamics of essences. Focusing upon a particularly obscure era in India's past to illustrate his ideas, Inden reconstructs the history of the Rashtrakuta kings. What happened can only be understood in light of particular circumstances where boundaries between communities and institutions "must be represented as *being* transacted, contested, and constantly reformulated." The very notion of castes, classes, or ethnicities as "substantialized essences" acting in society is seen as a distortion due to Western scholarship. Nowhere have such distortions been more rampant, in his view, than in that branch of Orientalism called Indology.

Inden is uncomfortable with how Western scholars have looked

27. Ronald Inden, *Imagining India* (Oxford: Basil Blackwell, 1990), 86-87.

at India: "Most Westerners still see South Asia as a society immobilized by age-old religious prejudice, whose polity and economy are on the verge of dissolution, as caste, region, clan and tribe conspire to rend it apart. The media repeatedly return to such topics as bride-burning and untouchability, implying that the Indian is still governed by pre-rational urges. Modern academics seem to say something similar." Inden accuses scholars at his own university (Chicago) of being too preoccupied with the "Indian" or "South Asian Mind" as this has been informed by ancient non-dualistic *(advaita)* philosophy. This perspective, he feels, has rendered distinctions between moral codes and physical substances meaningless. At other universities, Indian nationalism and caste identity have been made into intellectual playthings.

Inden's historical rhetoric is not inhibited by, nor does it blush in the presence of, contradiction or even outright ignorance. After tracing "Orientalist thought" to "Anglo-French imperial formation" in the late eighteenth and early nineteenth centuries, Inden holds the "Christian and utilitarian vision" of James Mill and his contemporaries responsible for the defective polity of India. Mill, the disciple of Jeremy Bentham, would probably have cringed at finding himself depicted as a Christian. Nor does Inden seem to realize that "India" had never known such a thing as a single polity, nor even such a concept as "India," prior to British rule. No doubt utilitarians did view caste as subversive to the workings of rational government. Inden describes German historical philosophers such as Hegel and Schlegel as having added an Enlightenment-engendered rationalist perspective by asserting that "India was trapped by Hinduism at the level of the pre-rational mind." Yet Inden fails to see that Indians themselves have been among the most avid consumers of such views; that they themselves may even be the authors of such thinking; or that thinkers everywhere have had a propensity for the same kind of thinking about themselves. As recently as the 1971 *Census of India,* Indian officials and scholars described tribals as "innocent children," tribal women as "native charmers," tribal men as "rugged types," and low-caste groups as "generally dirty." The selecting and large-scale murdering of Sikhs in Delhi the night of Mrs. Gandhi's assassination have been attributed to "a well-known criminal tribe" which had been known to British rulers and to Mughals before them, rather than to goondas let loose by local political bosses. The view, even since the last days of the Raj, that India is "a vast sponge which absorbs all that enters it without ceasing to be itself,"[28] or that it is a wild jungle requiring the rule of science and reason "to keep it orderly,"[29] is as much alive in India today as ever.

Descriptions portraying India as a dream society, potent and creative rather than partly defective, a place where rationality is subordinate to imperatives of ritual purity and where spiritual essence is all-pervasive, are as attractive to Indians as they are to Western thinkers. Among those who stressed nativistic spirituality, few were more outspoken than the philosopher and later president of India, Sarvepalli Radhakrishnan. Even Marxists in India, Inden might concede, have reproduced this kind of rhetoric, with "ruling classes" and "modes of production" replacing "caste," "brahmins," and "mystics" as causes of stagnation.[30]

Inden's attacks upon "stubborn" assumptions of Indological and/or "Orientalist discourse" receive an equivocal response from C. A. Bayly, one of the most prominent younger historians: "If at times he appears in the guise of the many-armed goddess Kali, strutting through the scholarly carnage sporting a necklace of academic skulls, his goal is still Regeneration. He specifically disowns the currently fashionable post-modernist retreat into nihilistic relativism, where history and the historian merge into one. Nor, as in Edward Said's *Orientalism* with which this can be compared, does Inden ever espouse an overtly political aim. He wants history and anthropology to continue as disciplines based on the analysis of evidence. Nor does he assert that only Indians should be allowed to write about India. But he wants the discipline to be radically reoriented."[31] Clearly not all are agreed on the role that history as rhetoric plays.

*　　　*　　　*

For some, the "past" is a battleground. It is the "place" of struggle. It is where control of the past and culture and consciousness in society are in ceaseless conflict. It is *the* war zone: the locus of mental territory, where what is

---

28. Thomas G. Percival Spear, *India, Pakistan, and the West* (New York: Oxford University Press, 1967).

29. Charles N. E. Eliot, *Hinduism and Buddhism: An Historical Sketch* (London: Routledge & Kegan Paul, 1954).

30. C. A. Bayly, "Elusive Essences," a cogent review of both *Imagining India*, by Ronald Inden, and another book with the same title by Richard Cronin, *Times Literary Supplement*, 7-13 December 1990.

31. Ibid.

accepted, believed, or understood is booty, a prize to be fought for and won. It is not, and never has been, as some so long held, the place where only contingent understandings might serve as a means for an ongoing quest for what might actually have happened, or for sifting information in order to correct understandings of what has happened. It does not require thorough investigation, critical detachment, or modest skepticism (or humility) in the face of facts. For those who participate in wars of rhetoric, contingent or contradictory facts are not admissible. The practice of history as rhetoric requires scant concern for "conventional" or "old-fashioned" kinds of discipline. That kind of intellectual activity which focuses concern upon human activity as it has actually taken place in a particular time and in a specific place, activity that is coherent, intelligible, and purposive, is not a central issue. That kind of study that focuses concern upon complex sequences of choices that are by definition unpredictable or that necessarily call for mind and will; that kind of research that also strives to discover what accidents, coincidences, contingencies, and unexpected turns or unpremeditated happenings might have led to prodigious and unforeseen events; or, finally, that kind of exercise that strives to *learn* something authentic about events (and actions) and that requires a willingness, in the absence of evidence, to admit that one does not (and, indeed, cannot) know what actually happened: such issues are often of peripheral or secondary importance for those who practice history as rhetoric.

For those who hold history to be rhetoric and nothing but rhetoric, other kinds of history hold no essential validity. Also not valid, where past is battleground, are distinctions between what is known or understood about events or "what minds have done in the past" and knowledge as merely a "reenactment of past thought in the historian's mind." In other words, the past can be nothing but a place of battle between contesting minds, a place where human consciousness and culture are no more than booty. Where events are not seen as real or where events cannot be known, rhetoric is an arsenal from which weapons are taken and then deployed for the battles that are to be fought. For that kind of history, for those who believe that "all is discourse and nothing is real," rhetoric is all important.[32]

32. Ross McKibbin, "Capitalism Out of Control: Writing Total History in a Global Century," review of *Age of Extremes: The Short Twentieth Century, 1914-1991,* by Eric Hobsbawm, *Times Literary Supplement,* 24 October 1994, 5. For further probing beyond the epistemology of Michel Foucault, see Gilles Deleuze, *Difference and Repetition,* trans. Paul Patton (London: Athlone, 1994), and the review of it in the same issue of *TLS,* 26.

*Conclusion*

# History as Belief:
# A Perpetual Predicament[1]

*The ultimate purpose of a historical inquiry is not in the establishment of certain objective facts, such as dates, places, numbers, names and the like, as much as all this is an indispensable preliminary, but in the encounter with living beings.*

Georges Florovsky, 1959

## I

History, as we have seen, has a double meaning. As commonly used, the term pertains both to "events" and to the "understandings of events." But events are things that "happen." Events — myriads upon myriads of them, far beyond counting — happen, have happened, are happening, and will continue to happen. They happen continuously. They happen anywhere and everywhere. Of most events we are not even

---

1. For many insights found in this chapter, I wish to acknowledge my debt to Professor Mark Noll. His eloquent and insightful paper, "Practice and Presuppositions: History," presented at a conference cosponsored by the Institute for Advanced Christian Studies (IFACS) and the Institute for the Study of American Evangelicalism (ISAE), Wheaton, Ill., June 2-6, 1987, has served to reinforce and to clarify my own conclusions. See *Christian Scholar's Review* 17, no. 4 (June 1988): 343-44 for a summary of this paper by Keith E. Yandell.

conscious. Many, indeed, most events, are themselves parts, remnants, or segments of yet other events: larger events consist of smaller events. Most events — which have happened, which are in the process of happening, or have yet to happen — escape awareness and go unnoticed. Other events attract attention. In so doing, events also obscure or distort capacity to see yet other events. Among events deemed worthy of notice, only a tiny fraction are ever considered significant. Even among such events, for one reason or another (so blatant, conspicuous, or insistent are they), only a very few are heeded; and only a few that are heeded are ever really studied. Some such events are marked, or selected. They become "facts." For one reason or another, they begin to "mean" something — at least some *one* thing, to some *one* person or community, in some *one* place, at some *one* time.

Events that "mean" something, or that have previously meant something, do so in many degrees, and in varying ways. What makes us attach so much significance or worth to some events, and not to others? Why do some events mean so much, and others so little? Why do they interest us at all? Questions like this are fraught with complexity. They are related to what we think is real, or unreal. What we hold to be "real," we value and cherish (or abhor and reject). What we hold as real serves to confirm our own identity and to shape our destiny. We confirm and shape who and what we are in relation to "real" events. "Reality," and how we hold it, is what we live by — it is what we *believe*.[2]

Events — in units, one by one, or in boxes within boxes, in clumps or collections within sequences, or in paradigms or patterns, or however they may be grasped — can often be "full of sound and fury, signifying nothing." Events can also be so full of meaning, so rich with significance and texture, that we celebrate them in song and verse. We raise memorials and monuments so that all may remember them; we recount details about them over and over again, so that we ourselves may again understand and affirm their significance. It is because of what we believe and what we value that we give them such attention. Among each person's, each community's, and each society's most cherished "posses-

---

2. Beliefs can be categorized and denoted under different labels, each with its own kind of affirmative or pejorative or rhetorical connotations and weight — such as "doctrine," "faith," "ideology," "world view," and so forth.

sions" are understandings of events: things that really "matter."[3] Such cultural treasures as these, understandings held as possessions, we call *history*. Why else would we bother to celebrate birthdays, visit cemeteries, or try to remember and recount certain special events, such as battles, victories, and turning points in life? Why else are records kept, or scholars engaged in sifting through details to look for tiny bits of evidence concerning exactly what may, or may not, have happened — on *that* particular day or in *that* particular place?

Whoever marks an event, any event whatever, does so for reasons. Reasons can also be "marked." They are "understandings." They may be rational and sound, or irrational and fatuous, even romantic, sentimental, or altogether zany. Yet those reasons invariably also will be uniquely particular, or else comparable to reasons generated elsewhere. No one else, either here or in some other society, can have had exactly the very same or identical reason, even if it may seem so.[4] Different reasons can be very similar or they can be very dissimilar. Different kinds of reasonings and sentiments obviously can bring about different responses to the same events. No one will notice the same event in exactly the same way. Also, what is noticed may be an entirely individual matter, due to some idiosyncratic inclination. Again, what is noticed may be in some way "representative" of community or corporate "feelings." As likely as not, what is noticed comes from a jumble of mixed emotions, feelings, inclinations, and motives — and/or "reasons," however logical or illogical these may be.

Yet the fact remains that history as an understanding of what has happened — even consciousness of events (History as Reality in some larger sense) — is always a "possession." Some person, some single or individual entity, some personal or public being, "holds" or "possesses" it. History, we remind ourselves again, always concerns events. It is always about "things that happened."[5] History, as such, is not primarily concerned with the timeless truth of principles or of verities — except as such ideas are treated as intellectual or mental events (or objects). Verities, or beliefs, are important; but they are important because they serve as criteria

3. But we also remind ourselves, again, that one person's or one community's treasure can be another's trash.

4. Because the very holding of a reason is itself an event and, as such, unique.

5. It is not some metaphysical abstraction or rational principle about "things that happen" — or about "how things happen" or "why things happen," or "how or why things might tend to happen" in some more general sense, or in scientific theory.

by which events are understood to be real and why some events are selected, structured, or synthesized.

Such being the case, we pause to observe and ponder how events attract notice.[6] Never before, as far as we know, have so many persons, and peoples, been so assailed by assertions and claims about events. Never, as far as we can tell, has the din of "news" about "new events," or the cacophonous clamor over conflicting accounts of such events, been so loud or so insistent as today. Moreover, never have such commotions of beliefs (often accompanied by dogmatic explanations and/or theories), each claiming to possess or to represent the "real story" and to answer the "real questions" — about mankind and about changes in the conditions of human existence or of human destiny — so jostled for attention and acceptance. Yet there is little evidence to show that modern mass communications — with mounting torrents of electronic words in the "information super-highway," clamoring for attention and competing with printed words for attention — have improved the quality of historical understandings, or have diminished the sum of historical nonsense. The intrinsic nature of historical understanding has not changed: the overall capacity for truly understanding events remains as problematic as ever. Old historical understandings still get lost, and important events often still remain unknown (or are overlooked). Older historical understandings also still remain "undiscovered": they are often "recovered" either by dint of some reawakened interest or by some accidental stumbling of research. Whatever happens to such understandings, their condition depends upon how much they were (or are) treasured and how well they have been treated. What happens to historical understandings — however much they are distorted or refined by fresh information or better logic — has tended to depend, in large measure, upon underlying approach and belief, upon convictions about the underlying nature of reality.

## II

Here we face a paradox: namely, that historical understandings and beliefs about underlying structures of reality are both inseparable and incompat-

---

6. This is based partly upon personal observation and readings of observations made by others, together with inferences drawn from such observations.

ible. Just as historical understandings are never free from underlying belief structures, so some belief structures are not possible without underlying assumptions or understandings about the verity of certain specific events. (To fully and properly expand upon these propositions calls for more argument, with clarifying of nuances and obscurities, than will be expanded or fully explored here.) In simple terms, the argument here is that every historical understanding comes out of a particular bias and that such understanding depends upon some particular perspective arising out of some particular ground or system of belief. No particular event, not even all events in general, can be known or seen apart from some frame of reference. Just as belief and bias generate the very interest without which historical events would ever be noticed, so it is that belief and bias also bend and distort all understandings of events, so that those understandings are always, in some measure, incomplete and imperfect, conditional and contingent. Belief and history are, to repeat, at once both incompatible and inexorably linked.

Of course, an assertion such as this may not escape unchallenged. There are some — true "believers" and genuine "historians" alike[7] — who will contest such linking and will dispute the implications of such thinking. Yet the argument put here is that, sooner or later, in one way or another, the practice of history and the presuppositions of history not only remain in contact but are interdependent, even if they are never in perfect sync. Even making a statement such as this is a reflection, in itself, of a bias and of a belief. Nor can the issue of belief-cum-bias, whether consciously or unconsciously held, ever be avoided.

Fundamental beliefs are understandings about the nature of reality. As such, they are taken as true (rather than false). They are matters that, in some sense, are held to possess inherent validity. Their validity may be seen as philosophical or religious in the same way as they might also be taken to be scientific. That is, beliefs as understandings can be held to be true whether or not what is so held is inherently and necessarily, or timelessly, true: i.e., whether or not something is true at any time and in any place and regardless of any event.[8] Such an understanding (of truth),

---

7. Can there be a historian who does not, underneath, believe in something and hold any assumption about the nature of reality?

8. "Believed" truths, in other words, may or may not be dependent upon events for validation.

whether it concerns something of natural or supernatural reality (non-theistic or theistic verity), is no different, in essence, than when it (understanding that is philosophical or scientific) is viewed as being rational or irrational (whether theistic or nontheistic). Belief, in short, concerns that which is taken or assumed to be true; that which is understood to be so: that which is thought to possess intrinsic (or *a priori*) veracity. How understandings concerning events, how historical understandings that are seriously held or "believed," can be in any way different, or might be held in any way so as to contradict underlying philosophically held assumptions and beliefs and convictions, not to mention ideological doctrines, is something no historian, *as a historian,* can fully or properly explore. Such activity is not the kind of activity in which historians engage. Nor is that kind of inquiry considered to be historical inquiry.

The historian, as a historian, knows that it is never possible to possess a complete understanding of any event. What has happened can never be *fully* known. Historical understandings are always contingent and dependent understandings. They are always qualified: qualified by the limits of each particular event; by the limits of its contexts (in space and time); by the limits of evidence in hand; by the limits in powers of possible examination; by the limits in analytical power brought to bear; by limits of capacity to perceive the full meaning of evidence; and by the limits of underlying structures of belief and value which might have brought the particularity of an event to notice. Thus, no historical understanding, as such, can fly in the face of fundamental beliefs. History and belief, to reiterate, are inextricably linked — and yet undeniably separate. Without belief, awareness of an event or its meaning becomes impossible. Without some sort of understanding about an event, certain kinds of belief also become impossible. This is a conundrum. It may seem so obvious that it looks simplistic, if not boring, inane, or mundane. Yet this conundrum lies at the heart of that enigma that is the predicament of history.

The problem, however, is also more complex. "Important" or "real" questions about events always have to do with what is believed to be true, what system of beliefs is embraced, and on what grounds beliefs about events are held to be true. Here one comes face to face with matters which, in every age, possess contemporaneity.[9] Contemporary

9. By which I mean that beliefs or pressing questions at issue in any given time are those unique to the time in which they are held both in relation to each other and

beliefs — whether they are sophisticated theories, mindless (if oft-repeated) stereotypes, popular notions, or simple common sense — are often held with great tenacity. They are like graven images of the mind, upholding dogmas against which no contrary argument can be allowed. Historical understandings are further complicated when, as so often happens in intellectual exchange, there is too much "slipping and sliding" of usages: ubiquitous but ill-defined labels for categories of beliefs result in all sorts of conceptual imprecision. What is now, in current jargon, rather loosely referred to as "discourse" is often so arcane that it lies beyond comprehension. The climate within which fashionable historical understandings have been constructed in recent times has too often been anything but open-minded. Moreover, within our own age, as within every age, lying just beneath every kind of historical understanding[10] is one or another particular set of beliefs. Beliefs have occupied the central place and played a dominant role in the establishment of ruling historical orthodoxy. No previous historical understandings can be properly or fully understood, nor can our own age itself be understood, without taking into consideration the central role of belief. Within each historical context, the dominant role played by ruling historical orthodoxies, as beliefs, becomes obvious. Nor is it just in past ages that this tendency toward enshrined historical orthodoxy can be found. In some sense, previous beliefs are parts of that "past as a foreign country" which we can never fully know.[11] In the same sense, beliefs within our own age may also be parts of the "present as our own country" which we also do not fully know, and may never fully understand.[12]

---

in relation to events, both of their time (contemporary) and of previous times with which they are concerned.

10. As described in more detail within various previous chapters.

11. David Lowenthal, *The Past Is a Foreign Country* (Cambridge: Cambridge University Press, 1985).

12. Herbert Butterfield, chap. 4 of *The Whig Interpretation of History* (London: G. Bell & Sons, 1951), 9ff., poses the dilemma neatly: "The primary assumption of all attempts to understand the men of the past must be the belief that we can in some degree enter into minds that are unlike our own. If this belief were unfounded it would seem that men must forever be locked away from one another, and all generations must be regarded as a world . . . unto themselves. . . . In reality the historian postulates that the world is in some sense always the same world and that even the men most dissimilar are never absolutely unalike."

Once such complications are taken into account, it is important, if not imperative, to ask careful questions about the underlying belief structures that have informed historical understandings in our own age. For all the narcissistic reflexivity of our age, attempts to "look through a glass darkly" have not been all that successful. In any examination of how underlying belief structures have served as the foundations for various historical understandings in our own time, shadows from the past still lurk. Different approaches during the past century or two show how much each difference in perspective has reflected a particular earlier tradition. Yet, as the world itself continues to shrink, such perspectives have entered the global village. Increasingly integrated into a world culture aided by accelerating networks of modern communication, historical understandings have also increased in complexity. The implications of such changes are, at the very least, enormous and have yet to be fully explored.

## III

History and belief, in other words, are continuously, if not inherently, in a dialectical, or dialogical, relationship. As already noted, they are both incompatible and inseparable — ceaselessly at odds and inextricably linked. Notwithstanding this seeming contradiction, certain basic categories of underlying assumptions or presuppositions about the nature of historical understandings have long held precedence. These categories are not difficult to detect and identify. Each in its own way may be described as inherently ideological: that is, each reflects an underlying kind of belief structure which is, in essence, ideological. However much this charge may be denied (by those who espouse one set of presuppositions or another), this is a common feature that seems undeniable. Paradoxically both at odds and in consonance, certain categories of presuppositions with respect to forms of historiographical understanding seem always to have been ascendant. In variously changing forms and under differently colored banners, this can certainly be traced back through many centuries, if not into the mists of historical antiquity. Yet these distinct presuppositional categories also seem to have become more distinct and pronounced and assertive within recent times, especially during the past fifty years.

Among different systems of historical belief, philosophy, or theory which have become complete or sufficient in themselves, certain sets of categories can be identified. Each of these is linked to specific doctrinal and ideological positions. Each reflects a kind of world view. Each such category of historical presuppositions, with its own distinct convictions as to the nature of historical events and of historical understandings, has also possessed an inherently determinist and historicist view of events. Features inherent within any one set of presuppositions, when taken to their logical extreme, have put that set of presuppositions into logical conflict or defiance of other sets. Each, in certain circumstances and times or in one way or another, has also become fashionable, if not dominant, within some intellectual community. It can be seen as having held sway among a constituency of influential historians. For the sake of analysis, the number of such approaches or categories of presuppositions, each with its own perspective on the validity of historical thinking, can be arbitrarily reduced to three.

These three categories, here metaphorically described as a trunk out of which two branches have grown,[13] can conveniently if somewhat simplistically be labeled as follows: (1) the *triumphalist* (doctrinal or ideological); (2) the *positivist* (scientistic or "verificationist"); and (3) the *nihilist* ("negativist" or, more moderately, pragmatist or relativist).[14] As can be shown, persuasive and practical forms of historical understanding have, almost invariably, consisted of some blending of elements from all three of these categories of presuppositional belief. In subtle blendings, each practicing historian tends to combine elements in such a way that points of historical understanding and deeper belief (world view) structures can be seen to intersect. Distinctions, often belabored and overlapping, at least for working historians, make these categories difficult to separate neatly. Yet, approached with care, caution, and circumspection, simplified caricatures of these three underlying categories can be sketched briefly.

The first category, as already indicated, encompasses others. In one way or another, it reflects a recognition, whether tacit or otherwise, that

13. It is important to recognize that the second and third of these three categories are, in reality, powerful branches (or subcategories) of the first set of presuppositions.
14. While what is presented here differs slightly in approach and interpretation, I am indebted to Mark Noll and his unpublished paper, "Practice and Presuppositions: History," for breaking down and condensing the main categories of historical presuppositions into this simple and paradigmatic (or pedagogically useful) triad.

every historical understanding is a vehicle for conveying some belief system. History mirrors the culture and interest of those who produced it. History is a means by which one can see the power and reality of events. As also already indicated, for the purposes of this analysis, this category of understandings can, arbitrarily if somewhat misleadingly, be labeled as "ideological" (or as "doctrinal"). This kind of approach is, quite explicitly, an open concession, if not a confession. It is an acknowledgement of the belief-centered nature of all historical understandings, as such. This most pervasive of all categories of historical understanding reflects, in one form or another, the kind of belief system that was instrumental in its very creation. Since every kind of historical understanding could by definition be lumped under this category, some might see such lumping as a meaningless exercise, a *reductio ad absurdum*. Nevertheless, this category is both noteworthy and useful, not only as a means of distinguishing and measuring the two other categories, but also as a foundational feature, something basic to all historical understandings.

The basic presupposition underlying this category is that all historical understandings, whether consciously (and purposefully) or unconsciously, reflect underlying structures of belief and conviction in such a way that history "speaks" for itself *within* events. Events can be understood *only* in the light of, and can *only* be informed by, convictions about ultimate verities already held. This kind of assumption presupposes that those who attempt to construct or reconstruct understandings of events have never been able to escape (even if they had wished to escape) their own earlier presuppositions about the nature of reality and that such earlier presuppositions have logically arisen out of previously held and already deeply rooted belief structures (with their epistemological, ontological, and metaphysical underpinnings). This assumption would hold such as having been so even if and when underlying convictions themselves may have been in the process of being modified and changed by events, by what has been learned from experience or from the studying of events. Ever since historical thinking and understanding first began, say those who hold this kind of presupposition, this is the way people have always approached the understanding of events.

This kind of approach, to repeat, is the most commonly and widely held, the one most often used. It is a kind of assumption which, in its most simplistic and extreme forms, rests upon two further presumptions.[15] First, it assumes that events occurring in the present (or in the future) are going to be very much like events that have occurred in the past — so that recent events or contemporary events (events happening today) can be seen as *resembling* events that have occurred before (or somewhere else); and so that events, even in their *uniqueness,* can also be seen as *comparable* (and/or similar) to events that have occurred in other times.[16] Second, it assumes that events occurring in the present are, in some way, a *consequence* of events that have occurred in the past — so that events can be discovered and understood to have been so.

This category of presuppositions, as already noted, is neither new nor rare. Open acknowledgement of the role of belief systems in determining what can and what cannot be known about events is usually, but not always, explicit. As seen in previous chapters of this book, this category of historical understandings has almost always been dominant. Under one banner or another, it is as old as historical understanding itself. Presuppositions underlying histories coming down to us from ancient times — from Egypt and Mesopotamia, Greece and Rome, India and China — fit into this category. From Moses (and Herodotus) to Marx (or Christopher Hill), events understood from some ideological standpoint have, in one way or another, been ascendent. This, in another context, is what Herbert Butterfield called "the Whig Interpretation of History."[17] Events as History, by such reckoning, are meant to show who or what was and is just and right.[18] They are meant to show how, in the end, "realities" have always triumphed and how "justice" has been vindicated.

15. Butterfield, *The Whig Interpretation of History.* See also Noll, "Practice and Presuppositions," 7-8.

16. And that, therefore, different events may be marked, noted, or measured.

17. Butterfield, preface to *The Whig Interpretation of History,* v: "the tendency in many historians to write on the side of Protestants and Whigs, to praise revolutions provided they have been successful, to emphasize certain principles of progress in the past and to produce a story which is the ratification if not the glorification of the present. This Whig version of the course of [H]istory is associated with certain methods of historical organization and inference — certain fallacies to which all history is liable, unless it be historical research. The examination of these raises problems. . . ."

18. As described by Frederick Jackson Turner: "To a large class of writers, represented by Hume, the field of historical writing is an arena, whereon are to be fought out present partisan debates. Whig is to struggle against Tory, and the party of their writer's choice is to be victorious at whatever cost." Quoted from "The Significance of History," in *Frederick Jackson Turner: Wisconsin's Historian of the Frontier,* ed. Martin Ridge (Madison: The State Historical Society of Wisconsin, 1933), 51.

This kind of perspective on events has not lost its sway in modern life: it is as contemporary and common as today's newspaper. Many modern historical writings can be seen as resting upon a moderate or reasonable form of this kind of history. Countless historians, nonprofessional and professional alike, have practiced it, or continue to practice it. Sometimes apologetic, sometimes apocalyptic, sometimes a blending of many shades of ideology, this "triumphalist" kind of history has often tended to lean toward historicism: linking past and future, remote antiquity to remote destiny, as a closed chain of inevitable events — a chain of inevitable (even necessary) continuity and (logical) consequences.

There is a temptation among some in our day to scorn history of this kind — to see it as old-fashioned and time-worn — or, in a word, *traditional.* Yet this attitude is not fully reasonable. All history, after all, reflects some belief system or ideology. All history rests upon assumptions and presuppositions. This is so whether or not underlying assumptions are fully and self-consciously understood. Open acknowledgement of this fact is, perhaps, one of the most self-critical and honest confessions a historian can make. Failure of self-awareness, in this essential regard, can lead to self-delusion; and self-delusion, or lack of self-critical detachment, can lead to scorn. Historical understandings are scorned when failure to make underlying belief systems, ideological agendas, and presuppositions fully explicit can be seen as leading to arrogantly, blindly, or dogmatically held conclusions. When ideological attitudes become manifest in extremist or intolerant modes, when they result in crass, reductionist, simplistic, or self-serving claims, rational inquiry is nullified and conclusions become dubious. Yet, as already noted earlier in this chapter, a self-consciously open-minded and modest acknowledgement of perspective, an admission that historical understandings would never be possible were they were not driven or motivated, in one way or another, by some belief, some perspective, some standpoint from which to look at an event, usually suffices to dissolve such scorn — and to allow for a suspension of final judgment.

In functional as well as in practical terms, it is *interest* that focuses our eyes in the direction of events and prompts us to select which events are important. Without interest, we would not be able to decide which events are more relevant, and which events need to be remembered or more closely studied. Whether inquiry about events is done on behalf of some family, nation, church, other corporate entity (e.g., business firm, profession, or academic discipline), or ideology makes no difference. It is out of some "common" or "natural" interest, arising out of some belief or conviction or presupposition with its intrinsic epistemology and ontology (however consciously or unconsciously held), that the eyes of each beholder turn toward one event and not another. It is interest that informs each perception of that event. So seen, the fact that each attempt to attain historical understanding arises out of some point of view is just an inescapable fact. It is also, quite essentially, a virtue. It helps the observer to make sense of a select few out of an impossible number of jumbled events and impulses. Rational capacity, sense or sensibility alike, requires this sort of selective filtering.

To repeat, only when any one set of ideological presuppositions becomes too extreme and too intolerant, only when its expression becomes crass and crude and when its findings lead to self-deception and delusion, does this kind of history become dangerous and destructive. What in some circumstances might compel more careful and critical examination can, when not done with due constraint, blind eyes and prevent open or critical inquiry. Even partial blindness to events can distort what is seen. As a consequence, approaches to historical understanding that become too extreme can miss the danger signals and become far-fetched. In the twentieth century, ideological presuppositions have done as much to darken as to enlighten our understanding of events. Like "bad coin driving out good," dogma in the garb of belief or in the guise of theory has contributed to an untold amount of blindness and has led to enormous human suffering and tragedy.

The second category of presuppositions is itself, like the first, also a form of bias. Sometimes labeled "positivist," sometimes "verificationist," "scientistic," "empiricist," or even "physicalist," this category is intrinsically just as much an ideology as any other. Positivism in its more extreme forms has also been secularistic and antisupernaturalistic. Its underlying presupposition has been that no valid understanding of any event is possible that does not come to us directly from empirical observation. Only findings modeled by empirical methods and verificationist procedures, especially those utilized by the physical sciences, have been seen as sufficient or valid. Coming into vogue during the Enlightenment and becoming increasingly popular among historians during the nineteenth century, this view has consisted in a belief that *methodology,* in and of itself, could bring about a more *perfect,* if not a more total, comprehension of events. At last, a fully "objective," "pure," and "untainted" grasp of events could be possible. Cleansed of all bias and preconception, especially of anything supernatural or theological, a historian could distill "true facts" from more solid data. Solid data, taken from validated evidence, could produce facts. Facts of pristine authenticity, once established and rigorously tested, could speak for themselves.

Here again was an absolutist system of belief — a ground of wonderful certainty. It was possible for "the whole truth and nothing but the truth" to be established once and for all. "At the very beginning of all conquest of the unknown," Burton Adams told the American Historical Association in 1908, "lies the fact, established and classified to the fullest possible extent." The historian was to avoid mere speculation and to discover and record "what actually happened," nothing more and nothing less.[19]

The credibility of this category of belief, especially in its more extreme (triumphalist) forms, has long since waned. And yet its allure lingers. Historians who identify themselves with social sciences and social theory (especially in sociology and social or cultural anthropology); and those for whom materialist analysis (Marxist analysis), new social history, *Annales* historiography, or cliometric technology is especially appealing have been attracted to it. Some devoutly sincere and valiant historians remain convinced that scientific method and scientific veracity *alone* can produce any truly trustworthy or "scientific" history.

Again, scorn or intolerance is not an appropriate response. Historical positivism, at the very least, can be credited with solid and significant contributions. Positivists have taken the reality of events seriously. By treating evidence of events with great care, they have continually raised fresh standards of historical inquiry. They have made history into a much more rigorous and critical discipline. By approaching each event on its own terms, by insistence upon keeping an open mind, by recognizing that what can be known about any event depends upon perception and perspective rather than preconception, they have made a lasting contribution to historical understandings. This contribu-

19. Cited by Mark Noll in "Practice and Presuppositions: History," 6, 18 n. 13. Adams's address was published in *American Historical Review* 14 (1909): 223, 226.

tion is of supreme importance. Critical self-awareness remains crucial to historical understandings, even if no one can fully measure up to such demands and even if no one is ever entirely free from preconceptions. Since positivists have taken events seriously, they have also taken everything in the world seriously. The inhabited universe, with all of its consistencies and regularities, has been perceived as being governed by fixed laws, principles that are discoverable. Assuming that events are at least in some measure predictable, positivists have held certain views in common with those very supernaturalists and theologians whose views they have often decried.

The problem with positivism, as already noted, can be found in its myopia. Due to narrowness of vision, its exponents have often failed to see that the very technologies by which historical judgments are formed are, in themselves, never as completely objective or value-free as they would like to think. The very acts of "discovering" historical "facts," in other words, have themselves always been driven by agents, and those agents were always capable of exercising free will. Inability even to consider the possibility that events, certainly human events, might not be irrevocably locked into predetermined patterns from which there can be no escape is the Achilles' heel of positivism. Those who hold this doctrine, in its extreme forms, fail to see that the historians themselves, as human persons, are the very ones who have produced historical understandings. This they themselves have done, whether consciously or not. Thus, historians have been and are ever and inescapably enmeshed within the biases and blindnesses of personal convictions of their own making. Moreover, in their own most important functions, positivists have overlooked the possibility that it is they themselves who, as historians, have made some of the real choices and decisions. Choices and decisions have consequences; and, in some measure, these have shaped understandings of the very events that positivist historians have sought to comprehend with such detachment.

The third category of presuppositions about the nature of historical understanding is "nihilistic." This might just as aptly be described as "negativistic," "opportunistic," "pragmatic," "relativistic," or "utilitarian." It is a kind of presupposition that reflects an attitude or belief concerning the very reality of events themselves — or the reality of any valid links between understandings and events. Like the other two categories of presuppositions, this too is an inherently ideological (or doctrinal) view. And, as such, it also possesses inherent strengths and inherent weaknesses. However, this third leg of our triad of categories stands in sharp contrast to the other two. Presuppositions of this sort deny the possibility of ever being able to fully or truly understand events. In more extreme forms, this kind of "historical" thinking rests upon a prior assumption that observations are so biased, so warped by prior prejudices, so corrupted by hidden motives, and so jaded by subconscious inclinations that no totally "objective" or truly "real" (much less "scientifically valid") understanding of a human event can ever be possible. Nothing meaningful can ever be clearly or definitively known about what has happened in the past (or in the present, for that matter). Perceptions of events are too tainted and warped. They are bent and distorted. They are products of "imaginative reconstruction" by "interested parties." Those who bend and distort are partisans who are driven by political aspirations. They are the myth-makers who, in their quests for power, have used facts about events as excuses for "colonizing" the bodies and minds of less fortunate fellow human beings. They have dominated and exploited not only people but also all natural resources within an expendable and limited global environment. Historians, in short, have either been hopelessly corrupted or inherently deluded (or duped).

The roots of this kind of belief about the understanding of events, as shown in previous chapters, go back many centuries, if not to remotest antiquity. It is a perspective that is inherently inward looking, if not pensive and resentful. It is an ideology that has tended to discover permanence and reality within: to explore inner elements. Reality lies within each person's sense of self. It lies within what may be called romantic or subjective impulses. It is idealistic experience that matters. By stressing what goes on within each person, by searching for reality within "essences" and "meanings" of inner experience, where persons are linked together in some sense of collective and organic community, its proponents look into the very nature of human consciousness itself for deeper understandings about events.

The lineage of this kind of thinking is Continental (European). Traces of the view that perceptions of events are little more than mere exercises in self-delusion or irrelevance can be found in some of the ideas of Friedrich Nietzsche (1844-1900). Less explicit forms of its expression can be found in the ideas of Max Weber (1864-1920), Wilhelm

Dilthey (1833-1911), Leopold von Ranke (1795-1886), G. W. F. Hegel (1770-1832), Immanuel Kant (1724-1804), Gottfried Herder (1744-1803), Giambattista Vico (1688-1744), and even in that founder of modern philosophy, René Descartes (1596-1650). Within our own age, it can be found in the views of Carl L. Becker. Twenty years before the appearance of his celebrated work on *The Heavenly City of the Eighteenth Century Philosophers* (1932),[20] Becker had already made clear his conviction that perfect detachment is impossible and that events can never really be fully understood.[21] "Mr. Everyman," he had explained, has always been "his own historian"; and historical verity is nothing more than what lies only in the eye of the beholder. Repeating these views in his presidential address to the American Historical Association in 1931, he declared that since it comes out of the defective memory of each person or community, history can never be more than "an imaginative creation, a personal possession which each of us, Mr. Everyman, fashions out of his individual experience, adapts to his practical or emotional needs, and adorns as well as may be to suit his aesthetic tastes."[22]

This same category of historical presuppositions, with its strongly ideological and polemical biases, is perhaps as strong today as it has ever been. Tracing itself back to Ferdinand de Saussure (1857-1913) and Martin Heidegger (1889-1976), as also to Paul de Man (1919-83), Jacques Derrida (1930- ), and Michel Foucault (1926-84),[23] its champions have gone so far as to deny the possibility of any kind of valid knowledge, much less historical understanding.[24] Deconstructionists, as

20. Carl L. Becker, *The Heavenly City of the Eighteenth-Century Philosophers* (New Haven and London: Yale University Press, 1932).

21. Carl L. Becker, "Detachment in the Writing of History," *Atlantic* 106 (1910): 524-36.

22. Carl L. Becker, "Everyman His Own Historian," *American Historical Review* 37 (1932): 228, reprinted in Carl L. Becker, *Everyman His Own Historian: Essays on History and Politics* (Chicago: Quadrangle Books, 1935), 243. I am grateful to Mark Noll for also reminding me to look again at Becker. However, I am inclined to add a cautionary note: Becker, taken in the context of his argument, was doing more than simply restating commonly held shibboleths about the limits and constraints which inhibit all historical understandings, a view with which any practicing historian can hardly quarrel.

23. Michel Foucault, *The Archaeology of Knowledge and the Discourse on Language* (New York: Pantheon, 1971).

24. A polemical and simple, straightforward, if also stylized, summary of this set of perspectives and presuppositions can be found in Keith Jenkins, *Re-Thinking History* (London and New York: Routledge, 1991).

also postmodernists and post-Orientalists, have taken historical presuppositions into the murky vales of self-indulgent subjectivism or onto puffy clouds of pure fantasy and fiction.

This school of thought trumpets human incapacity. It not only denies that anything can be known about past events, but in so doing, it thereby also implies that nothing can be known about the present. The same logic applies to all events. If nothing can be validly known about events other than that they are expressions of private longings, urges, interests, and ideologies — disguised attempts to acquire or to retain political power — then there is nothing at all that can be known. If science is nothing but a disguised mechanism for achieving the same results, what remains are mere gestures and self-conscious minglings of defiance and despair. If hard understandings are impossible, then understandings of any kind are impossible. Understandings of any sort amount, quite literally, to nothing. All that can be learned from exercises in rational inquiry, some would even try to argue, are the depths of self-deception into which supposedly rational people can plunge. In short, events of any kind — past, present, or future — simply cannot be known or understood. If nothing more can be known and nothing more can be anticipated but ultimate oblivion (called "death" or "annihilation"), one might as well "eat, drink, and be merry." Self-indulgence and self-fulfillment are all that remains — all that is real. The self alone, the *atma* of Vedic verse, by such reckoning, is inextricably linked to the timeless and motionless *Brahma* — the Cosmic All of the universe. Nothing, by such reckoning, matters.

# IV

How then does one deal with these three sets of categories? Which one of them is more correct? For anyone who holds beliefs or convictions about a reality above and beyond the immediate "here and now," beyond the realm of sensate feeling, this is no small question. Nor is the answer simple. None of these categories of presuppositions, in itself, is sufficient. At the same time, all of them are useful and necessary. All help to provide, if only in part, more adequate understandings of events. In other words, no presuppositions about events rooted exclusively in doctrine, philosophy, or theory are, in themselves, sufficiently adequate and complete. Each is prone to reductive over-simplification. None is capable, in itself, of fully explaining events. What can be understood, findings taken from perceptions of events (from data, evidence, etc.), are never complete. They are always less than fully comprehensible and always contingent upon the possibility of further findings. Yet, at the same time, each of these sets of presuppositions, despite inadequacies or dangers of generating distortion when taken too far, is also a necessary if not sufficient precondition for the possibility of understanding more about what may or may not have happened in past events.

Historical understandings of any kind, we have argued, are informed by beliefs or convictions about the very nature of reality: the very nature of events occurring in space and in time. Yet, the very nature of the historical understandings of events are themselves, however much they may be founded upon prior structures of belief and conviction, also the grounds on which the verification of those very same beliefs and convictions are established or founded. Herein lies a tautology: a circular kind of argument, that "a rose is a rose is a rose" — something that leads nowhere and says nothing. Yet, here also perhaps is dialectical mental process: a realization that historical understandings are formed and reformed by a constant and continuous spiral, an oscillating interplay between events or perceptions of events on the one hand, and belief structures (or conviction) and conceptions (epistemologies, ontologies, etc.) on the other. It is this oscillating interplay, this polarity between the unknown and the known, that lies at the very heart of historical understandings.

Historical understandings, and beliefs or convictions about the reality of events, are always partial. They are bounded and constrained by what there is about "what has happened" that is *not* known, by what there is about an event that is still *not* understood. What is not known and what cannot be known screams too loudly and insistently for any historical finding to be altogether final or conclusive. To lay claim to any more than a partial comprehension of what may or may not have happened when an event occurred is to reach beyond the limits of what a historian can know, and of what can be known. The historian, after all, is merely mortal. Full or total understanding of an event is always shrouded. Its totality remains hidden. To some degree, it remains a mystery. A mystery, even a partial mystery, can be very frustrating. For some kinds of thinkers, partial understandings of events are an affront.

Knowledge that remains contingent and conditional can be an affront to human curiosity, if not to human dignity, and, most of all, to human pride. Hubris itself is offended and violated. Deepest yearnings for certainty and for safety, among the most profound of all human needs, are not satisfied. Crucially important events, never fully or sufficiently well understood, continue to engage, fascinate, and beguile the best minds. Such beguiling has been occurring for as long as mankind has exercised conscious emotion, purpose, and reason. Whatever the human event may be, we "see through a glass darkly," knowing only in part and seeing in part what we would like to see and know in full. There is always more to an event than what meets the eye, more than has ever met the eyes of any mortal (or of all mortals together).

What undergirds our best historical understandings is a triad. Better yet, it is a humble three-legged stool *(tripos)*. The seat of this stool is upheld partially by each of the three legs — the three sets or categories of presuppositions summarized above. The options confronting the careful and conscientious historian are not limited to a simple choice of having to select one or another of the three genres of presuppositions. Rather, of necessity, historical understanding embraces and is tied together by all three of these kinds of conceptualizing frameworks, conditioning circumstances, and levels of comprehension. Moreover, at least two of these sets of doctrine can be seen as somehow incompatible with one of the others. The three legs of this stool are antinomies. No self-respecting rationalist, nor any philosopher or theorist, much less a systematic theologian, would deign to combine these sets of belief within any single frame of reference. This is because no system of logic can abide contradiction. Half-truths and paradoxes are not their meat. Thus, while each set of presuppositions provides one essential angle of reference by which an event (or events) might be understood, not one of them is adequate, in itself, to explain an event fully or sufficiently. Historical understandings are not merely arbitrary constructions, even though they are all of that. Nor are they simply logical abstractions, complete and consistent in every detail of comprehension. They are both much more and much less. Human understanding cannot inform events unless, in some way, those same events inform human understanding, enabling the mind to "make sense" of those events. Events having to do with the deepest mysteries of human life, in other words, are never fully understood.

But what are these mysteries? And what are the meanings we attach to events that we do not and perhaps cannot fully or properly fathom? Here lie some of the very issues of life and death — the stuff of relations, relationships, and relativities. No person, nor any group or society of any size, can learn of some historical event without being confronted with what it means to be human. When we learn that some little child or youth, whether girl or boy, has been stealthily enticed, dragged, or drugged into captivity, mutilated, tortured, and then wantonly killed, something within each of us cries out with anguish and pain. We realize that such an event could have happened to any one of us, or to one whom we deeply cherish, one whose disappearance from our lives would forever diminish that quality of our lives, both as individuals and as members of a larger community (which is its essence). To the degree that our reactions to such an event are not completely consumed by anguish, horror, outrage, and revulsion, we feel that something in us is less than human. Such feelings, as convictions, are multiplied beyond counting when a similar event, or a complex of such events, happens to millions of persons at once. In our own lifetime, certainly within this century, more persons have been wantonly done to death by their fellow human beings than has happened, as far as we can ascertain from records we possess, in all of the centuries and millennia that went before. This huge assertion takes our breath away. But we can document it with masses of detail beyond counting. Historians have commonly held that just the events of World War II in Eastern Europe brought violent death to over fifty million persons. Now, with the end of the Cold War, estimates of such deaths in Russia alone have been revised upwards from twenty to fifty million persons. Such calculations do not begin to include what happened in the death camps and gulags of the Nazi Empire, the Soviet Empire, or the Chinese Communist Empire during the rule of Hitler, Stalin, and Mao Ze-dong, or what happened in the killing fields of Cambodia, Ethiopia, Rwanda, and many other places. Worst of all, when informed that over half of all instances of death, torture, and violence that happen in our world have been inflicted upon persons by other persons who were known to one another, usually within the confining domestic embrace of their own families, our attempts to understand events are confronted by a mystery of iniquity, a depth of darkness and evil that lies deep within each and all of us who are supposedly "human" beings.

Evil and attempts to evade evil are at the heart of all notable human events. No human events can be fathomed that do not come to grips with this reality. The quality of human relationships is the very stuff of historical inquiry. But even when such perceptions are granted, most certainly and immediately, anyone who attempts to confront this issue must also confront the manifold and imaginative ways by which persons and communities and nations have attempted to evade responsibility for their own actions. The persistence, truculence, and virulence of such attitudes, the imaginativeness and inventiveness in the way deceptions have been carried out, can only fill the serious observer with wonder and awe. The ways in which corruption creeps or is foisted upon others, the suspecting and unsuspecting alike, can evoke restless and sober reflection. Some can evade issues of darkness and evil by focusing attention almost exclusively upon the "natural goodness" of mankind or upon unfortunate environmental conditions.

Constructions such as these are often built upon the bones and ruins of partially uncovered events. Used to define and explain evil, they are capable of evoking strong delusion. Endowed with politically correct or pseudo-divine righteousness and enshrined as icons in public consciousness, such constructions are capable of provoking actions that have led to enormous amounts of pain, suffering, and death. Dogma paraded as philosophy, theory, or ideology can be wondrously perfect in beauty and logic and yet deadly in consequence. Molded and re-molded so as to meet every possible objection, such systems of thought have then been loosed upon the world. Some inner compulsion in human beings makes them strive to embrace and to grab hold of "The Truth." This truth, once "discovered" or "captured," is "held" or "kept," if not "imprisoned" or "possessed." Then it is endowed with absolute certainty, packed into a neat box, and wrapped in persuasive rhetoric so that it can be conveyed to the ends of the earth.

This kind of truth is one of those recurring sorts of events that awakens the interest of historians. Historians — those who practice the craft — discover, dissect, and examine the entrails of such events. Enshrined ideas, as "man-made" inventions, acquire an almost divine status. They become "graven images." High and lifted up, they become objects of intellectual veneration and worship. They are among the chief forms of idolatry in each age. No community or nation, whether secular or sacred, seems to be without its own ideological icons. None is immune from the dangers of devotion to its own particular kind of "Truth." This truth, a mingling of partially false and partially true beliefs, always runs the danger of turning into an idol. As interpretative instruments, dogmas in the guise of theory or philosophy can be used to pronounce upon the meanings of events with awesome and totalistic certainty. They can be used to show how this or that institution (culture, nation, empire, etc.) within the collective life of humankind has achieved a special and paramount majesty, how it has surpassed the worth of anything that had ever before existed, and how therefore all of mankind is now obliged to acknowledge it and render due obeisance. There are no institutions constructed by the ingenuity of human agency that do not run the danger of becoming objects of idolatry. All such institutions, moreover, have embodied understandings of events within their innermost structures of belief.

Beneath and beyond the evil and idolatry discovered and embodied in events, one can also uncover, albeit always and only partially, elements of further meaning. One of these, by whatever name it may be known, is "consequence" or "judgment." Somewhere deep within lies the innate human capacity for dealing with adversity. This capacity, call it "courage," is that persistent refusal to give up or to lose hope. The capacity to find hope in the darkest of events has, like a coin, two sides. First, there is some sense that, however much events may ever be only partially understood, events possess some inexorable logic of their own and that, within the working out of this logic, forms of evil and idolatry have a way of bringing self-destruction upon their perpetrators. Few practicing historians, especially professional historians of the academy, dare to consider the possible existence of an "iron law of consequences" lying outside those events which they are seeking to understand. Certainly, they would not feel that the existence of such a law is definitively warranted by evidence, by what can be understood about human events. And yet, by such thinking as this, events can be seen as showing that individuals and institutions "reap what they sow," so that "those who sow the wind reap the whirlwind."[25]

Second, there is some sense that behind all events lies a slow but inevitable working out of an inexorable logic, that behind all events

25. In the rhetoric so used, the foundations and structures of heaven and hell are built, brick by brick, out of small events.

there lies some majestic design, or sovereign pattern. Events themselves, by such reckoning, have a way of eventually and ultimately leading to some sort of final resolution, some kind of "redemption" or "rescue." Whether or not this redemption, this rescue from seemingly hopeless situations that are seen as consequences of wickedness and idolatry, concerns individual persons or institutions led by persons can be a matter of endless debate and discussion.[26] The point at issue, however, is not whether there is some form of intelligibility behind events, but rather how events which are seen as human catastrophes and confusions in this world are to be understood. Without answers, without a sense of hope undergirded by some sense of judgment, events become meaningless.

The three-legged stool or triadic approach to basic presuppositions, combining the categories described above, has some distinct and practical advantages. First, as already indicated, it reaffirms the proposition that all we can know about events comes from within a frame of reference grounded in fundamental belief structures — or, conversely, that no events are perceived in a vacuum. History cannot be wholly detached from ideologies grounded in belief. Second, it affirms the proposition that human events occur within a real and objectively observable world. However biased or incomplete information concerning any event may be, it can be better understood if it is examined, as much as humanly possible, with critical detachment. The best methods and most rigorous tools of analysis available can further such understanding. And, third, because events may never be totally understood and because they are always biased, incomplete, partial, and contingent, events will always remain shrouded, however little or much, in mystery. There will always be some elements within events that can never be fully known. To some degree, a *complete* or *full* history will always remain unattainable.

In short, the very fact that each category of presuppositions that have influenced historical thinking over the past two centuries tends to make excessive claims underscores one of the deepest and most intrinsic features of historical understanding: namely, its paradoxical and mys-

---

26. Whether or not such a thing as an "iron law of consequences" exists, or can be found apart from events, is a matter that few practicing historians today, certainly few of those who are professionals within the academy, care to address. A question of this sort is not perceived to be an "historical" question. The issue is not considered to be one which historians, as historians, can properly address.

terious nature. Both the triumphalist (or "ideologicalistic," to coin a term) and the positivistic ("verificationistic") forms of presuppositions posit a comprehensive system (or a world view) which allows for neither compromise nor contradiction. Yet each, by denying room for the contingency, incompleteness, and uncertainty of what can be known about human events and by a lack of modesty about what can and cannot be known about human events, fails to fully comprehend the essence of historical understanding. The nihilistic (or negativistic) approach to historical understandings is, in no lesser degree, a comprehensive system of belief. It too, in comparable measure, brooks no contradiction. Denial of the very possibility of meaningful or useful knowledge about human events constitutes a denial and a repudiation either of the reality of events themselves or of the reality of the world in which events take place. All three of the categories of presuppositions, as systematic belief structures, are inadequate and cannot stand alone. None are capable of adequately explaining the combined reality and mystery of events, those paradoxes that can never be fully understood.

## VI

What, then, are the boundaries between history and belief? Between the limits of historical understanding vis-à-vis belief and the limits of belief vis-à-vis the understanding of events lies an enigma. What cannot be known about an event, however real that event may be, can be massive. Part of each event, especially each human event, remains cloaked in mystery. It lies shrouded in darkness because so much of what we would need to understand about it is still so contingent. There is always something more to be discovered, something yet to be explored. Much will always remain hidden from view. What we know about an event can be radically altered with just one or two more facts. When something new is uncovered or when new insights are developed, we find that there are still unresolved but nagging puzzles and riddles. Alternative readings of evidence remain persuasive and rational. Existing interpretations, due to limited and partial completeness of data, often fail to do justice to understandings of an event. At such points of frustration, all three basic categories of presuppositions fail. When this happens, much depends upon how two kinds of further questions are handled: questions of relevance/significance and of authenticity/validity.

First, regarding relevance and significance, questions vary according to interest and perspective. Those who ask the questions determine the focus and scope of historical understanding. Frederick Jackson Turner's view that "each age writes the history of the past anew with reference to the conditions uppermost in its own time"[27] is apropos. But questions about the relevance and significance of an event are also both elastic and partial: each history can be broadened or narrowed, stretched or shrunk, simplified or elaborated upon in manifold and untold ways. As with each age, so also with each world, each people, and each place (or interest). One person's history is not necessarily another's. The history of one place is never the history of another, no matter how small or large that place may be. Moreover, distinctions can always be made between events of a *particular relevance* and events of a more *general significance*. One physician's records, for example, do not reflect how medicine is practiced by another. Nor can one hospital's history of crisis management ever be identical to that of another. During one stretch of time, events may or may not have been noticed; and, if noticed, may not even have possessed the same meaning. Processes of particular relevance for those interested in looking back upon a particularly and peculiarly specific sequence of events do not carry equal weight for every person. On the other hand, some events are of common and general and widespread concern; they are perceived as having a significance that applies to everyone, or to a wider constituency of human interests.

Second, even when the particular relevance or general significance of an event is recognized, the authenticity or validity of what might be known about that event will never be total. Since no historical understandings of any event are complete, the history of all events remains incomplete. What is known is always conditional, always contingent upon what might yet become known (and, hence, upon what remains unknown). Findings are always provisional, and never perfect. This does not mean that the actual (or objective) reality of any event can be nullified.[28] What has happened has happened. It can never be altered,

27. Turner, "The Significance of History," 53.
28. The actual birth or death of a person, for example, cannot be nullified, or invalidated. Events, in that sense, cannot be "undone" or "reversed." But the occurrence

annulled, or undone. It belongs to the past, however fathomable or unfathomable that past may be.[29] Alternately, what can or cannot be known or understood about what has happened can vary extremely: it can range from almost nothing at all to almost everything. What is known and understood, seen on a relative scale, always falls somewhere between zero and one hundred percent. But in abstract terms, it can never encompass absolutely everything. Moreover, in a very large proportion of events having to do with human affairs, the authenticity and validity of historical understandings can vary widely within that scale, insomuch that what can be known will often be extremely limited.

To put this in terms other than historical, whether in theological or theoretical terms of reference, complete and total historical knowledge or understanding of an event is a practical impossibility. Were it otherwise we would be more than mortal: we would be omniscient, omnipresent, and omnipotent, if not everlasting. We would, in short, be taking to ourselves more than we are — more than the image of our Maker. We would be making ourselves into gods, capable of claiming equality with God.[30] Records are replete with instances in which human beings, or persons claiming to represent one corporate entity or another, have made such claims. The past is littered with the remains of such attempts. Ruins of monuments proclaim what has happened to human pride. Cities and empires of awesome size and splendor have vanished, so that even the memory of some human achievements is gone. Thus, even if we accept Turner's dictum that "History is all the remains that have come down to us from the past, studied with all the critical and interpretative power that the present can bring to the task,"[31] we do not escape the enigma. Inherent limitations in the understandings of historical events remain.

Yet there is also that "spark of eternity," that urge for ultimate immortality, if not for perfection, which lies deep within consciousness and which burns deep within each mind. The very mortality of each

---

of an event can often be falsified, or made into a "non-event," an event that is no longer allowed public acknowledgement. The "deconstruction" of such an event does not nullify its having actually happened.

29. This kind of *a priori* understanding is an assumption that is taken as true.

30. More knowledge than the deceptive promise of the serpent: "You will be like gods, knowing both good and evil" (Gen. 3:3b).

31. Turner, "The Significance of History," 54.

person itself stands as an affront to human aspiration. Each event that captures interest calls for understanding. Total understanding is what is coveted. Each mind strives to grasp "what really happened," to fully capture events that matter — whether of politics, of religion, of society, of art, or of any other kind. Each mind, at the same time, can also recognize, if perhaps only dimly or intuitively, and perhaps inferentially, that all categories of events and divisions between events are artificial: that no breaks exit between the continuities and extensions of events and that what has actually happened is part of the fabric of a total reality. Minds can imagine, *a priori,* that all of reality is a seamless and unified whole, where all events are somehow inextricably interconnected (both in time and in space). Yet in pragmatic terms, the utility and the technology of keeping books and records so as not to allow collective memory to be lost are recognized as essential and practical, not just for providing information necessary for routine, day-to-day functions, but also for capturing some sense of what it is that constitutes human identity. These are things that can be acknowledged, even as minds grope and try to come to grips with a very slippery whole.

When all of the arguments made above are taken into consideration, many events seen as historic for one person or group are not seen as historic for another. What one community holds to be both real and true may not be so for another. What one community thinks is important may not be seen as such by another. Relative senses of reality, truth, or importance in an event or sequence of events, convictions about its relative authenticity and validity, or of its relevance and significance, can vary considerably. The glass of understanding may be half full, or it may be half empty. For one person, there may be much less certainty or understanding, while for another, there is much more. The very ground for understandings held by one may be seen as questionable by another. Yet, since there can never be more than incomplete and partial understandings of any event anyway, those who believe in the certainty of an event that they do not fully understand are obliged, by the very enigmas of historical understanding, to hold their convictions with some measure of modesty. Modesty is mingled with certainty. Historical certainty in what is understood about an event is never fully free from contingency or from critical review in the light of what is not yet known about that event.

## VII

Finally, how the validity of occurrence of an event is to be understood
— how its actuality or reality is to be believed when the very actuality
or reality of that occurrence is itself a matter of debate and doubt — is
perhaps the most difficult of all questions. How the historian is to deal
with those kinds of events in which empirical evidence is difficult or
even impossible to obtain, in situations where validation is anything but
certain, is always a matter of critical, if not crucial concern. Such concerns become even more critical, if not crucial, when dealing with claims
concerning the occurrence of any "special" or "supernatural" event. How
does the historian deal with such claims?

In the light of what has already been argued above, answers to
such questions are always directly linked to questions of relevance and
significance. In human affairs, for example, one could make a strong
argument that among all events concerning human affairs — where
events concerning *relationships* between persons as individuals or between persons as institutional aggregations of individuals are at issue
— none have been more important than those centered in *forgiveness*.[32]
No other events in human experience, by such reckoning, have been
more crucial, more noteworthy, or more consequential. Any evil,
whether or not manifested in overt actions, is a historic event. Even
when an evil has consisted of no more than intentions of the mind, it
can still be an event of consequence, whether that consequence be
deemed actual or potential, trivial or momentous. If evil is an event
momentous in consequence, so also is forgiveness. Forgiveness, indeed,
is an event even more momentous in significance. Out of depths of evil
imaginations and intentions that have occurred as events within their
own minds, human beings have wreaked destruction upon each other.
When human beings have caused damage and done evil to one another,
chain reactions of tragic consequence have resulted. Calamities and
disasters wrought by humans upon other humans happen, have hap-

---

32. Implicit to any advent of forgiveness, however, is the prior occurrence (and
existence) of events of *evil*, on one hand, and on the other, of concurrent or subsequent
*rescue* (or what J. R. R. Tolkien labeled "eucatastrophe"). C. S. Lewis, in elaborating upon
these themes in *The Weight of Glory* (London: Macmillan, 1949), felt that consequences
and ripple effects of what human beings do to other human beings are of such weight
that they outlast all empires, kingdoms, and other human institutions.

pened, and continue to happen. But efforts to combat evil have also inspired grand achievements and noble efforts which, in turn, have produced chain reactions of consequence. Indeed, events of creative and redemptive worth represent triumphs of the human spirit and signal victories, however incomplete or partial, of good over evil.

The great struggles for freedom in the past have been struggles in which individual persons or groups of persons, even whole nations of persons, have sought to rescue themselves, if not all mankind, from the consequences of evil. But, even so, the main struggles have continued to remain within the human heart and mind. "It is ordained in the eternal constitution of things," wrote Edmund Burke some two centuries ago, "that men of intemperate minds cannot be free. Their passions forge their fetters." He went on to suggest that "men [humankind] are qualified for civil liberty in exact proportion to their disposition to put moral chains upon their appetites. . . ." Events arising out of human hearts and minds have resulted in deeds and efforts of heroic and momentous consequence for breaking the bonds of systemic and institutionalized evil. Events in which creative imaginations have devised ways to break such chains of bondage, however imperfect and partial these ways may have been, are enshrined among the noblest of all historical understandings. Understandings of such events — repeated line by line, in remembrances sung and told — are the very fiber of historical narrative. They are celebrated both in verse and in prose. But the story of humankind can also be found, at its very heart, to be neither more nor less than a profoundly moving tale of forgiveness. Without forgiveness, fruits of bitterness and evil have remained and multiplied and reigned supreme, with destruction following in their train and spiraling out of control, so that, ultimately, all that is human, if not life itself, has become threatened.

But *forgiveness* — in response to damages done, deceptions and destructions perpetrated against fellow human beings — has never been free. This sweeping and breathtaking fact, as an insight, is itself a product of historical understandings. As a generalization, it is supported by the evidence of events. Such events, closely observed, can be traced back into remote antiquity. Of course, like all historical understandings, this kind of understanding is necessarily contingent. It is always partial, ever subject to revision in the light of contrary evidence. Yet, though contingent and partial, it stands because contrary evidence has yet to be found. A sweeping generalization such as this cries aloud for someone to show, in some smallest of instances, that this was not so and has never, ever been so. Many historians may evade or disregard this issue, perhaps merely on the ground of its not being relevant to matters with which they are preoccupied, and hence of little personal or historical significance. Yet no historian has yet ever come forward to deny or refute this historical proposition. None indeed have advanced evidence to suggest any contrary argument. None can deny the occurrence or consequences of events that were evil; and none deny the dreadful costs of events inspired by evil. None, likewise, can show that forgiveness is free.

Therefore, if evil has always, as far as we know, entailed loss and suffering, so also has forgiveness, and if forgiveness has always entailed cost, those costs are events that can be understood historically. Costs of forgiveness have invoked events which, in themselves, can be considered to have been some forms of "counter-action" or "counter-event." Actions counteracting evil, in chains or sequence of events, are actions of judgment, atonement, or redemption: they are historic events that have the potential of balancing the scales of justice, of weighing the fine dust of right and wrong, and of restoring inner harmony, integrity, and peace. Forgiveness, therefore, entails atonement, or redemption. Atonement or redemption, where or whenever it happens, and whatever its cost, is invariably a historic event. But when such an event has occurred, it has, thereby, acquired a special moral relevance or spiritual significance. Such an event has acquired a particular and special importance, a meaning qualitatively differentiating it from other, more mundane events. At that point, historical understandings become matters not just of life and death, but of immortality.

At this point, discourses about events rise to a different level. Systems of belief (or world views) founded upon the historicity of events which lie beyond the limits of *total* historic certainty are historical in the sense that they lay claim to specific events, or sequences of events, as the very foundations upon which their belief systems rest. Thus, when great monotheistic systems, not to mention those more recent "mono-nontheistic" systems (nationalisms, socialisms, and marxisms) which have emerged out of the monotheistic traditions, offer narrative accounts of human life and or human events, they have done so in ways that have suggested, in Niebuhr's words, that "all facts and antinomies are comprehended." The relative authenticity, certainty, or validity of evidence offered in support of such accounts has varied. What can never be understood concerning events, which can be crucial to belief concerning the actuality or reality of any event, has also tended to vary greatly, depending upon how much supporting evidence could be marshalled and how much persuasive rhetoric has been employed in support of arguments on its behalf.

But in the end, all who have believed in the historicity of any event, however mundane or extraordinary the character of that event, have had to confess to the limits of human understandings concerning that event. Beliefs and convictions concerning its actuality, however total may be the logic behind such beliefs and convictions, rest upon no more than partial understandings. Moreover, at some point, boundaries between what can be seen as acceptable (admissible or veridical) evidence or persuasive argument and what cannot be so seen become smudged, so that differences between events described as natural and events described as supernatural (or beyond the natural) become issues of debate which cannot be entirely resolved by rational means. Given the limitations of historical understanding, such boundaries are themselves often all too arbitrary and far from absolute. Many who concede that no event can be completely fathomed or totally understood are too quick to dismiss possibilities concerning the nature or origins of events which go beyond the bounds of empirical observations within the purely natural or physical world. Those who are so dismissive also often fail to acknowledge how incomplete and inconclusive may be the evidence or arguments supporting their acceptance of many historical understandings of more mundane events in the past, understandings which they have long taken for granted.

If then, with respect to events both mundane and supernatural, one person's historical fact is another person's fiction, so that what one person sees as an actual occurrence becomes what another sees as no more than a mere superstition, no more than an illusion, a flawed perception, or an irrational belief, those who are careful historians will exercise restraint. They will not, hopefully, be too quick in rushing to final judgment. For all historians, indeed, final judgments are never really possible. Judgments are always, in some measure — whether more or less — suspended. If the certainty or historicity of one particular or mundane event in the recent past remains shrouded in mystery, insomuch that it remains a focal point of ceaseless controversy, how much less than mystery can be expected to surround the historicity of a certain event in the more remote past, however ostensibly mundane or supernatural that event may have been deemed to be? For an event to be defeasible is one thing. For it to be definitively deniable is another. For the orthodox monotheist (Christian, Jew, or Muslim), all events, however great or small, are under the ultimate control and sovereignty of an Almighty God who, as Creator, Sustainer, and Redeemer, has made (or allowed) those events to occur. This is a matter of theological belief. This is also a matter of rational understanding, of conclusions drawn from long and careful observation of events and from various kinds of apparatus devised for the preservation of human memories of such observations in the past.

The Apostles' Creed of the Christian Church consists of a number of such historical understandings. Each of these is believed; and each is held as being rationally plausible (if not defeasible). Each is also an understanding that remains shrouded in mystery. That any historical understanding should remain a mystery is hardly strange. The contexts within which such events are believed to have occurred are not exactly the same as the contexts within which a biochemist can verify the advent of a new and virulent form of disease within a blood cell. Yet even so, the events that occur within the blood cell of a human being are also cloaked in more mystery than anyone is yet able to fathom. Events as mysteries can be partially described. But they cannot be fully explained. For the historian as a believer and the believer as historian, therefore, a blending of critical skepticism with genuine humility is hardly an option. Open acknowledgment and confession of that perpetual predicament, that mystery which conditions and contextualizes what can be known about events, are important stepping stones to historical understanding.

> Now we only know in part. . . . But when that which is perfect is come, then that which is in part shall be done away. . . . For now we see through a glass darkly, but then face to face. . . . Now I know in part; but then shall I know even as also I am known.

> 1 Corinthians 13:9-12

# Bibliography

Adams, Burton. Presidential Address. *American Historical Review* 14 (1909): 223, 226.

al-ʿAim, Sadik Jalal. "Orientalism and Orientalism in Reverse." *Khamsin: Journal of Revolutionary Socialists of the Middle East* 8 (1981): 5-26.

Albright, W. F. *From the Stone Age to Christianity.* Baltimore: Johns Hopkins University Press, 1941.

Alexander, Lovelace. *The Preface to Luke's Gospel: Literary Convention and Social Context in Luke 1:1-4 and Acts 1:1.* Cambridge: Cambridge University Press, 1993.

Ankersmit, Frank, and Hans Kellner. *A New Philosophy of History.* Chicago: University of Chicago Press, 1995.

Aristotle. "On Philosophy." In Jean-Pierre Vernant, "The Crises of the City: The Earliest Sages," in *The Origins of Greek Thought.* Paris: Presses Universitaires de France, 1962; Ithaca: Cornell University Press, 1982.

Babb, Lawrence. *The Divine Hierarchy.* New York: Columbia University Press, 1975.

Bann, Stephen. *The Clothing of Clio: A Study of the Representation of History in Nineteenth-Century Britain and France.* Cambridge: Cambridge University Press, 1984.

Barker, John. *The Superhistorians: Makers of our Past.* New York: Scribner's, 1982.

Barnes, Harry Elmer. *A History of Historical Writing.* 1937; reprint, New York: Dover Publications, 1962.

Barth, Karl. *The Resurrection of the Dead.* Trans. H. J. Stenning. London: Hodder & Stoughton, 1933.

Barzun, Jacques. *Clio and the Doctors: Psycho-History, Quanto History, and History.* Chicago and London: University of Chicago Press, 1974.

Basham, A. L. "The Kashmir Chronicle." In *Historians of India, Pakistan and Ceylon,* ed. C. H. Philips, 57ff. Oxford: Oxford University Press, 1961.

————. *The Wonder That Was India.* London: Sidgwick & Jackson, 1955.

Bayly, C. A. "Elusive Essences." Review of *Imagining India* by Ronald Inden and *Imagining India* by Richard Cronin. *Times Literary Supplement,* 7-13 December 1990.

————. "Rallying Around the Subaltern." Review of *Subaltern Studies,* vols. 1-6, ed. Ranajit Guha. *The Journal of Peasant Studies* 16, no. 1 (October 1988): 110-20.

Becker, Carl L. "Detachment in the Writing of History." *Atlantic* 106 (1910): 524-36.

————. "Everyman His Own Historian." *American Historical Review* 37 (1932): 221-36; reprinted in *The Historian as Detective: Essays on Evidence.* Ed. Robin Wink. New York: Harper & Row, 1969.

————. *The Heavenly City of the Eighteenth-Century Philosophers.* New Haven and London: Yale University Press, 1932.

Benjamin, B. S. "Remembering." *Mind* 65 (1956): 312-31; reprinted in *Essays in Philosophical Psychology,* 171-94. London: Macmillan, 1967.

Berlin, Isaiah. *The Hedgehog and the Fox.* London: Weidenfeld and Nicolson, 1953.

Berne, Eric. *Games People Play.* New York: Grove Press, 1964.

Bhattacharya, Subysachi, and Romila Thapar. *Situating Indian History.* New Delhi: Oxford University Press, 1986.

Bloch, Marc. *The Historian's Craft.* Trans. Peter Putnam. New York: Alfred A. Knopf, 1953.

Blomberg, Craig. *The Historical Reliability of the Gospels.* Downers Grove, Ill.: InterVarsity Press, 1987.

Bok, Sissela. *Lying: Moral Choice in Public and Private Life.* New York: Pantheon Books, 1978.

Borkenau, Franz. *End and Beginning: On the Generations of Cultures and the Origins of the West.* New York: Columbia University Press, 1981.

Bowes, Pratima. *The Hindu Religious Tradition.* London and Boston: Routledge and Kegan Paul, 1977.

Bradley, F. H. *The Presuppositions of Critical History.* Oxford: James Parker & Co., 1874. Reprinted in *Collected Essays of F. H. Bradley.* Oxford: Clarendon Press, 1935.

Breasted, James Henry. *Ancient Times.* Boston: Ginn, 1944.

————. *The Battle of Kadesh: A Study of the Earliest Military Strategy.* Chicago: University of Chicago Press, 1903.

————. *The History of Ancient Egypt: From Earliest Times to the Persian Conquest.* London: 1920; 2nd ed., fully revised, 1951.

————, ed. and trans. *Ancient Records of Egypt: Historical Documents from the Earliest Times to the Persian Conquest, Collected, Edited, and Translated with Commentary.* 5 vols. 1906-7; reprint, New York: Russell & Russell, 1962.

Breisach, Ernst. *Historiography: Ancient, Medieval & Modern.* Chicago: University of Chicago Press, 1983.

Brown, David. *The Divine Trinity.* La Salle, Ill.: Open Court Publishers, 1985.

Brown, T. S. *The Greek Historians.* Lexington, Mass.: D. C. Heath, 1973.

Brundage, Burr C. "The Birth of Clio: A Resume and Interpretation of Ancient Near Eastern Historiography." In *Teachers of History: Essays in Honour of L. B. Packard,* ed. H. Stuart Hughes, 199-230. Ithaca, N.Y.: Cornell University Press, 1954.

Budge, E. A. Wallis. *The Book of Opening the Mouth: The Egyptian Texts with English Translations.* New York: Arno Press, 1980.

————. *The Book of the Dead.* 2nd ed. London: Routledge & Kegan Paul, 1977.

————. *Egyptian Magic.* London, 1899; reprint, London & New York: Routledge, 1988.

Bultmann, Rudolph. *Kerygma and Myth.* Ed. W. H. Bartsch. London: S.P.C.K, 1953.

Burns, Timothy, ed. *After History? Francis Fukuyama and His Critics.* Lanham, Md.: Rowman & Littlefield, 1994.

Burridge, Richard A. *What Are the Gospels? A Comparison with Graeco-Roman Biography.* Cambridge: Cambridge University Press, 1992.

Bury, J. B. *The Ancient Greek Historians.* London: Macmillan, 1909; New York: Dover Publications, 1958.

Butterfield, Herbert. *Christianity and History.* New York: Scribner's, 1949.

————. *Man on His Past: The Study of the History of Historical Scholarship.* Cambridge: Cambridge University Press, 1955; Boston: Beacon Press, 1960.

————. *The Origins of History.* London: Methuen, 1981.

————. *The Origins of Modern Science.* London: G. Bell and Sons, 1950; revision, New York: Free Press, 1957.

————. *The Whig Interpretation of History.* London: G. Bell & Sons, 1951.

Cannon, G. *The Life and Mind of Oriental Jones: Sir William Jones, the Father of Modern Linguistics.* New York: Cambridge University Press, 1990.

Carnley, Peter. *The Structure of Resurrection Belief.* Oxford: Clarendon Press, 1987.

Carstairs, Morris G. *The Twice Born.* Bloomington: Indiana University Press, 1961.

Chadwick, Owen. *The Secularization of the European Mind in the Nineteenth Century.* Cambridge: Cambridge University Press, 1975.

Childe, V. Gordon. *What Happened in History.* Harmondsworth, Middlesex: Pelican Books, 1942.

Clive, John. *Not by Fact Alone: Essays on the Writing and Reading of History.* New York: Alfred A. Knopf, 1989.

Cochrane, C. N. *Thucydides and the Science of History.* Oxford: Oxford University Press, 1929.

Coe, Richard N. "The Anecdote and the Novel: A Brief Enquiry into the Origins of Stendhal's Narrative Technique." *Australian Journal of French Studies* 20, no. 1 (January-April 1985): 7.

Cohn, Bernard S. *An Anthropologist among Historians and Other Essays.* New York: Oxford University Press, 1987.

Collingwood, R. G. *The Idea of History.* Oxford: Clarendon, 1946.

Cornford, F. M. *Greek Religious Thought.* London: Dent & Co., n.d.

————. *Thucydides Mythhistoricus.* London: Arnold, 1907; reprint, New York: Greenwood Press, 1969.

Craig, William Lane. *Assessing the New Testament Evidence for the Historicity of the Resurrection of Jesus.* Lewiston, N.Y., and Queenston, Ontario: Edwin Mellen Press, 1989.

————. *The Historical Argument for the Resurrection of Jesus during the Deist Controversy.* Vol. 23 in Texts and Studies in Religion Series. Lewiston, N.Y., and Queenston, Ontario: Edwin Mellen Press, 1985.

Crossan, John Dominic. *The Historical Jesus: The Life of a Mediterranean Jewish Peasant.* San Francisco: Harper San Francisco,
1991.

Danto, Arthur C. *Narration and Knowledge.* New York: Columbia University Press, 1985.

Deleuze, Gilles. *Difference and Repetition.* Trans. Paul Patton. London:
Athlone Press, 1994.

Dentan, R. C., ed. *The Idea of History in the Ancient Near East.* New
Haven: Yale University Press, 1955.

Derrett, J. Duncan M. *Religion, Law and the State in India.* London:
Faber & Faber, 1968.

Derrida, Jacques. *Specters of Marx: The State of the Debt, the Work of
Mourning, and the New International.* Trans. Peggy Kamuf. London: Routledge, 1995.

de Souza, J. P., and C. M. Kulkarni, eds. *Historiography in Indian Languages.* Delhi: Vikas, 1972.

Dickey, Laurence. *Hegel: Religion, Economics, and the Politics of Spirit,
1770-1807.* Cambridge: Cambridge University Press, 1987.

Dilthey, Wilhelm. *Pattern and Meaning in History: Thoughts on History
and Society.* Edited and introduced by H. P. Rickman. London:
George Allen & Unwin, 1961.

Dirks, Nicholas B. *The Hollow Crown: Ethnohistory of an Indian Kingdom.* South Asian Studies, no. 39. Cambridge: Cambridge University Press, 1987.

Donagan, Alan. "Explanation in History." In *Theories of History,* edited
(with introduction and commentary) by Patrick Gardiner, 428-43.
New York: Free Press, 1959.

Doniger, Wendy (O'Flaherty), ed. *Karma and Rebirth.* Berkeley and Los
Angeles: University of California Press, 1980.

Douglas, Mary. *Cultural Bias.* London: Royal Anthropological Institute,
1978.

———. *Purity and Danger: An Analysis of the Concepts of Pollution and
Taboo.* London: Arkon, 1984.

———. *Risk and Culture: An Essay on the Selection of Technical and
Environmental Dangers.* Berkeley and Los Angeles: University of
California Press, 1982.

———. *Rules and Meanings: The Anthropology of Everyday Knowledge.*
Harmondsworth, U.K.: Penguin, 1973.

Dray, William H. *Philosophy of History.* Englewood Cliffs, N.J.: Prentice-Hall, 1964.

Dumont, Louis. *Homo Hierarchicus: The Caste System and Its Implications.* Chicago: University of Chicago, 1970; rev. ed., 1980 (from French original edition in 1966).

———. "Origin Myths and Theories of Kingship." In *Religion, Politics and History in India: Collected Papers in Indian Sociology,* 70-88. Paris and The Hague: Mouton Publishers, 1970.

Durant, John. "Is Science a Social Invention?" *Times Literary Supplement,* 15 March 1991, 16.

Earle, William. "Memory." *Review of Metaphysics* 10 (1956): 3-27.

Edersheim, Arthur. *The Life and Times of Jesus the Messiah.* 3rd ed. London: Longmans, Green & Co., 1886.

———. *Sketches of Jewish Social Life.* London: Fleming H. Revell Co., 1878.

———. *The Temple and Its Worship.* London: Fleming H. Revell Co., 1874.

Eliade, Mircea. *Cosmos and History: or, The Myth of the Eternal Return.* 1954; reprint, Princeton: Princeton University Press, 1971.

———. *Patterns in Comparative Religion.* Trans. Rosemary Sheed. New York: New American Library, 1975.

———. *The Quest: History and Meaning in Religion.* Chicago: University of Chicago Press, 1969.

Eliot, Charles N. E. *Hinduism and Buddhism: An Historical Sketch.* London: Routledge & Kegan Paul, 1954.

Elton, G. R. *The Practice of History.* London: Methuen, 1967.

Eribon, Didier. *Michel Foucault.* Trans. Betsy Wing. London: Faber, 1993.

Fain, Haskell. *Between Philosophy and History.* Princeton: Princeton University Press, 1970.

Farrar, Cynthia. *The Origins of Democratic Thinking.* Cambridge: Cambridge University Press, 1988.

Faruqi, Nisar Ahmed. *Early Muslim Historiography: A Study of Early Transmitters of Arab History from the Rise of Islam Up to the End of the Umayyad Period (612-750 A.D.).* Delhi: Idarah-I Ababiyat-i Dilli, 1979.

Feenstra, Ronald J., and Cornelius Plantinga, Jr., eds. *Trinity, Incarnation, and Atonement: Philosophical and Theological Essays.* Notre Dame: University of Notre Dame Press, 1989.

Ferreira, M. Jamie. *Skepticism and Reasonable Doubt: The British Naturalist Tradition in Wilkins, Hume, Reid and Newman.* Oxford: Clarendon Press, 1986.

Finley, John H., Jr. *Thucydides.* Cambridge: Harvard University Press, 1942.

Finley, M. I. *The Ancient Greeks.* 1963; reprint, Harmondsworth, Middlesex: Penguin, 1981.

―――――. "Christian Beginnings: Three Views of Historiography." In *Aspects of Antiquity.* London: Chatto & Windus, n.d.

―――――. *The Greek Historians: The Essence of Herodotus, Thucydides, Xenophon, Polybius.* New York: Viking Press, 1959.

Fischer, David Hackett. *Historical Fallacies: Toward a Logic of Historical Thought.* New York: Harper & Row, 1970.

Fitzsimons, M. A. *The Past Recaptured: Great Historians and the History of History.* Notre Dame: University of Notre Dame Press, 1983.

Florovsky, Georges. "The Predicament of the Christian Historian." In vol. 2 of *Christianity and Culture: The Collected Works of Georges Florovsky.* Cambridge, Mass.: Nordland Publishing Company, 1974.

Foucault, Michel. *The Archaeology of Knowledge and the Discourse on Language.* New York: Pantheon, 1971.

Gadd, Cyril John. *The Early Dynasties of Sumer and Akkad.* London: Luzak, 1921.

―――――. *The Fall of Nineveh: A Newly Discovered Babylon Chronicle.* London: Oxford University Press, 1923.

―――――. *History and Monuments of Ur.* London: Chatto & Windus, 1929.

―――――. *Literary and Religious Texts.* London: British Museum, 1963.

―――――. "Seals of Ancient Indian Style Found at Ur." *Proceedings of the British Academy.* London, 1932.

―――――. *The Stones of Assyria.* London: Chatto & Windus, 1936.

Gallie, W. B. *Philosophy and the Historical Understanding.* New York: Schocken Books, 1968; 2nd ed., 1969.

Gardner, Charles S. *Chinese Traditional Historiography.* Cambridge: Harvard University Press, 1938; reprint, 1961.

Gardner, John, and John Maier. *Gilgamesh: Translated from the* Sîn-Leqi-Unninnī *Version.* New York: Alfred A. Knopf, 1984.

y Gasset, José Ortega. *Historical Reason.* Trans. Philip W. Silver. New York: W. W. Norton, 1985.

Gaur, Albertine. *A History of Writing.* London: The British Library, 1984, 1987.

Gearhart, Suzanne. *The Open Boundary of History and Fiction: A Critical Approach to the French Enlightenment.* Princeton: Princeton University Press, 1984.

Gellner, Ernest. *Plough, Sword and Book: The Structure of Human History.* Chicago: University of Chicago Press, 1989.

————. *Postmodernism, Reason, and Religion.* London and New York: Routledge, 1992.

Gordon, R. L., ed. and trans. *Myth, Religion, and Society.* Cambridge: Cambridge University Press, 1981.

Gottschalk, Louis. *Understanding History: A Primer of Historical Method.* New York: Alfred A. Knopf, 1950.

Gross, Alan G. *The Rhetoric of Science.* Cambridge: Harvard University Press, 1991.

Gruneberg, Michael M., Peter E. Morris, and R. N. Sykes. *Practical Aspects of Memory.* London: Methuen, 1978.

Guha, Ranajit, ed. *Selected Subaltern Studies.* New York and Oxford: Oxford University Press, 1988.

————. *Subaltern Studies: Writings on South Asian History and Society.* Vols. 1-6. Delhi: Oxford University Press, 1982-1988.

Gundy, G. B. *Thucydides and the History of His Age.* 2 vols. 2nd ed. Oxford: Basil Blackwell, 1948.

Gurney, O. R. *The Hittites: A Summary of the Art, Achievements and Social Organization of a Great People of Asia Minor during the Second Millennium B.C., as Discovered by Modern Excavations.* London: Penguin Books, 1952, 1975.

Halbwachs, George. *The Collective Memory.* New York: Harper, 1980.

Halpern, Baruch. *The First Historians: The Hebrew Bible and History.* San Francisco: Harper & Row, 1988.

Hanson, Norwood Russell. *Patterns of Discovery: An Inquiry into the Conceptual Foundations of Science.* Cambridge: Cambridge University Press, 1958; reprint, 1965.

————. *What I Do Not Believe, and Other Essays.* Ed. Stephen Toulmin and Harry Woolf. Dordrecht: Reidel, 1971.

Harbison, E. Harris. *Christianity and History.* Princeton: Princeton University Press, 1964.

Harris, Murray J. *Grave to Glory.* Grand Rapids: Zondervan, 1990.

Hart, H. L. A., and A. M. Honore. *Causation in the Law.* Oxford: Clarendon Press, 1959.

Hartog, Francois. *The Mirror of Herodotus: The Representation of the Other in the Writings of History.* Trans. Janet Lloyd. Berkeley and Los Angeles: University of California Press, 1988.

Harvey, Van Austin. *The Historian and the Believer: The Morality of Historical Knowledge and Christian Belief.* New York: Macmillan, 1966, 1969, 1975; London: S.C.M. Press, 1967.

Hebblethwaite, Brian. *The Incarnation: Collected Essays in Christology.* Cambridge: Cambridge University Press, 1987.

Hegel, George Wilhelm Friedrich. *The Philosophy of History.* New York: Dover Publications, 1956.

Hempel, Carl G. "The Function of General Laws in History." In *Theories of History,* ed. Patrick Gardiner, 344-56. New York: Free Press, 1959.

Hengel, Martin. *Earliest Christianity.* London: SCM Press, 1974.

Henry, Carl F. H., ed. *Jesus of Nazareth: Saviour and Lord.* London: Tyndale, 1966.

Hermann, Siegfried. *Time and History.* Trans. James L. Blevins. Biblical Encounter Series. Nashville: Abingdon Press, 1977.

Herodotus. *The Histories.* Trans. de Sélincourt. Harmondsworth: Penguin, 1971.

———. *History of the Persian Wars.* 4 vols. Trans. A. D. Godley. Loeb Classical Library. Cambridge: Harvard University Press, 1920-24.

———. *History of the Persian Wars.* Trans. George Rawlinson. New York: Random House, 1942.

Himmelfarb, Gertrude. *The New History and the Old: Critical Essays and Reappraisals.* Cambridge and London: Harvard University Press, 1987.

———. *On Looking into the Abyss: Untimely Thoughts on Culture and Society.* New York: Random House, 1994.

Hirsch, E. D. *Validity in Interpretation.* New Haven: Yale University Press, 1967.

Hobsbawm, Eric. *Age of Extremes: The Short Twentieth Century, 1914-1991.* London: Michael Joseph, 1994.

Hopper, R. J. *The Early Greeks.* New York: Barnes & Noble, 1976.

Hudson, W. H. *Far Away and Long Ago: A History of My Early Life.* London: Everyman, 1939.

Hughes, H. Stuart. *History as Art and as Science: Twin Vistas of the Past.* New York: Harper & Row, 1964.

Humphreys, R. Stephen. "The Historian, His Documents, and the Elementary Modes of Historical Thought." *History and Theory* 19, no. 1(January 1980): 1-20.

———. *Islamic History: A Framework for Inquiry.* Rev. ed. Princeton: Princeton University Press, 1991.

Hunter, Ian M. L. *Memory.* Rev. ed. Harmondsworth, Middlesex: Penguin, 1964.

Husserl, Edmund. *The Phenomenology of International Time-Consciousness.* Ed. Martin Heidegger. Trans. James S. Churchill. Bloomington and London: Indiana University Press, 1973.

Inden, Ronald. *Imagining India.* Oxford: Basil Blackwell, 1990.

Jacobsen, Thorkild. *Literary and Religious Texts.* London: British Museum, 1963.

———. *The Sumerian King List.* Chicago: University of Chicago Press, 1939 (reprinted 1964).

———. *Treasures of Darkness: A History of Mesopotamian Religion.* New Haven: Yale University Press, 1976.

Jacoby, Felix. *De Fragmente der Griechischen Historiker.* 16 vols. Leiden: E. J. Brill, 1923-1958.

Jenkins, Keith. *Re-Thinking History.* London and New York: Routledge, 1991.

Jenner, W. J. F. *The Tyranny of History: The Roots of China's Crisis.* London: Allen Lane/Penguin Press, 1992.

Johnson, Paul. *A History of the Jews.* London: Weidenfeld & Nicolson, 1987.

Josephus. *Works of Josephus.* Vol. 1: *Against Apion;* vol. 2: *The Jewish War,* Books 1-3. Trans. St. J. Thackeray. Loeb Classical Library. Cambridge: Harvard University Press, 1926.

Kähler, Martin. *The So-Called Historical Jesus and the Historic, Biblical Christ.* Ed. and trans. Carl E. Braaten. Philadelphia: Fortress Press, 1964.

Kant, Immanuel. *Critique of Pure Reason.* Trans. Norman Kemp Smith. 2nd ed. London and New York: Macmillan, 1958.

Kaufmann, Yehezkel. *The Biblical Account of the Conquest of Palestine.* Jerusalem: Hebrew University (Magnes Press), 1953.

Kejarjwal, O. P. *The Asiatic Society of Bengal and the Discovery of India's Past, 1784-1838.* Calcutta: Oxford University Press, 1988.

Kerr, Philip. *Ways of Lying: Dissimulation, Persecution and Conformity in Early Modern Europe.* Cambridge: Harvard University Press, 1991.

King, L. W. *Chronicles concerning Early Babylonian Kings, Including Records of the Early History of the Kassites and the Country of the Sea.* London: Luzac and Co., 1907.

Kitto, H. D. F. *The Greeks.* Rev. ed. Harmondsworth, Middlesex: Penguin, 1979.

Kopf, David. *British Orientalism and the Bengal Renaissance.* Berkeley and Los Angeles: University of California Press, 1969.

—. "Hermeneutics versus History." *Journal of Asian Studies* 39, no. 3 (May 1980): 495-505.

—. Review of Ronald Inden's *Imagining India.* In *Journal of the American Oriental Society* 112, no. 4 (1992): 674-77.

Kracauer, Siegfried. *History: The Last Things before the Last.* Oxford: Oxford University Press, 1967.

Kramer, Samuel N. *Enmerkar and the Land of Aratta: A Sumerian Epic Tale of Iraq and Iran.* Philadelphia: University Museum, University of Pennsylvania Press, 1952.

—. *History Begins at Sumer.* 1956; reprint, Philadelphia: University of Pennsylvania Press, 1988.

—. *Lamentations over the Destruction of Ur.* Chicago: University of Chicago Press, 1940.

—. *Mythologies of the Ancient World.* New York: Doubleday, 1961.

Kuhn, Thomas S. *The Structure of Scientific Revolutions.* 2nd ed. Chicago: University of Chicago Press, 1970.

Ladd, George Eldon. *I Believe in the Resurrection of Jesus.* Grand Rapids: Wm. B. Eerdmans, 1975.

Larson, Gerald. "Karma as a 'Sociology of Knowledge' or 'Social Psychology of Process/Praxis.'" In *Karma and Rebirth,* ed. Wendy O'Flaherty (Doniger). Berkeley and Los Angeles: University of California Press, 1980.

Lévi-Strauss, Claude. *The Savage Mind.* London: Weidenfeld & Nicolson, 1966; Chicago: University of Chicago, 1966.

Lewis, C. S. *God in the Dock: Essays on Theology and Ethics.* Grand Rapids: Wm. B. Eerdmans, 1970.

—. *Studies in Words.* Cambridge: Cambridge University Press, 1967.

————. *The Weight of Glory.* London: Macmillan, 1949.

Loftus, Geoffrey R., and Elizabeth F. Loftus. *Human Memory: The Processing of Information.* Hillsdale, N.J.: Lawrence Erlbaum Associates, 1976; distributed by the Halstead Division of John Wiley & Sons, 1976.

Lowenthal, David. *The Past Is a Foreign Country.* Cambridge: Cambridge University Press, 1985.

Luckenbill, Daniel D. *Ancient Records of Assyria and Babylonia.* 2 vols. Chicago: University of Chicago Press, 1926, 1927.

————. *The Annals of Sennacherib.* Chicago: University of Chicago Press, 1924.

Mackay, Donald M. *The Clockwork Image: A Christian Perspective on Science.* Downers Grove, Ill.: InterVarsity Press, 1974.

Majeed, Javed. *Ungoverned Imaginings.* Oxford: Clarendon Press, 1992.

Majumdar, A. K. "Sanskrit Historical Literature and Historians." *Journal of World History* 6, no. 2: 288-92.

Majumdar, R. C. "Scientific Spirit in Ancient India." *Journal of World History* 6, no. 2: 265-73.

Mandelbaum, Maurice. *The Anatomy of Historical Knowledge.* Baltimore and London: Johns Hopkins University Press, 1977.

————. *The Problem of Historical Knowledge.* New York: Liveright Publishing, 1938.

Martin, C. B., and Max Deutscher. "Remembering." *Philosophical Review* 75 (1966): 161-96.

Mayer, Adrian. *Caste and Kinship in Central India.* London: Routledge, 1960.

McCullagh, C. Behan. *Justifying Historical Descriptions.* Cambridge: Cambridge University Press, 1985.

McGrath, Alister E. *Iustitia Dei: A History of the Christian Doctrine of Justice.* 2 vols. Cambridge: Cambridge University Press, 1986.

————. *The Making of Modern German Christology from the Enlightenment to Pannenberg.* Oxford: Basil Blackwell, 1986.

McIntire, C. T., and Ronald A. Wells. *History and Historical Understanding.* Grand Rapids: Wm. B. Eerdmans, 1984.

McIntire, C. T., ed. *Herbert Butterfield: Writings on Christianity and History.* New York: Oxford University Press, 1979.

————. *God, History and Historians: Modern Christian Views of History.* New York: Oxford University Press, 1977.

McKibben, Ross. "Capitalism Out of Control: Writing Total History in a Global Century." Review of Eric Hobsbawm's *Age of Extremes.* In *Times Literary Supplement,* 24 October 1994, 5.

McNeill, William H. "A Defence of World History." The Prothero Lecture, delivered in the summer of 1981. In *Transactions of the Royal Historical Society.* London: Office of the Royal Historical Society, University College, 1982.

——. *The Rise of the West: A History of the Human Community.* Chicago: University of Chicago Press, 1963.

Miller, James. *The Passion of Michel Foucault.* New York: Simon & Schuster, 1993.

Miller, Joseph C. *The African Past Speaks.* Folkstone, U.K.: Dawson; Hamden, Conn.: Archon, 1980.

Moberg, Vilhelm. *A Time on Earth.* Translation of the Swedish *Den stund på jorden* by Naomi Walford. New York: Simon & Schuster, 1965.

Momigliano, Arnaldo. "Greek Historiography." In vol. 17 of *History and Theory: Studies in the Philosophy of History,* 1-27. Middletown, Conn.: Wesleyan University Press, 1978.

——. "The Place of Herodotus in the History of Historiography." *History* 43, no. 147 (February 1958): 1-13.

——. *Studies in Historiography.* London: Weidenfeld and Nicolson, 1966.

Monier-Williams, Sir Monier, et al., eds. *Sanskrit-English Dictionary.* Oxford: Clarendon Press, 1899.

Morenz, Siegfried. *Egyptian Religion.* Trans. Ann E. Keep. Ithaca, N.Y.: Cornell University Press, 1973 (first published in Stuttgart, 1960, under the title *Aegyptische Religion*).

Morgan, Timothy C. "The Mother of All Muddles." *Christianity Today,* 5 April 1993, 62-66.

Morison, Frank. *Who Moved the Stone.* 1930; reprint, London: Faber & Faber, 1968.

Morris, Thomas V. "Divine Necessity and Divine Goodness." In *Divine and Human Action: Essays in the Metaphysics of Theism,* 313-44. Ithaca, N.Y.: Cornell University Press, 1988.

Mulhall, Stephen. "Critic and Messiah: Derrida's Inheritance from Marx." *Times Literary Supplement,* 23 June 1995, 12.

Müller, C., and T. Müller. *Fragmenta Historicum Faecorum.* 5 vols. Paris: Didot, 1841-75.

Murray, A. T. *The Odyssey.* 2 vols. Cambridge: Harvard University Press, 1919.

Murray, Oswyn. "Greek Historians." In *The Oxford History of the Classical World,* ed. John Boardman, Jasper Griffin, and Oswyn Murray, 187-202. Oxford and New York: Oxford University Press, 1986.

Nakamura, Hajime. *Parallel Developments: A Comparative History of Ideas.* Tokyo and New York: Kodansha Ltd., 1975.

Neisser, Ulric, ed. *Memory Observed: Remembering in Natural Contexts.* San Francisco: Freeman, 1982.

Newman, Fred D. *Explanation by Description: Essays on Historical Methodology.* Paris: Mouton, 1968.

Niebuhr, Reinhold. *Beyond Tragedy: Essays on the Christian Interpretation of History.* New York: Scribner's, 1937.

———. *Faith and History: A Comparison of Christian and Modern Views of History.* New York: Scribner's, 1949.

———. *The Nature and Destiny of Man.* 2 vols. New York: Scribner's, 1941, 1943.

Nilsson, M. P. *A History of Greek Religion.* Oxford: Clarendon Press, 1925; 2nd ed., 1949.

———. *The Minoan-Mycenaean Religion and Its Survival in Greek Religion.* 2nd rev. ed. London: Gleerup, 1950.

———. *The Mycenaean Origin of Greek Mythology.* Berkeley and Los Angeles: University of California Press, 1932; New York: W. W. Norton, 1963.

———. *Primitive Time Reckoning: A Study of the Origins and First Development of the Art of Counting Time among the Primitive and Early Culture Peoples.* Lund: C. W. K. Gleerup, 1911; 2nd ed., 1960.

Noll, Mark. "Practice and Presuppositions: History." Paper presented at the IFACS/ISAE Conference, Wheaton, Ill., 2-6 June 1987, and summarized by Keith E. Yandell in *Christian Scholar's Review* 17, no. 4 (June 1988): 343-44.

Novick, Peter. *That Noble Dream: The Objectivity Question and the American Historical Profession.* Ideas in Context Series. Cambridge: Cambridge University Press, 1988.

Oakeshott, Michael. *Experience and Its Modes.* Cambridge: Cambridge University Press, 1933.

Oppenheim, A. Leo. *Ancient Mesopotamia: Portrait of a Dead Civiliza-*

*tion.* Chicago: University of Chicago Press, 1964 (revised 1977 by Eric Reiner).

Otto, W. F. *The Homeric Gods.* New York: Octagon Books, 1954.

Pannenberg, Wolfhart. *Theology and the Kingdom of God.* Philadelphia: Westminster, 1969.

Parke, H. W. *Greek Oracles.* London: Hutchinson University Library, 1967.

Parker, Christopher. *The English Historical Tradition Since 1850.* Edinburgh: Donald, 1990.

Peters, F. E. *Greek Philosophical Terms.* New York: New York University Press; London: University of London Press, 1967.

Philips, C. H., ed. *Historians of India, Pakistan and Ceylon.* Oxford: Oxford University Press, 1961.

————. *The Young Wellington in India.* The Creighton Lecture in History, 1972. London: Athlone Press, 1973.

Piaget, Jean, and Bärbel Inhelder. *Memory and Intelligence.* London: Routledge & Kegan Paul, 1973.

Pinnock, Clark H. "On the Third Day." In *Jesus of Nazareth: Saviour and Lord,* ed. Carl F. H. Henry, 145-56. London: Tyndale, 1966.

Pitkin, Hannah. *The Concept of Representation.* Berkeley and Los Angeles: University of California Press, 1967, 1972.

Plumb, J. H. *The Death of the Past.* New York: Houghton Mifflin, 1969.

Pocock, David F. "Psychological Approaches and Judgments of Reality." *Contributions to Indian Sociology* 5 (October 1961): 44-74.

Pollock, Sheldon. "*Mīmāṃsā* and the Problem of History in Traditional India." *Journal of the American Oriental Society* 109 (1988): 603-10.

————. "Problems of Historicity in South Asian Thought." Unpublished paper prepared for SSRC/ACLS, Iowa City, September 1988.

Popper, Karl R. *The Logic of Scientific Discovery.* New York: Harper & Row, 1969.

————. *The Open Society and Its Enemies.* London: Routledge & Kegan Paul, 1950.

————. *The Poverty of Historicism.* London: Routledge & Kegan Paul, 1957.

Porter, Dale H. *The Emergence of the Past: The Theory of Historical Explanation.* Chicago: University of Chicago Press, 1981.

Poythress, Vern S. *Science and Hermeneutics: Implications of Scientific*

*Method for Biblical Interpretation.* Foundations to Contemporary Interpretation, no. 6. Grand Rapids: Zondervan, 1988.

Pritchard, James B., ed. *Ancient Near Eastern Texts Relating to the Old Testament.* 2 vols. Princeton: Princeton University Press, 1950.

Proust, Marcel. *Remembrance of Things Past.* 3 vols. Translated from the French work of 1913-27 by K. C. Scott-Moncrieff and Terence Kilmartin. Harmondsworth, Middlesex: Penguin, 1983.

Radhakrishnan, S., and C. A. Moore. *A Sourcebook of Indian Philosophy.* Princeton: Princeton University Press, 1957.

Rao, Velcheru Narayana, trans., assisted by Gene H. Roghair. *Śiva's Warriors: The "Basava Purāna of Pālkuriki Somanātha."* Princeton: Princeton University Press, 1990.

Rhem, Richard A. "Sleeping through a Revolution." *Perspectives* 6, no. 4 (April 1991): 8-14.

Rifkin, Jeremy (with Ted Howard). *Entropy: A New World View.* New York: Viking Press, 1980.

Robertson, Richard. "History and Historians: An Introduction to the Study of History." In *The Forum Series,* 1-13. St. Louis, Mo.: Forum Press, 1978.

Roghair, Gene H. *The Epic of Palnādu: A Study and Translation of "Palnāti Vīrula Katha, A Telugu Oral Tradition from Andhra Pradesh, India."* Oxford: Clarendon Press, 1982.

Rose, H. J. *Ancient Greek Religion.* London: Hutchinson's University Library, 1948.

Russell, Jeffrey. "Inventing the Flat Earth." *History Today* 41 (August 1991): 13-19.

Sacks, Kenneth S. *Diodorus Siculus and the First Century.* Princeton: Princeton University Press, 1990.

Saggs, H. W. F. *The Greatness That Was Babylon.* Rev. ed. London: Sidgwick & Jackson, 1988.

Said, Edward. *Culture and Imperialism.* New York: Alfred A. Knopf, 1993.

———. *Orientalism.* New York: Pantheon Books, 1978.

Schmidt, H. D. "Jewish Philosophy of History and Its Contemporary Opponents." *Judaism* 9, no. 2 (Spring 1960): 129-40.

Schmithals, W. "The Saving Event: Cross and Resurrection." Chapter 6 in *Introduction to the Theology of Rudolph Bultmann,* trans. John Bowden. London: SCM, 1967.

Schwab, R. *The Oriental Renaissance: Europe's Rediscovery of India and the East, 1600-1880.* New York: Columbia University Press, 1984.

Schweitzer, Albert. *The Quest of the Historical Jesus.* New York: Macmillan, 1968.

Sen, K. M. *Hinduism.* Harmondsworth, Middlesex: Penguin, 1961.

Shafer, Boyd C. "History, Not Art, Not Science, But History: Meanings and Uses of History." *Pacific Historical Review* 29 (May 1960): 159-70.

Shattuck, Roger. *Proust's Binoculars: A Study of Memory, Time, and Recognition in "A la recherche du temps perdu."* London: Chatto & Windus, 1964.

Shulman, David Dean. *The "King" and the "Clown" in South Indian Myth and Poetry.* Princeton: Princeton University Press, 1985.

Simeti, Mary Taylor. *On Persephone's Island: A Sicilian Journal.* New York: Alfred A. Knopf, 1986.

Southern, R. W. "The Historical Experience." *Times Literary Supplement,* 24 June 1987, 771-73.

Spear, Thomas G. Percival. *India, Pakistan, and the West.* New York: Oxford University Press, 1967.

Stagg, Frank. *Polarities of Man's Existence in Biblical Perspective.* Philadelphia: Westminster Press, 1973.

Stanford, Michael. *The Nature of Historical Knowledge.* Oxford and New York: Basil Blackwell, 1986.

Starch, Richard. *The Word and the Christ: An Essay in Analytic Christology.* Oxford: Clarendon Press, 1991.

Stein, Burton. "A Decade of Historical Efflorescence." *South Asian Research* 10, no. 2 (November 1990): 125-28.

Steiner, George. *After Babel: Aspects of Language and Translation.* New York: Oxford University Press, 1975.

————. *Real Presences.* Chicago: University of Chicago Press, 1989.

Sullivan, J. W. N. *The Limitations of Science.* New York: Viking Press, 1922.

Tenney, Merrill C. "The Historicity of the Resurrection." In *Jesus of Nazareth: Saviour and Lord,* ed. Carl F. H. Henry, 133-44. London: Tyndale, 1966.

Thapar, Romila. "Society and Historical Consciousness: The Itihasa-Purana Tradition." In *Situating Indian History,* ed. Subysachi Bhattacharya and Romila Thapar, 353-83. New Delhi: Oxford University Press, 1986.

Thompson, J. A. *Deuteronomy: An Introduction and Commentary.* Leicester: Inter-Varsity Press, 1974; Downers Grove, Ill.: InterVarsity Press, 1976.

Thucydides. *History of the Peloponnesian Wars.* 4 vols. Trans. Charles Forster Smith. Loeb Classical Library. Cambridge: Harvard University Press, 1928.

Tillich, Paul. *The Courage to Be on the Boundary: An Autobiographical Sketch.* New Haven: Yale University Press, 1952; New York: Scribner's, 1966.

————. "History as a Problem in Our Period." *Review of Religion* 3 (1939): 255-64.

————. *The Interpretation of History.* New York: Scribner's, 1936.

Tolkien, J. R. R. "Beowulf: The Monsters and the Critics." Sir Israel Gallancz Lecture, presented 25 November 1936, published in *Proceedings of the British Academy,* 3-53.

————. "On Fairie Stories." In *The Tolkien Reader,* 3-84. New York: Ballantine Books, 1966.

Torrance, Thomas F. *Space, Time and Resurrection.* Grand Rapids: Wm. B. Eerdmans, 1976.

Tosh, John. *The Pursuit of History: Aims, Methods and New Directions in the Study of Modern History.* London and New York: Longman, 1984.

Toynbee, Arnold. *An Historian's Approach to Religion.* Oxford: Oxford University Press, 1956; 2nd ed., 1979.

Trevor-Roper, Hugh R. *History and Imagination.* Valedictory lecture delivered in the Examination Schools of Oxford on 20 May 1980 by Lord Hugh Trevor-Roper, on the occasion of resigning his Chair and becoming master of Peterhouse, Cambridge (Oxford: Oxford University Press, 1980). Also published as "History and Imagination" in *Times Literary Supplement,* 25 July 1980, 833-35.

————. *History, Professional and Lay: An Inaugural Lecture Given before the University of Oxford on 12 November 1957.* Oxford: Clarendon Press, 1957.

————. "The Lost Moments of History." *New York Review of Books,* 27 October 1988.

Trigger, B. G.; B. J. Kent; D. O'Connor; and A. B. Lloyd. *Ancient Egypt: A Social History.* Cambridge: Cambridge University Press, 1983.

Troeltsch, Ernst. *The Social Teaching of the Christian Churches.* New York:

Macmillan, and London: George Allen & Unwin, 1931; Harper reprint, 1960.

Tuchman, Barbara W. *Practicing History: Selected Essays.* New York: Alfred A. Knopf, 1981.

Tulving, Endel. *Elements of Episodic Memory.* Oxford: Oxford University Press, 1983.

Turner, Frederick Jackson. "The Significance of History." In *Frederick Jackson Turner: Wisconsin's Historian of the Frontier,* ed. Martin Ridge, 48-62. Madison: The State Historical Society of Wisconsin, 1933.

Van Austin, Harvey. *The Historian and the Believer: The Morality of Historical Knowledge and Christian Belief.* New York: Macmillan, 1966.

Van Inwagen, Peter. *An Essay on Free Will.* Oxford: Clarendon Press, and New York: Oxford University Press, 1983.

Vansina, Jan. "Memory and Oral Tradition." In *The African Past Speaks: Essays on Oral Tradition and History,* ed. Joseph C. Miller. Hamden, Conn.: Archon, 1980.

————. *Oral Tradition as History.* Madison: University of Wisconsin Press, 1985.

————. *Paths in the Rainforests: Toward a History of Political Tradition in Equatorial Africa.* Madison: University of Wisconsin Press, 1990.

Vernant, Jean-Pierre. "The Crises of the City: The Earliest Sages." In *The Origins of Greek Thought.* Ithaca, N.Y.: Cornell University Press, 1982; originally published by Presses Universitaires de France, 1962.

Veyne, Paul. *Did the Greeks Believe in Their Myths?: An Essay on Imagination.* Trans. Paula Wissing. Chicago and London: University of Chicago Press, 1983.

————. *Writing History.* Trans. Mina Moore-Rinvolucri. Bridgeport: Wesleyan University Press, and New York: Harper & Row, 1985.

Viswanathan, Gauri. *Masks of Conquest: Literary Study and British Rule in India.* New York: Columbia University Press, 1989.

Walsh, W. H. *An Introduction to Philosophy of Religion.* London: Hutchinson, 1951.

Warder, A. K. *An Introduction to Indian Historiography.* Monographs of the Department of Sanskrit and Indian Studies, University of Toronto. Bombay: Popular Prakasham, 1972.

Warnock, Mary. *Memory.* London: Faber & Faber, 1987.

Weigall, Arthur. *The Life and Times of Akhnaton: Pharaoh of Egypt.* Rev. ed. London: Thornton Butterworth, Ltd., 1934.

Whiston, William. *The Life and Works of Flavius Josephus.* Philadelphia: J. C. Winston, n.d.

White, Hayden. "Between Science and Symbol." *Times Literary Supplement,* 31 January 1986.

————. *The Content of the Form: Narrative Discourse and Historical Representation.* Baltimore: Johns Hopkins University Press, 1987.

————. *Metahistory: The Historical Imagination in Nineteenth-Century Europe.* Baltimore and London: Johns Hopkins University Press, 1973.

————. *Tropics of Discourse: Essays in Cultural Criticism.* Baltimore: Johns Hopkins University Press, 1985.

Whitrow, G. J. *Time in History.* Oxford: Oxford University Press, 1988.

Wilson, John A. *The Burden of Egypt.* Chicago: University of Chicago Press, 1951; republished as *The Culture of Egypt* (Chicago, 1958).

Wink, Robin, ed. *The Historian as Detective: Essays on Evidence.* New York: Harper & Row, 1969.

Wolkstein, Diane. *Inanna, Queen of Heaven and Earth.* London: Rider Press, 1983.

Woodruff, Philip (Mason). *Call the Next Witness.* London: Jonathan Cape, 1945.

Wright, N. T. *Who Was Jesus?* Grand Rapids: Wm. B. Eerdmans, 1992.

Wuthnow, Robert, et al. *Cultural Analysis: The Work of Peter L. Berger, Mary Douglas, Michel Foucault, and Jürgen Habermas.* London and Boston: Routledge & Kegan Paul, 1984.

Yandell, Keith E. "The Logic of God Incarnate." Paper later published as "Some Problems for Tomistic Incarnationists." *International Journal for Philosophy of Religion* 30, no. 3 (December 1991): 169-82.

Yerushalmi, Yosef Hayim. *Zakhor: Jewish History and Jewish Memory.* Seattle and London: University of Washington Press, 1982.

Young, Richard Fox. *Resistant Hinduism: Sanskrit Sources on Anti-Christian Apologetics in Early Nineteenth-Century India.* Vienna: De Nobili Research Library (Indological Department, University of Vienna), 1981.

Young, Richard Fox, and S. Jebasnesan. *The Bible Trembled: The Hindu-*

*Christian Controversies of Nineteenth-Century Ceylon.* Vienna: De Nobili Research Library (Institute of Indology, University of Vienna), 1995.

Zimmer, Heinrich. *Myths and Symbols in Indian Art and Civilization.* New York: Pantheon Books, 1946.

———. *Philosophies of India.* Princeton: Princeton University Press, 1951.

# Index

Gospel proclamation (*kerygma*), 223, 224
Gospels, 107, 221, 222, 223, 224, 229
Government, 269
Gramsci, Antonio, 287, 293, 295, 299
"Great Wheel" (*Mahachhakra*), 274
Greece, 209, 314; anecdotes used in, 104; as classical civilization, 150, 152; cultural achievement of, 124; historical understandings in, 174-89, 192; truth claims in, 13
Greek empire, 231
Gregorian Calendar, 131
Gregory XIII, 131
Groups, 58
*Grundzüge der Christologie* (Pannenberg), 219
Guha, Ranajit, 294-95
*Guru* (leader/teacher), 163, 291
Gutians, 142

Halpern, Baruch, 193
Hammurabi, Code of, 143, 146
Hanson, N. R., 92
Hanukkah, 210
Hanuman, 166, 169
*Harshacharitra*, 170
Hastings, Warren, 113-16, 288
Hattusas, 145
Hattusilis II, 146
"Heaven, mandate of," 8
*Heavenly City of the Eighteenth Century Philosophers, The* (Becker), 320
Hecataeus, 184, 185
Hegel, G. W. F., 13, 28n.19, 251, 301, 320
"Hegemony," 283, 290, 294
Heidegger, Martin, 279n.1, 284, 320
Heliopolis, 134
Hellanicus, 185
*Hellenica* (Xenophon), 188
Hellenistic, 3, 213
Heraclitus, 251
Herder, Gottfried, 320
Hermeneutics, 279, 285, 286
Herod, 213
Herodotus, 22, 89, 101, 106, 174n.42, 175, 184, 185-86, 187, 188, 189, 191-92, 314

Herrmann, Siegfried, 135
Hesiod, 180
Hezekiah, 206
Hieroglyphic, 129
Hill, Christopher, 314
Himmelfarb, Gertrude, 278
Hindu India, 299
Hinduism, 292, 300, 301
*Hindutva* (Hinduness), 201
*Historia* (story, narrative), 23, 62
Historians, 192: and absolute certainty, 325; arrogance of, 247-48; and belief systems, 264; biases of, 318; biblical, 203, 204; Greek, 175, 192; and historical claims, 257; and interpretation of events, 11-18, 309; Jewish, 212-13; as narrators, 87-89; and positivism, 317; problems for, in anecdote, 101; and religious experiences, 236-38; restraint required of, 335; and resurrection of Jesus, 217, 224, 233-35; task of, 5-6, 8-11, 243, 216, 260; Thucydides as, 187; and trivial items, 56
Historicism: and deconstructions, 292; definition of, 6; and history, 193, 251, 312, 315; and historicity in God's revelation, 196; new, 282; and resurrection of Jesus, 218; validity of, 249-51
Historicity: of biblical events, 105-6; in classical cultures, 173; of historical claims, 12-14; and historicism, 196; and human understandings, 335; in monotheistic thinking, 193-94; problems of, in anecdote, 101-2; of the Resurrection, 217, 218-25, 230; subordination of, 94; and theological perspectives, 240n.43
*Historie*, 234
Historiography, 6-7; definition of, 256; in India, 170-71, 294, 280-302; and language, 9; *puranic*, 4; role of religion in, 2-3
History: "abstracted," 200; as all existence, 25-27; in ancient Israel, 208, 210; as anecdote, 96-122; as antiq-